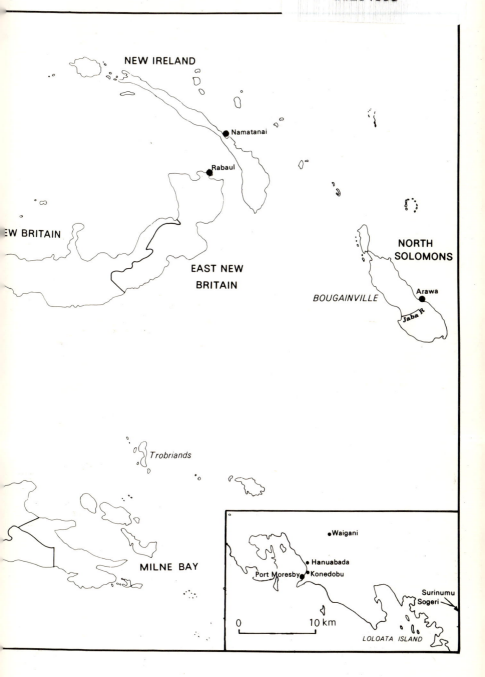

NEW IRELAND

Namatanai

Rabaul

NEW BRITAIN

EAST NEW
BRITAIN

NORTH
SOLOMONS

BOUGAINVILLE

Arawa

Jaba R

Trobriands

MILNE BAY

Waigani

Hanuabada

Port Moresby
Konedobu

Surinumu
Sogeri

0   10 km

LOLOATA ISLAND

Policy-Making
in a
New State

POLICY, POLITICS, AND ADMINISTRATION SERIES

General Series Editor

Patrick Weller

Forthcoming:

The Politics of Australian Defence Decision Making
by D. P. Ball

The Politics of Defeat: National Compensation in Australia
by D. M. Adams

Policy-Making in a New State

Papua New Guinea 1972-77

Edited by J. A. Ballard

University of Queensland Press

St Lucia • London • New York

© University of Queensland Press, St Lucia, Queensland 1981

Typeset by University of Queensland Press
Printed and bound by Warren Printing Co. Ltd, Hong Kong

Distributed in the United Kingdom, Europe, the Middle East, Africa, and the Caribbean by Prentice-Hall International, International Book Distributors Ltd, 66 Wood Lane End, Hemel Hempstead, Herts., England.

National Library of Australia
Cataloguing-in-Publication data

Ballard, J.A. (John Addison), 1930-
 Policy-making in a new state.

 (Policy, politics and administration series
 ISSN 0158-9016)
 Includes bibliographical references.
 ISBN 0 7022 1529 5

 1. Papua New Guinea — Politics and government.
 I. Title. (Series)

354.9507'2

Library of Congress Cataloging in Publication Data
Main entry under title:

Policy-making in a new state.

 (Policy, politics, and administration series,
 ISSN 0158-9016)
 Includes bibliographical references.

 1. Papua New Guinea—Politics and government—
 Addresses, essays, lectures. I. Ballard, J.A.
 (John Addison), 1930-.   II. Series.
 JQ6311.A55   1981   320.995'3   81-987
 ISBN 0 7022 1529 5   AACR2

Contents

Maps

Introduction by General Series Editor

Government activity is now pervasive throughout society. Government policies effect the way we live, the education we receive, the environment within which we operate, even the amount of earnings that we take home. Its administrative machinery can be found everywhere; whether in the guise of tax man, policeman, bureaucrat or lawyer. Its impact may be direct, in determining the structures and laws within which we live; or indirect, by regulating the way that corporations or other actors may behave.

Politics is always noticeable too — in the press, in the media, and in the daily arguments that occur with friends and neighbours about what should be done, how it should be done and when it should be done. The politics, the policies and the administration of government are important to us all.

But how much do we really know about them? How far can we understand, let alone anticipate, the effects of the policies that are adopted? How well do we understand the impact of administration on the way that policy is shaped and delivered? Often not much. And the cost of ignorance is high. Hopes can be ill-informed or misplaced; reforms based on incorrect assumptions will fail; plans for change may be frustrated. Disillusionment can easily follow. Knowledge of the way policy makers work is therefore essential.

In this series authors from a variety of disciplines — all complementary — have set out to discover how the processes of politics and government interact and how they effect decisions. Some studies will look at individual case studies or particular areas of policy; others will look at the mechanics, institutions or actors of politics and administration and their impact on policy. Some studies will be theoretical, others empirical: some will concentrate on one country, others will be comparative. But the objective will remain the same: to increase our awareness and understanding of the problems and performances of governments.

This volume, the first of the series, examines the operations of government and some areas of policy during the achievement of independence in Papua New Guinea. Some chapters were written by participants, others by close observers. They present an incisive look at an important period of transition which determined the very shape of government. The book provides a study of value both as political history and political analysis.

Patrick Weller

Contributors

John Ballard, having spent several years in teaching and research in Nigeria and French-speaking Africa, was resident in Papua New Guinea from early 1972 as Senior Research Fellow in Political Science in the Research School of Social Sciences, Australian National University. From 1974 to 1976 he served as Wills Professor of Administrative Studies at the University of Papua New Guinea. Apart from his research on political and administrative issues, he was an informal consultant to the government on questions of institutional change. Since 1977 he has been at the ANU in Canberra, with frequent visits to Papua New Guinea.

Tos Barnett arrived in Papua New Guinea in 1961 as a lawyer in the Public Solicitor's Office. From 1965 to 1970 he organized training for local court magistrates at the Administrative College, and he then became Senior Lecturer in Law at the University of Papua New Guinea. In February 1972 he joined the Department of the Administrator to organize the new Political Development Division, and transferred with his division a few months later to the new Office of the Chief Minister, where he was responsible both for negotiation of the transfer of power from Australia and for relations with the Constitutional Planning Committee. He retired from Papua New Guinea in mid-1975 to a rural community in Queensland.

Peter Bayne, after university teaching in Tanzania, became Senior Lecturer in Law at the University of Papua New Guinea from mid-1971 to mid-1974. From November 1973 he was also Legal Counsel to the House of Assembly, and from July to December 1974 he was its Senior Legal Officer. He then became Senior Lecturer in Law at La Trobe University in Melbourne, but from February to August 1975 served as constitutional consultant to the Minister of Justice, with a brief to assist the Leader of the Opposition.

Hal Colebatch, after two brief periods of political research in PNG, became Lecturer in External Studies at the Administrative College during 1969—

70. He returned in mid-1974 after doctoral research on the decentralization and recentralization of services in Kenya, and was Senior Lecturer in the College until October 1976. He then became Senior Research Fellow at the PNG Institute of Applied Social and Economic Research, where he carried out research on the Rural Improvement Program and on provincial and urban government. He is now Senior Lecturer in Politics at Kuring-gai College of Advanced Education in Sydney.

Jim Fingleton joined the Public Solicitor's Office as a lawyer in 1970. After secondment as research officer to the Commission of Inquiry into Land Matters in 1973, he became Principal Legal Officer in the Department of Lands, Surveys and Mines to work on implementation of the commission's report. From February 1976 until December 1978 he was Assistant Director (Policy and Research) in the Department of Natural Resources, and he is continuing with research into the registration of title to customary land in Papua New Guinea.

Ross Garnaut, who first visited Papua New Guinea for research in 1966, served as Research Fellow at the Australian National University's New Guinea Research Unit from early 1972 to early 1975. He was frequently involved as a consultant to ministers on economic policy, was a full-time adviser to the Finance Minister for a period in early 1973, and was a member of the Tariff Advisory Committee, consultant on the renegotiation of the Bougainville Copper Agreement, co-ordinator of the June 1974 anti-inflation campaign, and Finance Director of the Ok Tedi Development Company. During 1975 and 1976 he was First Assistant Secretary, General Financial and Economic Policy, in the Ministry of Finance. Since becoming Senior Research Fellow in Economics at the Research School of Pacific Studies in the Australian National University at the end of 1976, he has continued to provide economic policy advice to the PNG government under an agreement between the PNG Prime Minister and the Australian National University.

Mark Lynch served as a district administration officer in Papua New Guinea for eight years until 1967 and then joined the staff of the Administrative College. Appointed to the newly established secretariat of the Administrator's Executive Council in 1969, he became secretary to Cabinet and the various forms of Executive Council from 1972 to 1977. In 1978, he was secretary to the National Planning Committee of Cabinet and to the first Premier's Council, and in August 1979 he left Papua New Guinea to become director of Australia's Advisory Council for Inter-Government Relations.

Bob McKillop was for eight years from 1963 an agricultural field officer in the Highlands of Papua New Guinea and then was posted to Port Moresby, where he developed an extension research unit and was involved in the initiation of training programmes of the Department of Agriculture, Stock and Fisheries (later the Department of Primary Industry). He prepared several studies of the impact of extension services, and since leaving Papua New Guinea in 1976 he has continued research in this field through the consultant firm of McKillop Williamson and Associates, based in Sydney.

Bill Standish first visited Papua New Guinea for research in 1966, and from 1971 to 1974 he was Lecturer in Political Studies at the University of Papua New Guinea. From 1975 he has been a Research Scholar in Political Science in the Research School of Social Sciences at the Australian National University, but during 1977 was also Visiting Fellow at the PNG Institute of Applied Social and Economic Research. He has written frequently on PNG national politics, but his special area of concern has been political and social change in the Chimbu area of the Highlands, where he has carried out thirty months of fieldwork since 1972.

Tony Voutas served as a district administration officer in Papua New Guinea from early 1961, serving in Morobe District, Port Moresby, and Mount Hagen. In 1966 he was elected to the First House of Assembly in a by-election for the seat of Kaindi in Morobe, and in 1968 he was elected to the regional seat of Morobe. He was a founding member of the Pangu Pati, and from 1972 to late 1974, not having stood for re-election, he served as Principal Research Officer on the personal staff of the Chief Minister. Early in 1975 he returned to Australia to head the Policy Section of the Australian Development Assistance Agency, and in 1977 he became a Visiting Fellow at the Australian National University to write a political history of Papua New Guinea. He is currently a consultant on Papua New Guinea and China.

Editor's Preface

There are remarkably few detailed studies of the making of policy during the formative period of new states. During the late 1950s and the 1960s, when decolonization was under way in most colonial territories, political scientists were almost exclusively concerned with nationalist political activity or with policy stances of new states, particularly where these broke dramatically with the colonial past. Specialists in administration, with rare exceptions (e.g., Hyden, Jackson and Ikumu 1971, Murray 1970), were preoccupied with prescription, primarily within the context of foreign (usually American) technical assistance. Only in the 1970s, with the spread of concern with policy studies, have serious accounts of the processes of making and implementing policy in new states begun to appear; and most of these refer to well-established new states rather than to the period of transition.

Papua New Guinea, whose formal decolonization took place in the early 1970s, offers several advantages for the study of policy-making. Political stability within a competitive democratic framework has allowed for continuity in the working-out of policies. It has also made possible relatively open and honest government, with full public and parliamentary discussion of most major issues and freedom of comment within the confines of a small but heterogeneous elite, a single independent newspaper, and a national broadcasting system. For purposes of examining the formative years in retrospect, Papua New Guinea also presents the advantage of having a number of articulate commentators who played significant roles in policy-making or who were able to observe closely from within academic institutions.

The papers presented in this volume have been written by some of those who participated and observed (see notes on contributors), and who gathered for three days in January 1978 at the Australian National University to discuss several of the papers. Apart from those which appear here, papers were presented by Charles Lepani, director of the National Planning Office, Rabbie Namaliu, chairman of the Public Services Commission, and Ted Wolfers, former consultant to the Constitutional Planning Committee, none of whom had time available to revise his paper for publication. The paper by Jim Fingleton and those by the editor on policy-making in a new state and on provincial government were prepared later. Most of the papers are concerned with continuity and change in policy-making institutions, with the elaboration of a new regime, or with the development of policy on particular subjects. Each of these attempts to interpret the history of institutions and issues rather than to raise broader questions about the nature of policy-making. However, in the two papers that focus on specific programmes — those on rural development and on agriculture — there is an attempt to probe beneath the politics of formal policy articulation and to explore problems of maintenance and change in the patterns of committed resources. This is also the focus of the introductory paper on policy-making in new states.

The Research Schools of Pacific Studies and Social Sciences, and the Development Studies Centre, of the Australian National University were generous in the provision of funds and facilities for the conference at which the papers were presented. Mary Pearson, Margrit Sedlacek, Monica Follet, and especially Kath Bourke, of the Department of Political Science in the Research School of Social Sciences, were most patient and careful in preparing and typing various drafts of the papers. Ross Garnaut provided especially welcome comments and encouragement in the editing of the volume.

Abbreviations

AA	Area Authority
ABC	Australian Broadcasting Commission
AEC	Administrator's Executive Council
ASAG	Australian Staff Assistance Group
BCL	Bougainville Copper Ltd
BIPG	Bougainville Interim Provincial Government
BPC	Budget Priorities Committee
BSPC	Bougainville Special Political Committee
CILM	Commission of Inquiry into Land Matters
CIS	Corrective Institutions Service
CPC	Constitutional Planning Committee
CPO	Central Planning Office (later NPO)
DASF	Department of Agriculture, Stock and Fisheries (later DPI)
DCC	District Co-Ordinating Committee (later PCC)
DDA	Division of District Administration
DOET	Department of External Territories (Canberra)
DPI	Department of Primary Industry
FAS	First Assistant Secretary
FFP	Fresh Food Project
FUC	Follow-up Committee on Provincial Government
GFEP	General Financial and Economic Policy Division
HAD	House of Assembly Debates
IDCC	Inter-Departmental Co-ordinating Committee
LMC	Lowa Marketing Co-operative
MHA	Member of the House of Assembly
NEC	National Executive Council (Cabinet)
NIDA	National Investment and Development Authority
NPD	National Parliament Debates
NPEP	National Public Expenditure Plan
NPG	Nationalist Pressure Group
NPO	National Planning Office
OCM	Office of the Chief Minister

OIC	Officer-in-Charge
OLG	Office of Local Government
OPAC	Office of Programming and Co-ordination
PDD	Political Development Division
PDT	Provincial Development Team
PNG	Papua New Guinea
PPP	People's Progress Party
PSA	Public Service Association
PSB	Public Service Board (later PSC)
PSC	Public Services Commission
PWD	Public Works Department
RDF	Rural Development Fund (later RIP)
RIP	Rural Improvement Programme
SEP	Senior Executive Programme
SIPG	Simbu Interim Provincial Government
SOAC	Senior Officers Advisory Committee
SSCEP	Secondary School Community Extension Programme
UPNG	University of Papua New Guinea
VEDF	Village Economic Development Fund

Policy-Making in a New State

J. A. BALLARD

The flourishing of "policy studies" over the past decade has produced a considerable range of opinion about the scope and nature of *policy* and *policy-making*. Recent surveys of the field (reviewed in Hawker, Smith and Weller, 1979) reach no clear agreement on appropriate categories of definition and approach. Leaving aside the narrow and increasingly technical analysis and prescription of decision-making routines, applicable primarily to quantifiable choices in resource allocation, there appear to be two levels of focus, which may for present purposes be labelled those of "policy-making" and "policy".

Studies of policy-making are concerned with the structure and process of state activity. Studies of policy are concerned more broadly with the social outcomes of state activity or inactivity and with identifying the sources of these outcomes in the structure and process of policy-making itself or more widely in the socio-economic environment, in the distribution of power in society, and in prevailing ideas. The two levels of focus are obviously not exclusive. Environment determines the resources and values which are the substance of policy-making, while the individuals, institutions, and procedures of the state make their own imprint on policy outcomes. Only those who allow of no autonomy of the state see policy-making as a totally dependent variable and outcomes as pre-determined by social structure.

Against these analytical notions of policy must be set the common-sense usage of the term, for the usage itself is one of the forms of perception which shape policy-making. Even in states subjected to the most sophisticated policy analysis, policy is still commonly perceived as a matter of "decisions" made by politicians and implemented by public servants. If this is true in well-established states it is even more so in new states, where the sensitive issue of legitimacy is caught up in this image of policy-making. The ostensible point of self-government and independence for nationalist movements in colonial territories was that the people of a putative nation-state should determine their own fate. Kwame Nkrumah best expressed it for a whole generation: "Seek ye first the political kingdom and all things else shall be added unto you." The notion that a "transfer of power" heralds a radical transformation of both state and society remains widespread and is fundamental to the self-image of all new regimes, whether the transfer is revolutionary or peaceful.

Here we are concerned with the pattern of peaceful transfers from colonial rule in Africa, the Caribbean, and the Pacific, and with the period during which self-government and independence have been attained, together with the first years of independence. At the risk of gross and banal caricature it may be useful to rehearse briefly the common features of policy and policy-making in new states; it should at least be possible to improve on the generalizations and categorizations concerning new states that were produced in vast numbers in the 1960s and which read so quaintly today.

THE POLICY CONTEXT OF NEW STATES

Relevant environmental factors at the time of independence had a certain consistency among new states. Resource endowment might vary enormously, but the monetized sector of the colonial economies was organized primarily for export production, and infrastructure, productive resources, and state economic services were oriented accordingly. There was substantial variation among colonies in the proportions of production by settler, company or state plantations, and by smallholders and some variation in the pattern of commercial entrepreneurship. There was greater uniformity in metropolitan, usually private, control of marketing, shipping, and banking, and monetary policy was inevitably controlled from the metropole. Although there might be a choice of policies in a new state concerning the degree and timing of public or private national acquisition of control over these sectors, there was only very limited possibility for reorientation away from export production and from dependence on externally determined terms of trade. This meant effectively that new states had to depend on increased exports or foreign aid (or, in a few fortunate instances, on accumulated stabilization fund reserves) for uncommitted resources with which to initiate new programmes. Existing programmes, with their commitment in staff and infrastructure, were not readily susceptible to reorientation or even to restriction.

Colonial societies were by definition plural societies, in some instances made more complex by the presence of European settlers and non-indigenous Asian or African labourers. Although the legal racial barriers were normally removed at least a decade before independence, as one of the first steps towards formal decolonization, economic stratification remained along with patterns of social segregation and elite privilege. Uneven economic penetration laid a basis for unbalanced distribution of government and mission services, most significantly of education and openings for entrepreneurship, and resulted in substantial regional variations in mobilization. The decade before independence was usually one of rapidly accelerating social change, particularly in urbanization, incorporation into the cash economy, and demand for services. Increasing awareness of inter-personal and inter-regional inequalities was sharpened in new situations of competition for resources within emerging national arenas, and these situations served to mobilize ethnic and class identities. The patterns of mobilization varied among states, and there was also substantial variation in the extent to which mobilized groups were aggregated and channelled by national or sub-national parties and movements capable of securing support for leaders beyond the issue of independence. But even in new states with national political organizations capable of rivalling the public service, these organizations did not substantially reduce inequalities among persons and regions, or between urban and rural areas, in their capacity to articulate "public opinion" and influence policy.

The state itself was a colonial concept, imposed upon pre-colonial societies with disregard for their own structures and boundaries except where pre-colonial states provided useful adjuncts through indirect rule. The scope of state activity was exceptionally wide by metropolitan standards, since it was closely associated with economic penetration and was the only source, apart from missions, of modern social services. Despite this wide scope, state penetration of society was limited. Services were built within the scaffolding of generalist district administration, and in most colonies — even those in which native authorities and local governments were allocated substantial functions — the secretariat and generalist field administrator retained a co-ordinating and integrating role for all state activity. This was particularly true where colonies were largely self-financing and allowed to plan their own budgets. Where they were dependent on metropolitan subsidies, as in Papua New Guinea, metropolitan ministries of colonies claimed a greater role in co-ordination, planning, and budgeting, and less capacity developed within the colonies. Whatever the arrangements in this regard, however, in all colonies the state consisted of, and its resources were heavily committed to, a particular form of infrastructure and administrative structure closely integrated with the mobilized sectors of society.

Recruitment to formal policy-making roles, and particularly to the scaffolding of secretariat and district administration positions, was restricted to metropolitans until the last decade or so of colonial rule. It was expanded then only to admit natives who had been socialized into the values and orientation of the colonial public service through long experience in subordinate positions or "qualified" through higher education.

With the exception of those colonies where there was a tradition of assimilation through education, the provision of higher education was linked with preparation for self-government through localization of higher posts in the public service. Localization was seen as an essential element of capacity for self-government, in anticipation of an exodus of metropolitan staff, and localization was one of the few issues related to a transfer of power on which serious planning was undertaken before the transfer.

The pace and shaping of constitutional development in colonies varied widely, but in all cases the central issue was that of replacing the legal policy-making authority of metropolitan governments and their colonial agents with the authority of indigenous leaders. Whereas localization of the public service did not imply institutional change, localization of political authority required the creation of new institutions of state. The models chosen were almost inevitably those of metropolitan governments, altered to fit the needs of colonial administrative structures and the political constituencies they had shaped (e.g., federalism in Nigeria; see Ballard 1971). The recruitment of policy-makers through popular election, a concept as foreign as that of a career public service, was the essential qualification for self-government, and there remained only a transfer of legal powers to achieve the status of a "new state", with membership in the United Nations as evidence of international respectability.

But the notion that stages of constitutional change involved "preparation" for political roles was largely a matter of pretence and at most "a defective approach to ministerialization of responsibility and to popular political mobilization" (Schaffer 1978). The "political kingdom" that Nkrumah sought proved to be a state that had functioned without the intervention of politicians and in which public servants were much better prepared than politicians to defend their perceptions of policy. Nonetheless, the beliefs about authority being transferred and about constitutional formulae for ministerial control of policy were usually strong enough at the moments of self-government and of independence to give ministers legitimate scope for initiating change during their first months in office, though perhaps for no longer than the hundred days of grace said to be accorded new American presidents and British cabinets.

Such were the common lineaments of new states emerging by peaceful means from colonial rule. Despite the wide range of differences in their economic resources and pre-colonial social structures, similarity of policy context was perhaps inevitable given the narrow range of difference among metropolitan capitalist states in their colonial practice and given the common purpose of decolonization. The similarity of policy context in new states meant that many of the same issues arose, or failed to arise, in their policy agendas. The shape of the issues themselves together with common institutional features meant that there were common elements in the approach taken to policy-making.

POLICY-MAKING IN NEW STATES: AGENDA AND APPROACH

The scope of policy-making for governments and mobilized groups in new states was circumscribed in several important respects. As in all societies, there were, effectively, three levels of policy issues, corresponding to the three levels of power distinguished by Steven Lukes (1974). There were, first, *agenda issues* recognized as legitimate subjects of public, or at least official, discussion. There were *unconsidered issues,* perceived by individuals and groups that lacked sufficient access to public or official forums to gain agenda status for them. And there were *unrecognized issues,* those which failed to arise altogether since they were imbedded in assumptions, behaviour, and commitments whose legitimacy was not questioned.

Since the nation-state was essentially a colonial artefact, its patterns of resource commitment were largely determined by colonial assumptions and priorities. Much of what has been described above as the policy context of new states constituted *unrecognized issues* precisely because, like the boundaries and structures of the state, it was seen as essential to the state. In part this was due to the apparent solidity and power of the colonial state and to the assumption that it could be redirected or re-oriented but not radically reshaped. This assumption was common among politicians and public servants who took control of the apparatus of the colonial state and whose education and employment had been shaped by service to the state or by political roles sanctioned by the state. Just as they had incentive to treat colonial boundaries as sacrosanct, they also needed to maintain structures which, subject to limited constitutional redefinition, legitimized their roles. This was true generally of the mobilized sectors of society, since they were mobilized primarily in relation to the colonial state, even if in opposition to it. Where there were well-mobilized nationalist parties, party structures offered alternative sources of legitimacy, but in almost all cases parties in office tended to wither or to accommodate to state structures (Zolberg 1966).

Unconsidered issues were determined by inequalities of access within society. In new states the crucial inequalities were based on the structural advantages of urban over rural areas, on regional imbalances, and on differential assimilation of groups and individuals to colonial values. In practice this meant that rural areas, less penetrated regions, and unassimilated groups generally were disadvantaged not only in the resolution of those issues which reached the agenda level, but also in defining the issues that qualified as agenda items. The alternative courses of action available to such groups and individuals are imaginatively analyzed by Schaffer and Lamb (1974).

Here we seek to discern the special features of new states which help determine the kinds of policy issues that arise at the level of public and official agenda.

In an illuminating discussion of policy-making in Latin America, Albert O. Hirschman distinguishes between pressing and chosen policy problems, those which are forced on policy-makers and those which are more or less autonomously chosen by them. He goes on to argue that "the more firmly established the power of the state, the more its managers feel without power to affect the course of events as they just keep busy 'putting out fires' " or "muddling through". But "when control weakens and the existing social and political structures are under serious attack, then the state, challenged to adapt the old order to new circumstances or to build a new order, is more likely to engage in a spate of autonomous policymaking" (Hirschman 1975, pp. 389—90). Hirschman is primarily concerned with economic policy-making, for which his distinction is a valid one in new states, but as an assessment of the whole agenda of policy-making it understates the weight of concern with regime maintenance through crisis management.

Although seldom if ever labelled as an agenda item for policy-making, maintenance of the regime was never far beneath the surface of explicit consideration and overrode all other policies in a new state where the basis of accepted authority was being re-established. The fragility of roles and linkages at this time was in sharp contrast to the unquestioned and unambiguous nature of the colonial state and produced what James O'Connell has labelled "the inevitability of instability" (O'Connell 1967). The insecurity of ministers in coping with the range of tasks they confronted on taking over the colonial state meant that they were readily preoccupied by political crises that could prove crucial to the existence of the regime. In addition, both ministers and public servants were eager to prove their competence in managing the machinery and roles they had inherited. They were thus less willing and able than they might otherwise have been to exploit by radical reform the temporary vulnerability of the institutions and broader policy dispositions of the colonial state. They were also still engaged in, or freshly emerged from, negotiations over the transfer of authority which placed them in a contractual stance *vis-a-vis* the metropole, which most often continued to provide essential finance and staff and effectively to control the military and police. Even those regimes which were relatively well assured of internal political support went through a "critical phase" (Pratt 1976) in which the scope of attention to innovation was severely restricted by preoccupation with the formal concerns of transfer of power and constitution design, and with political crisis management. The length of this phase varied, but it was likely to leave traces in the perceptions and style of policy-making.

Inevitable policy issues in all new states were those relating to the elaboration of the state itself. Some of these arose as agenda items, depending on the programme for the transfer of power, the nature of constitution-making, and the development of linkages between politicians and the public service. Where the transfer of power was "in bulk", colonial administrative structures were most often taken over without substantial change, although central secretariats were dismantled in the process of ministry formation (Wettenhall 1976) and generalist field administrators — the base of the scaffolding of colonial authority — were vulnerable to political replacement. Where the transfer took place piecemeal, there was in theory a chance for reconsideration of the appropriate form for government functions, but in practice the exercise was essentially administrative, concerned only with fitting functions and functionaries into conventional bureaucratic formats. Constitutions in British colonies were subject to considerable protracted negotiation during and even after the transfer period in the effort to obtain agreement among all recognized political groups on the appropriate distribution of institutional power. Since constitution-making was central to politics and policy-making during this period, it had the potential for creating commitment to the constitutional bargain during the first years, a commitment lacking in states where the initial constitutions were designed in Paris or London and subject to proclamation rather than negotiation. Nevertheless, any serious challenge to the regime or to national unity tended to produce an authoritarian response which displayed the fragility of limitations on power and, by example, invited intervention by the military.

Many of the transfer and constitutional issues were framed in terms of "control", and ministerial control over the public service was seen as the essential condition of a new state. But beyond assertion of ministerial control as a constitutional principle, the problem of shaping effective authority was difficult to frame in policy agenda items. Localization of the public service was already in progress for other reasons, and ministers could insist on accelerating the pace and on making appointments to senior advisory positions in the expectation of obtaining greater loyalty and responsiveness from national public servants. Conversely, they often insisted on retaining "white advisers" in positions of trust. The problem at senior levels was essentially one of creating networks of trust to replace those with which the colonial state had functioned, and this was a matter of time rather than of legislation.

There was considerable reluctance, however, to penetrate beneath the surface of the public service. In part the notion of a non-political, career public service was deeply imbedded in the inherited concept of the state, and in the self-interest of a large portion of mobilized society. But then, too, the colonial state had appeared powerful, encouraging the assumption that it needed only to be redirected from the top and made more responsive to the interests of the politically mobilized; implementation would follow, and capacity itself was not at issue. Dissatisfaction with administrative performance in the provinces produced various essays at decentralization even in the first years of independence, but these seldom achieved a substantial redistribution of allocative authority or change in the quality of services. They were undermined by demands for increased central control in the name of efficiency and especially of sound financial management. Beyond localization and attempts at decentralization, reform was limited to training, the introduction of modern management techniques, and cosmetic restructuring, usually under the aegis of foreign consultants who helped to link the public service to international standards and networks (Schaffer 1978).

Some measure of control over "the economy" was a primary objective in new states and, beyond those aspects of control which were acquired almost automatically through the transfer of power, it was in this area that governments were most likely to engage in "a spate of autonomous policy-making". There was in any event pressure to acquire some of the most obvious symbols of colonial plural society, such as settler plantations, and to obtain at least a share in the control of major resources and commerce. But the way in which economic issues presented themselves, and the approaches taken to them, depended on a wide range of variables: on the commitment of leaders, advisers, and parties to state or private enterprise, on the influence of national entrepreneurs, on the leverage of aid donors and foreign investors, and on more short-term factors: the current state of the economy and the current state of economic theory, as represented by international consultants. For states late in the decolonization queue, the economists may have been particularly influential in framing issues based on their interpretation of the previous experience of other new states. In almost all new states "development planning" was part of the colonial heritage, but the planning exercise was typically a display of the failure of linkage among politicians, economists, and administrative capacity rather than an effective means of formulating priorities and obtaining commitment to them (Helleiner 1972).

A propensity for autonomous policy-making in the macro-economic sphere arose chiefly from the tempting array of levers and tools a new government could employ, ranging from monetary controls through taxation and incentives to nationalization. In the absence of a capacity within the public service or elsewhere to evaluate wider costs within a comparative framework, policy initiatives that appeared to provide control or to transfer resources were likely to be adopted. In this field, as in the allocation of finance, governments were in a position to express most directly their predisposition for national growth and redistribution from foreigners to nationals, without revealing, even to themselves, the extent to which their policy yielded to influence from privileged groups and increased inequality among nationals.

Another area open to autonomous policy-making was that of foreign policy, where few commitments were inherited and few costs were apparent. But in those policy areas in which the new states inherited heavy commitments in infrastructure, staff, and expectations, the possibilities of reorientation were limited. This was true of most services and particularly for education, health, and agricultural extension, which typically consumed most of the recurrent budget. Demands in these areas were for increase rather than change, and agenda items almost inevitably arose through formal departmental channels. Commitment to infrastructure and staff made it difficult to conceive of, promote as agenda items, and implement programmes that were not essentially bureaucratic in orientation, and the limitations of incremental policy-making in these fields infected efforts to undertake new schemes of rural or urban development (cf. Moore 1976). Political parties were the source of "self-help" initiatives to escape from community dependency on colonially devised services, but where these were actually undertaken and began to succeed they were most often incorporated eventually into the state and became a technique of bidding for the allocation of state resources (Colebatch 1974).

If it is possible to make general observations on the patterns of approach to policy-making in new states, perhaps the most that one can say is that certain policy areas — those of regime elaboration, economic policy, and allocation — were most likely to receive priority because of their relative urgency and tractability. All were subject to regulation, and once formal "decisions" were articulated on paper, the problems of implementation were largely formal. Developing or reorienting services, however, meant developing new capacity to spend funds. It required substantial commitment to changing the impact of services — and therefore of state impact on society — to alter inherited patterns, and this normally depended on mobilized political will outside the confines of the public service.

THE POLICY CONTEXT IN PAPUA NEW GUINEA

Papua New Guinea shared most of the features common to other colonies, and its most striking differences were essentially geographical. Extraordinarily rugged topography, the small scale of pre-colonial societies, and the absence of readily exploitable resources made penetration slow by world standards and contributed to assumptions about limited capacity for nationhood, which delayed steps toward self-government and placed Papua New Guinea late in the queue for formal decolonization. The fact that its metropole was relatively near by and had no other external territories encouraged close supervision from Canberra and assimilationist assumptions in policy and administration (Ward and Ballard 1976).

Urbanization and higher education were recent phenomena in 1972, which meant that the village was still seen by mobilized Papua New Guineans as a viable and desirable social unit. The small urban elite had not lost its village roots, and almost all of its members were employed in a public service whose dual salary structure kept elite life-styles within reach of village as well as expatriate levels. Nonetheless, stratification was promoted by urban incomes and by rural extension activities based on capital-intensive technology which favoured individualism. European control of plantations and commerce, and Chinese prominence in commerce, set models and targets for prospective and ambitious Papua New Guinean entrepreneurs.

Regional differentiation, particularly between the more heavily penetrated Islands and Papuan coast on one hand, and the Highlands and New Guinea mainland provinces on the others, was moderated by the conscious attempt to reduce inequalities during Paul Hasluck's term as Australia's Minister for External Territories, but perceptions of inequality were heightened by an explicit colonial policy of economic concentration from the mid-1960s. Ethnicity tended to be focused at the provincial level (Ballard, forthcoming), but political mobilization was low and in the years before 1972 was most active in the two furthest developed provinces, Bougainville and East New Britain. A sense of nationalism was largely confined to the public service, the defence force, students, and a small party group in the House of Assembly who were opposed there by a majority strongly influenced by expatriate businessmen and planters.

The structure of policy-making under post-war Australian rule became exceptionally bureaucratic. In part this was due to Australian finance for the growth of services in Papua New Guinea and to insistence by Hasluck, during his thirteen years as minister (1951–63) on his personal responsibility for policy on all issues. This view, reinforced by his successor's department head, assigned a largely instrumental role to the administrative machine in Papua New Guinea, where a co-ordinating secretariat was not permitted to develop and agents of specialist departments were expected to displace field administrators. Policy-making based on Canberra encouraged the adoption of Australian precedents and style in administration and was reinforced by application of the Commonwealth's complex public service establishments system. This fitted with assumptions that Papua New Guinea social and political structures were of no value for administrative purposes. Local government was treated as an adjunct to central administration, and law, lands policy, and extension services were increasingly oriented towards economic individualism.

A centralized and bureaucratic system of administration was extraordinarily ill-adapted to change. It bore all of the characteristics of "mechanistic" organization, identified by Burns and Stalker (1966) as appropriate to a stable environment, whereas a flexible "organic" network was needed for at least some areas of policy-making in approaching the transfer of power. The mechanistic approach was carried to absurd extremes as late as 1970 in the rigid isolation of public service management from financial policy and general administrative activity. Apart from the inordinate delay in routine action incurred by reference to Canberra, change of policy in such critical areas as localization became almost impossible to negotiate, and department heads were effectively encouraged to indulge in autonomous policy-making. From mid-1970, with the appointment of Les Johnson as Administrator, flexibility was officially sanctioned and change in some areas became negotiable, but the bureaucratic and assimilationist style was well established and had not been shaken by April 1972, when the first Coalition government led by Michael Somare took office.

The policy context in Papua New Guinea was also distinguished from that of other new states by the presence of an academic community which developed, during the late 1960s, a role as critic of government policy and a number of close links with nationalist politicians. The University of Papua New Guinea and the Australian National University's New Guinea Research Unit provided the new government with access to advice alternative to that of the public service and helped to break the isolation of Papua New Guinea from the experience of other new states. Complementing the close links between ministers and the first generation of university graduates, this was to prove crucial to the capacity of government to frame policy choices, particularly in breaking away from inherited and assimilationist assumptions. This special feature of the policy context depended in part on the small size and intimacy of the educated elite in Port Moresby.

POLICY-MAKING IN PAPUA NEW GUINEA

At the time the Coalition government was formed, the size of its potential agenda was formidable and its linkages with the public service were strictly formal. Tony Voutas points out elsewhere in this book that Canberra still planned to frame legislation on major issues: the transfer of power, public service control and localization, lands policy, and economic policy. In fact no clear proposals had been formulated in Canberra and the varying electoral commitment of the Coalition parties to act on these issues and on a new constitution was not shaped beyond their manifestos. There was some agreement on what the issue labels were, but no one was effectively prepared to give them shape. The agenda issues and the absence of linkages were familiar in most new states, but beyond this obvious point it is difficult to generalize and compare, if only because of the absence of detailed accounts of the development of policy-making during the first years of post-colonial government in other new states.

What appear as exceptional about the first five years in Papua New Guinea are its development of a novel and effective system of macro-economic policy co-ordination and the style of self-restraint and compromise which the government developed in handling issues of regime maintenance and elaboration. Ross Garnaut's account of economic policy-making traces and interprets the evolution of co-ordination, while my own paper on policy-making concerning provincial government traces a central issue on which the government negotiated compromise and accepted limitations on the use of power. The most remarkable instances were its abstention from the use of force in coping with civil disobedience and three declarations of secession, and the concession of a substantial devolution of powers to provincial governments (and, after 1977, its proposals for a self-denying new leadership code). It is difficult to account for this style and to locate its causes among personality, political culture (cf. Voutas 1977), ideology, the structure of politics, and rational calculation.

In discussing the features of policy-making in Papua New Guinea during 1972–77, it is possible to distinguish four periods. Although these overlap, there were substantial shifts in the agenda, the approach taken to issues on the agenda, and the roles played by different offices during each period. The first period was one of shakedown, in which the major issues were those which had been perceived by the time the Coalition government was formed and in which various groping attempts were made to define priorities and strategies. The Office of the Chief Minister took a central stimulating role, but initiatives from many sources were encouraged and there was indeed a spate of autonomous policy-making whose costs were reckoned later. The second period was one of political crisis, running from early 1973 to early 1975 and peaking in mid-1974, during which conflict with the Constitutional Planning Committee (a product of the first period) was central to a number of disputes about the shape and orientation of the regime, and in which threats of secession by Bougainville and Papua were intermittent preoccupations. The approach was, perhaps inevitably, one of crisis management in which an "organic" network of confidence developed among ministers and officials in the central departments.

The third period was one of co-ordination, made possible by the growing political confidence of the government and its success in renegotiating the Bougainville Copper Agreement. The capacity of the Department of Finance to frame coherent macro-economic policy, and the adaptation of the crisis network to the assertion of policy control through the National Planning Committee and Budget Priorities Committee, were the preconditions for co-ordination and for effective collaboration between ministers and public servants. But while this new co-ordinating framework gradually pulled autonomous sources of policy initiative into line, the Cabinet, pressing beyond the requirements of compromise with Bougainville, autonomously (some would say gratuitously) committed itself to the devolution of power to provincial governments. This commitment to a new transfer of power entailed much greater policy adjustment than had the transfer of power from Australia. During this fourth period, dominated by preparation for provincial government, the Public Services Commission and the Department of Provincial Affairs, both previously outside the co-ordinating network, were cast in orchestrating roles for which they were ill equipped.

This brief outline of the sequence of central issues and structures emphasizes the fluidity and flexibility of policy-making in the initial period of a new state. It indicates that the interplay of "pressing" and "chosen" issues may be more complex than Hirschman suggests and that autonomous choices may be made in times of relative political stability. The sequence also reveals the potential for distortion in an analysis of policy-making which focuses on one issue or one institution.

Several themes can be followed through the sequence. Apart from the succession of prominent issues and institutions, there is the shaping influence each of these had on policy in other areas. It is also possible to trace the development of linkages and networks and to examine the strategies applied in shaping policy commitment and in shaking inherited commitments.

The institutions and networks that had the flexibility to cope with major new issues were based in those central departments that inherited few programme responsibilities and hence had few staff and structures committed to colonial policy. (In this sense it is fortunate that the Treasury at Konedobu inherited very limited functions in 1972.) The Office of the Chief Minister (OCM) was the earliest catalyst linking ministerial confidants with responsive generalist officials from the Cabinet secretariat. In the search for policy advice outside the public service, the ministers through Voutas farmed out whole policy areas to independent commissions, most notably the Constitutional Planning Committee (CPC) and the Commission of Inquiry into Land Matters; adopted the advice of the already commissioned United Nations Development Programme (Faber) team on development strategies; and incorporated resident academics formally and informally into the OCM's discussions. New official policy structures were also launched for political purposes: the Central Planning Office to replace a similar office committed to inherited policies, and the peculiar assignment of foreign investment policy to a statutory authority, as a means of breaking the People's Progress Party monopoly of economic portfolios. During this period of *ad hoc,* open policy-making, initiatives from many sources were accepted; one of the most imaginative, on self-help housing, came from the only specialist department possessing a policy unit. The only co-ordinating filters were the new Cabinet, whose gradual integration Mark Lynch describes in the following paper, and Voutas himself, although Tos Barnett's co-ordination of the transfer of power from Australia also gave the OCM an integrating role affecting many areas of government.

Under conditions of political crisis, there was perhaps even less critical assessment of autonomous initiatives. However, the increasing level of confrontation with the CPC which, given its narrower focus of concern, had become much more committed to objectives and formulae than had the Cabinet, forced the Cabinet and its chief policy advisers into a defensive posture. Although the direct response to the CPC remained the responsibility of the OCM, a network formed by officials and advisers drawn from the central departments was focused by David Beatty's crisis calendar. Beatty and his Central Planning Office, new and centrally placed actors at the end of 1973, were able to shape their activity to the immediate needs of crisis management and to perceived areas of neglect in policy-making. During a period in which key positions in the OCM were being localized, and while the Department of Finance was only beginning to formulate its broad economic strategy, no department was able to take the lead in co-ordinating policy. Beatty, however, was well placed to orchestrate a flexible response to crisis, and he also co-ordinated the highly concentrated work of ministers, officials, and overseas consultants on renegotiation of the Bougainville Copper Agreement. The success of renegotiation, together with the government's success in pushing its own constitutional proposals through the House of Assembly, created confidence within the Coalition and made possible the next period of more institutionalized consolidation.

The Department of Finance was prepared, with both integrated policies and a proposal for an integrating institution, the Budget Priorities Committee, to take advantage of the government's new political capacity for attention to economic policy. Composed of Papua New Guinean officials who had won the confidence of ministers in the National Planning Committee during the earlier crisis period, the Budget Priorities Committee effectively replaced the crisis network in 1975. Its simple formula for translating the government's Eight Aims into an evaluation of departmental budget proposals proved effective in imposing chosen priorities on budget allocations, though it took much longer to affect entrenched expenditure patterns. The style of careful elaboration which had gone into policy-making in the Department of Finance began to be required of other departments as they were pulled into orbit. The Central Planning Office worked in close collaboration with Finance and continued to staff crisis areas such as the Bougainville negotiations, but the Office of the Chief

Minister — apart from the Cabinet secretariat — was left in an increasingly peripheral position, and the semi-autonomous constitutional position of the Public Services Commission meant that it remained unaffected.

The major unresolved issue outstanding after independence in September 1975 was that of Bougainville, whose declaration of secession had been successfully ignored but whose demands for greater autonomy persisted. The government, having committed itself to some measure of devolution to provincial governments on an *ad hoc* demand basis, re-opened negotiations with the Bougainville leaders and eventually agreed to a major transfer of powers to all provinces, though demand for this was restricted to Bougainville and East New Britain. The Department of Finance was mobilized to ensure the compatability of the agreement with its policies, but this was not true of other departments, most notably the Public Services Commission, which had little articulate conception of its own policies. The commission, however, now became the chief engine for implementation of the agreement, under a new chairman, Rabbie Namaliu, who had been a consistent and persuasive proponent of substantial devolution. For the first time the network of senior officials in central departments, which had managed the elaboration of the regime and the co-ordination of policy-making, was confronted directly with problems that could not be resolved in Port Moresby. The 1972 tactic of resorting to a commission — in this case a firm of management consultants — was employed not merely to sort out the problems of central-provincial relations, but also to negotiate acceptance of its recommendations by ministers and officials.

The issue of devolution pervaded policy-making during the last year of the Coalition government. With the Budget Priorities Committee increasingly routinized, the National Planning Office was given control through the National Public Expenditure Plan over all new capital spending. In so far as a crisis network was still required, it was now composed of the graduate heads of central departments in close consultation with senior ministers. In many respects the network had become official and institutionalized.

One of the themes running through this account of central agendas and institutions is that of the linkage between ministers and those capable of providing technical advice required for framing policy choices. This was considerably easier for ministers in the central departments where there was more flexibility in choosing staff from outside the public service. As Chief Minister, Somare proved adept through Voutas, Beatty, and the graduates in locating and tapping expertise from various sources, but after 1974, as crisis management became less central and the Budget Priorities Committee took charge, the Office of the Chief Minister lost its role and its importance. Julius Chan, with a narrower brief, worked very closely with selected staff to develop the technical competence of

Finance. Other ministers who sought actively to promote reform met obstruction in the more heavily institutionalized departments. Bob McKillop in a subsequent paper gives examples of John Guise's efforts at the Department of Agriculture, and Peter Bayne shows how John Kaputin used academic lawyers to bypass his department in attempting to promote reform. Iambakey Okuk tried the same tactic at Transport and was similarly frustrated. (Okuk, Guise, and Kaputin were the Coalition's most ardent opponents by 1977.) One of the strengths of the Constitutional Planning Committee was its access to a loyal staff and through it to other expertise.

A related theme is that of the development of policy commitment. It was not a matter of great difficulty to obtain agreement among ministers late in 1972 on the Eight Aims, but although these served as useful weapons for anyone seeking to justify a policy choice, they implied no serious commitment to priorities until they were applied to budget allocation by the Budget Priorities Committee. The Bougainville Copper renegotiation exercise was perhaps the most concentrated effort of policy-making that ministers undertook. It was an instance of policy education in which the ministers' commitment to their choice of policy was able to withstand all the pressures a multinational corporation could bring to bear. The exercise may also have been an education in the possibilities of rational choice, paving the way for acceptance of the tough allocation formula recommended by the Budget Priorities Committee. The Constitutional Planning Committee clearly had developed the same sort of commitment to its major recommendations after its many months of deliberation and political education, and as a result the CPC was a remarkably cohesive bloc across party lines during the constitutional debates. Broader education of the public service to policy commitment could also be achieved, as Ross Garnaut shows in his account of the anti-inflation campaign of 1974 and the financial stringency campaign of 1975.

Commitment could also, however, grow out of the trauma of fortuitous events producing strong conflict. Peter Bayne suggests that this was the case with a prosecution for wire-tapping in 1972 which frightened the Department of Law away from an active role in promoting change. It seems likely as well that the radical devolution to provincial governments stemmed from the determination of Bougainville leaders to obtain full budget control after the dispute of April 1975 over the size of the provincial works programme.

The themes of agenda, institutional roles, linkages, and commitment have been traced through the policy issues that preoccupied the central departments and senior ministers. The focus thus has been on the more explicit and public policy drama of the period, and a large proportion of committed public resources remain out of focus. These were the resources tied up in the technical and service departments where the scope for radical reorientation was limited and policy-making was incremental. McKillop's paper shows the extent to which resources in agriculture were committed in terms of specific commodities, and Bayne and the present writer emphasize the entrenched nature of legal and public service structures. Even in a department like Education, whose senior officials were seriously concerned with rethinking the objectives of their service, the weight of existing structure and practice proved impossible to shift substantially.

Despite an awareness by ministers and their advisers that colonially designed services were in many instances inappropriate, the difficulties of devising alternative institutions and reorienting staff ensured that other more pressing and tractable issues reached the agenda. Members of the House of Assembly called for more rather than different services, and demands could more readily be met, as Hal Colebatch indicates for the Rural Improvement Programme (RIP), simply by increasing financial allocations. More funds, more staff, perhaps more training — these were the easy choices that could be made within existing institutions.

To the extent that there was an articulate demand for non-bureaucratic alternatives to the pattern of service distribution, it came primarily from political leaders of local movements for economic mobilization. Kaputin's New Guinea Development Corporation served as a local model, and there was considerable interest in self-help alternatives stimulated at the university in 1972–73 which gave broader legitimacy to a few other local efforts. The government was sympathetic to requests for help and established a Village Economic Development Fund (VEDF) initially in response to these, though like the RIP and most other sources of largesse it was captured by Finance and given an allocation formula. In 1974 an outspoken critic of the public service and adviser to the Chief Minister, Moi Avei, established a network of educated leaders of local movements in Papuan provinces through a Village Development Task Force, but the task force failed to obtain control of the VEDF and its ambitions to bypass the public service withered. By 1976 most of the movements had withered as well or had become institutionalized through the acquisition of expatriate businesses and plantations with government assistance.

More successful initiatives were those which attempted to foster the growth of village and clan institutions supplementary to, rather than in competition with, the public service departments. The concept of village courts had been promoted along with local government in the early postwar period, but institutions potentially alien to Australian concepts of justice and bureaucratic control were anathema to the Australian judiciary and to Hasluck, who vetoed proposals. Bayne discusses the problems of raising such proposals effectively even in the receptive climate of open policy-making during 1972 and indicates that their survival depended on the dedicated intervention of Barry Holloway. Holloway's political standing with the government, analogous to that of Voutas, and his independent position as Speaker of the House gave him an exceptional legitimacy to intervene as a catalytic agent, and he chose to promote village-level institutions, particularly village courts and Eria Komuniti (local councils within bureaucratized local government councils), with his own electorate of Kainantu as a seed-bed. He provided an exceptional link between the centre and the sub-district, one which was difficult to maintain or to replicate once the Constitutional Planning Committee had decreed that the province was to be the only legitimate level for decentralization and devolution.

The Bougainville Agreement of 1976 and its elaboration by the McKinsey consultancy of 1977 ensured that provincial governments would face many of the same problems of policy-making that the first Coalition government confronted in its first five years. Bill Standish's account makes evident the difficulties of creating a new arena for policy-making by politicians of limited authority where there were no broad political mobilization, no experience of administrative co-ordination within the province, and no clear signals from the central government. The aftermath lies outside the period of the present study.

Ropes, Rules, and Ring-Keepers: the Cabinet System as Policy-Maker

MARK LYNCH

The era of transition to and through political independence is, for any nation, a period demanding a confusing plethora of decisions, and a time of disruption for established patterns and networks of power and influence. Papua New Guinea from 1972 to 1977 was no exception. It was a potentially unstable time, the atmosphere full of hopes for the best and fears for the worst.

A multitude of forces and pressures were at work throughout the period, competing and co-operating to influence and shape the policies and practice of the Somare government and to point an infant Papua New Guinea in certain directions. This paper focuses primarily on the formal system of executive political decision-making that was developed to cope with the situation, the objectives that were in mind, and the constraints that applied. It should be possible to draw some conclusions about the effectiveness of that system for the task that was being confronted, and to explore the extent to which the system itself influenced the outcome of policy decisions.

The decision to establish provincial governments, to provide a locus of legislative and executive decision-making in each province of Papua New Guinea, means that many of the administrative, organizational, and political difficulties encountered at the national level in recent years will reappear in provincial arenas. Just as it was useful in 1972 to compare similarities and differences between Papua New Guinea and other recently independent ex-colonial states, so within Papua New Guinea itself an understanding of the national transitional experience should be of value to provincial politicians and officials.

As I was Cabinet secretary during 1972–77, and deputy secretary for three years before that, my own perspective on the years of transition is a particular and a privileged one. That perspective was most directly focused on the final stages of political decision-making, on relationships within the ministry, and on relationships between ministers and senior public servants.

THE INFLUENCES OF THE COLONIAL EXPERIENCE – 1968–72

It is necessary to begin by sketching in some pertinent elements of the background to the events of 1972–77. The second House of Assembly (1968–72) comprised eighty-four elected and ten official members. After nominations by a parliamentary Ministerial Nominations Committee, seven ministerial members and eight assistant ministerial members were appointed. The Administrator's Executive Council (AEC), the embryonic Cabinet, had twelve members and comprised the Administrator as chairman, three official MHAs, the seven ministerial members, and one other elected MHA. The only active political party in the House was the small group of Pangu Pati members in voluntary opposition. Most of the remaining members belonged to an amorphous "Independent Group" which toward the end of the term resolved itself into the United Party and the smaller People's Progress Party. Passage of government legislation required, in addition to the votes of those holding official seats or ministerial positions, the support of a further twenty-one out of the remaining sixty-eight members. While ministerial members in the AEC and back-benchers in the House sometimes managed to achieve modification of projected legislation, the administration did not normally have very much difficulty in mustering the numbers for passage of its bills. The presence of ten official members in the House, to inform members and to lobby on issues, helped ensure that the numbers were generally there. MHAs were viewed by their electorates and by themselves primarily as communication links between the people and the administration, and as lobbyists for their areas for a greater share of roads, schools, doctors, kiaps, business opportunities, and government attention. Very few elected members saw themselves as initiators of policy through legislative processes.

The ministerial appointees were a widely disparate group of individuals lacking any common background or ideology, drawn from all regions of the country. While ministerial members were designated jointly responsible with their departmental heads for the plans, policy implementation, and expenditure proposals of their departments, and represented those departments in the House and the AEC, they did not have the collective strength, or will, or common purpose to assert any significant control over the administration. Moreover, there was not sufficient willingness and awareness either among the public at large or within the bureaucracy to permit any such assertion. The ministerial group did not command the required degree of legitimacy for that, and in any case they were primarily identified with those parliamentarians who opposed early independence.

The administrative structure of government comprised departments of the PNG administration, the top echelon of which was virtually entirely expatriate, and the PNG extensions of Australian Commonwealth departments. The Papua New Guinea Public Service Board reported directly to the Ministry of External Territories in Canberra, as did the Administrator. Some two-thirds of the budget came from Australian funds, and laws of both the Australian and the Territory legislatures governed its administration.

Internal decision-making within the administration was structured around a series of committees and informal networks, the most important being the Inter-Departmental Co-Ordinating Committee (IDCC), chaired by the Administrator. It met about twice a month with a restricted membership of the most senior officials, and less frequently with a membership of all departmental heads. While basically a co-ordinating body, it was able to provide a Konedobu officials' view to Canberra on issues raised at either end. It should be recalled that, at this stage, even the standards of high school toilets were determined in Canberra.

The AEC had been somewhat uncomfortably fitted into this structure. Its statutory powers of advice to the Administrator on certain matters were clearly defined, and on such matters the Administrator was in effect required to accept the advice of his council. These aspects caused few problems, and no significant difficulties arose; occasionally the AEC did vary proposals placed before it, and the variations were accepted. Less clear-cut was the process of consultation with the AEC on matters outside its areas of responsibility.

But the pace of events began to quicken, forced by problems in Bougainville and the Gazelle Peninsula, by Gough Whitlam's visits, and by heightened Australian political interest in Papua New Guinea. The Australian government's demonstrated strategy was generally to transfer power and authority to PNG institutions in advance of demand. The Administrator began to consult the AEC more frequently, over an ever-widening range of issues. In addition, he chaired periodic meetings of all ministerial appointees. Increasingly the Department of External Territories required consultation with the AEC and acceptance of proposals before proceeding within the Australian government or Cabinet. But while the AEC gradually became more assertive over individual issues, and even began to initiate a number of proposals, it remained basically a reactive group, a sounding-board.

This situation did not substantially alter when ministerial members were made solely responsible for their departments, within the framework of government policy, for day-to-day administrative actions, nor when they were handed policy-making powers over some areas of their department's responsibilities. The large measure of responsibility proffered the ministerial appointees was illusory, for although their new powers were legally defined, control of finances and the public service remained with Canberra. This was amply demonstrated to AEC members on their early budget pilgrimages to Canberra, where they were met by officials and generally made to feel that they had little real influence over the size, shape, and emphasis of the PNG budget. They met with the Minister for External Territories at the end of the discussions, after the hatchet-work was over.

Ministerial members had few sources of advice other than their departmental heads, and little administrative support. The small AEC secretariat, established in 1969, serviced the IDCC and the AEC and its committees, co-ordinated the parliamentary programme for each sitting, and provided some administrative and advisory support to ministerial members. Most of the transfers of policy powers came too late in the parliamentary term to be acted upon even if the ministerial group had wanted to formulate a programme of specific policy initiatives. The Catch 22 in all this was that the more ministerial members became assertive over particular issues, the more they brought themselves into conflict with their own stance of deploring early independence. The reluctance to accept political responsibility did not always go hand-in-hand with a reluctance to direct. On a number of issues, ministerial members could express views just as "radical" as those of the Pangu opposition.

The 1970 appointment of Administrator David Hay as Secretary for External Territories, and his replacement as Administrator by Les Johnson, had positive results in both Canberra and Konedobu. Hay's appointment ensured a better understanding of PNG events in senior Canberra circles and resulted in ministerial members being accorded more appropriate courtesies on Canberra visits. Johnson brought to his appointment a considerable store of good will among Papua New Guineans of all political leanings, plus a thorough knowledge of the internal workings of the administration, and this helped him to defuse the growing tensions inherent in transitional arrangements both before and after the 1972 elections.

A host of difficulties was encountered during the early phase of transition. For ministerial appointees the increasing demands on their time for departmental, parliamentary, and AEC duties reduced to a politically unhealthy degree their availability to their own electorates, which had little understanding of what their representatives were doing while away so much. An allowance was granted to employ an electorate secretary in recognition of this and as an attempt to offset it. A number of those in the ministry were illiterate or poorly educated and had to rely on verbal briefings — and not all senior officials were fluent enough pidgin speakers to ensure effective communication. Within the AEC this meant that most business was thrashed out verbally, and usually in pidgin, and while this was a very healthy process it was also time consuming. A system of sub-committees was adopted to reduce the volume of detailed discussion in the

AEC and to involve the eight assistant ministerial members in decision-making. This latter group had complained frequently about their lower status and lesser involvement, and their disgruntlement had prompted occasional resignation threats from some of them.

Departmental Heads were all expatriate. Some proved more adaptable, and some more astute, than others in learning to work with, and later for, their ministerial members. They were also caught up with the problem of dual responsibility — to the Administrator and Canberra on some issues, to their ministerial member on others. There was also a general lack of experienced policy-development capacity within departments and a tendency for some departments to operate in isolation from the political and cultural realities of Papua New Guinea. Another legacy was the practice of preparing arguments and documents for digestion by officials rather than politicians, and an initial lack of appreciation (or acceptance) of the different perspectives and requirements of decision-makers politically responsible to PNG (not Australian) electorates.

A real problem was a lack of awareness and a lack of acceptance, by both many officials and the public, of the pace of change. To demonstrate more visibly what was happening, the AEC undertook a programme of meetings in district centres, using the opportunity to address meetings of councillors, leaders, students, villagers, and townspeople in scores of locations. Such public meetings had a clearly visible impact on both expatriates and nationals. For the first time, Papua New Guineans were seen to be in the front row, answering questions and arguing the reasons behind government policies in their areas of responsibility. These meetings tangibly demonstrated what self-government and independence would bring. They also served to heighten political awareness and to reassure the community that black decision-making was not synonymous with chaos.

Within the AEC secretariat a programme of informal secondments of a number of senior Papua New Guinean officers was organized, which enabled them to see at first hand the developing process of political decision-making and the problems of policy formulation. Probably more importantly, it also provided them with a frame of reference against which to anticipate the next stages of transition.

With the further transfer of powers to ministerial appointees in 1970 and 1971, conflict began to loom over the existence of structures like the IDCC, where departmental heads, now responsible in many respects to their ministerial members, met to discuss issues that were frequently now being passed on to the AEC for decision. The official members of AEC were also IDCC members and had two opportunities to participate. Departmental heads had to adjust to a number of new realities, as some matters passed from their control to that of the ministerial member, and other matters no longer had to be referred to Canberra.

Out of these experiences a set of principles emerged, and some ground rules were formulated by the AEC secretariat for implementation with the advent of the 1972 government, whatever its political complexion. The objectives, as far as the AEC secretariat was concerned, were to ensure that the process by which decisions were reached was widely regarded as legitimate, and that the decisions themselves were based on the best possible presentation of facts and issues. Nothing would be more likely to undermine progress to self-government and independence or to discredit a newly formed government than a spate of hasty, ill-informed, expensive, arbitrary, inconsistent, or unmanageable decisions. The ground rules were designed to avoid that, while at the same time permitting the greatest possible degree of openness to new ideas and concepts. Incoming ministers would need to recognize the constraints of manpower and money, the dangers of inconsistency in policy; departmental heads and officials needed to keep minds open to new approaches, and to accept that the changing political realities would demand from them flexibility and a willingness to reconsider past precedents and policy. It was also important to keep the decision-making system as uncluttered as possible, and to ensure that its logic and application would be as appropriate for newly promoted senior Papua New Guinean officers as for the more experienced expatriate officials, who would soon depart.

While the ground rules formulated for Cabinet decision-making were in most respects basic common sense, they were intended to convert the constitutional shift of powers to PNG ministers into realty, more promptly and more smoothly than a *laissez-faire* approach. Only the minister responsible, not his departmental head, would be able to introduce items to Cabinet. Submissions had to be tendered sufficiently in advance to provide all Cabinet members the opportunity to study them. A standard format for policy submissions required, in less than five pages, a brief opening statement of the purpose, a concise résumé of the facts and considerations, the views of the Minister for External Territories where appropriate, the views of other affected PNG ministries, an authoritative statement of costs and staffing implications, an assessment of any political repercussions, inclusion of relevant previous policy references, and finally a recommendation the sponsoring minister sought to have adopted as a Cabinet decision.

TRANSITION – 1972–77

Enter the 1972 National Coalition government: a new and almost entirely inexperienced ministry, generally better educated than previously but still ranging from the illiterate to the university graduate; a group somewhat suspicious of the bureaucracy, wanting to employ a considerable number of their own staff members; a hastily thrown-together coalition of three rather weak and weakly disciplined political parties and a group of independent supporters; no ready-made consensus on issues, and some suspicions across party lines as a legacy of the election campaign; but with a group determination to master the tasks of running the government, and to demonstrate the capability of Papua New Guinean leaders to govern in the interests of Papua New Guinea and its people.

The new AEC comprised the Administrator as chairman, ten of the seventeen ministers, and three official members. At its first meeting, Michael Somare, Chief Minister and deputy chairman of the AEC was appointed as acting chairman during any absences of the Administrator; this paved the way for Johnson's subsequent practice of absenting himself from meetings except when items for which the Australian government remained responsible were discussed. Three subcommittees were appointed to enable the AEC to concentrate its attentions on the more important and more contentious issues and to involve non-AEC ministers in decision-making, although final powers remained vested in the AEC itself. The proposed ground rules for Cabinet submissions were explained, accepted, and adopted, and soon afterwards a booklet was widely distributed to senior officials and ministerial staff, setting out Cabinet requirements.

Some of the main threads of the next five years were those of transfer of power and institutions from Australia to Papua New Guinea, widespread and vigorous participation in constitution-making, commencement of a programme to restructure and reform the public service, rapid localization of the public sector, conduct of several major negotiations, the defusing of potentially harmful secession movements, a basically successful fight against inflation, and, most importantly, the evolution of a set of national objectives and development strategies, with the parallel or subsequent development of major policies in priority areas.

Each of these threads represented an area of major activity. The transfer process involved a continuous round of negotiations with Australia on a rolling programme of power and institutional transfers. Despite a gradual loss of experienced expatriate staff, it was relatively easy to assume control of established departments (Agriculture, Health, Education, Police, etc.) and begin to boost their policy and planning capabilities. More difficult were transfers of functions formerly directly controlled by Commonwealth bodies, as new infrastructure had to be created and adequate interim arrangements made to allow for training of national staff (e.g., Civil Aviation, Defence, Foreign Affairs, etc.). Into a third category fell the transfer and acquisition of central, trading, and savings bank functions, the establishment of a single national and international airline based on segments of the TAA and Ansett fleets and personnel, the successful launching of a stable currency in times of world-wide high inflation, and the formation of new bodies like the National Investment and Development Authority.

Throughout the period, the volume of business resolved at Cabinet level was enormous. Initially, when fewer responsibilities had been transferred to PNG control, the volume was increased by the tendency of ministers, inexperienced themselves and in a coalition that had still to develop a working consensus, to refer matters to Cabinet to ensure Coalition support. Later, as ministers became more confident of themselves and the views of Cabinet as a whole, this category of business declined, but any slack was taken up by the new concerns generated by assumption of additional powers and by the need to tackle a number of significant internal political problems. Cabinet never degenerated into a formalized, routine decision-making group. Matters were talked through to a consensus; on the very rare occasions when a vote was taken, the issue at stake was not one likely to cause serious dissension in the Coalition. If agreement could not be obtained on more serious issues, they were generally deferred in an effort to find a satisfactory way around disagreements. There were party, regional, and personal loyalties influencing individual stands on issues, plus the conformity to certain principles by some ministers. For example, some placed great emphasis on the views of the minister particularly responsible for a matter; others would disagree in principle with reversal of Cabinet decisions.

Given that there were sufficient natural strains within a coalition Cabinet of this nature, in retrospect it was probably even more important than had been anticipated that ground rules had been laid down and generally enforced on how matters were to be placed before Cabinet. The process of consultation required meant that there was usually at least agreement on the facts behind proposals, if not agreement on the proposals themselves. The discipline imposed by Cabinet procedures forced officials to think through policy concepts thoroughly *before* they reached Cabinet level and, while there is no way of quantifying this, many suggestions were dropped at an early stage as being either unworkable or unacceptable. The same discipline also provided very useful safeguards against the schemes of various carpet-baggers who seemed to view an emerging Papua New Guinea as a hopeful prospect for the purchase of a wide range of novel concepts and products.

The enforcement of Cabinet requirements was a major trouble throughout the period. There was an extremely high turnover of staff in the senior levels of government, so that many submissions were first efforts drafted by individual officers. There was a constant demand for the admission of late papers to Cabinet, which placed the Cabinet secretary or the Prime Minister in a negative relationship with ministers before almost every meeting. Frequently, late submissions were also deficient submissions, and could be excluded on those grounds; others were deferred by Cabinet itself; and there were those that were in order, urgent, and unavoidably late. A number of devices were tried to screen late submissions: initially the permission of the Deputy Administrator was required, later the agreement of three senior ministers. It was constantly necessary for the Cabinet secretariat to judge where the line should be drawn between the maintenance of essential standards and the desirability of prompt Cabinet responses to problems. It was also necessary to reaffirm from time to time the validity of the requirements set. The treatment meted out in Cabinet to incomplete submissions that were admitted demonstrated to both Cabinet staff and ministers themselves that the ground rules were warranted. It was one matter for an official to remind a minister that he had failed to consult an affected fellow minister about a proposal — and quite another for that minister to be the butt of strong objections within Cabinet for overlooking his colleagues. It was not always sufficient for officials to say where the ropes were; it was occasionally necessary for ministers to test them by bumping into them, by being bounced off them, or even on occasions being tangled up in them.

While the secretariat devoted considerable energy to standardizing the format and procedures of Cabinet, this was far from being a purely negative role. Officials and ministers often welcomed suggestions that a certain overlooked ministry be consulted in advance, or that there were simpler, more direct ways to achieve an objective than proposing legislation to Cabinet. Officials were frequently assisted to frame their submissions in a presentation meaningful to ministers. A great deal of largely informal coordination took place, primarily designed to reduce potential conflict within Cabinet. The standardized submission format made it easier for all ministers, whether highly educated or semi-literate, to identify quickly the substance of an issue placed before them.

The discipline imposed on how matters were to be presented for final decision in Cabinet was accompanied by a very open environment within Cabinet itself, which permitted any minister to raise any idea, or matter of concern, for discussion. Such matters usually fell into three categories: (1) a subject that was the responsibility of another minister who either explained the situation or promised to investigate or act upon it; (2) an idea tossed around but not taken up; (3) an idea sufficiently interesting for the minister(s) responsible to be asked to prepare a Cabinet submission. Thus the discipline imposed in no way implied a bureaucratic control over what was discussed in Cabinet.

The ropes also needed periodic adjustment and alteration. Cabinet procedures became increasingly sophisticated as it became necessary to relate proposals to the Eight Point Improvement Programme, to legislative implications, and to the Independence Constitution. It is also true to say that the procedures were least adequate when it became necessary to digest at Cabinet level a massive report setting out lengthy recommendations and alternative approaches. Because Cabinet continued to operate in meetings at a verbal level rather than taking the written word for granted, such reports were largely indigestible unless the subject of very lengthy and detailed discussion. The problem could be eased by skilful summarizing, but not avoided.

A breakthrough in this regard was the introduction by David Beatty (Director, National Planning Office) of slide presentations to supplement Cabinet submissions on complex issues. Presenting data and options visually — in graphs, diagrams, and even cartoon format — made an enormous contribution to enabling an inexperienced Cabinet to come to grips with such difficult questions as the Bougainville Copper and Kennecott negotiations, formulation of oil and gas exploration policy, anti-inflation policies, etc. This technique also permitted the less literate members of Cabinet better to understand and participate in decisions. While there are limits to the effective use of an overhead slide projector (danger of over-simplification, over-use leading to diminished impact, etc.), this method of augmenting Cabinet submissions now has a valuable and accepted place in the system.

Occasionally Cabinet would establish committees to cope with particular problems — for example, the Cabinet committee on the Highlands Famine operated for some months until the crisis passed. The Cabinet Committee on Localization of the Public Service had a longer life, evolving into the Public Service Committee of Cabinet and ultimately being absorbed into the National Planning Committee, which had overlapping membership and which included senior national public servants as "advisory members".

The Cabinet committees established in 1972 were defined by the category of business they considered (the Legislation Committee, the Statutory Business Committee, etc.), but this type of break-up proved unwieldy. The system was revised to concentrate on policy rather than process (e.g., Localization Committee, Investment Committee, etc.), and this latter arrangement proved much more durable, useful, and meaningful to the committee members.

A vexing problem through the period was that of adequate co-ordination within the bureaucracy. There were periods when it seemed political co-ordination was more effective than administrative co-ordination. The old IDCC had faded out of existence, and there were inter-departmental committees on particular subjects, but the rapid growth of the public service, the high staff turnover, expanded responsibilities, and heavy workload left little time for senior public servants to co-ordinate their activities regularly and effectively. There were formal and informal piecemeal attempts to reduce the problem, some of them effective for a while, but they were always in danger of being seen as attempts to constrain ministerial control. There continues to be room for improvement in this area, although the establishment of the Budget Priorities Committee has, at the cost of considerable investment of time by those involved, brought significant improvement.

It was not until fairly late in the period that the Cabinet secretariat was able to begin any systematic follow-up on Cabinet decisions to determine the effectiveness of implementation. The results indicated a surprisingly good record of implementation, with very few breakdowns or undue delays. The secretariat's inquiries did occasionally prod departments on matters inadvertently overlooked, and they also indicated that as a general rule those decisions which had taken the public service by surprise had taken a little longer to be translated into action. Perhaps it is to be expected that a department not consulted beforehand is a department less ready and less willing to implement a new policy.

From the outset, the Cabinet secretariat deliberately adopted and maintained a stance of neutrality. It was responsible to the Prime Minister and to all ministers; it did not seek to provide policy advice but did work hard to ensure the best possible advice was available to Cabinet. It did not side with either ministers or departmental heads when arguments developed over Cabinet matters, but it did on occasion mediate in such matters. A reputation for neutrality and competence in servicing Cabinet did seem to assist the secretariat greatly in its more unpleasant tasks, such as rejecting sub-standard submissions and conveying unpopular decisions. While there were opportunities to become actively involved in policy formulation, it was felt that the limited capacity of the small secretariat should remain concentrated upon the tasks of servicing Cabinet, co-ordinating the government's affairs in parliament, and ensuring an effective localization of secretariat positions.

The question of financial power and responsibility over the period is worth considering briefly. Before 1972, ministerial members had found themselves by and large powerless when it came to questions of budget size and emphasis, and even internal revenue raising had to fit in with whatever the Australian government was doing. Raising income or company taxes in Papua New Guinea would be frowned upon if the rates were being lowered that year in the Australian budget. The first few years of the Somare government were complicated by the process of transferring Commonwealth institutions and functions, and the initial funds to run them. Papua New Guinea substantially increased its own revenue raising, largely through its beautifully executed renegotiation of the Bougainville Copper Agreement. But there was a basic problem. Australian aid remained, and still is, extremely important to the PNG budget. And Papua New Guinea could not complete its own budget until the negotiated aid figure was available, shortly before the Australian government brought down its own budget. This was unhealthy for several reasons. It obviously made forward planning difficult and sometimes forced last-minute arbitrary cuts which did not necessarily fit with the government's priorities. It weakened internal discipline over new expenditure proposals, as there was always the vague hope that aid funds plus revenue would cover them, and it is easier for a Cabinet to say yes or maybe than it is to say no under such circumstances. It also tended to encourage the attitude (a legacy of the earlier relationship) that if the Australian government was attracted by a particular proposal it would be more likely to fund it. The 1976 agreement negotiated with the Fraser government on the nature and extent of future Australian aid commitments meant that for the first time the PNG government knew in advance, within fairly narrow limits, what it would have to spend over the next few years. This cannot but enforce at the political level a greater degree of real financial responsibility, and the emergence of the National Public Expenditure Plan is concrete evidence of this. Real financial responsibility can only be exercised effectively when new expenditure is dependent primarily upon either cost-cutting or internal revenue raising, both politically painful.

CONCLUSIONS AND COMMENTARY

Given the constraints that operated during the first five years — complete turnover of departmental heads, an inexperienced Coalition ministry, a lack of accepted precedents or tradition about national decision-making by Papua New Guinean leaders, the heavy workload, the adjustment to frequent legislative and constitutional change, the training responsibilities to achieve effective localization, the need to sort out a *modus operandi* with a substantial number of ministerial staff and to ensure that Cabinet decisions were legally valid and reached through processes accepted as legitimate — there is no doubt that the PNG Cabinet support system proved its value. The secretariat provided a co-ordinating and stabilizing mechanism which enabled effective political control to be exerted at Cabinet level to the extent wished by ministers, based generally on well-informed decision choices. While there were bound to be mistakes, useful lessons were learnt from some of them.

It is also true that the system as such indirectly influenced the outcome of policy decisions by requiring consultation, costings, and agreement on facts before presentation. Enforcing consultation with both opponents and supporters of proposals had the frequent, intended, result of resolving conflict or achieving compromise before deliberation by Cabinet, which helped to conserve political energy and good will within the ministry. Even if one did not always agree with the results of that influence on a particular decision, one could take comfort in the knowledge that the resulting decision was usually the outcome most just to Cabinet as a whole, and therefore the one most supportable by the Coalition.

The momentum of events throughout the period — transfers of power and institutions, political crises, constitution-making, grappling with new issues presented by independence in 1975, as well as simply running a government — meant that Cabinet was heavily committed to coping with the business of the day, to which ministers added a substantial number of new policy initiatives of their own. There has been some criticism that the Somare Cabinet adopted a piecemeal approach to government, tackling a few issues thoroughly, nibbling at some, and totally ignoring others, and there is some validity in that as a description of the 1972—77 era. It is sometimes also implied that a different approach to Cabinet decision-making could have altered the situation, enabling a more coherent, planned, and ideologically consistent style of government to emerge. Such criticisms give insufficient weight to certain key and unavoidable elements. The ministry was a multi-faceted coalition, held together largely by the desire for early independence and to demonstrate that Papua New Guineans could control their own affairs. That agreed objective necessitated the immediate settling of many issues to facilitate independence. Thus Cabinet discussion tended to focus on specifics, perhaps in the unstated knowledge that the trial-and-error consensus that had gradually emerged from Cabinet decision-making was too fragile to withstand deep ideological debate. Another important factor was the limited capacity of the bureaucracy in coping with what was already a large measure of policy and structural change. Thirdly, some issues were raised and confronted simply because there was the right combination of capacity, expertise, and ministerial will in a particular ministry to have an issue raised, decided, and followed through; and this mix was lacking for other issues.

The evolution of the Eight Point Improvement Programme, or Eight Aims, late in 1972, was probably the closest the ministry came to expressing a general ideological stance. While those aims were in some ways vague, even to a degree contradictory, they were of value in prompting politicians, public servants, and the people to consider policies and issues rather than simply to seek independence and black control. But, like the Bible, the Eight Aims could be quoted in support of almost any proposal; and they did not provide an all-embracing ideological framework. Whether by inclination or because they were largely unfettered by the day-to-day responsibilities of government, those members of parliament involved in the Constitutional Planning Committee provided the main stimulus and forum for ideological debate in the immediate pre-independence period.

In the meantime, the Cabinet system and secretariat had to be designed to facilitate effective decision-making in the environment that existed. While that designing primarily took account of PNG circumstances, the secretariat staff had also had the benefit of observing Cabinet systems at first hand in several independent African states, of brief staff attachments to the Cabinet Office in Canberra, and discussions with Cabinet officials from Fiji and elsewhere. Perhaps the final commentary on whether the system as adopted and modified was suitable is that the system survived the five years, the political transition to and through independence was smoother than most observers were prepared to predict, and, with the appointment of a Papua New Guinean as Cabinet secretary in 1977, the secretariat was finally fully localized. No doubt the political environment will alter over the course of time, and it would be unrealistic to expect the Cabinet support system to remain static. The practices and procedures that have been established should be maintained and enshrined only to the extent that they continue to justify themselves to ministers and their public service and political advisers, to the extent that they are in the interests of continued responsible, effective, and accountable government. They were formulated during the period of transition and are very much a product of that era, but they cannot be dismissed as a colonial carry-over. They have worked through five years of major political and bureaucratic change, and they provide a sound basis for post-independence government.

Policy Initiative and the Pursuit of Control, 1972–74

A. C. VOUTAS

It was ironic that the Governor-General's speech, delivered to the newly assembled third House of Assembly on 20 April 1972, had to be prepared before the contest for parliamentary power was resolved in Papua New Guinea. Vice-regal addresses are usually occasions for giving broad indication of the legislation and policies that Her Majesty's government intends to put before the House. On this occasion the Governor-General was properly speaking on behalf of the Australian government, for no final powers had then been transferred to Papua New Guinea. But by intimating that Australia would present draft legislation to the House on land ownership and the public service, would table a White Paper on strategies for a new national development programme, and had already prepared a programme of legislative and administrative changes that needed to take place before self-government, the speech-writers revealed that they had not anticipated basic changes in the power structure of the House resulting from a Coalition victory. Notwithstanding the strictly legal position, there was no recognition in the Governor-General's speech that it would be politically embarrassing, if not disastrous, for Australian officials to promote legislation that did not have the support of the new Papua New Guinea government.

About an hour after the vice-regal party had retired from the chamber, a vote on the composition of the Ministerial Nominations Committee confirmed the National Coalition's right to govern. Four days later, on Monday 24th April, Michael Somare was to give his first policy speech on behalf of the National Coalition government. This speech had to be cleared over the weekend by the other Coalition leaders, Julius Chan, John Guise, and Thomas Kavali. The parties and individuals drawn suddenly into the Coalition had never previously worked together to formulate policies. The National Party didn't even have a declared election policy, being at that stage a Highland splinter group rapidly put together in the week before parliament met as part of the intense lobbying for power. Both Pangu and the People's Progress Party had declared election platforms, but there were clear differences in their platforms. The People's Progress Party emphasized that it was a pragmatic party whose policies would flow up from the needs of a grass-roots membership. The party did, however, specifically advocate the encouragement and protection of private ownership and the attraction of foreign investment into labour-intensive industries to provide employment. Pangu, on the other hand, spoke of restricting sectors of the economy to PNG nationals, and of changing the law to allow for communal participation in economic development on a clan or village basis, rather than on an individual basis. The People's Progress Party emphasized employment creation and rural improvement as the means of stemming the urban drift. Pangu, while also calling for rural improvement, came down heavily in favour of improved wages and houses for urban workers, and avoided reconciling the competing demands of urban and rural areas. Pangu's platform covered a number of specific matters not mentioned in the People's Progress Party platform — immediate self-government, import replacement, a national shipping line, and an expert committee to examine land matters.

The party platforms were the base documents for preparing Somare's speech, but they were not treated with doctrinaire reverence because they were expressed in broad general terms and the leaders felt that there was little connection between the detail of their national policies and their accession to power. The same small core of party stalwarts who had manufactured the platforms felt confident enough in the face of a relatively parochial electorate to tinker with the nationally declared party policies. Thus the process of synthesizing the first statement of Coalition policy was not very difficult.

Somare's speech pledged the Coalition government to distribute its development programme fairly among all districts, regardless of the strength or weakness of the representation of particular districts in the government. The ideological motive behind this pledge was reinforced by the political judgement that such a pledge might erode Highlands solidarity behind the opposition United Party. Echoing the People's Progress Party emphasis, Somare stated the Coalition would be pro-business and would continue the policy of seeking to attract overseas investment. He did add the important rider that foreign investment inflows would be balanced by measures to prevent foreign control of the economy. Again echoing the People's Progress Party position, Somare claimed that the Coalition believed the timing of self-government was not as important as deciding on the type of self-government best suited to Papua New Guinea. This remarkable concession on Pangu's part must be viewed against the background of the collective wish of the Coalition leaders *not* to frighten off possible Highland converts to the Coalition.

In the formulation of this first Coalition policy statement, there was no difficulty in obtaining the agreement of Coalition leaders that Canberra should be given the message loudly and clearly that it was not to take the running on major policy issues. In response to the Australian initiatives foreshadowed in the Governor-General's speech, Somare's statement quashed any prospect of Australian-inspired land legislation until after an extensive inquiry by an expert committee. He also cautioned that his government would not accept the Australian programme for movement towards self-government simply for the sake of achieving self-government quickly.

With this very general statement of Coalition policy, little more than an invocation or a statement of hopes, Michael Somare and sixteen colleagues stepped into ministerial roles. A significant number of the new ministers had a "will to power" and wanted to develop and implement policy, their party's or their own. But they had little notion at that time of the process by which their policy decisions might be translated by many micro-decisions of the public service into action affecting the public. Only three of the older ministers, who had been assistant ministerial members in the second House of Assembly, had any previous ministerial experience. The inter-party deals that had been made in forming the Coalition restricted an allocation of portfolios on the basis of relevant experience or assumed capacity. And the same deals made for potential dissension, since they placed policy control over economic affairs, an area of apparent difference between the main parties, fully in the hands of the four People's Progress Party ministers.

There was thus a very limited basis for unity or for consistency of policy among highly individualist ministers in the early months of the Coalition government. But, without ministers needing to think out the rationale, the institutional workings of Cabinet launched them on a learning curve in the arts of policy development, co-ordination, and control. Cabinet discussion ensured a collective position on most issues, particularly in the early days of the Coalition when ministers preferred to take most matters to Cabinet rather than make individual decisions. The process ate up an inordinate amount of ministers' time, but it helped to build a unity of purpose and direction where none had existed before.

DEVELOPMENT OF A BROAD POLICY FRAMEWORK

Policy control is logically a sequel of overall policy formulation. The Chief Minister and his ministers saw the need to agree on a broad framework of goals on which to base public policy. Most ministers did not favour the development philosophy propounded by Bill McCasker, director of the Office of Programming and Co-ordination. He was seen to take a view favouring maximum growth by directing government resources to those areas that would yield the quickest returns. Fortunately Mike Faber of the University of East Anglia had been commissioned early in 1972 by the Australian government to formulate proposals for future economic development in Papua New Guinea. With the assistance of a rather unconventional team of British economists, he produced a report that identified equity in the distribution of services and economic opportunities as the best strategy for economic development. Drawing on the ideas contained in the Faber Report, a small group of people working under the Chief Minister and the Finance Minister, mainly non-public servants, worked up draft aims for consideration by ministers. Quite deliberately, there was almost no consultation on these drafts with senior public servants. Some ministers bargained with the Chief Minister during the drafting stage, gaining modifications, but the final Cabinet paper on the Eight Aims was not generally circulated beyond ministers.

In December 1972, immediately after ministers made a Cabinet decision on the Eight Aims, I was designated by the Chief Minister to brief all departmental heads. I had taken particular care to have the aims circulated to the departmental heads in advance. After expanding on each of the aims I asked each officer to state how he viewed the prospects of devising programmes, consistent with his departmental responsibilities, that were in line with the aims. With some noteworthy exceptions, the majority of departmental heads were aghast that outsiders with little public service experience should have put a proposal to Cabinet on overall development philosophy without its first being vetted, modified, and agreed upon among departments. The very idea that an elected government had the right to devise policy guidelines, and to expect its public service to implement programmes within these policy guidelines, appeared completely alien to a number of departmental heads. I shared with Somare and his Pangu ministers the normative assumption that in a democracy, responsible ministers make policy and public servants carry it out. As we saw it, colonial rule under a distant and aloof Australian minister had allowed public servants to exceed proper limits in making policy. By imposing policy guidelines on the public service, the Somare ministry was democratizing government.

The Eight Aims were later developed on a number of fronts mainly by *ad hoc* committees that included non-public servants. These committees worked on such matters as national education, the informal sector, the Village Economic Development Fund, foreign investment, including mining policy and the renegotiation of the Bougainville Copper Agreement, the involvement of traditional groups in business, and village dispute settlement. Eliciting from each department specific programmes that would further the Eight Aims later became the institutional responsibility of the Central Planning Office. The powerful Constitutional Planning Committee boosted the process of commitment to agreed national aims even further by developing the Eight Aims and having them incorporated in Papua New Guinea's Constitution as a bipartisan statement of the philosophy behind the new state.

PERSONNEL AND INSTITUTIONAL CHANGES AS STRATEGIES FOR POLICY CONTROL

When the National Coalition came to power, Somare and his ministers were particularly suspicious of many senior Australian public servants, whom they had seen as obstacles to change during their period in opposition. Administrator Les Johnson and a few departmental heads were seen as "good guys" but, these exceptions apart, the interaction of minister and departmental head was seen as a contest of wills in which the scales were tipped in favour of the expatriate career public servant. It is not surprising then that in its pursuit of policy control the Coalition was, for a period, preoccupied with personnel questions. It was decided to strengthen the position of each minister by allowing him to appoint two personal staff of his own choosing, and the Chief Minister was allocated three staff positions. This was in contrast to the earlier practice whereby department heads hand-picked departmental officers to assist ministerial members.

People chosen as ministerial staff did not become members of the public service. This was to ensure that staff were taking the same political risk in undertaking their job as the minister. Their fate was directly tied to that of their political master. It was hoped that this situation would be conducive to total loyalty. Ministers could if they wished have public servants seconded to their office, and some ministers merely accepted staff foisted upon them by their respective departments. Most ministers, however, availed themselves of the opportunity to select competent staff from the community at large. In the face of a number of expatriate appointments, John Guise made a point of selecting only Papua New Guineans to his staff. One or two ministers selected staff because they had nice legs, although fortunately these people were good managers and perceptive thinkers. Admittedly in a few cases, people who could only be described as expatriate carpet-baggers wormed their way into a minister's good books and savoured the perquisites of office and power. Once independent staff were provided to ministers, there was unfortunately little attempt to develop them as a collective force, sensitized to the government's general aims, and operating as bridge-builders between ministers. Most simply served their minister within a fairly narrow context. Some became players in the national power game without passing the selection test of a general election.

Personnel rearrangement as a strategy for policy control did not stop at the creation of ministerial staff. A number of senior public servants were marked men in the eyes of the Coalition government. Tom Ellis, the number one kiap and secretary of the Administrator's Department, was one of these. Ellis was probably misunderstood by Pangu Pati. He was a man of loyalty — loyalty to whichever government was in power. Pangu's memories of Tom Ellis, however, based on its experience in opposition, cast the man in the stereotype of the all-powerful colonial kiap. The much publicized slogan "God is not dead; He is alive and well at Konedobu" was directed at Ellis. Because of this stereotype image of the man, Somare was adamant from the very first days of the Coalition government that Ellis should not exercise his legal right to attend Cabinet meetings. (Ellis's appointment as an official member of Cabinet again suggests that Canberra was expecting a different outcome to the 1972 election.) Ellis in effect withered on the vine, eventually took extended leave, and retired. Other personnel movements engineered by ministers may have been designed simply to settle old scores, as was probably the case with Lyle Newby, Director of Information and Extension Services.

At a superficial level, Pangu may have seen the slaying of Goliath as heralding in a new era of administration. But having crippled the leadership of the kiap department, Somare did not move forcefully to use this widely spread force of officers as his own personal unit of policy control. Paul Ryan, the secretary of the Chief Minister's Department, took several opportunities to build bridges between Somare and the kiaps (speeches to district commissioners, increases in kiap pay), but the momentum was not sustained. The most positive step came in late 1973 when Somare sent a circular to all relevant departmental heads and district commissioners, giving administrative authority to district commissioners to co-ordinate the activities of all other field officers within their district.

As well as replacing some key representatives of the old order, the Coalition government was concerned to find strategies that would somehow make the bulk of the public service more conducive to promoting and implementing reforms. Rapid localization promised to provide the shock treatment necessary to bring the majority of the public service into line. Pangu's forecast of the effects of rapid localization relied in part on the simplistic assumption that putting Papua New Guineans in senior positions would make policy control easier and more effective.

A disturbing statement by the Public Service Board in September 1972 prompted Somare to take a dramatic stand on localization. The board claimed that the number of expatriates in the PNG public service would have to be maintained until 1975. Somare responded by announcing that the number of expatriates would be reduced from their current level of over seven thousand to three thousand by 1975. The dramatic target of three thousand was deliberately set to shock the board and the various departmental heads into action. After considerable grumbling in expatriate quarters about the recklessness of Somare's localization policy, a surprising number of overseas officers came to terms with their limited career prospects. Encouraged by the security of the generous "golden handshake" that Australia then agreed to provide, they devoted their energies to supporting the Coalition government's policies.

The implementation of a rapid localization programme put many Papua New Guineans into senior positions, but it did not result in the policy control expected by Pangu. Some Pangu leaders, in both the party's parliamentary wing and its central executive, were soon talking about "tame" blacks being put in to run departments. The dangers of a collection of Papua New Guinean mandarins, steeped in caution and the Australian colonial tradition, was clearly perceived by some of the politicians. At the Pangu national convention in late 1973, "black skins, white masks" were assigned primary blame for the lack of Coalition policy implementation. That convention resolved that all senior positions within the public service should be politicized. This brought an outcry from many of the senior Papua New Guinean public servants already in powerful positions. Cabinet did not, however, consider it proper to make political appointments on the scale envisaged at the convention. But Cabinet did move in this direction, seeking to appoint Papua New Guineans who were both professionally competent and strongly sympathetic towards the government parties. The appointment of Father Ignatius Kilage, Joe Nombri, and Dawa Lynch as members of the Public Service Board was an example of this.

The Coalition government was quick to recognize the importance of the Office of Programming and Co-ordination as an instrument for achieving policy control. This was evident from the tussle between ministers and parties for control of economic planning. Somare finally resolved this argument by recommending that a special National Planning Committee be collectively responsible for this function. This committee was made up of the four Coalition leaders (therefore staving off demands for individual control) and three senior Papua New Guinean public servants who were there to provide technical and professional competence.

Gaining policy control through economic planning was, for the Coalition, both a question of personnel and institutional change. The incumbent economic czar, Bill McCasker, was identified with the old Australian approach to economic development. The Coalition government wanted to find a new national planner. Late in 1972, advertisements were placed internationally. Several accomplished economic planners with impressive track records applied. These included men who had served as senior economic planners in Mauritius, the Malagasy Republic, Uganda, and Botswana. Six applicants were invited to Papua New Guinea and interviewed by a large panel which reflected both the divided responsibility that would befall the national planner, and the political concern that senior Papua New Guinean public servants should participate in a selection process as important as this. The selection committee was looking for someone who would make a dramatic impact on planning and policy co-ordination. The committee took the advice of Sir John Crawford that, given the innovative and highly taxing nature of the job, it would be wise to appoint someone under the age of forty.

The selection committee eventually favoured a young Canadian, David Beatty. Before presenting its recommendation to Cabinet, the committee made sure that Cabinet ministers had the opportunity to talk to the leading applicants. I was drawn to Beatty not just because of his professional competence but because he was clearly sympathetic to the Eight Aims, and because he was Canadian. Pangu believed that the overwhelming predominance in the public service of expatriates from one Western country only made innovation and policy control more difficult. De-Australianizing the expatriate segment of the public service at senior levels with the right people would assist policy control. In the period up to Beatty's arrival in mid-1973 the Coalition government strengthened and re-organized the Office of Programming and Co-ordination, renaming it the Central Planning Office. In the restructuring, particular emphasis was placed on the social aspects of national planning and on preparation for district planning.

Institutional change, as a strategy for policy control, went further than restaffing the Public Service Board and the Central Planning Office. In late 1972 the Chief Minister initiated an inquiry into the reorganization of all public service departments. The committee was chaired by Norm Rolfe of the Public Service Board and comprised McCasker, a representative of Finance, and myself. Although the committee made substantive recommendations — including establishment of an Area Improvement Department which would have brought together all field officers concerned with rural development — its main political purpose was to sensitize departmental heads to the political reality that Somare, and not Canberra, was determining the pace of change, and that they were being invited to be innovative in pursuit of the Coalition's policy objectives.

Policy control relies ultimately on ministerial competence and appropriate ministerial management techniques. Unfortunately, some ministers believed that, simply given an order, the bureaucrats would carry out their instructions. One or two ministers, in particular John Guise, were able, through the force of their personalities and the way in which they put questions to senior bureaucrats, to achieve this. Others, such as Iambakey Okuk, merely succeeded in putting their departments off-side. Somare was keen to keep ministers on their toes, and to put key ministers in portfolios suited to their skills. He used ministerial reshuffles to do this. Admittedly these reshuffles were made also as a result of power struggles within the Coalition itself. In the early days of the Coalition, the National Party felt particularly badly done by, and so did a number of senior members of Pangu. The People's Progress Party monopoly of the economic portfolios was the target of much animosity.

The first change, announced in July 1973, was primarily a case of up-grading the relative strengths of both the National and Pangu parties within the Coalition ministry as well as bringing John Kaputin into the Justice portfolio in the hope that he could institute major reforms within the conservative Law Department. The reshuffle of February 1974 was directed at placing those ministers who had shown themselves to be good operators into key "development" portfolios. An example of this was John Guise's appointment to Agriculture after the uneasy tension between Okuk and his department. This reshuffle was also designed to demonstrate to ministers that their after-hours behaviour was not unnoticed by the Chief Minister.

In looking at policy control, it is worth focusing on the examples of two highly motivated ministers, Iambakey Okuk and John Kaputin, who pushed for major reforms within their departments. Iambakey Okuk wanted to place middle-man profits associated with coffee — the most important village cash crop — in the hands of Papua New Guineans. He wanted to prohibit all further expatriate coffee buying, restricting it to Papua New Guineans only. His department saw nothing but problems in doing this. Okuk therefore arranged for an academic outsider to prepare the drafting instructions and much of the background work. In piloting this policy proposal through Cabinet and parliament, he acted independently of his department. During his public hours at least, Okuk was an uncompromising man of vision. It was his performance after hours that raised doubts about the appropriate level for his political responsibilities. When Iambakey took up his new portfolio as Minister for Transport and Civil Aviation, a major battle ensued between him and his department head. This resulted in Cabinet's retrenching the departmental head, leaving the minister at odds with most of his department. Again, Okuk sought outside advice on matters such as standardization of vehicles and vehicular parts, and on alternative transport systems such as aerial ropeways.

John Kaputin, as Minister for Justice, was full of progressive ideas and again relied on outside advice for some of his major reforms, such as those involved in the National Companies Ordinance and the Business Groups Incorporation Ordinance. But he did not communicate often, or easily, with his department. This would probably have led to the resignation of another departmental head but for other issues which led to the Chief

Minister's removing Kaputin from the ministry. Other ministers worked at policy control in their own ways. The most successful at this were probably Somare, John Guise, Julius Chan, Albert Maori Kiki, and Bruce Jephcott.

CO-ORDINATION

Policy control in the early days of the Coalition had much to do with achieving consensus between the main political actors. In late 1972 and in early 1973, a meeting of the four Coalition leaders was arranged each Cabinet week to consider approaches to major issues and the allocation of responsibilities. The meetings of leaders often resulted in their presenting a united front in the Cabinet room or in their putting pressure on a ministerial colleague to take action in a particular direction. This process fell into disuse, mainly, I believe, because the servicing of the meetings was not integrated with the work of the Cabinet secretariat.

Bridging gaps within the Coalition had to be done not only at the Coalition leader level but also at the level of individual ministers who had different views and overlapping responsibilities. The problem of establishing policy control over foreign investment was a clear example. The ministers for Finance, Foreign Relations, Trade, Business Development, Justice, and National Development all claimed legitimate interests in foreign investment, and so a National Investment Committee of Cabinet was set up with Sir Maori Kiki as its chairman. Unfortunately this committee met only a couple of times, probably as a result of the sacking of John Kaputin, and of the naive belief on the part of Pangu ministers that National Development Minister Gavera Rea would be able to build the Pangu ideas of foreign investment into the operations of the new National Investment and Development Authority (NIDA), nominally placed under his control.

The prime policy issue over foreign investment was whether NIDA would be an instrument for localization of the economy or an agency for facilitation of foreign investment. Pangu leaders intended an emphasis on localization. The ordinance establishing NIDA had sufficient flexibility to be used in both ways. On the side of localization, NIDA had power to establish development corporations that would buy into, and eventually take over, foreign ventures. The Tanzanian approach served as a model here. On the other hand, NIDA was charged with the duty of preparing priority schedules to identify desirable types of foreign investment in each area. In practice, NIDA in its early years concentrated on licensing all existing foreign ventures in the country, processing new applications for foreign investment, and drawing up national investment priorities. No NIDA-instigated development corporations were established.

It should be said that the Coalition government created NIDA, as it created the Central Planning Office, to have a major co-ordinating and policy control function over all the disparate departments and instrumentalities that had direct interests in foreign investment. The board of NIDA brought together all these various departments with the intention of inducing them to reach consensus.

Another technique used by the Coalition government to achieve policy control and co-ordination was the establishment of various commissions and committees. The Constitutional Planning Committee and the Lands Commission were the most important here. They were important in softening up the bureaucrats and the public to accept major reforms, although it is possible to argue that on occasion the Constitutional Planning Committee was a barrier to internal policy changes lest they prejudice the final shape of the Papua New Guinea Constitution.

By far the most common technique for policy control was *ad hoc* working groups on particular problems. It was usual for these working groups to contain a mix of top bureaucrats and political staff. Among these working groups were those concerned with relations with Japan, foreign aid, inflation, education, law and order, tribal fighting, mining policy, and the renegotiation of the Bougainville Copper Agreement, the informal sector, and village courts.

What was particularly useful in policy control in the early years was the community of key backroom men and women backing up the ministers. Among the group I include Rabbie Namaliu, Moi Avei, Ross Garnaut, Charles Lepani, Anthony Martin, Steve Zorn, Jim Fingleton, Tos Barnett, Diana Conyers, Peter Fitzpatrick, Loraine Blaxter, Mark Lynch, and myself. Members of this community shared a sense of purpose and were fundamentally sympathetic to the general philosophy of the Somare government. At various times they worked for different ministers and for different parties, yet they spent a lot of time working with one another and pushing their collective conclusions in their separate departments. It was this group that provided an informal mechanism for policy control and co-ordination. In a fluid situation with many ministers pushing pet ideas, information passed relatively freely within the group, and this often enabled the Chief Minister to manage his ministerial colleagues so that they were, at least, running in the same direction. Members of the group often served together on *ad hoc* working committees within the public service. They reinforced one another in the operation of these committees, so that both by numbers and by logic they persuaded traditional bureaucrats to modify well-established positions.

By 1974, mainly through the pushing of David Beatty, a system was institutionalized whereby the core operators serving the Coalition talked to one another regularly. Beatty instituted the daily "crisis calendar" meeting. The technique was simple. A large white board stood in Paul Ryan's office with columns headed "crisis", "proposed strategy", "person responsible for action", and "date by which action to be completed". The core operators would meet for thirty minutes at eight o'clock each morning in Ryan's office. Progressively more Papua New Guineans were built into this core, and when particular subjects involved other departmental heads they were specifically invited to attend. Beatty was responsible for updating the calendar. Shared approaches and a team spirit developed from this. It was a very useful technique in ensuring that core operators sustained the agreed priorities. It proved a successful technique for handling a number of crises — inflation being one — but it did not endure beyond 1974.

From 1972 to 1974 expatriates were playing a dominant role in policy formulation and policy control. Frustrations mounted among a number of senior and middle-level Papua New Guinean public servants, some of whom publicly supported Kaputin and John Momis in their criticisms of white advisers. All the expatriates in the key backroom group were sympathetic to local officer involvement and local officer control. Most of them took action in different ways to involve local officers in policy development and control. The Chief Minister's Department organized twice-weekly staff meetings with Papua New Guinean staff members on the way up. At these meetings local officers were briefed on what had happened and were encouraged to vent their views. In addition, the Chief Minister's personal staff, after it was enlarged to include Rabbie Namaliu, Moi Avei, Meg Taylor, and Bill Kuamin, met regularly as a separate unit to exchange information and to agree on approaches to the Chief Minister and other ministers.

Normally a government's budget would serve as a primary instrument for policy control and co-ordination. In the 1972/73 budget, and also to some extent in the 1973/74 budget, the policy framework that the ministers, political staff, and public servants had thrashed out was not affecting the budgetary process. This was partly because of the traditional secrecy that had always surrounded the budget, particularly on the revenue-raising side, and partly because of the uncertainty of the level of Australian aid until the last moment. For the first two budgets, senior ministers had very little time between their first sight of the budget and their final approval of it. The budget formulation process seemed to restrict ministers to making piecemeal inputs when they considered the draft works programme or new initiatives in the rural improvement programme or other matters which came to Cabinet as separate papers. The opportunity for Coalition leaders to take a long, hard look at the global budgetary situation was simply not available institutionally in the early years.

The gap between policies, programmes, and the budgetary process was not fully bridged until the 1975/76 budget, but national plan documents began to have an effect earlier. The production by the Planning Office of the Improvement Plan of 1973−74 and the Strategies for Nationhood documents of December 1974 required innovative inputs from the various departments which were vetted by the Coalition government. By 1975 a rigorous budget priority-setting mechanism had been established which provided for the early involvement of departmental heads and ministers in shaping the whole budget.

The hardest thing for an observer to appreciate fully is the constant stream of absolutely urgent political problems which consume the time available to ministers and the core operators for policy matters. The Coalition was initially confronted with the two main unsolved political problems of the Gazelle and Bougainville. These and the later pressures from the Trobriands and Papua Besena took up an inordinate amount of ministerial and support group time. In the early years there were also other issues which arose because of the power of established interest groups, such as the expatriate lawyers through the PNG branch of the International Commission of Jurists. They were upset that the police had tapped a phone call between a private lawyer and his client who was defending himself against a criminal offence. The private lawyers were able to lobby both the government and the opposition to take up this cause and consequently considerable time was devoted to the production of the Protection of Private Communications Bill 1972 (see also the paper by Peter Bayne in this volume).

There were many necessary institutional decisions associated with the move to independence, such as the nature of the independent banking system and the establishment of a national airline. Much of my own time was taken up with the establishment of the national airline. The institutional decisions were formalized by the detailed legalistic negotiations on the transfer of powers that took place between the Australian and Papua New Guinea governments, with the Constitutional Planning Committee as a third party. I would argue that this was the most sustained distraction from the Somare government's effort to effect its national policies. Meticulous legalistic concern for a text-book transfer of powers from metropole to colony allowed Australia to determine the priorities for policy focus. This order of priorities started with powers that were not sensitive for Australia's interests and moved finally through to powers that were highly sensitive for Australia. This order of priority for instituting policy control had nothing to do with the priorities the Coalition government might have set if it had acted independently.

CONCLUSION

Barry Holloway, the Speaker of the House of Assembly, has said of the Coalition government from 1972 to 1974 that it made little positive impact on village people. He was critical that the government had not concentrated on policy development and implementation in those areas meaningful to village people. He advised the government to focus on dispute settlement and revamping local government. Similarly, Moi Avei was critical that the Somare government was merely muddling through. Someone else less committed to the Coalition government claimed that Somare had had the good fortune to have made the right mistakes, but asked how long it could last. University students said it was a period of rhetoric, no action, and hypocrisy.

There is some truth in each of these views, but in retrospect the positive steps taken in 1973–74 to develop policy control were an achievement. The shock treatment of the public service through localization and internationalization produced a mental attitude in much of the service which questioned the sanctity of established norms and which was conducive to initiating change. The use of *ad hoc* working committees and grandoise committees of inquiry sensitized key members of the public service to the direction the government wanted to take. The early decision on the Eight Aims and the establishment of the Central Planning Office were fundamental in starting to bridge the gap between policy formulation and policy implementation.

There were certainly shortcomings in achieving policy control. Informal interaction between the Chief Minister and his ministers was not frequent enough, and not adequately used by the Chief Minister to impose policy control. The formal institutional interaction of ministers in Cabinet and in Cabinet committees was so taxing that it reduced informal interaction. It could be argued that some ministers were ambivalent about the philosophy behind the Eight Aims. The pseudo-socialistic overtones of the aims were acceptable at the level of public rhetoric. They even appeared to be related to the traditional restraints that existed in village societies. But for some ministers I believe that repressed entrepreneurial ambitions whispered: "I don't want redistribution applied to me personally; I would rather be a millionaire businessman."

The most cynical interpretation that can be made of the general philosophy announced by the Coalition government in the Eight Aims and elaborated in the Constitution is that it reflected an intellectual trend of the late sixties and seventies keenly felt by the expatriate Western liberals and by the Papua New Guinean graduates and undergraduates. The politicians, however, merely clothed themselves with these ideas because other political purposes were served in doing so. If this interpretation is true even in part, then ambivalence reduced the capacity of the new government to achieve policy control.

The final point to be made on the negative side of the policy control exercise was how little success the Coalition government had in setting its own priorities during the period under discussion. The main reason for this was the almost blind acceptance by the government of the involved process of legalistic transfer of powers as the correct ritual for achieving independence. Other reasons were the frequency of urgent side-tracking crises and issues.

Policy control was a new and sudden task for the National Coalition ministers. Generally it was a new task for the advisers also. Notwithstanding the problems, the general movement was towards a system of overall policy control and co-ordination, eventually exemplified in financial year 1975/76, which must be the envy of many countries.

Policy-Making in the Transfer of Powers from Australia

T. E. BARNETT

Policy-making between 1970 and September 1975 was quite like the closing matches in a football season. Senior players were found wanting, with nothing more to contribute; former stars faded into retirement; new players flashed, some only briefly, to stardom; and other players began to build up their reputations. As the pace quickened, one outstanding player retired to become the referee, and fights and diversions broke out spasmodically. After the final ceremony, at independence in September 1975, the retired players, the referee, and the spectators went home, leaving the new team re-examining the rules for the matches ahead.

The story is told here, from no particular theoretical viewpoint, of how player after player grabbed the ball of policy and tried to run with it towards the goal. Although it did not always seem so at the time, in retrospect it is clear that all the players were on the same side, though occasionally kicking in different directions. The chapter is divided into sections named after the influential players of the moment: (*a*) the Minister and Department of External Territories (DOET) (before 1972); (*b*) L. W. Johnson, Administrator (until April 1972); (*c*) Johnson and Michael Somare, Chief Minister (April—September 1972); (*d*) Somáre (September 1972—April 1973); (*e*) The PNG government and the Constitutional Planning Committee (CPC) (April 1973—August 1975).

The discussion focuses on policy formulation concerned with the transfer of authority from Australia to Papua New Guinea, as well as with the reallocation of that authority within Papua New Guinea. Transferring assets, making financial and staffing arrangements, strengthening or establishing PNG institutions and public service departments, allocating ministerial responsibility, as well as enacting the Constitution and other laws to control the exercise of authority are all included as part of this transfer process. A detailed description of the policy process in action, as it concerned the transfer of just one of many powers — that of defence, is given as an appendix for illustrative purpose.

MINISTER AND DEPARTMENT OF EXTERNAL TERRITORIES

In early 1972 there existed a very good personal and working relationship between the senior officials in DOET and the new minister, Andrew Peacock. There was a willing acceptance of the concept of early self-government and early independence. The Liberal–Country Party government was quite anxious to avoid United Nations criticism for being the last of the colonial powers and was planning for a smooth transfer of authority. (On earlier policies and steps towards transfer see Bayne and Colebatch 1973.) A confidential plan known as "The Gearing-Up Plan" had been prepared by officials, purporting to list the major activities to be carried out before self-government day — tentatively projected for December 1975. Over fifty activities were divided into "essential", "highly desirable", and "desirable" and then broken down into a series of detailed steps to be carried out in Australia or in Papua New Guinea. These ranged from such things as the possible provision of a new house of parliament to the transfer of the defence force. The plan included innumerable diagrams and flow charts and attempted to co-ordinate, in both countries, such matters as policy development, inter-government conferences, draft Cabinet submissions, decisions, drafting of bills, enactment, transfer of assets, and training and provision of manpower. This very involved plan was kept highly confidential to avoid political embarrassment. The press particularly were to be kept out of it. Australian officials had nightmares about pressmen discovering an early copy of the very flexible timetable and publishing a list of missed deadlines.

An early version of the Gearing-Up Plan included the following major activities:

Public service. DOET contemplated a review of the public service organization and the enactment of legislation to simplify procedures and separate overseas staff before self-government. The review was to be conducted by a DOET committee on which the PNG colonial administration was represented.

Banking. The programme was based on the premise that a separate banking system would be required by July 1974. A PNG central bank would be necessary and detailed discussions with Australian banks, legislation in both countries, and merger of assets would be necessary.

Broadcasting. Australia felt it would be inappropriate for the Australian Broadcasting Commission to continue broadcasting in Papua New Guinea after self-government. It was thought advisable for a single PNG broadcasting authority to take over existing ABC and administration facilities. Legislation would be needed and key staff should be appointed in early 1974. (In the event, the PNG government appointed its own consultant and eventually established the National Broadcasting Commission, closely modelled on the ABC.)

Courts. A detailed study of the court system by DOET, the Attorney-General's Department, and the administration was planned, covering all aspects including legislative control, appeals to the High Court, and a Magisterial Services Commission. (This plan was overtaken by events and the matter was handled within Papua New Guinea by the Law Department and, later, by the CPC.)

Land border with West Irian. Detailed plans to settle this question included mapping and agreement on a negotiating position by the Australian government and the Administrator's Executive Council by June 1972. The working group was to include the Australian Foreign Affairs Department.

Border with Queensland. Similar steps were planned, but the PNG government of Somare quickly took over initiative on this matter.

Investment guidelines. The idea was to set up a study by DOET and administration officials on the need for an investment code to be enacted in Papua New Guinea before self-government. (This plan was upset when the Coalition government was returned, having its own ideas about investment.)

Commonwealth functions. There were separate plans for the future handling of functions of various Commonwealth departments in Papua New Guinea — Works, Shipping and Transport (navigational aids), Meteorology, Auditor-General, Bureau of Mineral Resources, and so on.

Australian High Commission. There were plans for the establishment of an office.

Foreign Office and foreign activities. There was provision for the training of PNG diplomats with Australian assistance and the establishment of foreign consulates in Papua New Guinea after self-government. (In fact, from Papua New Guinea's point of view, this heading was to involve the establishment of a department, the development of PNG policy independently of Australia, the location of PNG officers in selected Australian overseas missions, and the investigation of possible future international treaty relationships.)

Overseas telecommunications. The transfer of the function involved legislation in both countries, agreements about finance, staffing and training, and joining international bodies.

Currency. Plans for designing, introducing and controlling a PNG currency were linked with the establishment of the proposed PNG Reserve Bank.

Police. The plan for the transfer of the police force to PNG control involved legislation to separate the expatriate permanent and contract officers from Papua New Guinean officers. This eventually led to much discussion on whether to transfer at self-government and on improving the capacity of the force to ensure it could handle the increasing pressure upon it as unrest increased.

There were many other areas of activity. As can be seen from the above selection, some were purely of concern to Australia, some should have been purely of PNG concern, and others genuinely required joint action. Each project was broken up into a series of very detailed steps, and the timetabling and allocation of lead-in times for each project were inter-related. It was very much a Commonwealth plan, and there were officers in DOET detailed to keep it up to date by monthly amendments. To carry these steps out in an orderly fashion was to be a massive undertaking. It was realized that, as independence would be only a few years after self-government, the task was urgent; its complexity is illustrated in the discussion of the defence transfer provided in the appendix.

A major difficulty from the PNG side was that, in places where the plan really was relevant to PNG needs, there were often vital and unconsidered questions of PNG policy involved, but the government was not geared for major policy-making in many areas. Since Papua New Guinea was geographically so close to Australia, it had been the habit for DOET to direct PNG officials as though they were members of a section of DOET. In 1972 this was still being done by telephone, by lengthy telex directions from named Australian officials to named PNG officials, and by regular visits. Some PNG departments had no policy sections and, for matters such as defence and foreign affairs, there were no departments at all. Central policy co-ordination mechanisms were weak, and such policy-making capacity as existed was held almost exclusively by expatriates. At the beginning of 1972, Papua New Guinea's preparations for self-government consisted of visits by forward-thinking DOET officials from the Constitutional and Legal Section carrying their Gearing-Up Plan with its graphs and flow-charts. They would sit around the Administrator's conference table with a large PNG inter-departmental committee consisting mainly of officials who were either apathetic or hostile to the idea of self-government. All were expatriates. There were, of course, individual expatriate officials in various departments and in the Administrative College who were acutely aware that self-government would come and find the country unprepared, and they were committed to help prepare national public servants for that day. Their spirit, however, had little influence on that inter-departmental committee. The only PNG politicians interested in self-government seemed to be the small group of Pangu supporters and sympathizers gathered around Somare, but their rise to power was not foreseen, or even contemplated.

The experiment with ministerial members had not been a great success. Although they had technically been given "final power" over some unimportant matters (by ministerial determination under the Papua New Guinea Act), the departmental heads remained in full control of the departments and considered themselves responsible directly to the Administrator, which indeed they were. After the Administrator's direction for them to consult with their ministerial member had been largely ignored, the Administrator (L. W. Johnson) insisted that a place be provided at the foot of all policy submissions for the signature (or mark X) of the ministerial member and a statement signed by the departmental head that the submission had been seen by and explained to the ministerial member. Among the PNG electors, particularly in the conservative Highlands, the concept of self-government was an unknown or forbidden subject. Hostility to the idea was cultivated by some expatriate members of the House of Assembly and by some senior members of the Department of the Administrator. (Somare and his advisers were convinced that senior officers of the Division of District Administration campaigned actively against Pangu in the 1972 elections.)

L. W. JOHNSON: ADMINISTRATOR

Johnson had come to Papua New Guinea in 1962 as Director of Education. He was never an entrenched member of the class of colonial administrators and had the good fortune to be based among the educated PNG teachers and education officers. From this vantage point the idea of self-government and an independent Papua New Guinea run by nationals seemed natural and inevitable. He was seen by nationals to be one of the expatriates actively working towards this goal and, on appointment as Administrator in 1970, was well fitted to the difficult task of transition.

In February 1972 Johnson allowed the inter-departmental committee to lapse and created an Office of Constitutional Development headed by the present writer as First Assistant Secretary, directly responsible to the Administrator. This office expanded to become the Political Development Division (PDD). Its role was, originally, to plan and co-ordinate all necessary steps within Papua New Guinea to acquire self-government. Fairly rapidly this role was expanded to target upon independence. I had been a defence counsel and law lecturer with close associations with Somare, Kiki, and senior national public servants who had attended the Administrative College since 1965; with me in the PDD were a recent expatriate law graduate and expatriate clerk. After a few months of searching and negotiating, one of the ablest Papua New Guinean law graduates, I. F. Tarua, joined the staff. He eventually took charge of the division at the end of 1974.

Johnson's instructions were to sit down and work out all that had to be done to prepare for self-government, to advise him, and to make sure it was being done. He promised full support to stimulate a sense of urgency. In detail the Political Development Division was instructed to:

1. Re-examine the Gearing-Up Plan and rewrite it from the PNG viewpoint. Identify areas where PNG and Australian interests conflicted or where a potential for conflict existed, and ensure steps were being taken to develop *PNG* policy in these areas.
2. Analyse the existing government structure in Papua New Guinea and the officials and bodies presently exercising statutory authority.
3. Assess structural weaknesses and propose plans to strengthen structures and to initiate and co-ordinate their implementation — e.g., create departments to formulate policy for defence and foreign affairs and oversee the establishment of those departments. Set up suitable intelligence machinery. Check that talks on creating a Reserve Bank and a PNG currency were beginning and that deadlines would be met.
4. Arrange and chair working groups to plan details of transfers from Australia — e.g., transfer of assets from the Commonwealth Works Department to a PNG works authority. Arrange for transfer of the Department of Civil Aviation (a consultant was employed to advise on technical and policy matters and work on preparation of an agency agreement).
5. Prepare lists of all instances of statutory power under PNG laws and advise the Administrator on the reallocation of those powers.
6. Arrange and hold talks with Australian officials to co-ordinate activities connected with the transfer of powers in both countries.
7. Study Australia's international treaty arrangements and define the options regarding succession to treaties which would be open to an independent Papua New Guinea.
8. Identify gaps in PNG laws (where Australian legislation applied of its own force) and set in motion the action necessary to prepare draft PNG replacement legislation. (There were approximately a hundred Australian acts in force in Papua New Guinea. Co-operate with Australian officials on the Australian programme to repeal such legislation.

Areas of potential conflict between the two countries included fixing the borders with Australia and Indonesia, fisheries agreements, off-shore oil rights, future aid commitments, setting up a civil aviation authority and national airline, and setting up a PNG Reserve Bank and a separate currency. The PDD set about identifying the issues and ensuring that the necessary machinery for developing separate PNG policies existed. Thus, pending the creation of the Department of Foreign Relations and Trade, negotiations with Australia on the Torres Strait at the official level were handled directly by the PDD. Pending the establishment of the Department of Defence, an Australian officer was seconded to the Administrator's Department to work in close conjunction with the PDD. A position was created in the PDD for an officer to work on the succession to international treaties, and an overseas consultant was hired to advise him. Eventually these functions were handed to the new departments once they were established and settled. The PDD was originally intended to work itself out of a job at independence.

From the outset it was understood that time was very short. It was expected that the target date for self-government of 1975 set out in the Gearing-Up Plan would be advanced. Johnson inculcated a sense of urgency in the PDD and instructed that it be spread to other departments. In response to a direct question, Johnson instructed that the PDD should give priority to transferring authority over *existing* institutions as, in general, there would be no time for radical restructuring. This did not preclude policy development in specific areas such as public service organization, defence, broadcasting, etc., but institutional reform was subordinate to the yet-to-be-decided timetable for independence. Later, Somare's approach was to be very similar, and this may be seen as a major cause of the friction that developed between the PDD and the Constitutional Planning Committee, which tended to advocate institutional "reform" before "transfer".

It was Johnson's intention to hand real powers to the new ministry to be formed after the April 1972 elections. To this end he directed the PDD to prepare lists of statutory powers which he could delegate to ministers. This involved a major review of all existing legislation to identify the many hundreds of instances of statutory power. The nature of each power had to be analysed and a decision taken, by the Administrator, whether to retain the power himself or to delegate it to a minister or to the Executive Council. In many instances the ordinance gave the power to a departmental head or officer, in which case the Administrator divested him of the power in order to delegate it to a minister. The views of departmental heads were sought, but then, without further consultation, the final decision was the Administrator's. It turned out that some departments had only a hazy idea of what legislation they administered. This exercise continued almost until self-government and provided the subject of many of the early discussions (and confrontations) between Somare's ministers and their departmental heads. Johnson adopted the policy of delegating even minor and technical matters to ministers rather than to public servants and encouraged ministers to sub-delegate to public servants where retention of the power would mean flooding the minister with routine administration. Although initially this policy caused some blockages with papers building up on ministers' desks for signature, it was deliberately intended as a practical lesson for new ministers to find out the powers of the executive and to demonstrate to departmental heads that it was the ministers, not themselves, who held authority.

Just before the elections, there were regular meetings between the Administrator and the secretary of DOET, and between the PDD and

DOET officials planning the transfer of authority. For instance, one of the concerns at that stage was the phasing out of the Commonwealth Department of Works and the transfer of its functions and its assets to the PNG Public Works Department. On such matters, officials of both countries communicated with each other directly as had always been the case. The Australian minister no doubt received reports as did other Australian ministers, as the transactions involved Works and Supply and Treasury. The views of PNG ministers, however, were not a consideration. All PNG participants in official talks were expatriates, but Papua New Guinea's interests were put forward with dogged independence by the Administrator. In matters such as the rights of Papua New Guinean staff being transferred to the PNG administration from the Commonwealth department, their staunchest ally often seemed to be the DOET representative rather than the expatriate PNG officials. DOET frequently strengthened Papua New Guinea's position against other Commonwealth departments in bureaucratic battles over the transfer of housing, equipment, and the like, and especially over the transfer of the defence function.

JOHNSON AND SOMARE

The formation of Somare's National Coalition government after the April 1972 election came as a complete surprise. Australian strategy for decolonizing had largely been based on the need to push reluctant United Party ministerial members into accepting responsibility or at least acting so as to create that impression. The advent of "the radicals" to power started a process of profound readjustment in attitude in Canberra. Over the next months the PNG ministry began to assert control over all public servants in Papua New Guinea, and official and informal links between PNG officials and DOET were to be broken, one by one. In this sometimes painful process the role of Johnson was crucial. He was the man squarely in the middle. He himself remained subject to ministerial direction from Canberra, but he also had to stand as a buffer between DOET and PNG officials. He proceeded quietly but firmly to help Australian officials and senior expatriate officials in Papua New Guinea to realize that, whatever the constitutional situation might be from time to time regarding final PNG powers and reserve Australian powers, the loyalty of all public servants working for the PNG government, regardless of race, must be to the PNG ministry. The Australians in Canberra accepted this situation with good grace, almost with relief, as did many, but by no means all, PNG expatriates. DOET ceased to apply direct pressure on expatriate PNG officials, and policy negotiations were increasingly transferred to inter-government ministerial level. Whatever direct pressures were applied on Johnson, and they must sometimes have been considerable, he kept to himself.

The expatriate public servants found the process of adjusting to their new ministers far more traumatic. The first formal meeting took place in the Cabinet room. Somare and his ministers sat around the table with the Administrator, and he endeavoured to outline the constitutional position and the roles of the Administrator, the Chief Minister (then known as Deputy Chairman of the Administrator's Executive Council), the ministers, the heads of departments and statutory authorities, and the public servants. It was a complicated situation because, although Australia technically retained full authority over Papua New Guinea until independence and the Administrator was Australian representative, the Australian minister had determined that "final power" over governmental matters would progressively be transferred to PNG ministers. In relation to any one department, the PNG minister responsible would have final powers of direction over some of its functions, but not over other functions that remained as reserve powers for which the Australian minister was responsible. On those matters, Johnson explained, the PNG ministers would have "day-to-day direction" (whatever that meant) but not final control. Ministers were to have authority over their departmental heads, but, under the Public Service Ordinance, the head was to be responsible for the working of the department and its officers. There were questions about this very confusing situation, and Johnson offered his services, which were frequently required in the following months.

Meanwhile, the expatriate departmental heads who had been waiting in the passage for some time were ushered in to seats provided in rows away from the Cabinet table. Perhaps they were more red-faced than usual because of the unaccustomed indignity of being kept waiting, but the overall impression was of the startling visual contrast between the slender, gaily and informally dressed young ministers and the older, predominantly corpulent, florid-faced departmental heads in long white socks, shorts, and shirts. Referring to his list, Johnson called the name of the minister and the department(s) for which he was to be responsible. The minister would stand and the relevant departmental head would stand and introduce himself. As the ministers then left the table to mingle with the heads for a beer, the atmosphere was charged with apprehension and mutual suspicion. The ministers simply seemed to disappear into the crowd, swamped amidst their much larger colleagues. The contrast between the ministers and their departmental heads went far deeper than mere surface appearances, and it quickly became apparent that many could not work together at all. In a very short time it was the heads who disappeared, having been retired or "localized" and shifted sideways into "special projects" pending finalization of the repatriation scheme.

An early problem was caused by ministers trying to choose advisers within their department whom they found more compatible than their departmental head. Sometimes ministers chose outsiders, but sometimes it was possible to appoint an acceptable public servant onto the minister's personal staff on secondment. Whatever happened, relations with the departmental head were often hostile. Nor did this necessarily stop after the appointment of Papua New Guinean departmental heads, as many of these were solidly indoctrinated with the values of a non-political and hierarchical public service and objected strongly if their ministers sought advice from junior officers or outsiders. In the early days the role of Johnson was crucial in pointing out the facts of the new political life to expatriate officers, and Somare was usually able to help his ministers to modify their sometimes intransigent attitudes. Part of the problem was caused by the hostile attitude of expatriate departmental heads, but many ministers had little idea of the limit of their powers over the permanent public service and assumed that, as well as deciding policy, they would have day-to-day detailed control as well as unfettered power over promotions, transfers, and dismissals. It would have been better perhaps if more attention had been given to developing a form of public service with a clearer relationship between ministers, departmental heads, personal staff, and junior officers. There had, however, already been one Australian-initiated public service review (the Besley Committee), whose report was awaited, and there was shortly to be another (the Rolfe Committee), Even had these committees tackled these problems satisfactorily, any final decision would have had to await the report of the Constitutional Planning Committee, still over a year away. Meanwhile, the problems were tackled as they arose, with the only clear guidelines being the need to give effective power to ministers while maintaining the morale of the public service, and the need to avoid a split in the public service, with some officers owing allegiance to the Administrator and some to Somare.

The method chosen by Australia for transferring formal power was to make determinations under the Papua New Guinea Act, giving final power to Papua New Guinea over some subject matters while leaving others reserved to Australia. Thus, within the one department, the minister would have final authority to direct his departmental head over some aspects, but the departmental head remained responsible to the Administrator for other matters. Johnson managed partly to resolve this difficult situation by directing departmental heads not to approach him even on policy over reserved matters except through the relevant minister. In the meantime, all parties in Papua New Guinea tended to ignore the formal constitutional relationships and proceeded to operate as if power had already been handed over. Thus Somare was addressing "his" district commissioners as if they were already under his power, whereas their formal boss was Tom

Ellis, secretary of the Department of the Administrator, who was technically still responsible to the Administrator. This approach was generally accepted by DOET, although there was an anguished scream when Johnson delegated his statutory powers over certain reserved matters to PNG ministers, and there were often complaints when the Cabinet secretariat forgot to send Cabinet submissions dealing with reserved matters to Canberra.

Somare and Kiki and their political advisers, such as Tony Voutas, Paul Cowdy, and John Yocklunn, came to power very suspicious of the existing PNG public service, especially of the expatriates in senior positions. They had recent memories of opposition and insults from key officials. They probably assumed that they would face a hostile Department of External Territories as well. They were particularly suspicious of the PDD, which was close to Johnson with its fingers in many pies and its direct links to the DOET officials. After a period of uneasy silence, I met with Somare and Voutas to explain the activities of the PDD. It was quite clear that it could only function with Somare's support and direction. So at Somare's request it was agreed with Johnson that the PDD should transfer its allegiance completely to Somare and his Coalition government. It was agreed by all that I would keep Johnson informed of my activities unless there was a conflict of interest between Papua New Guinea and Australia or unless Somare instructed to the contrary. The duty statement of the first assistant secretary of the PDD was altered accordingly. It was a clean break, and Johnson scrupulously avoided giving directions to the PDD from that date. On the other hand, he used his personal relationship with me on occasions as an informal channel to Somare to make suggestions and to alert him to situations.

By this time Somare's plans to set up a Constitutional Planning Committee were well advanced. These were worked up on the advice of Voutas and Yocklunn together with John Ley (parliamentary counsel) and David Stone (an ANU academic), both of whom became advisers to the CPC. Part of my duty statement already included the giving of advice to the Chief Minister on constitutional matters; the then unrecognized potential for conflict between him and the advisers to the CPC was later, unfortunately, to be fulfilled.

To give Somare direct control over some active public servants, an Office of the Chief Minister was established under Paul Ryan, who had been secretary to the Administrator's Executive Council. It took in the Cabinet secretariat, Ministerial Services, the PDD, and the Chief Minister's personal staff. This group quickly fused into an effective team in which public service versus political staff divisions and questions of hierarchy were largely ignored. The team worked so well that nothing was formalized. Ryan, Voutas, Cowdy (press secretary), March Lynch (secretary to the Cabinet), and I were all expatriates but managed to work harmoniously with Tarua and usually with Leo Morgan, the only two senior Papua New Guinean officers there in the early days. The lack of senior Papua New Guinean officers close to Somare was recognized, but attempts to fill the gaps involved competition with other departments for the few available educated officers with administrative experience. Gabriel Gris came for a few days but was lured away to become Vice-Chancellor of the University of Papua New Guinea. Dr Alexis Sarei became principal private secretary but later was appointed a district commissioner. Rabbie Namaliu came for the crucial period prior to independence before being promoted out, as did Moi Avei. When the last "white advisers" left before independence, it became apparent that the complex arrangements with the Office of the Chief Minister had been made to work on the basis of the social relationships between the participants, black and white, regardless of public service status. No lasting internal organizational structure had been worked out, and the problem today seems still to be a very real one.

Similarly there was a failure to formalize the co-ordinating links from the other departments to the Office of the Chief Minister and to the Chief Minister himself. Regular daily meetings were held in the secretary's office to discuss a "crisis calendar" for a while, and during that time there was an improvement in communication and co-ordination. Initially this group consisted of the "white advisers" to the Chief Minister as well as David Beatty from the Central Planning Office and Anthony Martin from Finance. By early 1974 Papua New Guinean officers such as Namaliu, Avei, and Mekere Morauta had joined the group, which then spilled over "Melanesian-style" onto the floor. When these meetings ceased in mid-1974 after Ryan left the secretary's post in favour of a Papua New Guinean officer, the semi-formal gathering also ceased and was not replaced by any adequate substitute. The only more formalized mechanism that continued was the Cabinet secretariat, with a stable and experienced staff of Papua New Guinean officers under Mark Lynch. It played a major co-ordinating role for the consideration of Cabinet business by insisting that Cabinet submissions be circulated and written comments obtained. It also played an important informal co-ordinating role by being so much in the centre of things yet above the bureaucratic battle. Despite this, however, there was a real problem in co-ordinating the flow of inputs to the Chief Minister, and it was never resolved during the period before independence.

SOMARE

Since the 1972 PNG elections the Australian government, represented by the Minister for External Territories, Andrew Peacock, had been pressing

Somare behind the scenes to move towards self-government. The reason that the pressure did not become objectionable was that Somare and the Pangu and National parties were in even more of a hurry to obtain self-government than Peacock was to give it. Only the People's Progress Party had reservations, as were shown in discussions about setting the date. The choice of December 1973, however, was set without pressure from, or even consultation with, Australia. In fact, bringing the date forward by two years in this way put real pressure upon Australia to make the necessary arrangements in time. It also faced the PNG government and officials with a nearly impossible task, especially as the PNG government's definition of self-government came to include transfer of power over everything except foreign relations and defence, which was further than Australia had intended to go. There was later some hard negotiating on this issue, especially on the question of transferring authority for law and order at self-government.

The method of an orderly transfer of formal power bit by bit, as policy decisions, legislation, staffing arrangements, and asset transfers were worked out, was not questioned by the PNG government or its advisers. This methodical and rather rigid approach, originally conceived by Australia, was not seen as a problem because the transfer of *de facto* power over most matters was really effected as soon as a PNG minister chose to assert authority, whatever the formal constitutional situation. The Gearing-Up Plan was modified to accord with Papua New Guinea's priorities, and joint working groups of officials were set up.

The PDD endeavoured to co-ordinate these many activities, keeping a detailed check-list and timetable to see that PNG working groups had prepared submissions in time for the PNG Cabinet meeting which sometimes had to reach a decision by a certain date to allow drafting of legislation to be completed for a particular meeting of the House of Assembly. The fairly rigid timetable was often made even more inflexible as it had to tie in at various stages with similar processes in Australia in order to meet sitting days of the Australian Cabinet and Parliament. Inevitably the PDD was obliged to harry PNG officials and, over the signature of Somare (or Johnson if appropriate), to apply pressure also on PNG ministers to meet deadlines. The PDD was also in almost daily contact with officers of the constitutional and legal section of DOET.

Long before the April 1972 elections, officials of both countries had been tentatively planning a "post-election" meeting between ministers to agree on a transfer plan. This was enthusiastically accepted by Somare and, after a couple of months of energetic meetings of officials, Peacock met with the PNG ministers, the leader of the opposition United Party, and Father John Momis, the deputy chairman of the CPC. Before this meeting, as a result of intense activity of PNG officials as well as inter-governmental working groups, extensive background papers had been prepared for the PNG ministers by the PDD. When the novice PNG ministers were briefed during the two days before the meeting, they had had insufficient time to read the papers and seek advice. Some were not literate in English and therefore found it doubly hard. At the meeting, Peacock was well briefed, having had several months to work on the issues. Formal agreement was reached on transferring authority in some non-controversial matters, and it was agreed to put other issues to joint working groups of officials of both countries and await their report back to ministers.

After the meeting, some very angry PNG ministers turned upon the Chief Minister and the PDD and demanded to know what was going on when expatriate officials had planned such things directly with Australian officials, without adequate consultation with PNG ministers. It was a very stormy passage, but the PDD learned a very valuable lesson in how to work with the PNG ministry. New procedures were worked out and approved by the ministry whereby every relevant PNG minister was given background papers of all officials' meetings which concerned his ministry and was invited to attend such meetings or send a representative. Responsibility was firmly placed on each departmental head to keep himself informed of transfer-of-power negotiations concerning his department and to brief his minister. There was no further trouble of this nature between ministers and the PDD, and the PDD then set about teaching public servants of other departments, by example and comment, how to work with their ministers, whose duty it was to make decisions. As far as possible, direct official-to-official contact between the two countries was curtailed, but, for many departments, it was quite impossible to break off contact completely, as they were still integral parts of Commonwealth institutions, e.g., Defence, Fisheries, the ABC, Works, Treasury.

During the July/August 1972 meetings, Father Momis, deputy chairman of the embryo CPC, and the United Party voiced objections about too rapid a transfer of power over existing institutions. The United Party appeared negative and was really objecting to the whole idea of self-government until the country was more ready. Momis was more positively concerned that a headlong rush for self-government according to an Australian-inspired plan would pre-empt the work of the CPC, whose membership was not even finalized at that stage. In the event, it was already too late for the CPC to prepare constitutional recommendations for the enactment of a constitution by 1 December 1973, the date already chosen for self-government. The government was not going to budge from this date (and won parliamentary approval for it in September 1972), yet the CPC still embarked on a long-term process of public consultation and public hearings to prepare a self-government constitution. Had politicians and their advisers, including the PDD, been more realistic, it could have been accepted from the start that it would be an independence day constitution and, perhaps, much destructive hostility between government and CPC politicians and advisers could have been avoided.

At the July/August meeting, it was also made clear to Peacock that Somare would have real difficulty obtaining the approval of the House of Assembly to early self-government and, later, to independence. The transfer of authority over each matter was going to require approval by a substantial majority (75 per cent) of a House in which many of the members were Highlanders from very conservative electorates that were genuinely frightened of the idea of Australia handing control to educated coastal people. For the remainder of his term as minister, Peacock developed a close personal relationship with Somare and demonstrated a sensitive awareness of Papua New Guinea's internal problems. Peacock was very careful not to force the pace to the extent of stirring the opposition or breaking the Coalition. His successor, Bill Morrison, was less sensitive on this issue.

Somare realized at this time that many of the fears about self-government were based on ignorance of what was involved. He tended to blame the Political Education Branch of the Department of the Administrator for failing to "teach" the people about self-government. Consequently he transferred the Political Education Branch to the PDD, where it was reorganized as the Government Liaison Branch. This involved expanding its headquarters section to improve its capability to produce such materials as pamphlets, videotapes, and posters. It also involved the replacement of most of the expatriate kiaps, who were detailed to political education work, by educated Papua New Guinean officers recruited from various departments. Emphasis was given to creating a two-way communications system from national headquarters through government liaison committees in districts and sub-districts to village leaders contacted regularly by well-briefed field workers of the various departments (teachers, medical assistants, etc.). Information about government and self-reliance was fed into this system from the constitutional section of PDD. Much greater use was also made of other media such as the ABC, government radio stations, the Department of Information and Extension Services, the *Post Courier* newspaper, and various other local publications. Eventually the Government Liaison Branch sponsored an ambitious "Operation Nation-Building" programme which involved many departments and was a co-ordinated public relations campaign to publicize national leaders and projects aimed at stimulating confidence and pride in the concept of Papua New Guinea as a nation. It is not really possible to assess the effectiveness of such a programme, but during the next two years public opinion did focus more on, and accept, the idea of independent nationhood. When the CPC was ready to consult with the people, the Government Liaison Branch was directed to work full time to assist the CPC in its task, which it did to the satisfaction of the CPC, by preparing materials and using its field network to arrange meetings and discussion groups throughout the country.

In April 1973 the Chief Minister was formally given authority over the Department of the Administrator, which was renamed the Department of the Chief Minister and Development Administration, and Johnson gracefully withdrew from active participation in executive government. In the course of a couple of months Johnson's office, from being the busy centre of activity, became a quiet haven for public servants and politicians to seek experienced counsel. Officers had to be reminded to send him Cabinet papers as a matter of courtesy. Somare's office, on the other hand, became a hive of activity day and night. The action did not return to the Administrator's building until he had handed it over to Somare and moved to a new office up the hill as embryo High Commissioner.

Things were becoming hot for Somare as unrest in several regions, an inheritance from the last years of colonial administration, posed a threat to national unity. There was trouble in the Gazelle Peninsula between the Mataungan and Warbete Kivung groups and supporters of the suspended Gazelle Peninsula Local Government Council. The Bougainville secession movement was becoming more and more insistent and threatening sabotage. The Papua Besena separatist movement seemed to be moving from strength to strength, and unrest in the Highlands was manifest in serious tribal fighting. Somare felt all these things were aggravated by fear and uncertainty about self-government; he was confirmed in his determination to achieve it in December 1973. In this he was strongly supported by Bill Morrison, the Minister for External Territories under the newly elected Australian Labor government. The CPC, on the other hand, was still aiming to produce a home-grown constitution for self-government. Yet its deliberations were already behind schedule, and as a succession of timetables were revised because of missed deadlines, the CPC began to exert pressure to delay self-government.

THE PNG GOVERNMENT AND THE CPC

Somare undertook an enormous workload as he strove to develop and implement the government's political philosophy, run Pangu Pati, hold the Coalition together, and negotiate with the Australian government, with the Bougainville Copper organization, and with activists on Bougainville. He neglected his relationship with the CPC and only very rarely attended a meeting. Deputy Chief Minister John Guise, the other remaining minister on the CPC after the death of Paulus Arek, also failed to attend meetings. In consequence, a serious communications gap developed and many CPC members became very suspicious of Somare's motives for rushing into self-government. At first, criticism was levelled at Morrison and at Somare's white advisers, and the CPC boycotted a meeting between Morrison and Somare in April 1973. The incident made it clear that relations between the CPC and the government and between their respective advisers had deteriorated badly. A compromise solution was agreed upon which provided for formal self-government at 1 December, to be followed by the enactment of a self-government constitution in April 1974. (This also proved unworkable and was later abandoned with further loss of good will as the CPC was unable to prepare its draft report until June 1974, and the process of debate, drafting, and enactment was actually not completed until 15 August 1975.) By this time the realities of the time factor were appreciated by Somare and he was privately sounding out the CPC's reaction to abandoning the concept of a self-government constitution in favour of a constitution for independence. This was not accepted, however, and the CPC's hostility grew and was eventually focused squarely on Somare and his ministers.

The conflict between the CPC and its advisers and government officials did not occur so much over the transfer from Australia of matters with clear constitutional implications, such as the courts, the prosecution function, police, and defence. In these matters there tended to be early and adequate consultations, and the constitutional issues were left alone until the CPC had considered them. Thus a CPC representative attended the meetings on the establishment of an intelligence system; the transfer of the Supreme Court and the creation of a Minister for Justice were delayed until cleared by the CPC; and the CPC views on higher organization of the Defence Force were the basis of the PNG position in the wrangles over this issue. The conflicts tended to be most intense in nebulous areas where there was no clear agreement that the CPC had a legitimate interest. This was partly because the CPC took a much wider view of what should go into a constitution than was at first realized by Somare and his advisers. It gave much weight to a very wide-ranging set of "national goals and directive principles" as well as to a stringent leadership code and detailed human rights provisions. In the CPC view, nearly all matters concerning government organization and functions and economic and social development were intended to be influenced by the wording of the Constitution and the spirit behind it. I personally did not realize the full implications of this factor until the draft final report started to appear in dribs and drabs, with the national goals and directive principles provisions appearing towards the middle of 1974.

This lack of understanding was a direct result of poor communications which in turn were caused mainly by the sheer pressure of work. When there are so many practical things for politicians and administrative officials to do, so many rigid deadlines, and when there are so many philosophical and practical things for a constitution maker to think about, it is easy to neglect communications. Easy, but potentially disastrous. The matter was compounded at a very early date, perhaps even from the beginning, by the fact that some CPC members and advisers were so suspicious of the motives of all government officials, and particularly the "white advisers" around Somare, that the CPC meetings were closed to them and minutes of meetings were delivered very belatedly, sometimes months after the event.

Another problem was that the PDD was used by Somare as an independent source of advice on legal matters involving political as well as constitutional matters. I became involved with negotiations in "trouble areas" such as the Gazelle Peninsula and Bougainville. Such activities quite likely raised suspicions amongst CPC members who had vital interests in these areas.

A further cause for friction may have been that the PDD had also interpreted its role widely and was actively involved in matters not strictly related to the transfer of formal powers to Papua New Guinea. Thus when it became clear that the CPC would recommend a system of provincial government and that this would almost certainly be accepted by the Constituent Assembly, the PDD advised Somare that unless preparations were begun immediately the sudden switch-over from a very highly centralized to a decentralized state would impose immense burdens on his public service and the decision-making and delivery mechanisms generally. Advised by his departmental head, Paul Ryan, Somare issued directions for all departmental representatives in a district to co-ordinate their activities and, where possible, to make district decisions as a team under the leadership of the District Commissioner. I chaired an inter-departmental committee to try to urge all departments to analyse their activities and to see at what level decisions were then being made. They were urged to make preliminary assessments about which of their functions should be considered national and which could be devolved to the district level. A study was also initiated to determine the actual cost of carrying out each government function in each district. Somare's aim was to move towards administrative decentralization as soon as possible and to create district teams to co-ordinate district activities. After provincial governments were established, they would then have an existing public service team to direct. Although the CPC had sent a representative to these meetings, the initiative ran into heavy fire from the CPC and was eventually dropped. In retrospect, it seems likely that, having a fair idea that it would be recommending the abolition of the position of District Commissioner, and of the concept of kiaps generally, the CPC feared that the officials were fighting a rearguard action to perpetuate the district commissioner system and to emasculate the powers of the proposed provincial governments. In the event, several years were wasted during which the country could have been moving towards provincial government, solving administrative and financial problems in the process. This incident caused hostility on one side and bitterness and frustration on the other.

A more general weakness in government policy-making also affected relations with the CPC. This was the increasingly difficult position of expatriate officials who continued to fill most of the criticial posts, even after localization of department headships and district commissionerships. During 1973 a large number of senior and middle-range expatriate public servants caught the "plague" and became lethargic sources of festering contamination to others. The "plague" in these cases was the mental and emotional realization that their PNG careers were over and that they faced a momentous readjustment of their personal lives in another country. At the very time they began to weaken, their PNG subordinates and political masters began to resent them and become abusive, especially the politicians who were not in government and thus not relying on their assistance. The symptoms of "plague" were general disorientation, lack of motivation concerning PNG affairs, and preoccupation with personal, particularly financial, affairs. Some managed to struggle on better than others, but *all* were affected to some degree. They remained in key positions or were side-slotted into sinecures, but they could not be retired without great expense to the PNG government. It was for this reason that Somare had actively involved himself in 1972 in urging Australia to accept responsibility and announce the retirement scheme (the Employment Security Scheme) which would give the PNG government the right to dismiss, and public servants the right to resign, with the Australian government bearing the heavy cost of the process. The presence of disaffected, worried officers was a potent cause of trouble within the service and a real constraint on policy formulation and implementation. The problem was particularly severe in the Chief Minister's own department, as expatriate field officers not only faced the retirement problem but had become aware that the CPC was questioning the continued existence of the kiap. This fact was also very unsettling for Papua New Guinean kiaps who had waited eagerly for appointment as district commissioners.

The racial question became more noticeable in the Chief Minister's own office in mid-1973. Middle-level indigenous officers were active in the Cabinet secretariat and the PDD, but they were headed by expatriates. A Papua New Guinean officer headed the Ministerial Services Division, but its attempts to become a policy section had not been successful and it mostly concentrated on co-ordinating replies to parliamentary questions and on housekeeping functions for ministers. The Chief Minister's personal staff were expatriates — Voutas, Cowdy, and Yocklunn — as was the secretary, Ryan. Policy advice was handled by expatriates working under pressure, as a sort of informal club: myself, Voutas, Ryan, and Lynch, advised by expatriate lawyers Bill Kearney (the Secretary for Law) and Joe Lynch (the Legislative Counsel), on professional matters. Tarua of PDD became increasingly an active member of this group. On wider issues of economic planning and aid talks there was then the Central Planning Office headed by David Beatty, supported by other expatriates. From Treasury there was Harry Ritchie, accompanied increasingly by Morauta, gaining confidence and eventually the first national Secretary for Finance.

All the expatriates concerned were acutely aware that circumstances had thrown them forward to fill a gap existing because of Australia's failure to encourage the emergence of an experienced class of indigenous administrators. As young Papua New Guineans joined the office, straight out of the university, they resented the "white advisers" who also became the target for attacks by students, nationalists, and all opponents of the Coalition government. To increase participation by Papua New Guinean officers, Ryan organized regular weekly conferences of divisional heads and the more senior Papua New Guinean officers, and these were often very outspoken discussions. One sympathized with young graduates who were reduced to advocating "black power" in their own country against their own Chief Minister. Voutas tried to reduce his profile by sliding into a research position and Alexis Sarei and later Moi Avei and Rabbie Namaliu were sought for Somare's personal staff and rapidly became active and very effective advisers. Ilinome Tarua also began to have direct access to Somare. There seemed however no option but for expatriates to hold key positions for a little longer and to try to be of as little embarrassment to Somare as possible.

It also became clear that Australian officials and politicians took far more notice if they felt they were hearing the genuine view of Papua New Guineans and not those of some white adviser. This was dramatically demonstrated during the second talks held in Canberra on the PNG/Queensland border issue. The PNG team consisted of Oala Oala Rarua (later High Commissioner to Australia), Benson Gegeyo, a district commissioner, and a middle-level national fisheries officer. The team had been well briefed and was advised by two white advisers who sat behind them but did not talk. Despite their inexperience at such conferences, the Papua New Guinean delegates spoke with fluency and assurance, and their effect on the Australian departmental heads present, who were used to seeing expatriate officials and perhaps a silent Papua New Guinean junior or two, was quite evident. The message received was that they were dealing with a foreign nation seeking its own best interest. Previous inter-governmental talks at ministerial level had usually been, to a large extent, prestructured by officials and then formally conducted by ministers with white advisers participating at their side, and the atmosphere was quite different. This meeting was in marked contrast also to the meetings then still being held regularly in Port Moresby before budget time, in which Australian DOET officials met with PNG officials to pick in detail through the PNG budget proposals, seeking Australian aid approvals. I recall storming (quietly) out of one such meeting as late as mid-1974 to advise Somare to look at the colour of the people fiddling with his budget. All twenty or so participants were white, and independence was, at that stage, planned for December 1974. The then very active national advisers had still not penetrated to the centre where the financial decisions were being made.

As well as the white advisers with long-term PNG connections, there were a few officers of the Australian public service who were specially seconded at the request of the PNG government to work on policy development in particular projects in Papua New Guinea. Colin McDonald, a serving Foreign Affairs officer, was seconded to assist in the establishment of the PNG Foreign Affairs Department. He succeeded in obtaining a wide measure of acceptance in Papua New Guinea until substantive "conflict" issues such as the PNG/Queensland border issue came to the fore. At that stage the difficulty of his position was realized by all parties and he was subject to a degree of friendly exclusion. More difficult was the position of Nick Webb, a young serving officer of the Australian Defence Department who was sent up both to establish and to run the PNG Defence Department. This officer, naturally, saw his future in the Australian department and was dealing with serving officers of the Australian Defence Force. His role in establishing the PNG department must have been difficult for him, as this involved vital policy decisions about higher organization on which Australian department headquarters and PNG-based serving Australian officers tended to disagree. It was never clear to what extent he remained subject to direction from his Australian superiors, if at all, and this doubt probably contributed to his problems.

By contrast, another Australian Defence Department officer, Ted Mulholland, succeeded in gaining a high degree of acceptance among PNG politicians and public servants. Mulholland was a former serving officer with extensive combat experience and experience in Intelligence. He came with a written instruction from his Australian superior *not* to report to Canberra and to consider his first loyalty to be to the PNG government. Being close to retiring age in any event, he had no need to fear for his future career in Australia and was able to identify more completely with the PNG government. He came to assist in setting up a co-ordinated intelligence-gathering service, but in fact was largely used by the PNG government as an independent source of advice on defence force organization and hardware. In this regard he played a hard-hitting and key role in negotiations on the transfer of the defence force and in matters of internal security generally. On one occasion, so trusted had he become that his PNG minister, Sir Maori Kiki, asked him to field the technical questions at an inter-government conference with the officer's Australian minister (Lance Barnard) and senior Australian officers, who must all have been somewhat bemused to see their own man apparently leading the PNG team at Kiki's request.

In the period from just before self-government until independence, policy direction seemed often to be the result of the interaction of the established Somare ministry and the more radical and ambitious members of the CPC — ambitious some for themselves and others for their country. When the hectic months of August/September 1973 were past, it was clear that the official parliamentary opposition had been won over to the idea of self-government, and approval for transfer of almost all remaining powers had been given. Everyone accepted that independence would occur by 1976 at the latest, but the exact timing remained open. Against all advice from practical realists, Somare publicly opted for December 1974, for which he wished to get things lined up. He was supported in this by Morrison — some say even pushed into it. But the only difference between Somare and Morrison on the question of desirable speed was that Somare was far more sensitive to the reality of internal PNG politics and was not prepared to risk national unity by undue pushing. Morrison sometimes seemed less concerned with this.

Delay in the publication of the CPC report effectively stopped Somare's plans for independence in December 1974, though he gave up reluctantly and only after he had been forced by combined CPC and United Party opposition to agree that there could be no independence until after the Constitution was enacted. During this period the suspicion and hostility between government and CPC deepened still further. When the CPC report was released in June 1974, the real issues of PNG politics surfaced at last and active CPC members formed themselves into a Nationalist Pressure Group to fight the government head-on over those issues which concerned who was to exercise power once it was transferred from Australia. The controversy centred on chapters dealing with:

1. The National Executive. Should there be an institutional head of state and should the Prime Minister be answerable to a large Executive Council when making all decisions, or should he be given the flexibility to confer with a smaller "inner" group of ministers?
2. The national parliament and the role of permanent parliamentary committees. The report recommended several powerful committees with permanent staff and the power to call and cross-examine witnesses, including public servants and ministers. To many ministers this proposal seemed uncomfortably like an expensive proliferation

of more powerful versions of the CPC, intended to act as permanent watchdogs over the executive.

3. Provincial government. Fresh from bitter and nearly violent disputes with the Bougainville Constituent Assembly, many ministers saw the spread of provincial governments as a real threat to their power and an unsustainable burden on Papua New Guinea's administrative and financial resources.

4. Citizenship. The CPC proposals were considered racist and objectionable by many (but not all) ministers. The CPC proposals used the weapon of denying citizenship to keep expatriates and many persons of mixed race out of positions in government and to put them at a disadvantage in private enterprise.

Before the CPC report was published, Father Momis and Somare made several attempts to achieve consensus for the sake of national unity while Cabinet and the CPC met to discuss the report. The issues dividing them, however, seemed unbridgeable. Somare and Guise confirmed the breakdown of negotiations by issuing a minority report, later reformulated as a White Paper, setting out the issues over which the government would fights. Now at last the national ministers, politicians, and public servants felt at home with home-grown issues. They were able to enter this debate without the technical or moral support of white advisers and did so. During the months following the publication of the CPC report there was a rapid withdrawal of the active white advisers. Tarua took over the PDD and I took leave, Voutas and Ryan retired and left the country, and Cowdy followed shortly afterwards. Yocklunn had long since moved to a less prominent position and gone overseas.

In the weeks preceding and during the House of Assembly debate on the CPC report, there were party and group meetings all over Port Moresby while politicians were briefed and sought to trade for support on particular issues. It was a lively demonstration of the PNG parliamentary process in action. During this time the government was briefed by Papua New Guinean lawyers led by Tarua. After the report (as amended by government proposals and negotiated compromises) was accepted, the draftsman, Joe Lynch (who had been in direct contact with the CPC during the preparation of the report), was supervised by Papua New Guinean lawyers in the government and the draft constitution was vetted by a drafting committee of Papua New Guinean officers.

By Independence Day in September 1975 all powers were transferred and the Australian control of day-to-day government had ceased. The hostilities generated at the centre during the process of transferring power and enacting the Constitution had been intense at the time and seemed destructive of national unity. The whole period seems, in retrospect, more like one of intense participation: by the people during the CPC consultation process and by Papua New Guinean leaders during the debate and as they gradually dominated, and took over from, the expatriates involved at the centre. The personal scars seem now to have healed; former enemies are now friends, and *vice versa*. It remains to be seen to what extent the institutions and procedures transferred, and the constitutional principles and institutions adopted, will be appropriate for the new country.

APPENDIX: TRANSFER OF THE DEFENCE POWER

Until independence, the PNG Defence Force (army, navy, and air force) was an integral part of the Australian Defence Force, and all personnel, Australian and Papua New Guinean, were employed directly by the Commonwealth. The commander was directly responsible to his superior officer in Australia, and policy was decided in the Defence Department in Australia. In 1972 there were two Papua New Guinean officers who had reached the rank of major; Australian officers and other ranks were integrated into all units. Policy and administrative matters were handled from Canberra according to Australian legislation and procedures.

On the formation of the Somare government, it was accepted that Australia would continue to control the Defence Force until independence, but it was realized that there were some matters in which the PNG government would have a legitimate interest before independence. Somare therefore became Spokesman for Defence. Nick Webb, an Australian Defence Department officer, was seconded to the Chief Minister's Office to set up a defence policy cell to advise him. Webb worked closely with the PDD, which was looking at what would be involved in transferring the PNGDF to Papua New Guinea. The task seemed daunting. One of the very early policy questions that arose concerned the future size of the force. The new PNG government did not wish to be saddled with a large, expensive and underemployed defence force — for obvious reasons. The Canberra Defence Department and the Papua New Guinean serving officers seemed to take a different view. This raised, early on, the questions of the nature of the threat and the role of the force. Papua New Guinea wanted to see military assets such as engineering units, airplanes, and men used as well for a wide range of civic projects, and even considered the possibility of flying the force by Air Niugini when it was formed. The serving officers were fiercely opposed to this. Papua New Guinea wanted accounting and purchasing procedures to be standardized with PNG civil procedures. This was clearly going to take time.

A meeting was held between Somare and the Australian Minister for Defence, Lance Barnard, their civilian advisers, and the chief of the Joint Chiefs of Staff, and as a result a joint steering committee was set up to meet alternately in Port Moresby and Canberra. As Papua New Guinea had as yet no Defence Department, I, as head of the PDD, was chairman of the meetings in Papua New Guinea and was advised by Mulholland as executive officer. The first meeting occurred in June 1973 and was attended by representatives of the Australian departments of Defence and External Territories, including headquarters serving officers. On the PNG side were myself, Webb, and representatives of the PNGDF, Treasury, District Administration, Police, and a member of Somare's personal staff. For the first few meetings, all were expatriates. Mulholland attended as executive officer, recorder, and occasional active participant. Four working parties were set up to make proposals on the following:

1. The concept of the higher defence organization. The contentious issue was the question of civilian paramountcy in the relationship between minister, commander, and department head.
2. Defence legislation — the Defence Act and regulations for the control, maintenance, and administration of the force. This included the regulations applicable for military aid to the civilian authorities during declared emergencies which had to be geared in with the constitutional arrangements. This group also was to make proposals for a status-of-forces agreement which would be necessary because of the large number of Australian servicemen who would remain in Papua New Guinea after independence.
3. Financial and administrative procedures for the Defence Force which would be compatible with PNG civil arrangements.
4. Arrangements for the transfer of assets such as buildings, land, and weapons to PNG accountancy control and the return of some assets to Australia.

It was difficult to find Papua New Guinean officers with experience in these issues to provide satisfactory indigenous representation on all the working parties.

In addition, a proposal for establishing a Joint Services Training College was floated at the Joint Steering Committee and followed up by a one-man working group consisting of Mulholland. A Cabinet submission was prepared and approval was received four weeks later for the college to be established in barracks at Ingam, near Lae, for the joint training of officers of the Defence and Police Forces and of the Corrective Institutions Service. The officers were to share academic training and administrative facilities and to separate for relevant professional training. The first intake of seventy-five men began training in January 1974, six months after the Cabinet approval. The fact that accommodation, staff, administrative matters, and recruiting were completed in six months gives a fair impression of the speed and urgency of events at that time, even the more remarkable as it involved co-ordinated decisions by both governments and the various services.

The working groups met more or less continuously for the next twelve months and reported back to the Joint Steering Committee meeting at about two-monthly intervals. The last Steering Committee meeting was held in September 1974. During that time, as well as the urgent push to put forward policy proposals, action was being taken to establish a PNG Defence Department and to staff and accommodate it and to appoint a minister to control it.

During the course of 1974, the character of the meetings changed markedly. At the start they were friendly meetings of white Australians working affably on a joint project. As differences of policy surfaced, and as Papua New Guinean ministers exercised tighter control over their officials, the joint group became composed of adversaries fighting for different countries. The sense of PNG nationalism developed more strongly after the appointment of Noel Levi to understudy Webb as secretary of the new PNG Defence Department and the inclusion of more indigenous officers in the meetings. At the end of the deliberations, the PNG team refused to allow officials of the Australian government to work with them on the PNG Cabinet submission, although it concerned the PNGDF which was still Australian-controlled. As the Papua New Guinean representatives saw it, the submissions concerned the future PNGDF after independence.

On the major policy questions of higher organization and aid to civil power in security operations, the differences were not only between Papua New Guinean and Australian teams; the teams divided among themselves. Serving officers of the PNGDF who were on the PNG team strongly pushed for an organization whereby the commander would be the minister's senior adviser. Expatriate officers pushed this hardest but were supported by the indigenous officers who, however, remained fairly silent in the presence of their senior officers. Both the Canberra and PNG civilian officers pushed for civilian paramountcy. Throughout, the PNG leader was able to argue that the CPC had already opted for civilian paramountcy and nothing else would be acceptable. The final result was for the commander and secretary to have equal access to the minister. It would seem that this relationship is still causing troubles in Papua New Guinea, and if so it would be fair to say that the present senior PNGDF officers are merely continuing to push the same line as their predecessors. (It was never clear to me where the Australian service chiefs stood on the issue.)

On the other main issue — the role of the Defence Force in internal security situations — there tended to be a conflict between the PNG government, who argued for more early involvement of the Defence Force, subject to constitutional controls, when the police could no longer cope, and Morrison with his officials, who advocated strengthening police mobile squads to handle riots. At one stage Morrison seemed to favour the establishment of a paramilitary force rather than allow any active involvement of the Defence Force. The PNG government argued that it wished to control local civil violence by improving the services of the police in small rural police stations which could not be done if scarce resources were diverted to increasing the number of riot squads. The PNGDF officers for their part seemed willing to act in civil disorders but were not trained in, and not particularly interested in using, "minimum violence" police methods.

These and similar issues were hotly debated and served to strengthen the feeling that towards the end of 1974 two independent countries were negotiating. Papua New Guinea resented Australia's vigorous involvement in what was shortly to be independent Papua New Guinea's internal issue, and Australia argued that it still had control of the Defence Force and that even after independence its officers would be heavily involved. Australia was concerned that its officers with the post-independence Defence Force might be involved in possible counter-insurgency operations by that force. In the end the PNG Cabinet submissions and decisions were made independently but were no doubt modified by the year-long discussions. The final weeks of 1974 were a mad rush trying to finalize matters in both Australia and Papua New Guinea to achieve a practical transfer of the Defence Force by December 1974 as recently agreed between Whitlam and Somare. As it happened, the deadline was missed because financial arrangements and relevant legislation could not be ready in time. Transfer was effected in March 1975.

The situation of Noel Levi should be seen as fairly typical of the demands put upon the new Papua New Guinean departmental heads at this time. He was called from his job as DDA field officer about the middle of 1973 and attached to the new Defence Department to understudy Webb, who was acting as secretary. With no previous experience of defence matters, he was thrown immediately into the middle of an urgent and sometimes heated battle between senior defence officials and career serving officers. Within months he was running the department, leading the PNG negotiating team, and advising his minister. Whereas it could easily have happened that this experience would have undermined his confidence, in fact the reverse happened and he contributed a responsible "nationalist" point of view to the negotiations. Not all departmental heads came through similar traumatic experiences so well, but some did.

Reforming the Bureaucratic Heritage

J. A. BALLARD

All of us were brought up in a society where decisions are made by groups. None of us was born in Westminster, Washington, or Canberra. . . . We do not want an Australian or European-type Public Service, geared to 20th Century technology, nor can we afford to maintain such a Public Service.

Michael T. Somare
28 September and
16 October 1972

ADMINISTRATIVE REFORM IN NEW STATES

When a new state is formed within the scaffolding of a colonial admini-stration, under the political direction of a new government, there is a period during which radical structural change is expected and seen to be legitimate. This is one of the moments of bureaucratic vulnerability when administrative reforms are most likely to succeed (Schaffer 1978; Caiden 1975). But the opportunity for change during a transfer of power is restricted by limited capacity for action. A new government is inexperi-enced in setting priorities, and while it may be conceded exceptional au-thority to set new directions, its linkages with sources of information about the range of alternative programmes and structures are weak. Its real leverage is therefore much more constrained than the apparent scope of opportunity. As experience and linkages gradually improve capacity for setting priorities and overseeing the implementation of programmes, the area of legitimacy for radical change rapidly narrows. Other groups and interests gain confidence, and those responsible for maintaining and defending inherited bureaucratic traditions are among them.

There are certain kinds of administrative reform which are nonethe-less likely to be taken up during the transfer of power. Localization of the public service is seen on all sides as an inevitable concomitant of the transfer of power, and a certain amount of bureau shuffling is inherent in the transfer process itself. New constitutional settlements, particularly if they include new federal or quasi-federal arrangements, can also have significant implications for administrative restructuring. But it is exceedingly rare to find the basic pattern of organization, procedures, and values of the colonial administration substantially disturbed in the first years of a new state, even in revolutionary situations (Staniland 1969; cf. Pratt 1976).

By comparison with other objects of policy-making in new states, the structures of administration and the public service are perhaps the least tractable. Constitution-making, foreign policy, and macro-economic policy are new areas of activity with little inherited commitment and staff, and they can be shaped on the basis of a fresh assessment of opportunities, constraints, and preferences. Localization of the public service and of private economic activities, and the reshaping of private law, involve difficult adjustments but are amenable to decrees from new authorities. On the other hand, social and agricultural policy are already heavily committed in terms of trained staff and infrastructure, and there is limited scope for redirection of effort except through piecemeal supplementation and long-term retraining.

Redesigning the work and behaviour of public servants is difficult both in selecting the direction and means of change and in achieving substantial change. Not only must the government depend continuously on public servants for much of the framing and execution of policy, but the commitment to inherited bureaucratic values is most effectively imbedded in the structure of public employment through direct experience and through the socialization provided by an education system established to prepare for public employment. It is not therefore surprising that the apparent opportunity for redirection proves ephemeral and that such changes as do take place are the by-products of constitutional change and of policies with political momentum of their own.

THE AUSTRALIAN ADMINISTRATIVE INHERITANCE

Australian rule in Papua New Guinea had many assimilationist features (Ward and Ballard 1976). These were most marked in its public service arrangements, those designed most exclusively to meet the needs and preconceptions of Australian public servants. This did not necessarily have to be the case. In British colonies public service and administrative structures were substantially different from those of the United Kingdom, much of the difference stemming from the separate traditions of India in the nineteenth century. During the early post-war period in Papua New Guinea, while communications with Canberra were weak, *ad hoc* arrangements concerning recruitment, salaries, and work assignments allowed aggressive and innovative officials like the Director of Public Health, John Gunther, to develop services designed to fit PNG needs. Bureaucratization along Australian lines was introduced with the Public Service Ordinance of 1949 and was extended as official policy under Paul Hasluck, who insisted on the virtues of specialization of service in the field and complementary centralization of control in Canberra (Parker 1966, pp. 195–206). This was carried to unprecedented lengths under Hasluck's successor, whose ministry was preoccupied with rapid economic development. Increasing injections of Australian finance and staff into Papua New Guinea were thought to require increasingly tight control of policy in Canberra and routine implementation in the field.

The resulting administrative and public service structures in Papua New Guinea imported the full range of Australian complexity, reinforced by the determination of the Public Service Association (PSA) to obtain parity with Australian conditions of service. As the basis for a future PNG public service, the Australian model offered at least a few advantages. Unlike British colonial services it had no official class structure to be eradicated and there were no problems of integrating ministries with departments when generalist permanent secretaries did not have to be inserted; these were the primary administrative concerns of the British before transferring power. But the technical advantages of the Australian model were heavily outweighed by the lack of a secretariat for initiating policy and co-ordinating departments in Port Moresby and the districts, and by a system of public service establishments easily subject to inflexible operation, making organizational change and staff transfers remarkably cumbersome and career planning impossible. The highly instrumental approach taken by Canberra towards the PNG public service helped stifle such policy initiative as the Administrator and his inter-departmental committees might have exercised, and also promoted an unrealistic demarcation between politics and administration (Schaffer 1970).

The most difficult problem raised by Australian-based public service arrangements was their incompatability with localization of the service (Ballard 1972; Parker 1972). Extraordinarily complex negotiations between Hasluck, the PSA, and the official and expatriate leaders of the Legislative Council produced an unsatisfactory compromise in the Public Service Ordinance of 1963 (a chapter notably missing from Hasluck's detailed account of his stewardship; see Hasluck 1976). The ordinance provided for separate salary scales for Australians and Papua New Guineans within a unified public service and made preference in selection for Papua New Guineans dependent on exceptional arrangements. At the same time Hasluck promised compensation to expatriate public servants for loss of career. The PSA was able to insist during the following decade that preference for Papua New Guineans, and therefore localization, must depend on elaboration of a satisfactory compensation scheme. There was little incentive for Canberra to produce such a scheme during a period in which the slow development of PNG education for public service meant a substantial increase in expatriate recruitment to meet Canberra's demand for rapid economic development (cf. Schaffer 1965). In practice there was relatively little real pressure for more rapid localization from PNG public servants, whose orientation towards their employment was focused in industrial terms by the protracted arbitration of their salary scales; but many of the ablest expatriates departed because of the absence of an adequate compensation scheme.

Dissatisfaction with public service policies was a recurrent, even dominant, theme in the House of Assembly after 1964 and one of the few that united expatriate and nationalist members. An ordinance replacing the Public Service Commissioner with some measure of PNG control over a Public Service Board was disallowed by Canberra, but in 1969 a board and a Public Service Conciliation and Arbitration Tribunal were finally established. The new Public Service Board (PSB), with responsibility for "promoting and co-ordinating the implementation of localisation policy at departmental level and to ensure as far as possible a uniform approach to the question of standards", remained fully responsible to the minister in Canberra and provoked even more intense controversy. Two of its four members were Papua New Guineans, the first to be appointed to senior posts, but the board was dominated by its chairman, Gerald Unkles, who was determined to maintain Australian standards at all costs.

Under Unkles the board maintained only formal diplomatic relations with the Administrator, refusing to participate in inter-departmental committees and moving its offices away from Konedobu in an assertion of full independence from the public service which it supervised. Within the administration this meant that an enterprising department like Education evaded the board's red tape and the delay of reference to Canberra by setting up its own localization programme, rearranging establishments informally and sequestering teaching staff from board control through a new Teaching Service Commission. The rigidity of Unkles at the board and George Warwick-Smith, secretary of the department in Canberra, further politicized public service issues. The House of Assembly overrode Unkles's renaming of the Administrative College (one of the few instances when future Pangu ministers found themselves with majority support); there was widespread criticism of instructions to public servants not to participate in a Waigani Seminar on Politics in Melanesia; during the Prime Minister's visit PNG public servants demonstrated angrily against PSB opposition to salary awards; and the PSA severed relations with the board altogether over selection policy. The precipitate departure of Unkles in December

1970 and his replacement as chairman by Sere Pitoi removed much of the heat from these issues, but the board's formalist posture, its isolation from arenas of policy-making, and its image as an obstacle to change had been firmly established.

The PSB's fragmented internal structure reinforced resistance to change. Its various branches — Recruitment and Training, Establishments, Localisation, Industrial and Arbitration, the Administrative College, and the selection boards — reported separately to the four board members. Neither the "Manpower Planning Committee", composed of the branch heads, nor the board itself was concerned with planning or broad policy formulation, and the isolation of branches within the board was nearly as great as the isolation of the board from administrative departments. A board structure was suitable for impartial application of rules for recruitment and selection (the only role of a Public Service Commission in former British colonies) but it was inappropriate for innovating outside Australian traditions or for responding to Cabinet pressure in areas requiring policy change — localization, establishments, training, and industrial relations. Both its internal structure and its external relationships ensured that the board would serve as a force for maintaining the Australian public service inheritance against initiatives for change, and the board members perceived this as an appropriate posture.

CHANGING PERSONNEL: LOCALIZATION

Localization of the public service, like the transfer of power, was so much an assumed objective within Australian policy and among educated Papua New Guineans by 1972 that there was no discussion of the ultimate objective but consideration only of how and how fast to achieve it. There had been little real progress towards either localization or the transfer of power by 1972, but by 1975 both had nominally been achieved. In the case of localization, once certain arrangements had been made, the departure of expatriates and the expectations of Papua New Guinean public servants developed their own momentum and determined much of the pace and shape of localization, outside the control of the government and the PSB. The fact that localization was almost inevitably taking place was in itself a major constraint on other types of administrative reform and on the policy-making process itself.

At the time the Coalition government came to office the only senior Papua New Guinean officials were four statutory appointees — to the Public Service Board, the Teaching Service Commission, and one department headship — and one deputy district commissioner appointed on promotion. Other appointments of Papua New Guinean officers to senior second division positions had been blocked by failure to agree on the terms of a compensation scheme for expatriates. The PSB's new procedures permitting preference for local officers through "sideways" promotion (the "lateral arabesque") for displaced overseas officers had just come into effect.

Although the board had maintained a Localisation Section since its establishment in 1969, the section had been restricted to record-keeping and hypothetical planning. It had little relationship with the Training Section and the Administrative College, which reported to a different board member and which were responsible for the new Senior Executive Program (SEP) through which promising talent, identified by the Localisation Section, was to be trained in temporary acting appointments for senior posts. Proposals for an inter-departmental committee on localization were vetoed by the board on the grounds that this would infringe its territory. The Department of External Territories (DOET) in Canberra held full control over the Employment Security Scheme, but no one had responsibility for the eventual phasing out of overseas officers, and in the absence of an operating scheme, the abler and more employable overseas officers were already looking south for jobs.

Since a satisfactory compensation scheme was the *sine qua non* both for a programme of rapid localization and for maintaining overseas officer morale, attention within the administration was focused first on this. The Australian Cabinet had twice rejected proposals negotiated between DOET and the expatriate-dominated PSA, and the appointment of an independent commissioner, A. M. Simpson, was agreed upon in July as the means of persuading the Australian government to take full financial responsibility.

For the new ministers the compensation issue was merely an unacceptable excuse for delay in localization. They expressed their annoyance with the Public Service Board by forcefully rejecting its first submissions to the Administrator's Executive Council (AEC). During the first negotiations on the transfer of power in July–August 1972, the Australian minister Andrew Peacock, made it clear that localization policy was in the hands of the PNG ministers, even though the board remained legally responsible to Canberra until self-government. Events during the September budget session of the House of Assembly then gave the Chief Minister a chance to assert the government's new authority. The Public Service Board tabled a report on the first year's performance under its Accelerated Localisation and Training Programme, concluding that manpower needs and training output would require the employment of 7,000 overseas public servants in 1976, compared with 7,800 in 1971. This coincided with an opposition statement agreeing with the government's budget contention that the public service was too large for Papua New Guinea to support. A fortnight later the Chief Minister took advantage of the board's report and the opposition statement to present, without previous consultation with the board, the government's first major policy guidelines. Government functions and the public service would have to be reduced and overseas staff would by 1976 be cut not to 7,000 but to 3,000.

The figure of 3,000, chosen for its shock effect, had the desired result. Until Somare's statement the large expatriate community had shared the PSB's bland expectation that all the expatriates who could be recruited would be needed by the public service and that officials who wished to stay on indefinitely in their posts would have no difficulty in doing so. The best illustration of the shock effect was the sudden and complete cessation of all purchases of cars and consumer durables. The statement also had its effect in Canberra, where there was clear indication that a Simpson report with favourable compensation terms would now be readily accepted. The PSA, which might have been expected to react negatively, was mollified by the prospect of this acceptance. The Public Service Board itself was shaken into a realization that, whatever legal arrangements might link it to the minister in Canberra, the new ministers occupying the board's old office in Konedobu were now setting priorities.

Paul Ryan, the director of the new Office of the Chief Minister, had earlier worked with the PSB and he took a leading role in attempting to bring the board into closer communication with the ministers and to overcome its tradition of splendid isolation. Sere Pitoi, the board's chairman, was invited to join the four Coalition leaders in an AEC subcommittee on the public service. A new advisory committee at official level was the first on public service matters to include a few Papua New Guinean public servants. It was to oversee the work of revitalized departmental localization committees in planning and reviewing localization and overseas reduction, but effective communication was minimal. The crucial arrangements concerning the future position of overseas officers in relation to an indigenous public service were agreed upon in Canberra at the time the Simpson Report on an Employment Security Scheme was adopted. A meeting of officials from DOET and Papua New Guinea adopted arrangements (not unlike those initially proposed for the Public Service Ordinance of 1963) for an overseas auxiliary service to be removed entirely from the promotion system. This was the genesis of the Australian Staff Assistance Group (ASAG), which came to life with the formation of an indigenous public service at self-government.

The new machinery and guidelines could not compensate for lack of preparation, and the rapid change of direction took its toll. The crash programme response to the target of three thousand overseas staff by 1976 was the imposition of 15 per cent annual reduction targets on all departments, irrespective of the nature of their work or current progress in localization. Notification to individual overseas officers of the government's intention to retain them was disastrously slow. Uncertainty about the government's intention and about the dates of self-government and independence compounded the problems of confidence and co-ordination. Expatriates, including many whom the government wished to retain, left when they could find posts elsewhere. By June 1974, with the wastage rate well above 15 per cent a year, the Chief Minister revoked his target and the emphasis turned from reduction towards retention of expatriate skills. Meanwhile, because of the cost of further Australian recruitment, the Public Service Board had persuaded the government to begin tapping cheaper sources of staff in the Philippines, Britain, and New Zealand.

Localization from the other side, that of Papua New Guineans taking over senior posts in the public service, involved less explicit policy-making by the new government. The board's Senior Executive Programme, designed in 1971, provided counterpart attachments for thirty-five officers who were targeted on priority policy-making posts over a two-year period. Since there was little direction of the programme by the board, its success depended on departmental initiative, which varied from Education's well advanced programme, through the confused efforts of District Administration, to almost no programme at all among the smaller and more technical departments. There was considerable dissatisfaction expressed by the Papua New Guinean public servants in the SEP when they met in a seminar in October 1972. It was clear that Papua New Guineans played very little role in departmental policy-making, and this was compounded by the firmly centralized nature of decision-making within departments, which left the few senior Papua New Guinean field officers outside the exclusively white policy-making ranks at headquarters. A seminar for senior Public Health officials in December 1972 made this point most emphatically.

Although several of the new ministers, particularly those in Pangu, had been public servants themselves and had a wide acquaintance among senior Papua New Guinean public servants, few took firm initiatives in localizing the senior positions in their departments apart from John Guise, who forced the pace in Social Development and Home Affairs during 1973–74. Others frequently appeared to be more comfortable and confident in dealing with senior expatriate officials, and this was particularly evident in the case of the Office of the Chief Minister, where Somare came under fire from radicals and the Constitutional Planning Committee for his reliance on "white advisers". As a government, however, the ministers agreed to a PSB suggestion that Papua New Guineans public servants be involved in policy-making concerning the future of the public service. At first there was token representation of Papua New Guinean public servants on the Rolfe Committee of February 1973 (see below). Then major public service reform proposals were referred to a workshop of the

Senior Executive Program in April 1973, and this was followed by the establishment of a Senior Officers Advisory Committee (SOAC) to advise the Cabinet Public Service Subcommittee through the chairman of the PSB. The workshop was particularly important in giving senior Papua New Guinean public servants a sense of participation in major policy decisions affecting them. Both the PSB and the AEC formally approved the workshop's recommendations with minimal change, but there was no effective action on them by the board. Other early modes of participation, particularly SOAC, proved ineffective and frustrating.

Department headships and district commissionerships were the critical posts for localization, since they were regarded as the focal points for power and prestige within the existing public service. The PSB's September 1972 report on localization set targets for localization of these senior posts, and these targets were largely adhered to. In mid-1973 five Papua New Guinean department heads were appointed and by the end of that year several others and a few district commissioners were named. By independence all department heads, board members, and district commissioners were Papua New Guineans, along with most heads of statutory bodies.

The choice of the first Papua New Guinean department heads led the government to consider the terms for these appointments. The government already had before it a range of proposals concerning the public service, submitted by the SEP workshop. These included a proposal for adopting an establishments system based on personal classification, allowing flexibility in the deployment of the small number of senior Papua New Guinean public servants. The government decided to appoint department heads for three-year terms to avoid the possibility that these men might hold their posts for thirty years before reaching retirement age. It also reached a compromise between public service and political considerations by advertising the posts and allowing the PSB to advise on candidates before the AEC made its choice, with the relevant minister holding a power of veto in the selection of his department head.

Much of the intended flexibility in these arrangements was undercut when, in December 1975, the first major reorganization of departments was accompanied by a reshuffle of heads. Pitoi as chairman of the renamed Public Services Commission (PSC), was given authority to recommend the transfer of heads and did so without consultation, but some of the announced transfers were revoked when heads mobilized their ministers to protest against their transfer. One department head was removed from headship status altogether, but the Cabinet, in appointing him to a statutory body, allowed him to retain his higher department head salary. This reflected a general unwillingness within the government to impose individual sanctions.

CHANGING PERSONNEL: POLITICAL CONTROLS

The changes in personnel which took place in the process of localization did not remove a basic distrust between politicians and public servants. During the ministers' first year in office their distrust was focused on expatriate officials, although the two most prominent Papua New Guinean officials appointed by the Australian administration — Sere Pitoi, chairman of the Public Service Board, and Paulias Matane, secretary of the Department of Business Development — were also viewed with suspicion. Ministers initially sought alternative advice through their private staff. They inherited from the ministerial members provision for one class 5 officer as a private secretary, and they expanded and upgraded this provision. But talents available for recruitment to ministerial staff were very limited and, with few exceptions, particularly in the Office of the Chief Minister (Tony Voutas, Steve Zorn, Moi Avei, and Rabbie Namaliu) and Finance (Anthony Martin and Ross Garnaut), the posts did not attract staff competent to advise on departmental matters. There was, instead, ample scope for conflict between ministerial private staff and senior departmental officials, conflict which was not suspended when department headships were localized.

The Papua New Guinean public servants, on their side, were fully imbued with an Australian public servant's distrust of politicians and were watchful for any evidence of political interference in the very broad area considered to be the rightful domain of the public service. In Somare's absence John Guise was the only minister brave enough to confront the Papua New Guinean public servants at the first SEP workshop of April 1973, and he was bearded directly on the issue of political interference. It became increasingly apparent to some ministers, and especially to Pangu partisans, that even a localized public service was not going to be a compliant tool for changing policy directions.

The ministers were initially reluctant to antagonize the public service by making appointments on other than inherited criteria. In May 1973, when Alexis Sarei was appointed from the Chief Minister's staff to be District Commissioner for Bougainville, primarily to appease demands from Bougainville, the Chief Minister paved the way by meeting with senior Papua New Guinean field staff of the Division of District Administration. Shortly afterwards there were plans for appointing a politically acceptable kiap, Joe Nombri, as Commissioner of Police, but when these were leaked the government backed off in the face of protests from the Police Association. The issue of political appointments was taken up much more directly by the young graduate radicals of Pangu, who took control of the party organization at its convention in November 1973. Moi Avei, who had worked closely with John Guise at Social Development and

Home Affairs to promote new policies and rapid localization in opposition to department officials, became president of Pangu. A new party platform called for active participation in politics by public servants, political criteria for appointing department heads and district commissioners, and a political review of the organizational structure of the public service. Board chairman Sere Pitoi replied by asserting the need for an impartial and non-political public service, and he was supported by the People's Progress Party and the opposition, leaving the Chief Minister in a difficult position. "As the Parliamentary leader of Pangu, of course I agree with my party platform. But unless Pangu Party policy becomes Government policy, Mr. Pitoi is absolutely correct in his statement" (*Post Courier*, 11 December 1973).

At this point Moi Avei, Rabbie Namaliu, and a few other graduates joined the private staff of the Chief Minister, and there followed a year of in-fighting between them and Sere Pitoi, defender of the inherited traditions of the public service. The relatively weak political position of the government during 1974 meant that ministers were unwilling to confront the public service with the Pangu proposals, and Moi Avei's leverage was reduced after the ministerial reshuffle of February 1974, for which he was held largely responsible. But Pitoi's vulnerability was made apparent through the limitation of his appointment as board chairman to a series of three-month renewals, and it was only the government's fear of alienating further Papuan support that kept him in office. This vitiated the already limited willingness of the board to take any initiatives. In May the board's two expatriate members were replaced by Dawa Lynch and Father Ignatius Kilage, both known to be sympathetic to Pangu and neither having previous public service experience (the appointment of Kilage, a Highlander, was also a rare concession to regional representation). At about the same time three non-kiap district commissioners were appointed, including Tony Bais, a recent graduate who had served as principal private secretary to the Chief Minister. In August, when the CPC's final report and the government's answering White Paper produced alternative constitutional proposals, Moi Avei's hand could be seen in the more liberal provisions of the latter for political activity among public servants.

The tide began to turn in the board's favour during the latter half of 1974. Moi Avei turned his attention to the new Village Development Task Force in an unsuccessful attempt to circumvent the public service altogether by linking local associations directly to the Chief Minister. More significant was the government's first bitter taste of public servant involvement in politics. At the end of July Simon Kaumi, secretary of the Interior Department, publicly criticized his minister and his minister's white advisers for interference in departmental affairs and was initially removed from his post, then restored through Sere Pitoi's mediation. Two months later Kaumi, as leader of a radical Action Front, presided over a rally calling for the removal of the government and then led a protest march through Port Moresby. Kaumi, who was chairman of the Senior Officers Advisory Committee and who had recently been considered as a replacement for Pitoi as Board chairman, was immediately suspended and then dismissed from the public service after a board of inquiry. The Kaumi affair tempered the government's enthusiasm for any form of politicization. By June 1975, after Alexis Sarei as District Commissioner openly supported Bougainville secession, the Cabinet authorized the board to issue instructions requiring public servants to choose between the public service and party executive office. Moi Avei chose to resign from the public service and from the chairmanship of the Task Force, and Pitoi was reappointed for a full term as board chairman.

The battle over politicization reinforced solidarity among the senior Papua New Guinean public servants, none of whom were tempted to follow Kaumi and Moi Avei. Since early in 1973 the SEP workshops, the meetings of SOAC, and other less formal arrangements had established communication across departmental boundaries and a broad *esprit de corps*. The issue of political interference also created defensive solidarity behind Pitoi and the PSB, and Pitoi was increasingly called upon by department heads to help them in coping with pressures from ministers and ministerial private staff.

Many of the consultative arrangements which fostered solidarity were promoted initially by the board's Senior Inspector for Localization, Jack Baker. Like Paul Ryan, Baker was one of a few ex-kiap generalists with a strong political sense and a wide network of acquaintance among Papua New Guinean public servants and politicians. He was committed to the use of extension techniques, particularly a "team-building" approach and was able, with the support of Pitoi and Bill Lawrence of the PSB, to promote this approach through the SEP workshops and elsewhere. In November 1974 an attempt was made to confront the issues of minister–public service relations directly in a three-day retreat at Sirinumu held among six ministers, including Somare and Guise, and fifteen of the most senior Papua New Guinean public servants. The Sirinumu *kivung* produced little in the way of specific proposals, but it set a framework for improved relations between minister and public servants. Although Cabinet adopted in December 1974 a proposal from the Pangu graduates to provide each minister with up to ten private staff, this proposal was never implemented.

After 1974, as the government's political stability and confidence increased, the issue of political responsiveness faded. This was in good measure the result of activity by a small group of department heads, most of them graduates of UPNG, who had close political links with leading ministers and yet held firmly established public service roles. In place of

Moi Avei's programmes of politicization and circumvention of the public service, the young men in Finance and the Planning Office proposed effective bureaucratic control of departmental programmes through the Budget Priorities Committee (BPC). Working to the Cabinet's National Planning Committee, and thus with the support of all party leaders in the coalition, the BPC during 1975 became the focus of effective collaboration between ministers and senior officials.

The Public Service Board, which had survived intact the challenges of 1974, remained — despite its representation on the BPC — isolated from and insensitive to the main centres of policy initiative in Finance, Planning, and the Office of the Chief Minister. In part the board's problems in this respect stemmed from its lack of responsibility to a minister and from its diffuse internal structure. Despite its potentially critical control of establishments, it failed to contribute to discussion of the central issues of economic policy and provincial government and continued to be seen as an obstacle to any proposals for change. During 1976, as the government committed itself fully to the establishment of provincial governments, the board's failure to collaborate, stemming from its failure to participate in the networks of policy discussion, led to the most dramatic appointment made by the first Coalition government. In August Sere Pitoi was replaced as chairman by Rabbie Namaliu who, as principal private secretary to the Chief Minister in 1974, was one of the architects of politicization proposals and who had spent the previous months as a provincial commissioner, circumventing the public service while establishing a basis for provincial government in East New Britain. A group of Papuan department heads, suspecting that Namaliu's appointment was the first of a number of displacements, attempted briefly to mobilize support for Pitoi. They met with no success, were sternly lectured by Somare for engaging in politics, and quickly made their peace with Namaliu and the graduate department heads supporting him.

Namaliu's presence at the board succeeded in imposing the implementation of provincial government as its first priority. During the following months the board set the pace among departments in planning necessary changes. Namaliu's position within the political counsels of the government also ensured that the board took a more active collaborative role in other policy areas, but it would be difficult to claim that, below the level of chairman, the board had become effectively integrated into the central machinery of government.

CHANGING STRUCTURES

When the Coalition government came to office in 1972 Papua New Guinea had a total of eighteen departments and twenty one statutory authorities, apart from a substantial number of organizations that were run as branches of Australian Commonwealth departments. Bill McCasker's Office of Programming and Co-ordination had as one of its responsibilities an annual review of functions and priorities of government. In mid-1972, in conjunction with the Public Service Board, the Treasury, and the Department of the Administrator, McCasker proceeded to interview all departments on possible economies and reforms, coming up with proposals in August for a fairly limited rationalization of departments. Somare's localization statement of September called for a simplification of administration, and McCasker then produced a further proposal for reduction to fourteen departments. At the same time Graham Douglas of Finance, a rival to McCasker for control over planning, presented a much more radical scheme in conjunction with a comprehensive strategy and timetable for development. This advocated a reduction to nine super-departments including one for Area Improvement which would combine district administration and local government with agriculture, forestry, and business development. When this scheme was circulated as a Cabinet submisson, each department presented strong arguments of self-defence, and Cabinet in January 1973 referred the various proposals for reorganization to an inter-departmental committee.

The committee, chaired by Norm Rolfe of the Public Service Board and including Voutas, McCasker, and Douglas's successor, co-opted three Papua New Guineans from the officials committee advising on localization and produced within its one-month deadline a report, mistitled "The Report on the Restructuring of the Public Service". This favoured Douglas's proposal for a Department of Area Improvement but otherwise opted for a total of fourteen departments, preferring cabinet co-ordinating committees rather than super-departments for Human Resources and Natural Resources. It also recommended the absorption of smaller statutory authorities into departments and accepted a proposal from the Office of the Chief Minister for the establishment of a National Investment and Development Authority absorbing the Investment Corporation, Development Bank, and other business promotion activities. Despite the Chief Minister's assurance that no minister's responsibilities would be reduced by any restructuring, ministers and their department heads assumed a defensive stance. Since Cabinet also had before it a conservative and technical "Report on Arrangements Appropriate to a National Public Service" (the Besley Report), dealing with provisions for a future Public Service Ordinance, it was decided to obtain the views of senior Papua New Guinean public servants on both reports.

A two-week "policy workshop" of the SEP, enlarged to fifty-three members, was organized outside Port Moresby in April 1973 for this purpose. It was the first occasion on which Papua New Guinean public servants had been given an opportunity to consider the whole range of future administrative arrangements, and as it took place before they had been promoted into the highest positions in their departments, they were willing to make a fresh assessment outside the vested interests of office. They agreed that adoption of the Rolfe proposals would create confusion while localization was proceeding and that the restructuring of central government departments was of lower priority than the need for implementing the CPC's new outline proposals for district government. They also focused attention on problems overlooked in both reports. They recommended personal classification, rather than job classification, for senior posts so as to provide flexibility in posting; and they called attention to the problem of regional imbalance within the public service through the creation of district quotas for recruitment, training, and, to a limited extent, promotion.

The Public Service Board approved all of these proposals and forwarded them to Cabinet, which agreed to drop the Rolfe Committee proposals and was concerned primarily to get on with the appointment of Papua New Guinean department heads. It passed the more difficult reforms back to the board for further consideration. The officials of the board had more pressing current business than the design of complex changes in the inherited classification structure and procedures with which they had always worked. Apart from the compilation of statistics showing the very considerable imbalance of regional representation within the public service (Welch 1976), no further action was taken.

A number of structural changes in central government took place either as a result of the transfer of powers or to meet political needs within the ministry. Between 1972 and 1975 the transfer led to the taking over of existing branches of Australian institutions, such as the Bank of Papua New Guinea and the Papua New Guinea Banking Corporation, and to the creation of new ones, such as the departments of Defence and Foreign Relations, the National Broadcasting Commission, and Air Niugini. These were each dealt with as separate operations under the general policy guidance of Tos Barnett's Political Development Division in the Office of the Chief Minister. During 1973–74 there was also a tendency to create new organizations at least in part to provide ministers with portfolios. Creation of an Office of Minerals and Energy was both a means of organizing competence in a developing area and of giving a senior minister a distinct administrative domain; the Office of Cultural Affairs provided a portfolio for a weak minister, based on the opportunity created by a large Australian cultural grant; and the Office of Environment and Conservation was invented for a new minister after Information had been taken over by the Chief Minister. All of these arrangements were planned primarily by the Chief Minister's political staff. The more important

Central Planning Office and National Investment and Development Authority also grew out of initiatives by the political staff of the Chief Minister; their development is discussed at length by Garnaut and Voutas in this volume. Two other new organizations grew out of attempts to improve efficiency by aggregating departmental services in the Bureau of Management Services and the Plant and Transport Authority. Neither had proved a notable success by 1977, but the former was an essential preliminary step towards provincial government.

Many of these new organizations had come into existence by August 1974 when the issue of a general restructuring of central government was raised again by the Office of the Chief Minister, where the politicization campaign was still strong. The alternative institutional proposals of the CPC report and the government's White Paper, as well as the implications of the Provincial Government (Preparatory Arrangements) Act of July, made it necessary to consider future administrative arrangements coherently before independence. One of the government's new appointees to the Public Service Board, Ignatius Kilage, was named chairman of an inter-departmental committee composed largely of Papua New Guinean public servants and drawn only from the board, the Chief Minister's Office, the Planning Office, and Finance, in close liaison with Moi Avei's new Village Development Task Force. With reference back to the recommendations of the Rolfe Committee and the SEP's comments, as well as to constitutional and provincial government proposals, the Kilage Committee produced in December a detailed survey of all government activities. On most issues the committee took a centralizing line, justified largely in terms of efficiency. Thus, with the slogan, "One Nation: One Public Service: One Employer", it proposed to transfer all statutory authority staff into the public service and to absorb non-commercial authorities into departments; it repeated in modified and more detailed form the Rolfe proposals for a small number of super-departments; and it proposed to retain the Public Service Board in the fullness of its functions. This last was in response to the CPC's recommendation of the British post-colonial model, with an independent Public Services Commission limited to recruitment, promotion, and discipline, and with public service management confined to a ministerial department. On the other hand the Kilage Report dealt with the issue of provincial government by proposing to transfer all staff involved in provincial functions to a Department of Provincial Affairs, an adapted and more radical form of the Rolfe Committee's proposed Department of Area Improvement.

The Kilage Report was prepared in considerable secrecy. When it was submitted to the Public Service Board there was demand from senior public servants that they be consulted. Following the SEP workshop tradition, all department heads and representatives of statutory bodies were convoked for four days in February 1975 on Loloata Island near Port Moresby, where they were instructed by the Chief Minister to agree upon a definitive response to the Kilage proposals before leaving the island. Apart from complaints about the composition of the Kilage Committee and its lack of consultation with departments, the main areas of disagreement concerned the statutory authorities and the Department of Provincial Affairs. The Loloata Conference wanted banking authorities left outside the public service and some autonomy for commercial statutory authorities, and it argued for a more flexible approach to the transfer of powers to provincial governments, allowing departments to deal with provinces directly concerning the transfer of functions and staff, rather than through the intermediary agency of a Department of Provincial Affairs. Whereas Bougainville's experience had made it apparent to advocates of provincial government that negotiation with individual departments was a recipe for obstruction (Conyers 1976), the department heads were far from eager to relinquish control over their field operations while the future shape of provincial government remained in doubt. The heads at Loloata also revised a number of Kilage's proposed departmental amalgamations. On the whole the board supported the Loloata amendments.

Cabinet took no action on these proposals until after the final constitutional debates, but by independence in September 1975 the Chief Minister was in a position to push forward both a ministerial reshuffle and a full restructuring of central government along lines adapted from the Kilage/Loloata/PSB proposals. This was announced on 11 December. It included a reduction to fifteen departments and absorption of non-commercial statutory authorities into departments. Although Somare was able to make his ministerial changes in portfolio stick for the moment, to the extent of dismissing recalcitrants, Pitoi's single-handed reassignment of department heads met successful resistance on the part of two who lobbied through their ministers. Until September the newly retitled Public Services Commission had been given no clear indication of Cabinet's preferences concerning the form of eventual restructuring, and when the December announcement was made only outlines of the restructure implementation had been prepared. It was not until February 1976 that *Gazette* notices and circular instructions could be issued, and even then department heads had no clear notions of their responsibility in relation to statutory authorities placed under their care. A "Restructure Digest" was prepared, but, apart from useful departmental organization charts, it was more confusing than helpful and provided no rationale for the changes being made.

After all the work that had gone into the rethinking of central government organization, and after nearly two years of readjustment following the restructuring exercise of December 1975, the primacy of politics in determining administrative structure reasserted itself after the 1977 elections. The demand for Cabinet representation from each province made it necessary to appoint twenty-two ministers, and within a very short time ministers had successfully insisted on having separate departments to fit their portfolios. The long process of pruning in 1975 proved to be merely a prelude to the reflowering of departments in 1977.

CONCLUSION

Three approaches to making bureaucracy responsive have been traced through the history of the first Somare government. The government's overall objective was a fairly clear one: that of taking control of an inherited administrative system and directing it towards new ends. There were those in Bougainville, in the CPC, and associated with Moi Avei's Village Development Task Force who believed that the system could not be successfully reoriented, and that new ends — particularly those of community-based development — could be achieved only by subverting or circumventing the public service and by developing local political institutions. But Cabinet decisions were based on an assumption that control and redirection were feasible.

Localization was a once-and-for-all process like the transfer of power, of which it was seen as an inevitable concomitant. Those who favoured a rapid transfer also favoured rapid localization. But while the CPC forcefully questioned the desirability of an unthinking transfer of colonial institutions, no one effectively questioned the value of simply substituting Papua New Guineans for Australians within public service establishments. It was easier to conceive of alternative institutions and functions of government than to think outside the only known conventions of public employment; "policy" here was a matter of conventional expectations.

Once an acceptable compensation scheme was available for overseas officers, localization as a process of expatriate departure developed its own momentum. The pace of localization itself began to determine much of the behaviour of the public service, and there were unanticipated by-products. As senior Papua New Guinean public servants were promoted through several posts to department headships and district commissionerships in the course of a few months, they escaped full socialization into the roles of their predecessors and were more ready to develop new networks of co-ordination. Less senior staff in the provinces were promoted and transferred and sent on irrelevant training courses so frequently that established routines and networks broke down, with inevitable retreat into formal, office-based activity. The unplanned outcome of localization, then, was a net improvement of co-ordination and responsiveness to political direction at the top and a sharp decline in effective performance and responsiveness to policy objectives in the field.

Various other strategies were employed to give ministers a political grip on the public service, through ministerial private staff, political criteria for appointment to senior offices, and encouragement of political activity by public servants. Apart from the programme put forward by the Pangu graduates in 1973, it could not be said that these strategies amounted to a policy of politicizing the public service. They were, rather, a range of devices available to ministers for use depending on the political situation and the climate of relations with the public service. Once a responsive link between the government and senior public servants had been established through the Budget Priorities Committee, the Cabinet increasingly relied on it to obtain compliance with directives and had few occasions for resort to more direct political methods.

Structural reform of the central administration was a less direct approach to responsiveness, and tended to reflect other concerns. The only important innovations at the centre, the Planning Office and the Budget Priorities Committee, arose not from the comprehensive programmes of the Rolfe and Kilage committees, but out of sharply perceived needs for specific improvement in the machinery for planning and co-ordination. Other changes reflected accommodation to the transfer of power or to immediate political needs, and it was apparent that efficiency in administrative structure was subordinate to the Chief Minister's constraints in designing and allocating ministerial portfolios.

Still other major structural reforms were those proposed by the Constitutional Planning Committee, which was concerned not with responsiveness to ministers but with public accountability and direct responsiveness to local public interest. Although the committee failed to establish strong parliamentary committees in the Constitution, it succeeded in its proposals for an Ombudsman Commission and for a Leadership Code covering senior public servants as well as political office-holders. The main thrust of the CPC, however, in reshaping the administrative inheritance of colonial rule lay in its proposals for political control by provincial governments over all field staff. The shaping and effect of these proposals is discussed in the following paper.

There were other strategies that might have been more effective in reorientating public service behaviour towards the expressed goals of the government, but they required complex planning of change by the Public Service Board, which was cast as a bastion of tradition rather than an agency of reform. The only critical examination of the values implicit in an Australian-model public service was the short-lived effort by senior Papua New Guinean public servants at the SEP workshop of April 1973, and the board was not equipped to act upon the workshop's recommendations. Public service training, another potential weapon of reorientation, was centralized in the Administrative College, under the board's control, but its primary task was that of upgrading trainees for established positions. There was no serious consideration of training as a strategy for reform, and no coherent support for the few imaginative efforts at the college and in departmental training institutions to reorient extension activities. As Hal Colebatch shows elsewhere in this volume, local officials and institutions tended to reshape government programmes to suit their own interests. And, as Bill Standish shows, the hopes of the Constitutional Planning Committee that devolution of powers to provincial governments alone would reorient the public service were simplistic. By the end of the first Somare government, localization, political control at the centre, and restructuring to suit political needs had been achieved, but the evidence available concerning public service behaviour suggests that improvement in responsiveness was limited to the aggregates within the grasp afforded to the government by the Budget Priorities Committee.

Policy-Making as Trauma: The Provincial Government Issue

J. A. BALLARD

In this volume's introductory paper, "Policy-Making in a New State", I explore the problems of altering the committed pattern of resources inherited by a new government from its colonial predecessor. Most of the papers in this collection focus on changes proposed and introduced by the new government, although Hal Colebatch and Bob McKillop emphasize instead the dominance of policy maintenance. Here I examine the most striking example of traumatic change in the inherited structure of commitments in Papua New Guinea: the decentralization of control over substantial resources to newly created provincial governments.

The process by which decentralization was effected was basic to the politics of the period from 1972. It proceeded in several arenas, often with little communication among them. Since it involved well-mobilized groups outside the government, much policy-making took place by negotiation, frequently in conditions of crisis. For the major actors concerned with decentralization at different times, the adjustments to new commitments often required traumatic reorientation, but there were many areas of government, and many districts, where adjustment to newly declared patterns of policy was minimal. There were, in addition, the side-effects of traumatic change, the casualties of disorientation in a sense, particularly the career officers of district administration, about whom no one was willing or able to make effective future commitments.

Diana Conyers, who was closely involved in and strongly committed to attempts to introduce provincial government, has analyzed much of the history of the period to 1976 regarding the issues and administrative problems of decentralization (Conyers 1976). In another paper in this collection Bill Standish examines the impact of decentralization on policy-making in one province. Here I attempt to unravel the development of perceptions and commitments within the national government and other mobilized groups concerned with the issue. In adhering to an essentially chronological narrative of a complex process of negotiation and change, I inevitably run the risk of distortion through simplification and the attempt to make intelligible the discontinuity, inconsistency, and ambiguity which are inherent in the process. This may, nonetheless, be the only approach which allows "decisions" and "crises" to be located within their wider contexts.

DECENTRALIZATION UNDER COLONIAL RULE

When the Somare Coalition took office in April 1972, it inherited the structures and personnel of Australian territorial administration and an agenda of perceived but unresolved problems. The governing parties were preoccupied with the timing and shaping of self-government and the localization of the public service and private enterprise. They had no firm notions about the kinds of changes they wished to make in the administrative system they inherited, though there was a general bias in favour of decentralization as a means of achieving greater responsiveness in government, but also a determination to maintain national unity.

The issue of decentralization was not a new one. Generalist field administrators (kiaps) who were concerned with the establishment and maintenance of Australian law and order had found their primacy in the districts challenged in the 1950s by Paul Hasluck's preference for centralized specialist administration on the Australian model, and by the rapid growth of specialist extension staff in the districts. The major inquiries into administrative reform during the 1950s and 1960s were concerned with the future role of the kiaps, and in 1961 Hasluck considered their replacement by local government authorities. Although circulars reaffirmed the responsibility of district commissioners for co-ordinating planning and development activities in their districts, there was no effective support for this role from specialist department headquarters in Konedobu or from Canberra (Parker 1966, pp. 195–206). Kiap headquarters developed no capacity for generating policy initiatives, and kiaps with political and planning talents (e.g., Paul Ryan, Mark Lynch, Tim Terrell, Jack Baker) found promotions more readily in other departments. The few district commissioners who succeeded in creating effective interdepartmental teams did so by force of character and by promoting a sense of district loyalty overriding departmental identity. Only in the Eastern Highlands and the Southern Highlands had a commitment to teamwork among departments been firmly established by 1972.

Although the kiaps' Division of District Administration within the Department of the Administrator was itself well decentralized, the specialist departments remained firmly centralized and experimented only with regional offices as agencies of field control distinct from the kiaps' district framework. A special case was the Department of Education, which carried out a thorough reorganization in 1970, incorporating mission teaching staff and establishing District Education Boards with political representation and substantial controls over the allocation of resources.

The Office of Local Government (OLG), a weak and unloved step-child of District Administration, supervised the activities of Local Government Councils. These were first established in a few areas in the 1950s and by 1972 they covered 92 per cent of the population. From the mid-1960s, district-level Combined Councils Conferences were organized by district local government officers, and these constituted the first district-level political bodies. Councils also began to provide the majority of members in appointed District Advisory Councils, previously the preserve of expatriate economic and mission interests. None of these district bodies had more than advisory functions, their meetings were infrequent, and they were largely dominated by district officials. Local Government Councils themselves held very limited service and taxing powers and they varied widely in the measure of authority accorded to them by officials and by their electorates.

For purposes of representing local and district interests at the centre, more effective spokesmen had begun to appear in the territorial House of Assembly. Most of the members were primarily concerned to promote parochial interests both within the House and through informal lobbying with department headquarters and district administration. In exceptional districts like the Southern Highlands, MHAs were marshalled as a district team, to support the district administration in its dealings with headquarters. MHAs were invited to attend meetings of Combined Councils Conferences and District Advisory Councils, but these were often composed largely of defeated candidates for the House of Assembly, and rival claims for district spokesmanship were already apparent in some districts (Gerritsen forthcoming; Griffin 1977).

Apart from these institutional arrangements, there was a multitude of unofficial associations and mobilized groups that attempted to promote local, district, or regional interests in collaboration with, or in opposition to, the administration. Some were populist and were usually dismissed by the administration as cultist. Others were controlled by small groups of big-men or an educated elite claiming to speak for larger numbers and seeking to control access to government resources (Gerritsen 1975; May 1975). These groups also promoted their economic interests through local and district councils, and they were best mobilized in some districts to benefit from decentralization. (On the evolution of district and regional identities, see Ballard forthcoming.)

Those groups that caused greatest concern to the administration had leaders who were able effectively to oppose government proposals for development. In Bougainville and the Gazelle Peninsula, where education and cash cropping were particularly well advanced, there were groups

(Raluana, Navuneram, Hahalis) that fought the establishment of councils in the 1950s and maintained a tradition of opposition to the administration. Then from 1967 to 1970 long-simmering dissatisfaction was mobilized in both areas against what was seen as arbitrary action by Konedobu: the imposition of a Multi-Racial Council, coupled with delays in the return of alienated land, in the Gazelle and compulsory acquisition of land for copper mine facilities, with very limited compensation, in Bougainville. These produced not only forceful reaction at the local level but also articulate demands from educated men and some MHAs for greater control over decisions at the district level. In September 1968 a group of Bougainville students and MHAs at Port Moresby demanded a referendum on secession before self-government; "secession" (for which there had earlier been occasional demand) became within Bougainville the accepted formula for expression of dissatisfaction with the administration and the mine. In the absence of mobilizing issues and capacity at the national level, the events in Bougainville and Gazelle were central to the development of nationalism in Papua New Guinea and linked nationalism with decentralization. Opposition to Australian rule was opposition to the centralized, arbitrary control exercised by Canberra and territorial headquarters at Konedobu. When MHAs from Papua took up the cause of separate status for Papua in 1971, this was also based in good measure on complaints that a national allocation system had disadvantaged Papua, and that the transfer of power to a New Guinea—dominated national government would produce more of the same (Griffin 1973b).

The Australian government was committed to an eventual transfer of power to a single national government in Papua New Guinea, and the response of Canberra and Konedobu to demands for local autonomy was a campaign of political education in the advantages of national unity and a programme for developing national symbols. There was also some recognition of the need to give politically advanced areas the possibility of obtaining some measure of local self-government, without frightening the people of regions such as the Highlands, where development and the chance of catching up was seen as dependent on the maintenance of Australian kiap control. At the District Commissioners' Conference in 1969 the notion that disparities in political development be given institutional recognition, and that political units such as the Gazelle be permitted to vary from the kiaps' district boundaries, was firmly opposed by Tom Ellis, then head of the Division of District Administration (DDA). But Canberra and some officials at Konedobu saw value in the proposal. When Prime Minister John Gorton visited Papua New Guinea in 1970 and announced the first significant steps towards a transfer of power, he was sufficiently impressed with the force of sentiment in Bougainville and the Gazelle to propose that more substantial powers be devolved to regional or district authorities.

What resulted from Gorton's proposal was an amendment to the Local Government Ordinance providing for the establishment of Area Authorities at district or lower levels. Those, particularly in District Administration, who had hoped that the authorities might provide a significant third tier of government, were disappointed by announcements that they were to be merely a lateral extension of Local Government Councils, excluding MHAs and district officials from membership, and were initially to be given only planning and a few advisory functions. The OLG was given responsibility for oganizing the Area Authorities in those areas that wished to have them, and late in 1971 the OLG began consultations in a few districts.

INITIAL DISPOSITIONS, 1972

The formation in April 1972 of the National Coalition government around Michael Somare's Pangu Pati, which had opposed the administration's central planning and its actions in Bougainville and the Gazelle, meant that there was from the start a general commitment towards the recognition of local demands for greater control. The new government attracted the initial support, or at least the tolerant good will, of most active proponents of local autonomy and secession. All four Bougainville MHAs supported the government, and Paul Lapun and Donatus Mola became ministers, while Father John Momis was given senior posts in the House of Assembly and soon became deputy chairman of the Constitutional Planning Committee. The Mataungan Association MHAs from the Gazelle also supported the government but refused ministerial appointment. Josephine Abaijah, the MHA for Central Province who had most directly espoused the Papuan cause during the election campaign, maintained an independent stance, but other Papuan spokesmen took places in the ministry.

Pangu had always supported stronger local government and had unsuccessfully proposed the formation of a separate department of local government, but had expressed strong doubts about Area Authorities. Its main Coalition partner, the People's Progress Party, warmly supported Area Authorities since Julius Chan's political base, New Ireland, had been chosen as the pilot Area Authority. This was formally inaugurated in July 1972 and others were established during the course of 1972 and 1973. The only other programme of local initiative the government inherited was the Rural Development Fund, which was intended to provide matching funds for projects proposed and managed by Local Government Councils (often, in practice, by their kiap advisers). The government poured substantially increased funds into the renamed Rural Improvement Programme (RIP).

As Area Authorities were established, they were gradually given powers over the allocation of RIP funds among council proposals, under the final control of Julius Chan's Department of Finance.

The new government's attitude towards district administration was much more ambivalent. Not only were district commissioners the paternalist mainstay of colonial administration in the districts, but some had been active in support of the United Party opposition. One of Somare's first actions as Chief Minister was to insist that Tom Ellis be excluded from meetings of the Administrator's Executive Council. When the expatriate district commissioners and a few Papua New Guinean understudies assembled for their annual conference in July, they were uncertain of their future. Somare, while warning them against overbearing attitudes and stressing the need for greater sensitivity, declared that some system of generalist field administration was essential and that he intended to reform it only gradually as a part of his own department. Whereas the legitimacy of kiaps in the field was thus confirmed, the government's antipathy to Ellis and the lack of planning capacity at DDA headquarters meant that the agency most concerned with decentralization made no effective input to policy on decentralization.

Although the Bougainville Combined Councils' Conference and Paul Lapun repeated their request for a referendum on secession in July 1972, the area that posed the greatest immediate concern for the new government was the Gazelle. There the elections had exacerbated tensions among three rival Tolai groups. After a visit by Somare to the Gazelle in July, staff from the Office of the Chief Minister (Tony Voutas, Alexis Sarei, and Tos Barnett) entered into negotiations for some form of accommodation among the groups involving a devolution of powers to a joint authority. They did so with the realization that they were setting a precedent by proposing special arrangements for one area, but they hoped that this might provide a model for more widespread devolution of powers. A traditional Tolai model, the *likun*, was proposed by one of the Gazelle MHAs, John Kaputin, and this served as the basis for special legislation giving a Gazelle authority more substantial powers than were provided for Area Authorities. The legislation was introduced in November and passed in March 1973 against opposition from the Tolai pro-council group, and it had little effect in reducing local antagonisms.

Meanwhile the government, in pursuit of Pangu's primary goal of self-government, had chosen to establish a new institution which was to play a major role in determining the shape of decentralization, the Constitutional Planning Committee (CPC). The initial conception for such a committee was that of Professor James Davidson, whose experience as a constitutional consultant elsewhere in the Pacific had encouraged distrust of metropolitan and administrative involvement in constitutional design.

Davidson's former student, David Stone, persuaded Somare and his chief political adviser, Tony Voutas, of the need for an independent committee of MHAs with a very broad brief and only formal contact with the territorial administration. After considerable delay, occasioned by opposition demands for greater representation and by controversy within the government over the selection of consultants, the CPC was eventually established in September 1972 with Davidson and Stone among its consultants. The CPC's terms of reference were "to make recommendations for a constitution for full internal self-government in a united Papua New Guinea with a view to eventual independence", and among the matters on which it was asked to report were "central — regional — local government relations and district administration".

Although the Chief Minister and two other ministers were nominally chairman and members of the CPC, they were rarely able to participate, and the committee's most active and vocal members were its deputy chairman (and *de facto* chairman), Father John Momis of Bougainville, and John Kaputin of the Gazelle. Momis and Kaputin were the two best educated Papua New Guinean MHAs and the most articulate radicals in the House, and they shared the government's initial distrust of the Australian administration and its potential for interfering in constitutional arrangements. The CPC was immediately concerned that negotiations between the new government and Australia concerning the transfer of power not be allowed to pre-empt the committee's options.

A unique feature of the transfer of power in the case of Papua New Guinea was its piecemeal nature, involving negotiation over each government function and a continuous process of legislation rather than a single ordinance transferring all but reserved functions, as in British and French transfers. Barnett's Political Development Division in the Office of the Chief Minister was responsible both for the PNG side of these negotiations and for liaison with the Constitutional Planning Committee, and the committee's suspicions about the transfer of power infected its relations with the government from the start. In November 1972, members of the CPC attempted to block the transfer of district administration and local government to PNG control, and eventually agreed to the transfer only after extracting a promise that the government would not attempt any restructuring until the CPC had examined the constitutional implications. By early December, tensions between the government and the CPC were open knowledge and Somare and his staff were privately referring to the CPC as an albatross.

The CPC chose three of its terms of reference — citizenship, central-district-local government relations, and legislative-executive relations — as its top priorities. At its first substantive meetings, held early in December, a paper on the possible division of powers among central, regional, and local governments was presented by one of the consultants, Ted Wolfers, a young political scientist with considerable experience in Papua New Guinea. John Kaputin described the "district government" with taxing and other powers being considered for the Gazelle, and its possible extension to the whole of East New Britain District. After two days of discussion the CPC reached its first conclusion: that it favoured some form of strengthened local and district government. Momis announced this publicly (*Post Courier*, 20 December 1972) and Nigel Oram, an experienced British colonial official and long-term resident critic of Australian administration, was engaged as a part-time consultant to work with Wolfers in developing proposals on the subject.

Up to the end of 1972, initiatives for programmes of decentralization were taken on several fronts. The Office of Local Government was busy establishing Area Authorities and attempting to persuade central departments to hand over some minor powers to them. A few of the more enterprising of the district commissioners encouraged the new Area Authorities as politically legitimate allies in the cause of district coordination and planning, while others treated them as irrelevancies. The Office of the Chief Minister found itself increasingly preoccupied with the management of political crises and had little time for planning, while the CPC was asserting its exclusive right to pronounce, and its right to control initiatives, on all subjects within its purview. The government, under seige from the opposition over its timetable for self-government, tacitly accepted this assertion. At this point, however, a new force emerged to set its own terms for decentralization.

TAKING STANCES, 1973

In December 1972 a district-level assembly, the first of its kind in Papua New Guinea, met in Bougainville. It was convoked as a seminar on the district's problems by Bougainville students at the University of Papua New Guinea, with the support of the Combined Councils Conference. Delegations from all the Local Government Councils and from non-council areas met to hear the Bougainville MHAs, Leo Hannett, John Kaputin and other speakers. None of them openly supported the students' cherished aim of secession, but at the end of the seminar a petition for a referendum on secession received wide support (Griffin 1973*a*).

Then at Christmas two senior Bougainville public servants were killed in instant "payback" in the Eastern Highlands after their car had run down a child. This inflamed Bougainville sentiment against mainland "redskins", and when Somare visited Bougainville early in January he was greeted in all parts of the district with demands for secession. With Momis's support,

Somare asked that Bougainville submit specific proposals to the CPC, and he appointed Leo Hannett as his liaison officer in Bougainville.

As a student at UPNG, Hannett had been one of the most articulate of early nationalists and helped formulate the 1968 call for Bougainville secession. During Somare's tour he was the most outspoken of Bougainvilleans, and his appointment was a calculated risk for the government. Hannett met with the MHAs and other senior Bougainvilleans in Port Moresby to work out a strategy for mobilizing public support for a form of district autonomy rather than secession. Then at a meeting of the Bougainville Combined Councils Conference late in February, after intensive lobbying and despite reluctance by the more conservative northern councils, the Bougainville Special Political Committee was formed. It was composed of thirty-six representatives from the councils, from non-council areas, and from other associations, with Hannett as its chairman (Mamak and Bedford 1974, pp. 19–24). The formation of the Bougainville Special Political Committee (BSPC) added to the CPC and the Office of the Chief Minister a third body concerned with planning for what was by now widely called "district government".

During January and February the CPC formulated its conception of district government, based on discussion papers prepared by Oram and Wolfers. These raised for the first time such issues as the structure of district executives and assemblies, the division of functions between central and district governments, and control of public servants, finance, and local government. At the end of February the CPC issued a press statement favouring some form of district government, including district assemblies stronger than the Area Authorities, established within existing district boundaries. Beyond this it merely specified a range of options for political structures on which it sought submissions, particularly during the CPC's forthcoming tour of the districts.

At the same time the Office of the Chief Minister sought to exploit the vulnerability of established patterns of administrative behaviour during the transfer of power both by reorganizing at the centre and by pushing through a decentralization of central department powers to district officials. A committee on the restructuring of government departments was established under Norm Rolfe of the Public Service Board, and this worked to a tight schedule during the month of February. It recommended that District Administration and Local Government be incorporated with the Office of the Chief Minister as the Department of the Chief Minister and Development Administration. It also, in anticipation of district government, proposed the amalgamation of extension field staff from various departments in a Department of Area Improvement.

The CPC was reluctant to allow any reforms to go forward and refused to allow Boyamo Sali, Minister of State for district administration and local government, and Ilinome Tarua, Barnett's proposed liaison agent, to attend CPC discussions of district and local government. On 27 March Somare himself attended a meeting of the CPC and argued the need for administrative decentralization as a preliminary step to give Area Authorities responsibility and to reorient public servants by making them responsible to Area Authorities. He reminded the CPC that its job was to recommend structures for self-government, but that his was to govern effectively and to prepare machinery and procedures to implement the committee's recommendations. This approach succeeded and gave the Office of the Chief Minister a charter for limited reforms and further studies. Within the following week the new Department of the Chief Minister and Development Administration was gazetted and Somare was able to instruct the district commissioners at their annual conference that their responsibility was to ensure that district departmental staff worked as a team to Area Authorities.

The CPC went through its most serious crisis at this point, when the opposition refused for a fortnight to participate in the committee. There was a serious possibility that the committee might collapse altogether, a prospect causing no great distress to the Office of the Chief Minister. The crisis proved temporary, but it exacerbated tensions, and at the end of April a series of misunderstandings provoked by the Whitlam government's pressures for rapid decolonization led Momis, in the name of the CPC, to issue a public attack on Barnett and the Australian government for bypassing the committee. A major source of tension was removed when it was agreed that the CPC's draft constitution need not be ready for self-government on 1 December 1973, and the committee went off to tour the districts better unified than before.

In June the Office of the Chief Minister established the District Organization Steering Committee to undertake, under Barnett's co-ordination, a number of studies in preparation for district government. Apart from initial consideration of financial allocation arrangements, pilot projects were begun in several districts to test and improve the capacities of Area Authorities and district administration. The costs of all government activities in Bougainville and the Southern Highlands were calculated; the Northern District Area Authority was closely scrutinized; an experiment in the unification and simplification of departmental management services was undertaken in Madang District (providing a model for the future Bureau of Management Services); and an experiment in district planning in Morobe District was given official support. Barnett also took over from the OLG its abortive efforts to obtain from other central departments a devolution of powers to Area Authorities as interim district governments, and by July he had negotiated proposals for giving Area Authorities power to set policy for all department extension services and to control some

RIP and other limited funds. The Rolfe Committee's proposal for a Department of Area Improvement unifying all extension services had been opposed by departments and rejected by Cabinet and Barnett's attempt to persuade departments to give district commissioners the powers of department heads was unsuccessful, resulting only in an ineffective joint circular calling for full collaboration of district departmental staff with the District Commissioner and Area Authorities. All of these efforts were aimed at preparing both the central departments and district administration for effective collaboration with district political authorities, but there was no evident change and the Public Service Board notably failed to act or to plan for administrative decentralization.

During the same period, Hannett and the executive of the BSPC were active building commitment to their own concept of district government, which replaced secession as a popular solution for Bougainville's grievances. Hannett's dual role as liaison officer for the Chief Minister and chairman of the BSPC caused some embarrassment to the Office of the Chief Minister, particularly through his public diatribes against other officials. The OCM accepted the necessity of special consideration for Bougainville, whose contribution to the economy became increasingly apparent as Bougainville Copper Ltd (BCL) produced its first profit statements. In response to repeated demands for the replacement of non-Bougainvilleans in senior posts, it was agreed that Alexis Sarei, a Bougainvillean serving as principal private secretary to Somare, be appointed District Commissioner for Bougainville. This was cleared by Somare with senior national kiaps, but the Public Service Association protested against what it saw as the first "political" appointment to a public service post. Sarei, as the Chief Minister's official representative in the district, and Momis, representing the CPC, were present when the BSPC executive held its first large assembly in May, aimed at creating solidarity behind district government "on their terms". A further mass meeting considered reports from local committees organized by BSPC members and adopted a coherent set of proposals (Mamak and Bedford 1974, pp. 28—50).

Late in July the CPC, touring since late May, made its formal visit to Bougainville, this time with Somare attending as chairman. In other districts local discussion groups had been organized in advance to consider questions issued by the CPC and to meet with its touring members, but only from Bougainville did the CPC receive a district-level submission with organized political commitment behind it. With an emotive preface — "Hear our cries, hear our shouts, take notice of our feelings, take notice of our strong thoughts and our thinking" — the BSPC called for district government by 1 November 1973, a month before Papua New Guinea's self-government, and for recognition of the right to determine in future whether or not it wished to remain within Papua New Guinea. It proposed a strong district executive and assembly with substantial legislative and allocative powers as well as power to direct public servants and to establish district and village courts and village governments based on traditional leaders. Going well beyond the financial options suggested by the CPC, the BSPC demanded for district governments the right to raise taxes, including a company tax on BCL, to receive mining royalties as well as compensation for the extraction of non-renewable resources, and to collect all income and excise taxes. In conclusion, while emphasizing the deadline of 1 November, the BSPC offered a compromise which had been proposed by Hannett: if the CPC recommendations for district government were not available for legal enactment by the deadline, a special purpose authority would be an acceptable interim substitute (text in Mamak and Bedford 1974, pp. 73–79).

The BSPC submission was seen as a deliberate overbid (*Age*, 1 August 1973; Griffin 1977, p. 54) and the Somare Cabinet, refusing special legislation for Bougainville, took up the compromise option by offering Bougainville a special purpose authority pending the CPC report. Barnett and Gabriel Gris were sent to Bougainville with strict Cabinet instructions to argue that only the additional powers and very limited finances being proposed for Area Authorities were feasible for the moment. This was unacceptable to the BSPC, which reasserted its demand for substantial powers and finance by 1 November. Hannett led a delegation to Port Moresby to seek political negotiations, but Cabinet, which had recently taken a hard line in opposing renewed demands for Papuan autonomy, and which had not previously had occasion to consider district government, was reluctant to jeopardize national unity or to treat Bougainville as a special case. The Bougainville ministers Lapun and Mola, who had suffered virulent criticism from their former electoral rivals on the BSPC, gave its proposals no support. The CPC intervened to suggest that an interim form of provincial government would be acceptable, but only after several Cabinet meetings did Somare persuade his ministers to accept the concept of substantial decentralization, and then only on condition that it be made available to all districts (Somare 1975, p. 119).

There followed several weeks of intense tripartite negotiation by delegations from the BSPC (Hannett, Moses Havini, and Aloysius Noga) and the CPC (Momis, John Ley, and others), and political representatives of the OCM (Voutas, Sali, and Gris). Barnett was unacceptable to the CPC and Hannett, and he and his staff did not participate directly. Up to this time each of the three bodies concerned had developed its own notion of district government in relative isolation, but the negotiations between late August and early October forced mutual consideration of the hard issues posed by the BSPC model. Although collaboration between Wolfers and Barnett meant that the CPC and OCM delegations started with the same brief, the negotiations quickly moved into new territory. The structures of district government raised no serious issues, and there was agreement that district government should be safeguarded in the Constitution; but, while the division of legislative powers proved complex and open to further negotiation, the financial proposals of the BSPC were quite specific and proved most difficult to negotiate. The Bougainville delegates conceded that the public service and tax collection should remain under national control, but they held firmly to their demand for copper royalties and substantial other funds (cf. Mamak and Bedford 1974, pp. 54—55). On finance, which became the central issue, the negotiations boiled down to bargaining between Hannett and Voutas over the sum necessary to prevent secession.

During the negotiations, tension remained high. At a meeting of Barnett's official steering committee, John Kaputin, who had recently become Minister for Justice, bitterly attacked the involvement of expatriate officials and their attempts to initiate administrative reforms in anticipation of the CPC's plans for district government. Kaputin's attack had a traumatic effect on several public servants, and CPC hostility took much of the steam out of Barnett's various initiatives, effectively undermining the legitimacy of official co-ordination and planning for district government. Thereafter officials maintained a very low profile on the issue and confined themselves to purely technical roles, with the effect that Cabinet had no continuing source of advice and information on decentralization options. Late in the negotiations, Hannett broadcast an attack on the two Bougainville ministers for failing to support the BSPC position, and he was promptly dismissed by Somare as his liaison officer, though the tripartite discussions continued.

At the conclusion of negotiations, Voutas drew up for Cabinet consideration proposals on interim district government. It had been agreed in the talks that district government should not be imposed uniformly, but would be available on the basis of political demand from individual districts, with Area Authorities, or no district institutions at all, as alternative options. Where demand arose, some existing political group broadly representative of the district would be recognized as a preliminary district government to begin planning for district government. A range of options based on CPC suggestions was offered for the political structures of interim district governments, which were entitled to appoint two staff of their own, a district planner and assistant district planner. The District Commissioner would become District Secretary, responsible to the district government for transferred functions and otherwise to the central government. The district government would have a voice in his appointment and in that of other public servants posted to the district. It would plan future government activities in the district in accordance with national guidelines and would control the execution of government functions transferred to it. These functions were yet to be determined but were to include in the first instance those which Barnett had proposed for Area Authorities as well as a power of veto over foreign investment proposals.

The financial provisions were most precise. Each district government would receive an untied grant equivalent to what was spent by government in its district during the fiscal year 1973/74, adjusted upward with the level of general budget expansion. It would receive all royalties on copper and timber apart from the percentage guaranteed to local land-owners, as well as contributions to a Non-Renewable Resources Trust Fund providing the equivalent of royalties, these to be fully controlled by the district government. An additional grant would be allocated according to a formula favouring poorer districts, and each interim district government would receive an initial grant covering its operating expenses and the salaries of its two staff.

The Department of Finance and other government departments not involved in the negotiations were shocked at the extent to which national resources were to be surrendered. In the light of their comments, revised proposals for the government were circulated at the end of October, with considerable tightening of provisions for finance and the public service. The notion of a clear division of functions between A (central government), B (negotiable), and C (automatically available for transfer to district governments) lists was introduced. The untied grant would be limited to the cost of C functions and, to avoid divided loyalties among public servants responsible to both governments, those staff concerned primarily with C functions might be transferred to a Department of Area Improvement containing a division for each district. Contributions to a Non-Renewable Resources Fund, and a possible compensatory grant for Papua, were isolated as special political grants which should not become part of the general formula for district government.

Because of the BSPC's deadline and the need to maintain the credibility of the recent negotiations, rather than to allow more radical secessionists to promote insurrection, Cabinet agreed on 2 November 1973 that district constituent assemblies preparatory to interim district government could be established administratively without waiting for legislation, and that two staff members would be funded (a provision designed for Hannett and Havini). But despite the pressure to present some form of legislation to the November House of Assembly, the full proposals for interim district government were not considered until 23 November, when Cabinet agreed to a much more cautious set of arrangements. These incorporated the CPC's recent choices on political structures for district government, which had been refined from the earlier wide range of options and which called for election by Local Government Councils and other recognized groups (but added a provision for dissenting areas, e.g. northern Bougainville, to opt out of interim district government). The definition of A, B, and C functions was assigned to an interdepartmental task force with CPC participation, which was also responsible for designing legislation for interim district government. Public servants working on B and C functions in the districts would work as a team to the District Secretary under the direction of the interim district government, but this arrangement would be referred to senior public servants for comment, against the CPC's wishes. While the CPC wanted funds transferred to district governments, it was decided that the Department of Finance would control all funds and districts would only be entitled to expend. Despite arguments that a grant of royalties and the Non-Renewable Resource Fund be approved as a cheap price for keeping Bougainville within Papua New Guinea, Cabinet deferred action and agreed only that interim district government should be established in Bougainville, and in a Papuan and a Highlands district as well. Cabinet's insistence that Bougainville not be treated as a special case was to limit severely the government's options in later planning and negotiation.

The CPC was fully consulted in the revision of these proposals and there was disagreement only on details. On the same day that Cabinet considered Somare's final submission on interim district government, Somare as *ex officio* chairman of the CPC presented its Second Interim Report to the Administrator. The report outlined in detail the political structures recommended for district government, citing frequently the CPC's discussions in the districts as the source of legitimacy for its choices (although the discussions were based on the CPC's discussion paper, which assumed the creation of district governments and specified options only concerning their form). It rejected proposals from Papuan and Highlands groups for regional government, as well as comment from the Speaker of the House, Barry Holloway, that district government would crush the development of community self-government associations blossoming in various forms in the country and add a new tier of bureaucracy. The report proposed a symbolic break with the colonial term *district*, and its replacement by the term *province*, hence "provincial government". On the tough issues of public service control and provincial government powers, the CPC was undecided and was prepared to participate in the government's task force on A, B, and C functions. On the crucial issue of finance it remained silent (PNG 1973*b*). During the week before self-government on 1 December, Somare announced to the House of Assembly the terms agreed to for interim district government, and the CPC's Second Interim Report was made public.

By the end of 1973 Papua New Guinea had arrived at self-government, and the best-mobilized groups in the country – the government, the CPC, and the BSPC – had reached a limited measure of understanding on the

outlines of a programme of decentralization, although the BSPC considered the initial Hannett-Voutas proposals as the legitimate programme. The
Bougainville leaders were angry with the failure of Cabinet to approve the
terms agreed to in negotiation, but Hannett was persuaded by Wolfers
and others that real power lay in planning the district's works programme,
and he accepted appointment as Bougainville's District Planner. Those
political groups — e.g., Papua Besena and the Highlands Liberation Front
— which had doubts about the utility of provincial government for their
purposes, were insufficiently mobilized within or outside government
councils to have any impact. There were other elite groups, especially
students (Ballard 1977), who had adopted the district as the most appropriate framework of political organization and who lent support to the
concept of provincial government. Ministers and their departments, who
had most to lose from decentralization, had begun to be aware of the
potential impact of provincial government on their powers, and several
non-Pangu ministers had developed positions of firm opposition to the
concept of provincial government. Perhaps most important at this stage
was the fact that a model of policy-making in this area had been established: political negotiation between Bougainville and the representatives
of the Chief Minister had displaced administrative planning for a gradual
evolution towards provincial government appropriate to all districts.

ELABORATION BY CRISIS, 1974

At the start of 1974, while the Bougainville leaders began to organize
their interim district government and to plan the district's future development, the CPC turned to the drafting of its final report due in February.
The government, on the other hand, had developed no firm commitment
to provincial government and hence no clear interest in working out a
coherent approach in the midst of many other preoccupations. In the
absence of political support, the technical work of the Task Force on
Interim District Government, that of carving up all government functions
into A, B, and C lists and of devising legislation, was left to a subcommittee of lower-echelon expatriate functionaries. When senior Papua New
Guinean public servants, and particularly the kiaps, became aware of the
extent of changes being proposed, they sent a delegation to the Chief
Minister, strengthening the resolve of his office against a rigid formula
for provincial government and in favour of a flexible range of options
adapted to the needs of all districts, to be made available on demand.
Even this limited measure of devolution proved unacceptable to ministers
when functions, lists, and minimal draft legislation for interim provincial
government were submitted to Cabinet early in March.

While the OCM became persuaded of the need for provincial options and gradual evolution, the CPC, increasingly distrustful of the government's real commitment to radical reform through the Constitution, sought to entrench all its proposals for change and settled on a programme of immediate uniform devolution of powers to Bougainville-model provincial governments. At this point the Commonwealth Secretariat was asked to supply, on very short notice, advice on international experience with decentralized systems of government. Two political scientists, William Tordoff and Ronald Watts, arrived early in March to spend a month looking into the CPC and Task Force proposals and the early Bougainville experience. Their report clarified a number of confused issues, particularly on administration and finance, introducing the specification of revenue sources, and the notion of a Fiscal Commission. It was most useful in reconciling the OCM and CPC positions by recommending that provincial government be conceived of in three stages: administrative devolution with advisory political bodies, political decentralization to interim provincial governments, and full provincial governments with responsibility for all administration. This allowed for flexibility and district initiative in the first stages while holding to the CPC's model as the ultimate form of provincial government. Although joint CPC-Cabinet discussions on the CPC's draft constitutional proposals lasted only a fortnight before breaking up in disagreement, the Tordoff-Watts proposals defused the provincial government issue for the moment, and antagonism was focused on the less negotiable issues of citizenship and control of the executive.

When the CPC draft report was finally tabled in the House of Assembly at the end of June 1974, its recommendations on provincial government, claiming to "embody the views of the overwhelming majority of our people", followed the lines set out in the Second Interim Report but sought to ensure through detailed provisions fully independent powers and finance for provincial governments. It adopted the phasing suggested by Tordoff and Watts but insisted that interim provincial governments be set up without delay in all districts (PNG 1974a, 1974b). When the definitive CPC report appeared in August, its chapter on provincial government, the longest in the report, declared that "our people envisage no alternative to what we have described as Stage 3 Provincial Governments . . . [W]e warn against those who might seek to undermine our proposals by arguing — falsely — that the three stages we provide for can be seen as alternative answers to the people's needs" (PNG 1974c, p. 10/5).

The government's response was outlined in the brief minority report appended by Somare and Guise to the draft final report in June. Provincial government should be available to any province requesting it through a properly representative body, but should be limited to those powers authorized by national legislation. Only the principle of provincial government should appear in the Constitution, with details left to ordinary legislation. These positions and others put forward by the government in opposition to the CPC were then fully discussed in meetings with government backbenchers, which created a measure of political commitment to the broad outlines of a policy on provincial government. The minority report was amplified in the Government Paper issued with the CPC final report in August. This argued that "the type of near-federal system proposed by the CPC would create many legal and administrative problems if introduced suddenly", and warned against the danger of "little Konedobus being created at provincial headquarters, equally alienated from the village people" (PNG 1974*d*). The proposals of the United Party opposition, predominantly composed of MHAs from less advanced provinces, supported the government position on provincial government and suggested that the Tordoff-Watts Report serve as the basis for further detailed planning (PNG 1974*e*). The government's opposition to the CPC report was seen by the CPC as betrayal of a commitment to radical change of the colonial heritage, and most CPC members joined in an inter-party Nationalist Pressure Group to defend their proposals. Debate on the Constitution in the House of Assembly continued until December, when it adjourned until March 1975, having considered all but the chapter on provincial government.

Meanwhile the Bougainville leaders had pressed ahead within the framework of the arrangements agreed to in principle in November 1973. A Bougainville Constituent Assembly met in January and named Hannett as District Planner and another graduate, Moses Havini, as Executive Officer. With the aid of Diana Conyers, provided through the Central Planning Office, Havini worked out an administrative structure for provincial government (Conyers 1975, pp. 13–16; Mamak and Bedford 1974), and Hannett began to map out a provincial development plan. In February Bougainville Copper Ltd announced very high profits, touching off renewed demands for renegotiation of the 1967 BCL agreement and leading the Chief Minister to appoint a renegotiation committee, with Hannett as one of its members. Late in March Bougainville's draft Provincial Development Plan for 1974/75 was submitted to the national government. Cabinet, conceding the need to prove good will and to maintain Bougainville support during the BCL renegotiation, responded by approving, apart from mineral royalties, the financial grants proposed in the 1973 discussions. There were frequent visits to Bougainville not only by representatives of the Chief Minister but also in May by leading officials from Finance and the Public Service Board, who came away persuaded that decentralization had produced remarkable advantages in planning.

It became increasingly urgent to give the Bougainville Constituent Assembly and its officials legal status, so minimal outline legislation for interim provincial government, the Provincial Government (Preparatory Arrangements) Act 1974, applicable to all provinces was approved by Cabinet in June. Introducing the bill in the House of Assembly early in July — a few days after the tabling of the CPC draft report and the government's minority report, and at a high point in CPC-government antagonism — Somare spoke warmly of the achievement of the Bougainville leaders and of the restoration of public service morale in the district. The bill was passed immediately despite disagreement with Momis over the right of MHAs to attend provincial assembly sessions. By the end of July regulations for Bougainville under the new law were approved and the Bougainville Interim Provincial Government (BIPG) was officially established.

At this critical point there was a turnover in government staff responsible for handling the provincial government issue. During the bitter exchanges between the CPC and the government in July, much of the fire was focused on the "white advisers" to the Chief Minister and to the CPC. Partially in response to this pressure, Voutas withdrew from the OCM and was replaced in many of his roles by Rabbie Namaliu, principal private secretary to Somare. Barnett remained, but withdrew from negotiations and was preoccupied with other constitutional matters. Voutas and Barnett were the only national government officials who understood the extraordinarily complex system being proposed by the CPC. Paul Ryan, Secretary of the Department of the Chief Minister and Development Administration, handed over to Philip Bouraga, a district commissioner, while Jack Karukuru, another district commissioner, was also moved to headquarters and given responsibility for provincial government matters. The new men inherited little of the office's collective memory of the 1973 negotiations, and almost nothing of the network of contacts and confidence their predecessors had built up across political-official boundaries. The two kiaps were new to headquarters and were distrusted by the graduates on the political staff of the Chief Minister. Although Namaliu retained close links with Hannett, Momis, and Kaputin, his links with official planning were primarily with the newly arrived Canadians in the Central Planning Office (CPO), who had not as yet been directly concerned with provincial government matters. During the testing months that followed, the absence of effective linkages and continuity weakened national government coherence and provided fertile ground for suspicions in Bougainville.

Bougainville was already encountering ample frustration in attempting to persuade national departments to meet provincial rather than central priorities and in obtaining firm national government decisions on the shape of future provincial government (Conyers 1975, pp. 18—23). Many of these difficulties arose from the fact that no office was responsible for co-

ordinating provincial government matters once Barnett's Political Development Division had lost its legitimacy in this field. Provincial government
elections in Bougainville, initially scheduled for August, were repeatedly
postponed by the electoral office pending adoption of the provincial
government chapter in the Constitution. When Cabinet accepted the
Provincial Development Plan as the basis for the 1974/75 capital works
programme in Bougainville, provision for a local road serving the home
area of one of the ministers was inserted. These actions heightened
Bougainville suspicions of national government intentions, and in August
Momis warned that Bougainville would secede if provincial government
was not entrenched in the Constitution.

Hannett, as a member of the national government's BCL renegotiation
committee, agreed in the national interest to forgo a demand that the
agreement guarantee all mining royalties to Bougainville. When the renegotiation was successfully completed in early October 1974, ensuring a very
large increase in government revenue, officials agreed to submit to Cabinet
Bougainville's proposals for a share in this revenue, as well as for financial
adjustments covering nationally imposed projects and financial arrangements for 1975/76. Several weeks later, Cabinet offered to send a team of
officials headed by a minister to Bougainville for further discussions,
intending to meet any reasonable demands. This was interpreted by the
provincial government as a stalling tactic, and it refused further talks at
official level and insisted that the Cabinet itself come to Bougainville to
negotiate. Cabinet, which had already committed itself to provide $3.7
million to Bougainville in the 1974/75 budget − including $2.4 million
(the estimated royalties) beyond normal capital works "in recognition of
Bougainville's contribution to our revenues" (*HAD*, vol. III, no. 35, p.
4459, 24 September 1974) − appointed a Cabinet committee under Julius
Chan, the Minister for Finance, to negotiate on royalties and further
financial assistance. The BIPG, communicating only by broadcast and
press release, refused further negotiation and threatened to divert the Jaba
River, which serves the copper mine, and to secede if its demands were not
met. At this, Cabinet agreed explicitly to offer the royalties and immediate
action on the works programme issues and on BIPG staffing, and the
BIPG agreed to receive a Cabinet committee headed by Chan, claiming at
the same time that this was merely a face-saving formality. On 18 December at Arawa an agreement was signed transferring royalties uncondition-
ally to Bougainville from July 1975, adding $401,000 to the Bougainville
works programme and providing for additional funds for BIPG staff and
further discussions on tertiary educational institutions in Bougainville.
Although the national government had not in the end conceded much that
was not implicit in its September budget, the distrust generated by "betrayal" on constitutional issues made it difficult to persuade the BIPG that

financial promises were genuine commitments. The crisis instead convinced the Bougainville leaders that concessions could be won only by ultimatum.

BUILDING CONFRONTATION, EARLY 1975

Following the traumatic negotiations with Bougainville and in the face of requests from several Area Authorities that they be declared provincial governments, the Office of the Chief Minister became aware that, despite the government's commitment to provincial government in its constitutional proposals, it had no clear definition of the powers of provincial governments and no procedures for establishing them. Co-ordinated official planning had ceased when Barnett's efforts of 1973 were stifled by the CPC. Although responsibility for policy rested nominally with Namaliu and Karukuru in the OCM and with the Provincial Planning Branch of the CPO, none of these was actively involved until the final stages of the December Bougainville crisis.

Early in January 1975 Karukuru was assigned full time to provincial government matters and an interdepartmental committee was established to develop detailed policies on provincial government arrangements. Chaired by Karukuru, it was initially composed of earnest expatriate amateurs, with no previous experience in this area apart from that of Diana Conyers, who had helped organize Bougainville's provincial government. The committee outlined alternative approaches to the central and delicate issue of powers over public servants. Its submission was seen by David Beatty of the CPO as heavily weighted towards the Bougainville model, and it alerted Somare to the political and financial implications of spreading that model to other districts. Thus, when Momis and Kaputin reasserted the CPC's demand for entrenchment of provincial government in the Constitution and called for immediate recognition of local political movements as provincial governments, Somare argued for slow and steady progress. It was not possible to give all nineteen districts provincial government "straight off the counter". To do so would bankrupt the country within three months (*Post Courier*, 19 February 1975). The issue of costs had been firmly raised for the first time.

The amateurs were dropped from Karukuru's committee and replaced by Barnett, Ryan, and Michael Grey of the CPO, who focused their experience on the issues. They framed recommendations which for the first time placed the implications of provincial government clearly before Cabinet. Cabinet was warned that the transfer of powers to provincial governments would have greater immediate effect on the government than would independence and that some ministers would lose most of their powers over departmental field staff. Yet the government had committed itself in its constitutional proposals to offer provincial government to districts on request, arousing expectations in many districts. Failure to specify the powers available to provincial governments, even though the cost could not yet be known, would block what was described as excellent progress in Bougainville. On 4 March 1975, when the House of Assembly held its brief debate on provincial government provisions for the Constitution, Cabinet finally agreed to make C functions and related staff, equipment, and finance available to provincial governments requesting them.

In the House of Assembly Somare laid stress on the problems of provincial government and urged maximum flexibility. Other MHAs reflected clearly the public confusion over the nature and meaning of provincial government, accepting it as a hopeful answer to dissatisfaction with existing institutions but concerned about the potential for fragmentation and secession. Much of the passion over constitutional issues had been spent on the earlier debate on citizenship, and outside the House a compromise was struck between representatives of the government, the Nationalist Pressure Group (NPG) and the United Party, whereby the government accepted amendments safeguarding through an organic law the powers of provincial governments over C functions and adequate finance for these functions. The terms of the organic law were left to an interparty Follow-up Committee (FUC), and after very little debate the House adopted the amended provincial government chapter of the Government White Paper without division. This concluded debate on constitutional proposals, and the House adjourned until late May when it met as a Constituent Assembly to debate the draft Constitution.

The FUC assembled on 3 April and met almost daily for several weeks to settle detailed provincial government terms of the Constitution, the organic law, and other legislation. Whereas the NPG was represented by its stalwarts, Momis and Kaputin, advised by John Ley, the government team was led by Ebia Olewale, Minister for Justice, and Barry Holloway, Speaker of the House, neither of whom had been directly involved in previous provincial government discussions, counselled by Tarua, who had replaced Barnett in the OCM. Karukuru was preoccupied with Bougainville affairs, and Grey and Barry Stuart, the Planning Office members of the Karukuru committee, were drafted to provide government staff support, while Peter Bayne advised the United Party delegation; much of the FUC's work fell to the lawyers, Ley, Tarua, Stuart, and Bayne. The NPG delegation used the opportunity provided by the FUC to reintroduce the CPC's proposals on provincial government, while the government delegation had no clear brief to defend, and Bayne sought to hold the middle ground in terms of the Tordoff-Watts Report of 1974. Ronald Watts and another Canadian, W. R. Lederman, arrived as consultants to help convert the

FUC's agreement on structures and procedures into more detailed arrangements for an organic law covering the more controversial and crucial issues of financial and legislative powers.

At this point, late in May 1975, confidence between the government and other parties broke down over differences between House of Assembly instructions and the fourth draft of the Constitution, in which the government on its own initiative had inserted the Queen as head of state and diluted constitutional amendment procedures. This created an extended crisis and coincided with a rupture in relations with Bougainville.

The agreement on finance reached with the BIPG at the end of 1974 had left the provincial works programme for 1975/76 to future negotiation. In February 1975 the Bougainville Assembly approved a programme (which may initially have been designed as a three-year programme) costing $5.3 million and submitted this for national funding in 1975/76. The national government had stringent budget prospects despite its huge new copper revenues, which it had resolved to hold in reserve for stabilization. The Department of Finance, which was putting into effect the basic framework of its economic policies, pointed to the dangers of *ad hoc* precedents, and other national departments calculated that their Bougainville staff had capacity to spend no more than $1.37 million. This was a slight increase over funding for 1974/75. A delegation led by Karukuru was dispatched to offer this amount. Hannett and the young graduates in the Bougainville Provincial Secretariat rejected this as an insult to Bougainville, and the BIPG refused to consider funding any of the works programme from its royalties. When negotiations failed at the official level, an assembly of Bougainville leaders on 15 May threatened to secede from Papua New Guinea. When discussions with ministers led to an impasse, a further meeting voted on 30 May in favour of secession, citing both broken promises on works funding and the government's "tampering" with the Constitution. Although there were indications that Hannett was more determined on secession than Momis and Sarei, the BIPG maintained a united front in refusing to negotiate on any issue except the terms of secession. An improved offer from the government and tours of Bougainville by teams of government ministers and officials failed to undermine this unity. The Bougainvilleans, however, made it clear that they did not intend to use violence to achieve their aim and the national government, having successfully ignored Josephine Abaijah's declaration of Papuan independence in March, was not distracted from its primary concern with passage of the Constitution.

While the FUC and the mounting Bougainville crisis were proceeding in separate arenas, each extending the government's disjointed dialogue of previous years with the CPC and with Bougainville, other actors were becoming engaged in planning for provincial government, particularly departmental and district officials beyond the small circle of those in the OCM, the CPO, and Finance, who had so far been involved. During the last quarter of 1974 a committee of senior public servants, chaired by Ignatius Kilage of the Public Service Board, had inquired into national administrative and public service arrangements in preparation for independence. The Kilage Committee, working in camera, recommended *inter alia* the creation of a Department of Provincial Affairs to hold and coordinate all C functions and relevant staff pending the establishment of provincial governments. Early in February 1975 all department heads met for a week at Loloata Island to consider the Kilage Report and firmly opposed such a department as an unnecessary encumbrance. They foresaw instead the need for flexible negotiation for devolution to "fast" and "slow" moving districts which their departments could better manage directly. The Public Service Board attempted to compromise by recommending an upgrading of Karukuru's small co-ordinating secretariat.

Consideration of provincial government was also spreading in the districts. During 1974 all Area Authorities had asked for provincial government but, although the Provincial Government (Preparatory Arrangements) Act authorized the establishment of interim institutions, there were no set procedures for obtaining recognition. There were also no organized movements comparable to that of Bougainville, whose provincial government was seen in most districts as selfish and unpatriotic. Initiative thus lay primarily in the hands of the district commissioners, who were uncertain of their own future role under provincial government. Karukuru's committee drafted provisional procedures for establishing provincial governments, and the district commissioners were convoked on 23 April 1975 to discuss their role in instigating the planning of provincial government in the districts. Although the procedures were not formally adopted at this stage, because of opposition from the FUC, they served as guidelines for district commissioners and Area Authorities who wished to initiate activity. At the end of May the OCM sought from department heads and district commissioners information on the staffing, financial, and legislative implications of transferring the B and C list powers and functions. The costing exercise for the first time involved many senior public servants in consideration of the potential impact of provincial government.

The government was concerned to provide evidence that its intentions to decentralize were serious. On 20 June, a few days after the Constituent Assembly had finally approved the government's proposed independence date in September, Somare gave Olewale, the Minister for Justice who was chairing the FUC, additional responsibility as Minister Assisting the Chief Minister on Provincial Affairs. He also pledged that, as soon as the Constitution was adopted, the government would establish a Department of

Provincial Affairs and the institutions proposed in the CPC report: a Fiscal Commission, a provincial premiers council, and a parliamentary standing committee on provincial affairs (*HAD*, 20 June 1975, vol. 3, no. 46, pp. 893–94). The Public Service Board opposed immediate establishment of a new department but agreed to the creation of an Office of Provincial Affairs, approved by Cabinet in mid-July with Karukuru as director.

The Follow-up Committee approached its conclusion with the aid of the Watts-Lederman Report, issued on 9 July. One of the contributions of this report to further clarification was its movement away from the A, B, and C lists of functions towards the specification of legislative powers for provincial governments and of the sources of finance for them; but since the CPC Report provided the only firm proposals on legislative and financial powers, the Watts-Lederman Report resuscitated these. The Department of Finance, which was particularly concerned to avoid repetition of the annual haggling with Bougainville, had worked out the financial implications of alternative arrangements with the aid of Anthony Clunies Ross, former Professor of Economics at UPNG. The department agreed with the principle that financial provision for provincial governments should match their powers, but it suggested that national grants were likely to be of much greater importance than the taxes, derived revenue, and Fiscal Commission grants on which the NPG had focused the FUC's attention.

At what proved to be the final meeting of the FUC on 19 July, Somare took the chair and asked Grey and Stuart of the CPO and Ross Garnaut of Finance to explain the political and financial implications of the CPC model as developed in the Watts-Lederman Report. Garnaut presented the Clunies Ross calculations, which showed that distribution of royalties and export tax receipts for 1973/74 (a year of high prices) among the districts would have given K4.1 million to Bougainville and substantial amounts to other island districts, but only K2,000 to the Southern Highlands. Somare offered his own conclusion: that the FUC's model of provincial government favoured the better-endowed districts, while leaving the poorer districts stationary. The FUC appointed a subcommittee to consider the Watts-Lederman Report and frame an organic law, but apparently it failed to meet.

The Constituent Assembly reached part VII of the draft Constitution, dealing with provincial government, on 30 July, a few days after the Deputy Chief Minister, Albert Maori Kiki, returned from an unsuccessful last attempt at negotiation in Bougainville. Somare, opening the debate, emphasized the wide differences in financial and manpower resources among districts and argued that administrative decentralization would be preferable since most districts were not ready for provincial government. In the light of the Bougainville experience, he said "the time will come when we are being bled by our own provincial governments!" The leader of the United Party opposition and several other speakers supported the Chief Minister. Olewale, as the responsible minister and chairman of the FUC, regretted that, although he "believed in the provincial government system", the country could not afford it at present. A motion to omit part VII from the Constitution passed by thirty-nine votes to nineteen (National Constituent Assembly, *Draft Hansard*, 30 July 1975).

Somare's initiative caught his provincial government advisers completely by surprise. The decision to drop provincial government from the Constitution had been made at the last moment, when it was clear that the government had the numbers to support this in the Assembly, and Olewale's speech had to be rewritten during the debate. Public statements of explanation emphasized the financial and manpower costs of provincial government, but the sour experience with Bougainville and the general reluctance of ministers and their departments to relinquish control were also clearly influential (Conyers 1976, pp. 50, 65–70). Most public servants – particularly those responsible for provincial planning – had loyally followed what they took to be the government's firm commitment, but ministers were far from enthusiastic. Although Stuart and Grey of Beatty's Central Planning Office had been closely involved in the work of the FUC and the drafting of the Watts-Lederman Report, David Beatty himself (perhaps the single most influential adviser after leading the BCL renegotiation of 1974) felt that the political and financial situation meant that the time was not ripe for provincial government. Most Australian commentators considered any approach towards a federal system a grave mistake, and Somare frequently cited the recentralizing experience of Kenya, which had been forcefully put to him by D.N. Ndegwa and other members of a visiting UN Environmental Program mission.

RESOLUTION, 1975–76

During the week following 30 July 1975, the government reassured the Constituent Assembly, district commissioners, and Area Authorities that it intended to proceed with the gradual establishment of provincial governments under the Provincial Government (Preparatory Arrangements) Act. Towards this end K2,000 was immediately allocated to each district commissioner to finance district constituent assemblies based on Area Authorities or equivalent bodies. On the other hand, the Watts-Lederman proposals for an organic law on provincial government were quietly shelved, and the Public Service Board refused to approve staffing for Karukuru's Office of Provincial Affairs until government intentions became clearer. Karukuru and his small secretariat continued to promote activity in the districts, but among other national departments only

Finance prepared contingency plans suitable for either political or administrative decentralization. The Public Service Board limited its contribution to "team-building" workshops in the districts.

In the districts, which became provinces under the Constitution at independence, there had been desultory progress towards provincial government before the events of July 1975. This depended largely on the interest and energy of individual district commissioners (by now all indigenous officers), Area Authority executive officers (almost all expatriate kiaps), MHAs, and students. Following the draft guidelines for the establishment of provincial governments, the steering committees which had been organized in most districts had begun going through the specified steps towards qualification — each with the expectation that its members would become the dominant forces within interim provincial governments.

Two models of provincial government began to emerge at this stage. Young university graduates and students envisaged provincial government in the terms set forth by Bougainville and the CPC, as a means of mobilizing popular initiative to displace dependency on a colonial bureaucracy. To this end several graduates who had worked in the OCM returned to their provinces in mid-1975, most notably Rabbie Namaliu as District Commissioner of East New Britain, but also Moi Avei in Central Province, and Nahau Rooney in Manus. Tony Bais, the graduate District Commissioner of East Sepik Province, and a group of young graduates from New Ireland also took charge of mobilization in their provinces, and other graduates and students attempted with less success to do the same elsewhere.

An alternative model was developed by kiaps, both indigenous and expatriate, following the government's apparent preference for administrative decentralization and the gradual evolution of Area Authorities. This was most successful in districts with limited political mobilization where kiaps still held substantial authority as agents of development and points of contact with the outside world, particularly in the Highlands. The graduates sought to displace the Area Authorities, and the Local Government Councils on which they were based, as relics of an older generation's dependency. The kiaps, with support from ex-kiaps Bouraga and Karukuru in the OCM and Jack Baker and Joe Nombri at the Public Service Board, attempted to build on the existing institutions that were under their tutelage. The Eastern Highlands, which had been chosen early in 1974 as a pilot district, was the first to complete the various procedural stages, pushed by the expatriate Area Authority Executive Officer. In September 1975 the Area Authority submitted a draft constitution asking for no additional powers and thus provided a test of the government's commitment to provincial government. There followed a long delay in processing draft regulations, which suggested that provincial government on the Area

Authority model commanded no significant priority within the government.

The decision to drop provincial government from the Constitution had been the last straw for Bougainville. Four days later, on 3 August 1975, the Bougainville Provincial Assembly announced that it would declare the independence of the Republic of the North Solomons on 1 September, two weeks before Papua New Guinea's independence date. Momis was dispatched without success to Australia and the United Nations to seek recognition, and soundings were made on the prospects of federation with the neighbouring Solomon Islands, still a British Protectorate (Griffin 1976, Hastings 1976). Somare's advisers were divided on the appropriate strategy for dealing with the Bougainville situation. After a tour of the province, several young graduate department heads became convinced of the widespread popular commitment to autonomy and they counselled compromise. Others, including several ministers and Somare's department head, Bouraga, took a hard line. The government quickly plugged a gap in existing legislation by pushing through provision for the suspension and abolition of interim provincial governments, but it left open a door to reconciliation, providing $4.14 million for Bougainville, including royalties, in its 1975/76 budget. On 16 October the government suspended the BIPG, appointing a district commissioner to replace Sarei and a Bougainville Provincial Trust, composed of Port Moresby—based public servants, to administer funds. This led to demonstrations in Bougainville, a threat of civil conflict, and rejection of further overtures to negotiation, but a period of quiet ensued after a reorganization of the North Solomons executive in which Momis became chairman and Sarei chief secretary, with Hannett confined to the role of planner. The executive were allowed to remain in their government houses and offices, and they continued to control the well-funded Bougainville Development Corporation, established early in 1974.

The Somare government employed various stratagems to bring the North Solomons leaders to negotiation, but the latter resisted and attempted to maintain authority within the province. The situation came to a head after 16 January 1976, when the North Solomons Assembly issued an ultimatum demanding that it be paid royalties and other funds. On 26 January there was carefully managed violence against government installations at several centres in Bougainville, though typically there were no injuries. Two days later Somare and Momis agreed by telephone to a truce. Preliminary talks were held on 16—17 February in Bougainville by delegations headed by Somare and Momis, after which Somare, referring to a nation-wide desire for provincial government, announced his government's willingness to reinstate the BIPG. At further talks a week later in Rabaul the North Solomons delegation retreated from its stance of non-negotiable secession and presented a list of proposals calling for full implementation of the CPC model of provincial government. The government agreed to revive the constitutional chapter and organic law on provincial government.

Meanwhile, pressure had been mounting in other districts, and particularly in East New Britain, for rapid progress towards the establishment of provincial governments. Rabbie Namaliu, as Provincial Commissioner in East New Britain, had succeeded in bringing local factions together in a Tolai Government Committee to consider working within the framework of a provincial government. Somare's own province, the East Sepik, was also pressing for action. On 26 January, the day of violence in Bougainville, Somare appointed Oscar Tammur of East New Britain as Minister for Provincial Affairs, with responsibility for Karukuru's office and for local government. In early February the Tolai factions finally reached agreement and in the negotiations of the following weeks between Somare and Momis, Namaliu was a vital catalyst, loyal to Somare but a close friend of Hannett and a firm supporter of political decentralization.

During the following months, movement towards the definition and establishment of provincial governments proceeded on several fronts. While the national government and Bougainville teams carried on negotiations, other provinces led by East New Britain pressed for action on their own cases, and national government departments began slowly to mobilize to cope with the increasing reality of provincial government.

At Rabaul, Somare and Momis appointed a joint negotiating committee with Namaliu and Momis as joint chairmen. The North Solomons delegation was composed of leading politicians and members of the Provincial Policy Secretariat, while Namaliu was joined by Barry Stuart and Pedi Anis of the NPO, which served as the focal agency for negotiation, and by Paul Bengo, Somare's principal private secretary. The chief national government negotiators, Namaliu and Stuart, were firm supporters of the Watts-Lederman formula and were thus effective brokers between the North Solomons delegation and an interdepartmental task force at national headquarters.

During March and April momentum was maintained by the reinstatement of the BIPG, the transfer to it of royalties and other funds and additional powers under hastily enacted amendments to the 1974 interim legislation, and the introduction of a constitutional amendment on provincial government. Suspicion and tension in Bougainville arose, however, when the Electoral Commission delayed provincial government elections until mid-June and insisted on holding parliamentary by-elections for seats vacated by North Solomons leaders. Tensions were exacerbated by police initiative in evacuating teachers reputedly beseiged at Buin High School, just before a round of negotiations on control over education and police.

Although confidence between the negotiating teams survived these events, the climate of tension hardened North Solomons insistence on full safeguards.

By early July, preliminary agreement had been reached on a package of legislative powers for provincial governments, but an impasse had developed over North Solomons demands for power over natural resources, for direct executive authority over public servants, and for powers to tax produce and income and to borrow overseas. Somare and Momis, meeting at the inauguration of East New Britain's interim provincial government, agreed that these demands raised technical issues beyond the grasp of politicians and could better be resolved by lawyers. They therefore appointed Yash Ghai and Barry Stuart as their respective champions for the final phase of negotiation. North Solomons leaders had full confidence in Ghai, an East African who had served as visiting consultant to the CPC and who was finishing a six-month attachment to the Law Reform Commission. Stuart, a young Canadian who had been active in designing and resurrecting the Watts-Lederman formula, was felt by some public servants to be representing the wrong side in the negotiations.

Ghai was available for only three weeks further in Papua New Guinea, and this set a deadline for the urgent and hectic discussions that ensued. On the issue of control over public servants executing provincial functions, the Public Services Commission had no clearly conceived preferences, and a confused compromise was reached in the form of a Provincial Management Team, composed of political appointees from the provincial policy secretariat and national public servants including a residual provincial commissioner. The other outstanding issues concerned the Ministry of Finance, which alone among national departments had a well defined set of policies to defend and which had followed the negotiations closely. On the morning of 7 August, with Ghai leaving at midday, there was still no agreement on the financial issues, but in the final flurry of drafting the North Solomons leaders gave up their demands on taxation, borrowing and control over natural resources.

Although the agreement of 7 August referred specifically to arrangements for the North Solomons, many of its essential provisions were couched as draft proposals for organic laws on provincial government for general application. Several of the national government representatives involved in the negotiations were in a position to defend the interests of their own provinces, but these were the best developed provinces like East New Britain and New Ireland. There was no formal consultation of other provinces in the framing of the proposals, but Somare and the Ministry of Finance from their national perspectives had as one of their concerns the preservation of the national government's discretion to act in the interests of weaker provinces.

In formal terms the agreement remained within the framework of provincial government approved by Cabinet in March 1975. The legislative powers to be given exclusively to provincial governments were drawn from the old C list approved at that time, and in the case of concurrent powers national legislation was given precedence. The principle of a national public service was maintained, and the financial arrangements followed the principle of giving provincial governments full options over transferred functions without disrupting the national scheme of tight controls on total expenditure. Apart from the Non-Renewable Resources Fund the North Solomons would receive only those finances extended to other provinces. These included the proceeds of nationally levied royalties on natural resources and certain registration fees, a derivation grant equal to 1¼ per cent of the value of all exports from the province (less the amount of royalties received), as well as the power to tax retail sales, certain licences, entertainment fees, and land. The most important source of revenue would be an "unconditional" grant from the national government equal to existing levels of national expenditure on transferred functions in each province, with provincial governments given a limited measure of discretion to redirect funds among services. The national government would also continue to pay the salaries of public servants assigned to provincial functions. Finally a Fiscal Commission, allocating additional grants so as to help correct the imbalance in the level of services among provinces, would have power only to make recommendations to the national government.

North Solomons suspicions of the national government's political and administrative processes were written into the agreement in the form of strict deadlines for the transfer of financial, legislative, and administrative powers and the introduction of organic laws in parliament. The narrow margin of success in completing the negotiations meant that Somare and his advisers, as well as the Ministry of Finance, were committed to carrying through this programme without substantial variation, and ministers and departments with reservations were warned of the dangers of provoking renewed secession. The most important task of implementation was the translation of the agreement's often fuzzy compromises into an organic law. The Department of Law had shown no capacity for imaginative work in this area and the Commonwealth Secretariat was once again called upon by Beatty to provide talent. Roland Brown, former Attorney-General to Nyerere in Tanzania and a consultant to the PNG government during the renegotiation of the Bougainville Copper Agreement, arrived on short notice and worked within a deadline set at the end of October, by which date the agreement's timetable required that the draft organic law be published. Lobbying of ministers and national departments to persuade them of the necessity and desirability of accepting change was orchestrated by Beatty and Namaliu. The North Solomons leaders retained the right to approve the provisions of the organic law, and Yash Ghai returned to advise the provincial government in a final round of negotiations late in October.

The draft Organic Law on Provincial Government, published on 26 October 1976, clarified several points in the North Solomons agreement. On finance, the formula for "unconditional" grants was set at the cost of transferred services in each province for the fiscal year 1976/77, adjusted annually up or down according to the cost of living and available government revenue and thus giving the national government a means of reducing the grants in adverse circumstances. Detailed arrangements for the Fiscal Commission were also set, ensuring that the national government would determine the total amount of funds allocated by it. The area of greatest contention was that of public service controls, for here the agreement was unclear. In order to ensure that public servants assigned to provincial responsibilities were under the control and direction of the provincial government, and yet remained part of a unified national public service, the disciplinary powers belonging to national department heads were assigned to a "deemed department head" in each province. In the North Solomons, this post was combined with the national government functions of the Provincial Commissioner in the new post of Administrative Secretary.

Although the Organic Law was not finally enacted until March 1977, the North Solomons Provincial Government was formally established on the anniversary of secession, 1 September 1976, and took over full powers under a further extension of the Provincial Government (Preparatory Arrangements) Act. Although the Organic Law allowed for a range of possible arrangements in different provinces, the North Solomons had succeeded in setting the basic model for provincial government, and once this model was fully established in the North Solomons the province made little further contribution to its elaboration elsewhere. Within a few months of the August agreement the political unity of the provincial leaders was fractured: Hannett was dismissed as Provincial Secretary by the Premier, Sarei, and the Provincial Executive Council, then was reinstated, and was eventually defeated by Momis in the July 1977 parliamentary elections for the North Solomons provincial seat.

BEGINNINGS OF IMPLEMENTATION, 1976–77

In May 1976, early in the North Solomons negotiations, the national government established the Department of Provincial Affairs, incorporating the kiaps and other field operations of the Department of the Prime Minister, and Karukuru was named departmental head. Since he had first been given nominal responsibility for provincial government policy at the end of 1974, Karukuru had the thankless task of attempting to persuade national departments to collaborate with Bougainville and with the government's inchoate "policy" of decentralization. His small Office of Provincial Affairs had no political clout and was unfairly blamed by the North Solomons leaders for national government shortcomings. It remained on the margins of serious policy-making exercises like the North Solomons negotiations, even after the appointment of Tammur as Minister for Provincial Affairs. The chief work of the office had been to co-ordinate the conduct of provincial government consultations in other provinces, but the lack of capacity to provide clear answers concerning national government intentions — together with a related failure to obtain helpful responses to provinces from national departments — made Karukuru's office and new department a general whipping-boy.

To avoid a repetition of the failures of communication which had marked relations with Bougainville, Cabinet appointed at the end of June 1976 the Inter-Departmental Committee on Provincial Government. This was to co-ordinate policy on provincial government and Bougainville matters as well, replacing the informal task force supervising the negotiations. But the negotiations had developed a momentum of their own, and it was not until they were completed that the Committee, through its Bougainville Agreement Implementation Subcommittee, came to life. Even then, much of the activity lay not in Karukuru's department but in Finance and Planning, which were already well geared up for work on the crucial issues.

Many of the most difficult of the outstanding issues concerned public service matters. At the start of September 1976 the weakest of the central departments, the Public Services Commission (PSC), was brought into line with the replacement of Sere Pitoi as chairman by Rabbie Namaliu. Namaliu's appointment gave the North Solomons leaders, and the young graduates following the North Solomons model in other provinces, confidence that the agreement and the Organic Law would be firmly applied by the national government. With the departure of Stuart, as well as Beatty and Garnaut, from Papua New Guinea after the Organic Law was drafted, Namaliu made the PSC the focal point for provincial government policy, leaving the Department of Provincial Affairs and the Implementation Subcommittee on the sidelines once again.

A number of public service issues were immediately evident when Namaliu took over the PSC. His East New Britain government had pressured the PSC into funding through Provincial Affairs the six politically appointed Provincial Policy Secretariat positions which had been accorded to the North Solomons, and now the Organic Law specified that all provinces were entitled to six positions. In the better developed provinces the secretariats, under provincial secretaries like Leo Hannett in the North Solomons, were inevitable rivals of the provincial commissioners as chief advisers to interim provincial governments (Standish 1979). The role of the provincial commissioners in relation to provincial government had always been potentially invidious, and the experience of Benson Gegeyo as Provincial Commissioner in Bougainville during the period of secession convinced others that they were considered expendable. During secession the North Solomons Provincial Government had appointed its own field administrators, and when the agreement was signed Hannett asked Karukuru for the transfer of most kiaps from the province.

The role of kiaps had been in question since Hasluck's time, but in most provinces, particularly the least developed, they continued to serve as indispensable agents and co-ordinators of government-sponsored development. In the absence of mobilized groups, they were the chief spokesmen for provincial interests and were recognized as such within their provinces. But kiaps lacked an effective voice at headquarters, and proposals for administrative decentralization — such as that put forward by the Western Highlands Provincial Co-ordinating Committee, seeking devolution of staff, budget, and other powers in preparation for provincial government — brought no response from the PSC. Early in October 1976, the provincial commissioners were assembled to discuss the future role of kiaps (Ballard and Colebatch 1976). The Governor-General, Sir John Guise, a consistent opponent of provincial government, persuaded them privately that the government felt their role had come to an end. The provincial commissioners exploded at a meeting with Karukuru and Namaliu, refusing to accept assurances even from Somare. At Karukuru's instance, a committee on the future role of kiaps and of the Department of Provincial Affairs was appointed under Evertius Romney of the PSC. Although its report several months later recognized a continuing role for both, it evoked no response from the government and had only limited circulation. In the absence of any government policy, morale in the department and the field, already low, was further sapped and creative initiatives could not be expected from either quarter.

The PSC as a department was not radically transformed by Namaliu into a vital new centre of activity, but his office attempted to promote commitment to the devolution of administrative authority to provincial governments — primarily through the definitive carving up of national and provincial powers and through workshops for department heads at Sogeri in December 1976, for department heads and provincial government staff at Rabaul in March 1977, and for provincial planners at Lae in April 1977. Much of this activity was limited to the few provinces that had proceeded furthest with provincial government — North Solomons, East New Britain, Eastern Highlands, Central, and now New Ireland — and although others were gradually moving towards recognition as interim provincial governments, there was great reluctance on the part of national extension departments — Education, Public Health, Primary Industry,

Works — and within Finance to part with substantial controls over staff and finance.

On leaving Papua New Guinea in September 1976, David Beatty had persuaded Namaliu that the complexities of administrative devolution to provincial governments could not be dealt with effectively by the PSC and other departments, and that Beatty's former employer McKinsey and Co. (which had worked out a scheme of decentralization for Tanzania) were the most appropriate consultants. A McKinsey group paid an initial visit at the end of September, but the proprieties of tendering for a contract delayed their return until April 1977, when much of the flexibility of September had been lost.

The work of the McKinsey team extends beyond the scope of the present study, since its report was ready for presentation only after the elections of July 1977 and the appointment of Momis as Minister for Decentralization in the new Somare Coalition. The McKinsey formula for uniform devolution to all provinces, breaking with the principle of provincial initiative, was extended in a second report which led to the creation of the Office of Implementation within Momis's new ministry. The office, working to Bougainville-style deadlines, mobilized a crash programme which effectively transferred substantial powers by 1 January 1978 to all provinces (Conyers 1979).

CONCLUSIONS

The establishment of provincial governments constituted the most radical reform of inherited colonial structures in Papua New Guinea, and it was no mean achievement to devolve substantial power without disrupting national unity and a coherent economic policy. Yet it seems clear that at no time was Somare or his Cabinet fully committed to political decentralization. Why then did it become effective policy?

The easy answer is that a politically mobilized group in one district, making demands in the name of one formula of "provincial government" and having a capacity to issue credible threats to a major resource, forced the issue. This is certainly true, but it is not an adequate explanation of the national government's behaviour, and particularly of its forebearance from the use of force. A more complete interpretation, which may shed light on policy-making more generally under the Somare Coalition, requires examination of both the capacity of the government to focus on issues and to generate its own preferred programmes, and the value placed by Somare and his closest advisers on participation and compromise.

One of the consistent advantages held by Bougainville leaders and the CPC in dealing with the national government was their relatively narrow

focus of concern. While they could press for an ostensibly coherent programme of reforms, government ministers and their advisers were preoccupied with the maintenance of existing programmes and with learning the
tolerances of coalition coherence, political support, and public service
capacity. The transfer of power, the framing of a constitution, and the renegotiation of the BCL contract were major and pressing, but finite, concerns. Decentralization was much less bounded and much more difficult to
grasp in its implications. Accordingly, there was a reluctance to focus
attention upon it and a general hope that the issue would go away. Even
when ministers were forced by external pressures to reach "decisions"
ostensibly committing them to provincial government, their reluctance and
that of public servants was sufficient to ensure that implementation failed
to receive high priority.

Reluctance and low priority were reinforced by the absence of any
national government office having both responsibility for planning decentralization and legitimacy in the eyes of Bougainville, the CPC and the
public service. Once Barnett's Political Development Division was effectively disqualified by the CPC, there was a year's hiatus before Karukuru's
committee attempted to pick up the issue in a much less tractable situation. The national government might well have developed an effective
scheme of administrative decentralization had Barnett's exercise been
maintained and had the Public Services Commission been brought into
action, but this opportunity was not taken up during 1974, the Coalition's
period of greatest political vulnerability. Thus, when provincial government was dropped from the Constitution in mid-1975, there was no alternative programme to throw into the breach. Throughout the period the
government lacked programmes of its own on decentralization and could
only react to external initiatives.

At the level of political negotiation, too, the national government
suffered from lack of continuity. The experience accumulated by Voutas
and Barnett was eliminated by pressures from the CPC in 1974, which contributed to misunderstanding and the crises of late 1974 and mid-1975
with Bougainville. Namaliu and Stuart were involved in some planning and
negotiation from the end of 1974, but by 1976 they were dealing with
Bougainville leaders who had been refining their positions since 1972, and
they were themselves committed to political decentralization.

The lack of continuity and of focus on this issue reflected a more
general lack of capacity for analysis within the national government
administration, a legacy of Canberra's refusal to allow the development of
planning institutions in the colonial period. Apart from Barnett's PDD in
1972–73 and the Department of Finance in 1975–76, each relying
heavily on the talents of one man, there was very little organized effort
within the administration to consider wider issues and to assess with sub-

tlety and depth the options available to the government. For a particularly complex issue like that of decentralization, as for any kind of radical administrative reform, there was simply no readily available competence, and the government rapidly learned to fall back on external consultants in devising detailed arrangements. Non-Australian consultants had exceptional legitimacy because of the government's happy experience with the Faber team on economic development strategy in 1972 and with the succession of experts located through the Commonwealth Secretariat. The CPC had been equally pleased with Yash Ghai and with Tordoff and Watts. The Canadians in the National Planning Office also had an exceptional position as outsiders within the public service, politically dependent on their close relationship with Somare and Namaliu and therefore more readily perceived by the latter as loyal. By 1975 the Follow-up Committee was willing to accept fully the proposals of Watts and Lederman, and reliance on consultants was carried to the full in the handing over of the 1976 negotiations to Stuart and Ghai, and the 1977 implementation plans to McKinsey and Co. Meanwhile, among government departments, only Finance — recognized by 1975 as the central motor of government policy — had sufficient grasp of its own policy commitments to recognize the implications of provincial government proposals and to formulate arrangements compatible with its interests.

Apart from the government's problems with focus and planning, it is clear that the government's values — much more elusive for analysis — helped determine the outcome of the provincial government issue. The government began with a general commitment to wider, and especially local, participation in policy-making. This meant that, at least during its first year in office, it accorded special recognition to mobilized movements in the districts, negotiating some measure of autonomy for Gazelle institutions and encouraging Hannett's mobilizing efforts, which at the start were aimed at deflecting secession. Each case was initially dealt with on its own merits, but by mid-1973 there was an increasing tendency to incorporate local movements into more generalized national programmes. Hence John Kasaipwalova's demands for substantial grants to the Trobriand Islands were channelled into the new Village Economic Development Fund, and Papua Besena's strident call for secession led to the formation of Moi Avei's Village Development Task Force. The same logic led ministers to insist that Bougainville should be given no special legislative recognition.

Nonetheless, the BIPG had established its autonomous role by 1974, when the BCL renegotiation exercise helped guarantee this. At the same time the very denial of special provision for Bougainville under the Provincial Government (Preparatory Arrangements) Act 1974 ensured recognition for separate initiatives and mobilization within each of the other districts. This was maintained throughout the crises of the following year, and provincial initiative and variation became an important component of government rhetoric after the provincial government chapter was removed from the Constitution, encouraging the development of pressures from East New Britain and elsewhere. Only under the McKinsey formula was the notion of provincial variation and initiative curtailed through the imposition of uniform administrative arrangements.

The early commitment to local participation and initiative was significant, but of much wider importance were the values and personal qualities of Somare and his chief lieutenants, Voutas and especially Namaliu. They shared a preference for compromise which amounted to a determination to reach solutions through negotiation rather than confrontation, and Somare's increasing stature within the government enabled him to win over Cabinet colleagues who espoused a hard line during crises. This preference for compromise, often seen as a Melanesian cultural trait, was reinforced in the case of Somare and his lieutenants by a capacity to keep lines open to all parties in dispute and a willingness to take risks, such as the appointment of Hannett early in 1973 and of Stuart as sole negotiator in 1976. It also entailed a tolerance for ambiguity and a dislike of difficult decisions and crisp solutions, which tended to be left to the lawyers and consultants once a general compromise had been struck. While this characteristic was of considerable value in coping with the complexities of the transition to independence, it was a source of vulnerability to mobilized groups who knew what they wanted and were willing to engage in confrontation.

Legal Policy-Making

PETER BAYNE

The basic approach of Australian legal policy in Papua New Guinea during the two decades before 1972 is summed up in a memorandum of 1955 by the Minister for Territories, Paul Hasluck, concerning a proposal to establish village courts.

> In a dependent and primitive society, such as that in New Guinea, I think the individual native would have a greater expectation of justice in the fullest sense of the term, by arrangements which would make courts in the British tradition more easily accessible to him, with a bench appointed in the customary way, observing the customary forms, and patiently applying the laws applicable to "subjects" of the Crown, than he would have in village courts set up by an administrative officer, with a bench composed of village natives following variable rules and applying a variable body of customs (Hasluck 1976, p. 189).

The basic legal policy objective was that, as far as possible, and with the significant exception of juries, the Anglo-Australian legal system should be replicated in the Territory, both in substantive law and in the machinery for its administration. Professor Derham's 1960 report on the administration of justice confirmed Hasluck's views on the lower courts (Derham 1960, p. 31), and the Local Courts Act 1963 replaced the kiap courts with local courts to which all races were subject and which would be conducted by trained specialist magistrates. The change was, however, more apparent than real, for administration field officers continued to act as magistrates and in practice only Papua New Guineans were subject to the courts (see Bayne 1975*a*, pp. 22–25).

The basic policy objective can be seen in other reforms in the 1950s and 1960s. In the 1960s some saw a link between this objective and the policies on economic development advocated by the World Bank which had been embraced by the Australian government. Mr Justice Kerr, for instance, argued that Australian legal institutions would "follow to a large extent, upon the conversion of the New Guinea economy from a subsistence to a money economy" (Kerr 1968, pp. 10–11). Kerr argued too that an indigenous elite could play a vital role in this transformation, and that

Papua New Guinean lawyers had an especially important role to play. "Such lawyers in politics, administration and judicial administration could achieve real freedom from their former cultural ties at the high level of political and legal comprehension" (p. 20). Australian officials in the Territory took a comparable line when they argued that by replicating Australian laws in Papua New Guinea there would be created a climate in which foreign, and especially Australian, business would flourish while Papua New Guinea capitalist activity would also be encouraged (Paliwala, Zorn, and Bayne 1978).

The results of the policy supported by Hasluck and others in the period can be seen in a number of reforms. The gradual removal of racially discriminatory provisions in legislation and the repeal of the Native Regulations were necessary if an elite was to emerge, and both these measures were part of the reform movement. Commercial law reform was designed explicitly to accommodate Australian forms of business enterprise. Foreign investors were given specific legislative protection, and the law-and-order campaign of the late 1960s was linked with their activities. Those who designed and administered the system of legal education were clear that its objective was to create a legal elite that would be divorced from the village communities (Paliwala, Zorn, and Bayne 1978).

The general pattern of policy formulation and policy implementation in the pre-1972 period seems fairly clear. Hasluck's memoirs (Hasluck 1976) provide ample evidence of his interest in formulating policy on legal matters and his close attention to its implementation. Although his successors took little interest in such matters, the pattern of Canberra control was established and Canberra-based public servants assumed Hasluck's role. Canberra control was facilitated by the appointment of legal staff in the Department of External Territories who were concerned with legal policy in Papua New Guinea. Policy implementation was largely the responsibility of the Department of Law in the Territory, and although Hasluck complains of resistance to his policies on legal matters, they were on the whole implemented. A desire for closer Canberra control over both policy and its implementation in the late colonial phase may have motivated the appointment in 1969 to the position of Secretary for Law of an Australian public service lawyer, L. Curtis, whose experience had been on the executive side of the Commonwealth Attorney-General's Department (see Gyles 1975, p. 33). It is clear that the general pattern was that policy was to be decided in Canberra and that the Department of Law was to be responsible for its implementation under close supervision from Canberra.

In any event, the Department of Law was not in a position to play a developmental role in the creation of policy. W. Watkins, the Secretary for Law for a considerable period before the appointment of Curtis, was politically conservative, and other senior officials were not temperamentally inclined to a policy role, in part a consequence of their training as lawyers. There were some exceptions. W. A. (Peter) Lalor had a close relationship with Hasluck and was concerned with policy formulation, and C. J. (Joe) Lynch worked closely with senior administration officials outside the department. However, both men worked outside the mainstream of the department: Lalor, as Public Solicitor, was virtually independent, and Lynch, as parliamentary draftsman, worked in isolation from his Department of Law colleagues. Some younger lawyers who joined the department in the 1960s found it too confining; they (such as John Ley, who became counsel to the House of Assembly) were able to find an independent basis for a more policy-oriented role.

Lawyers outside the public service had little influence on policy. The private profession was concerned primarily with servicing the legal needs of the expatriate community and of Australian companies investing in Papua New Guinea and were moved to action only when their interests or those of their clients were threatened. The Faculty of Law at the University of Papua New Guinea was in general agreement with the thrust of the Australian government's policy, although some members were critical of some of its aspects.

1972: THE DIVERSIFICATION OF THE SOURCES OF INFLUENCE ON LEGAL POLICY

In the first year of the National Coalition there were several significant changes in the process of policy formulation and implementation on legal matters. Canberra control was loosened significantly, and the sources of policy initiated both inside and outside the government in Papua New Guinea diversified. The extent to which Canberra control was relaxed, and the problems faced by the National Coalition, its advisers, and pressure groups in Port Moresby in attempting to operate in the vacuum thereby created, can be illustrated by comparing two sets of cases that came before the courts in 1971 and 1972.

The first set of cases, the prosecutions that followed the killing in late 1971 of Jack Emmanuel, the District Commissioner of East New Britain, provide a dramatic example of the degree to which the department in Canberra maintained supervision over day-to-day administration in Papua New Guinea in the late colonial period. As a consequence of the killing, thirteen persons were charged with murder. The decision to charge such a large number was criticized because, as Gyles has noted, "it appeared to most observers from an early stage that there were in fact two clear 'principals' involved in the killing, the remainder being (at most) 'aiders and abettors' " (Gyles 1975, p. 34). Criticism mounted when the Department of Law pressed on with the *ex-officio* indictments of those accused who had been discharged at the committal stage. "It was widely believed in legal circles that the decision to try so many accused, leading directly to the vast proportions of the case, was made in Australia against some local advice" (Gyles 1975, p. 35). The decision of the Supreme Court to allow *ex-officio* indictment was also criticized (Kassam 1974).

However, by June 1972, when the trial of those charged with the murder concluded, relations between Canberra and Port Moresby had changed. The election of the National Coalition and the appointment of Andrew Peacock as the Australian minister resulted in a situation in which "although Australia retained constitutional power and control over the administration of justice, Canberra in practice would not exercise such power and control without the concurrence of the local ministry" (Gyles 1975, p. 36). But the local ministry was not equipped to operate in the changed situation. This was of course true for the ministers, none of whom had any experience of operating in a system where they had real executive responsibility. It was also true for key advisers like Tony Voutas, whose experience of administration was limited. At the same time, department heads and other officers in the administration who might have been expected to cope were unused to a situation where they were responsible to a local minister, or even responsible for taking decisions without referral to Canberra. The situation with regard to the Department of Law was complicated by the fact that there was no local minister with responsibility for the significant functions of the department.

The difficulties faced in this situation by the National Coalition ministry, and by those putting pressure on the ministry to act in one way or another, can be illustrated by a second set of cases. The cases began with the prosecution of an Australian named Boxtel for the rape of an Australian woman. During the course of their investigation, police tapped the telephones of Boxtel and one of his lawyers. On the basis of the evidence so obtained, and on other evidence, this lawyer and another lawyer involved with Boxtel were charged with certain offences. In the event, Boxtel and the two lawyers, both of whom were Australian, were acquitted or not proceeded against. What is of interest about the whole episode is what it reveals about the process of policy-making in Port Moresby.

The telephone taps and the decisions to prosecute the two lawyers, which were made by or known to senior officials in the Department of Law, roused the opposition of the private legal profession, some officers in the Public Solicitor's Office, and some judges. In various ways, this group brought pressure to bear on the Chief Minister's Office to institute a judicial inquiry into the Department of Law, and sought to influence legislation the government wished to introduce concerning telephone tapping. Roger Gyles, an Australian lawyer who acted for one of the lawyers who was prosecuted, has provided the only account of the activities of this group. (It should be said, however, that Gyles does not indicate that any judges were involved. (Gyles states that the minister in Canberra was prepared to order a judicial inquiry if the National Coalition did not object, but that, contrary to early indications, the National Coalition did object. Gyles speculates that opposition from the Department of Law, or from the Constitutional Planning Committee, may have produced the change of mind (Gyles 1975, pp. 39–40).

It is difficult to take speculation about motives any further, but it can be concluded that the issue revealed the vacuum created, in matters of legal policy making at least, by the loosening of Canberra control. Tony Voutas has acknowledged that the matter distracted the National Coalition's attention in its early months, and it must have been particularly irksome that only expatriates were involved. The Coalition's inexperience was no doubt a factor leading to delay. The Department of Law was also unused to a policy role, but in any event its capacity to advise on these issues was compromised by the fact that it might be the subject of the inquiry. Gyles's account reveals too the difficulties faced by those who wished to bring pressure on the Coalition. The channels of communication to Australia, both to politicians and to lawyers, were no longer adequate, but neither was it clear who influenced and made the decisions in Port Moresby. A wide range of lawyers and non-lawyers in Port Moresby were involved, and the episode indicated to them all just how open the system had become.

The episode contributed to a weakening of the role of the Department of Law. One cause of its decline was bitterness between the office of the Public Solicitor, which was formally within the department, and the prosecution side of the department. The events surrounding the rape prosecution "acted as a catalyst to unite the Public Solicitor's Office lawyers and the private profession in opposition to the Secretary for Law and those responsible for prosecutions in his department" (Gyles 1975, p. 39). The potential for conflict between the Public Solicitor and other branches of the department was inherent in their respective roles. The Public Solicitor was at issue with the department in all significant criminal proceedings and in respect of several key land cases. In the best of circumstances, there would have been tension in the relationship, but the situation was exacerbated by the personalities involved. The weakening of Canberra control probably served also to unleash old hostilities and ambitions. In spite of all this, the department might have taken a leading role in policy formulation, but the prosecutions in these cases served to put the department very much on the defensive; they also consumed a great deal of attention and energy over the latter part of 1972. The threat of a judicial inquiry was a very real one and probably served to inhibit the enterprise of key Department of Law staff.

Two other developments in the government weakened the department's role in policy formulation and even in its implementation. Sections of the Chief Minister's Office became interested in legal development, particularly as it related to constitutional and economic development. The creation of a Political Development Division within that office was particularly important. This division was headed by Tos Barnett, a lawyer who had close links with key National Coalition politicians. His position involved him directly in legal development on constitutional matters and indirectly in relationship to a wide range of other issues (for example, tribal fighting in the Highlands). Non-lawyers close to the Chief Minister also became involved in legal policy when they were appealed to concerning the telephone tapping cases. The other development was the growth in influence of the legislative draftsman, Joe Lynch, which was facilitated by the establishment of a separate Office of Legislative Counsel within the Chief Minister's Office in June 1972. Lynch had been one of the few administration lawyers prepared to challenge Canberra and was in a position to offer clear alternatives when the National Coalition showed itself receptive to change.

The sources of influence outside the department also diversified. The private profession remained in general quiescent, although it did exert itself when two of its members were prosecuted. The judiciary became involved in policy-making through participation in bodies or committees concerned with legal matters, particularly in regard to legal education, and the network of informal contacts that some judges had with some of the government lawyers were occasionally used to influence policy. Leading politicians such as John Guise had always taken an interest in legal matters, and with the liberation of Port Moresby from Canberra control the influence of the politicians increased. As ministers, they had access to independent legal advice. One important source of influence was the Constitutional Planning Committee. The committee opposed the proposals for a judicial inquiry into the Department of Law, partly from concern that it might find its own view on the administration of justice pre-empted, and its desire to preserve its influence generally brought it into conflict with others. The principal legal adviser to the Committee was John Ley, an administration lawyer who had become counsel to the House of Assembly, from which position he was seconded to the committee. The committee's other lawyer was Bernard Narakobi, whose influence grew as independence approached and who has played an important role since 1975.

The Faculty of Law at the University of Papua New Guinea also changed significantly during 1972. At the beginning of that year it was dominated by Australians, most of whom had no prior experience in law teaching and who were committed to a substantial amount of private practice. In the course of 1972 a number of these people resigned and there was an expansion of the faculty. Several of the new appointees had prior experience teaching in Africa, and particularly in Tanzania during a period of substantial post-colonial reform. There began a long and sometimes bitter debate within the faculty about the nature and purpose of legal education. Professor A. B. Weston wrote in the 1973 university *Calendar* that law professionals needed elements of a general education so that they would not "view themselves or their jobs in isolation from the constant social change within Papua New Guinea or the general patterns of change in the rest of the world" (UPNG 1973). Other lawyers in Papua New Guinea saw the change differently. Commenting on the developments during 1972, Gyles has argued that "there was a trend developing which placed emphasis on teaching law as a general education for administration, rather than as a training for the actual practice of the law. An object would be to train people to assist in running a State operated economy and legal system along the Tanzanian model" (Gyles 1975, p. 39). Those members of the faculty who were interested in the role of law and lawyers in social change were also close to politicians and their advisers and began to have some influence on policy.

1973–77: INTERACTION OF THE SOURCES OF INFLUENCE

The manner in which these sources of influence interacted varied from issue to issue, although in time alliances formed which remained relatively stable. Analysis of examples of interaction is limited here to a number of particular issues. Underlying each of these lay a more fundamental question concerning the nature of the PNG legal system: the choice between development on the Anglo-Australian model and development reflecting the needs and values of modern Papua New Guinean society. The centrality of this question was stressed by the Chief Minister in an address to the 1973 Waigani Seminar: "We do not want to create an imitation of the Australian, English or American legal systems. We want to build a framework of laws and procedures that the people of Papua New Guinea can recognise as their own – not something imposed on them by outsiders" (Somare 1975, p. 14). The sentiment that the legal system imposed by the Australian government was antithetical to the values of Papua New Guinean communities was articulated by politicians whenever legal issues were discussed in the House of Assembly and remained evident in the period after independence (see especially Kaputin 1975).

It must be recognized too that what are identified here as legal issues occurred in the course of day-to-day political life and that the outcomes were influenced by that context. In the first place, the legal issues were themselves political in that different opinions on these issues can be traced ultimately to different political objectives or ideologies. Some issues were more obviously political and in relation to them the debate was more bitter and sometimes of significance to the wider political process. The debate over the citizenship law is perhaps the most obvious example, although it is not discussed here (see Wolfers 1977, pp. 301–97); of the issues discussed, the debate over legal education is one where some of the disputants made their broader political position reasonably clear.

Secondly, disputes over legal issues were sometimes influenced by disputes over distinct political issues. Thus, the opposition within the National Coalition ministry to John Kaputin during his term as Minister for Justice, which was manifest in the controversy over the appointment of judges to the Supreme Court, can be traced to the conflict between the Constitutional Planning Committee, for which Kaputin was a leading spokesman, and the ministry. This conflict was a result of differences of opinion on issues such as citizenship and foreign investment, and was also a clash of personal ambitions.

In this discussion of issues of legal policy the general political dimensions are identified, but the primary focus is on the sources of influence on the legal issues, and particularly on the role of the lawyers.

Village Courts

The first major policy initiative of the National Coalition in legal matters concerned village courts. The Australian administration belief that any system of courts administered by ordinary Papua New Guineans would be inimical to the administration of justice seems hardly to have penetrated into the consciousness of Papua New Guineans. John Guise articulated the feelings of many when he argued for recognition to be given to the village systems for settling disputes (International Commission of Jurists 1970, p. 44; Young 1971, pp. 60–62). In addition, a few administration officers had never accepted the official line and had kept the issue alive during the 1950s and the 1960s (Fenbury 1979, chap. 6; Lynch 1965 and 1972).

Perhaps in response to these views, or perhaps because of a genuine change of mind, the Australian administration began to review its position in 1971. In February, the minister initiated a review of the lower court system which included examination of the possible appointment of village justices and village law enforcement officers. By December 1971 a senior Canberra officer and the Secretary for Law had concluded that some link with the villagers by means of village justices was necessary and had drawn up detailed terms of reference for a review. However, it is doubtful that the reforms eventually introduced by the Village Courts Act 1973 would have been so substantial if the National Coalition had not been elected.

The advent of the National Coalition gave a strong impetus to the review of the local court system. The Coalition appointed two District Court magistrates, one an expatriate and the other a Papua New Guinean, to make recommendations concerning village courts. Their recommendations were accepted by the government, whose White Paper was endorsed with enthusiasm by the House of Assembly in November 1972. In April 1973 the Department of Law circulated a set of proposals for legislation and invited discussion. The discussion that resulted showed that some elements of the legal profession remained unconvinced. On a rare excursion into the general field of public policy, the Council of the Law Society advocated that village courts should so far as possible be kept within the national judicial system and that they should be limited to homogeneous rural groups. They were also concerned that the proposed legislation would weaken the Human Rights Ordinance (Law Society [1973]). Of greater weight was the opposition expressed at the 1973 Waigani Seminar. The Chief Justice, a Papua New Guinean District Court magistrate, and a Papua New Guinean lawyer all expressed agreement with a view that had been advanced by a visitor to the seminar, Mr Justice Georges of the Court of Appeal of Trinidad and Tobago. Georges advocated that it might have been better to pursue an alternative system in which the local court system was expanded rapidly and linkages established between those courts and village arbitration procedures (see Bayne 1975b).

For whatever reason, the first draft of the Village Courts Bill was "a very weak instrument which did little more than provide official recognition for existing unofficial mediatory procedures" (Oram 1978, p. 27). At this point political intervention became crucial. Nigel Oram, who was actively involved in the process of revision of the bill, has outlined what occurred: "Dissatisfied with its provisions, Barry Holloway, Speaker of the House of Assembly, called a series of meetings of Ministers, senior officials and others to discuss the drafts. Nearly all proposals for strengthening the courts were accepted by the Secretary of Law, W. Kearney" (Oram 1978, p. 28).

The Village Courts Act 1973 demonstrated that the National Coalition was prepared to accept radical change to the legal system. Although the act declared: "The primary function of a Village Court is to ensure peace and harmony in the area for which it is established by mediating in endeavouring to obtain just and amicable settlements of disputes" (sec. 19), the courts are clothed with ample powers to adjudicate and to make orders for compensation, fines, or the performance of community work. There are no formal qualifications set for village court magistrates. The sections of the act concerning the law to be applied represent a radical departure from the logic of the 1963 reforms which created the local courts. A village court "is not bound by any law other than this Act that is not expressly applied to it but shall . . . decide any matter before it in accordance with substantial justice" (sec. 30). However, section 29 provides that village courts must apply relevant custom as determined in accordance with the Native Customs (Recognition) Act. Custom may be applied notwithstanding that it is contrary to some other law, and a local government council may make rules declaring the custom of its area. The act was passed by the House of Assembly in late 1973, but the first village court was not established until February 1975. The establishment of "unofficial" village courts in Barry Holloway's electorate, Kainantu, and in other areas probably served to force the hand of the Village Courts Secretariat, which did not initially pursue the objectives of the scheme with any vigour (N. Oram: personal communication).

There were, and remain, significant political dimensions to the debate over village courts. The "official" Australian government line of the 1950s and 1960s was related to its conception of the desirable kind of political framework for Papua New Guinea, and some supporters of this line saw clearly the link between this framework and the broader economic and social system. On the other hand, some of the supporters of village level courts were advocates of a different kind of social system, one in which Papua New Guinea's local communities would have greater influence. They were aware that village courts would be a means of affording recognition to villages as political units, and thus a means of weakening the administration in both Port Moresby and Canberra and of sponsoring Papua New Guinean political development. Easy passage of the Village Courts Act of 1973 may be seen as manifestation of an emerging Papua New Guinean nationalism.

However, the debates in the House on the bill reveal another political dimension which may influence the future development of the courts. A point stressed in the debates by leading political figures such as John Guise and Oscar Tammur was that the courts would be an instrument for strengthening the hand of the village elders against youthful dissidents (*HAD*, vol. III, nos. 21, 23, and 24). Conversely, and outside the House, some younger Papua New Guineans argued that village courts were not an appropriate means of regulating the conduct of those who had become accustomed to an urban life-style (see Bayne 1975*b*). The seeds of conflict are evident, and they also appear in the work of the local land courts, which adjudicate on customary land disputes and which work with mediators drawn from the local community.

The First Minister for Justice and Judicial Appointments

On 30 August 1973, John Kaputin was appointed the first Minister for Justice. (On the evolution of the ministerial system and the transfer of executive power in Papua New Guinea, see Bayne and Colebatch 1973.) When the first National Coalition ministry was formed in April 1972, most of the functions of the Department of Law remained under Australian control. In addition, the Secretary for Law, William Kearney, the public service head of the department, remained as one of the four official members of the House of Assembly and as one of the three official members on the Administrator's Executive Council. Although as a matter of law he was obliged to accept direction through the Administrator from Canberra in respect of those functions of his department not transferred to Papua New Guinea, the Australian Minister for Territories made it clear that the Australian government would consult with the Administrator's Executive Council on the exercise of these functions. The Secretary for Law remained a member of the AEC until Kaputin's appointment, and it therefore received its advice from a person who would have been quite understandably diffident about intruding into policy matters. Thus policy on most legal matters had been treated in a different fashion from most other functions of government.

Kaputin came into a situation fraught with ambiguity as to the extent of his powers, those of the Secretary for Law, and those of the Australian government. Moreover, as has been seen, some members of the legal fraternity in Port Moresby had taken advantage of this situation to lobby Canberra directly on matters relating to the administration of justice. After Kaputin's appointment, some ambiguity remained. Kearney ceased to be a member of the AEC, and Kaputin became responsible for a substantial measure of the department's functions. But Kearney, and through him Canberra, retained policy responsibility for a number of significant areas, including the judiciary. The subtleties of the constitutional situation were appreciated by only a few people and would in any event have hardly mattered to Kaputin, who was concerned to use his position to achieve broad social objectives.

During his year in office, Kaputin alienated his ministerial colleagues and a significant number of lawyers both inside and outside the government. The opposition of many lawyers can be traced, in part at least, to a speech Kaputin made at the Papuan Hotel in November 1973, in which he described the law as "a colonial weapon" (Kaputin 1975, p. 4), and in that vein commented on various aspects of the law and of the work of lawyers. Kaputin's relations with his department became strained rather quickly, and it is clear that a relationship of trust and confidence was not established. Kaputin was not able to procure the appointment as his personal adviser of Ikenna Nwokolo, a Nigerian lawyer resident in Port Moresby who had acted for the Mataungans in the Rabaul "keys case" (see below and Gunther 1970, p. 30). On the other hand, a senior officer of the department who produced a paper outlining possible policy initiatives after a meeting between Kaputin and senior officers was not encouraged by Kaputin to proceed on these initiatives. The difficult relationship between the minister and the department was partly a result of personalities, partly a result of the fact that the minister was distracted by the general political situation.

Kaputin's disaffection with his ministerial colleagues can be traced partly to some of his policy initiatives. For example, his proposal for "a special division in my Ministry to deal with and co-ordinate with other functional ministries the legal aspects of international trade and investment questions" (Kaputin 1975, p. 7) angered the Minister for Finance, Julius Chan. In addition, Kaputin maintained his leading role on the Constitutional Planning Committee which by the middle of 1974 had clashed with the Coalition, and in particular with the Chief Minister, over policies concerning citizenship and foreign investment. Kaputin at one point voiced a lack of confidence in Somare.

Kaputin's term ended with his dismissal on 15 October 1974. In a speech to the House of Assembly on the reasons for his dismissal, Kaputin dwelt in particular on the question of the appointment to the Supreme Court of two West Indian judges, both of whom had visited Papua New Guinea at the invitation of the Faculty of Law to attend the Waigani Seminar in April 1973, and who had met with the Constitutional Planning Committee. He stated that he was opposed to the appointment of Mr Justice Georges of Trinidad and Tobago as Chief Justice, but consented to the appointment of another West Indian, Mr Justice Cross, after the Chief Minister had assured him that the appointment would only be for three years. He then observed: "I leave to you to establish why they have not turned up when both had indicated to the system that they were willing to come" (*HAD*, vol. III, no. 37, 17 October 1974, p. 4763). This remark is difficult to interpret. My understanding is that Mr Justice Georges was committed to remain in Trinidad and Tobago, and that the negotiations with Mr Justice Cross broke down over the question of salary and other conditions of appointment, he having been offered a salary substantially lower than that of his counterpart Australian judges and of several administration lawyers.

Kaputin's more serious claim was that his recommendation that Paul Quinlivan be appointed as an acting judge for two months was overruled and that, instead, "Konedobu and Canberra came up with Mr Justice Edmunds and Mr Justice Denton for the positions of acting judges" (ibid.). He claimed too that Peter Lalor was appointed as an acting judge for twelve months over his express opposition. It is difficult to comment on these allegations without access to files both in Port Moresby and in Canberra, but enough evidence is available to provide amplification.

One early initiative from Kaputin was the advocacy of a policy to appoint expatriate judges from among those whose main legal experience was in Papua New Guinea. Kearney responded to a request for proposals with a paper which was sympathetic to the policy and which canvassed possible appointees. Quinlivan's name was included, as was that of Lalor. However, at some point (possibly when Kaputin was abroad) the matter was removed into the Chief Minister's Office and the decision not to appoint Quinlivan, and to appoint Justices Edmunds and Denton instead, was made ultimately by the Chief Minister. All these decisions were made without the knowledge of Kaputin, who did not, moreover, know that Justices Edmunds and Denton were being considered. One view taken by the Chief Minister's advisers was that judicial appointments were, as a matter of general constitutional principle, ultimately decisions for the leader of the government. English practice provides some support for such a principle (Hood Phillips 1973, p. 332), while Australian practice in relation to High Court appointments is unclear (Sawer 1967, pp. 35–36), but in both these countries the minister with political responsibility for the judiciary has a key role in making recommendations.

However, the precise constitutional position in Papua New Guinea at the time was not clear, and the Australian government could claim an interest in the matter. The Australian Attorney-General's office was involved in this episode, at least to the extent of advising on the availability of Mr Justice Edmunds. The Office of the Chief Minister also took advice from the judges of the Supreme Court of Papua New Guinea, and the opposition of at least one of the justices to Quinlivan's appointment was of considerable significance to the Chief Minister's decision not to appoint Quinlivan.* The appointment of Mr Justice Lalor occurred some time after the episode just described. Kaputin was firmly opposed to his appointment, possibly at least partly because of Lalor's involvement as Public Solicitor in a Matupit land matter. Kaputin was given only very short notice by the Office of the Chief Minister of the proposal to appoint Lalor.

* Quinlivan was Stipendary Magistrate in Rabaul in the years 1967–70, a time when the Tolai and, in particular, the Mataungan Association (with Kaputin among its leaders) were in conflict with the administration which, on some occasions, had the support of other Tolai. One such conflict led to three Mataungan leaders being charged with the theft of the keys of the Rabaul Council Chambers. Quinlivan S.M. dismissed the stealing charge on the obvious ground that the three had no intention of keeping the keys permanently. In dealing with another charge of obstructing staff of the council, which arose out of the same incident, Quinlivan criticized the administration's handling of the situation, found ground for Mataungan frustration, and used his discretion under the applicable law to dismiss the charge without proceeding to a conviction (see Gunther 1970, p. 30). Less than a year later Quinlivan was, by action of the administration, removed from Rabaul. It has been alleged that his removal was due primarily to his decision in the "keys case", and indirect evidence of this is the statement in the Australian House of Representatives by Kim Beazley that "quite high officers of the Administration" had not denied this allegation when it was put to them (*House of Representatives Debates*, vol. 66, 12 October 1970, p. 359).

Although Kaputin's specific positions on judicial appointments may not have been crucial to his dismissal, general policy on appointments was a significant indicator of legal policy in the period to 1977. In several respects there were changes to the policy favoured by Hasluck, and continued by his successor, of appointing experienced barristers from the Australian states. In the first place, the Papua New Guinea Act was amended in August 1973 to permit the appointment of non-Australians to the Supreme Court; however, only one such appointment had been made up to 1977. Secondly, following a recommendations of the Constitutional Planning Committee, section 167 of the Constitution permits the appointment as assistant judges of Papua New Guineans whose experience does not qualify them for a full appointment. Again, however, this provision has had little effect, for up to 1977 no such persons had been appointed (see Ross 1977, p. 10). Finally, the government has in practice adopted the policy favoured by Kaputin of appointing to the National Court and the Supreme Court Australian lawyers whose experience has been largely in Papua New Guinea.

Policy on judicial appointments is probably determined ultimately at the political level in Cabinet, but there is little public evidence about what factors influence policy. It is possible that the government might be influenced by the argument advanced by the Public Solicitor in his 1976 report that the encouragement of foreign investment required that expatriate judges be retained on the Supreme Court, which is the ultimate court of appeal in Papua New Guinea (see Public Solicitor 1976, pp. 8–9). It is known too that discussions with Kennecott broke down partly because the company insisted that any disputes it might have with the government should be settled by a body outside the PNG judicial system. This was possibly a bargaining ploy, but it is significant that it was thought credible enough to advance as a reason for the breakdown in negotiations.

Legal Personality for Papua New Guinean Forms of Enterprise

The history of legislation permitting a new form of legal personality for "customary" group activity illuminates policy-making on a significant legal issue. Before 1972 there were proposals for legislation to facilitate business activity by customary groups, the most notable being a draft bill prepared in 1969 by Joe Lynch (see also Lynch 1969 and 1970). However, the Registrar of Companies had expressed strong opposition to the concept of customary group incorporation in an address to the 1969 Waigani Seminar and argued that a Companies Act based on Australian legislation was necessary to facilitate foreign (especially Australian) businesses and local entrepreneurs (Healy 1969). Advisers to the National

Coalition brought the issue back to the fore. Tos Barnett was responsible for attaching to the Office of the Chief Minister Peter Fitzpatrick, an academic lawyer who, under the auspices of the New Guinea Council on Legal Research, was studying the law relating to indigenous business. Fitzpatrick's brief was to prepare legislation for the incorporation of customary groups and he was advised by Barnett to work through the Department of Business Development rather than through the Department of Law. The Law Department was at best indifferent to the proposals, and one advantage of working through Business Development was that the minister, Donatus Mola, was enthusiastic. By February 1973 Fitzpatrick had drafted a General Purposes Corporation Bill and Cabinet had approved a set of instructions which were designed to implement the draft.

But the legislation passed by the House of Assembly to implement the policy objective was substantially different from Fitzpatrick's draft. In a statement to the House in April 1974 Ebia Olewale, the new Minister for Commerce, explained that he had been concerned at the length and complexity of Fitzpatrick's draft and that the matter had been referred back to the First Legislative Counsel, Joe Jynch. A considerably shorter Business Groups Incorporation Act was passed by the June sitting of the House.

According to Fitzpatrick, senior officers in Business Development became hostile because he had assisted Iambakey Okuk, as Minister for Agriculture, to draft legislation that excluded expatriates from coffee buying, and for this reason they were disposed to an alternative approach. Their draft of the Business Groups Incorporation Act was based partly on the drafts of the Land Groups Bill which had resulted from the Commission of Inquiry into Land Matters Report and also appears to draw inspiration from Lynch's 1969 draft legislation.

The details of these events remain unclear, but some conclusions of general significance are apparent. The Department of Law had little to do with one of the most significant developments in legal policy during this period; indeed, the Office of the Chief Minister had kept the department out of the way. Fitzpatrick, a non-public service adviser in the OCM played a significant role, but the public servants in the Department of Business Development were able to assert their preferences, largely because of a change in ministers. The Legislative Counsel and a lawyer in the Lands Department, Jim Fingleton, probably had the greatest influence on the actual shape of the eventual legislation.

Fitzpatrick's interest in this kind of legislation can be understood as part of his more general argument that the law should be adapted, either by the enactment of new laws or the repeal of existing ones, to stimulate "informal sector" activity by Papua New Guineans who found it difficult or impossible to operate within the confines of the Australian-influenced commercial and licensing laws (Fitzpatrick and Blaxter 1974). It is possible that disaffection towards Fitzpatrick was due to the fact that he took a more comprehensive and radical stance on legal and economic issues, but this is not apparent with regard to the legislation concerning business groups. The shorter final version of the legislation is just as effective a vehicle for achieving Fitzpatrick's objectives as his longer original bill.

Fitzpatrick's conflict with public servants in Business Development is instructive because it is illustrative of the problems raised for public servants by the role of non-public service advisers to National Coalition ministers. Some part of such conflicts may be traced to personal antagonism, but there were deeper causes. Public servants were concerned that the advisers had access to files without being subject to normal public service restraints. The files contained commentaries, working papers, and notes which were not written for circulation and which were potentially embarrassing to the authors and to others. Some senior officers considered keeping two sets of files. There were also problems of status which concerned some junior offices in particular. Such difficulties played a part in obstructing co-operation on substantive policy issues.

Legal Education: Two Issues

Before independence in 1975, Papua New Guineans influenced legal policy formulation only indirectly and occasionally. One important exception concerns the amendments to the Local Courts Act and the District Courts Act which conferred a right on certain categories of law students to appear in these courts.

Early in 1973 a group of law students acting on their own initiative began a legal aid scheme in the Port Moresby area. In the words of three of its promoters the scheme had two aspects: first, "going out into the settlements and participating in what would be called legal education"; secondly, "going into the Local Court and participating in the client-service aspect of the legal profession" (Sam, Passingan, and Kanawi 1975, p. 163). Some local court and District Court magistrates became upset that law students were appearing for hitherto unrepresented persons, and the District Magistrate in Port Moresby announced that the students would not be allowed to make appearances. Although this magistrate was an expatriate, he was supported by several Papua New Guinean magistrates who resented the students' presence. The students approached the Secretary for Law, who responded by organizing a meeting between students, university lecturers, and magistrates, at which some common ground was reached. The necessary amending legislation was prepared in a class at the Faculty of Law, and when it appeared to the students that the Department of Law was dilatory in producing the legislation, they approached a private member of the House of Assembly who promoted its passage.

This development within the Faculty of Law was taken a step further by the Report of the Committee of Enquiry into University Development (1974), which recommended that all university students should, as part of their degree, engage in work experience, preferably in their home areas. The Faculty of Law responded with a proposal for reform of the Bachelor of Laws degree that would split academic study by a year's work (Weisbrot and Paliwala 1976, p. 197). The subsequent history of this proposal reveals with more clarity than is usual the clash of interests and ideologies that often surround issues of legal policy.

Although these proposals were endorsed by both the Faculty of Law and the Academic Board of the university, they were deferred by the University Council, "in part because of opposition by elements of the organised bar, and the bench, which have claimed that diplomates would be, in effect, 'half-baked lawyers', incapable of providing legal services of acceptable quality. One Judge went so far as to condemn the modular approach as a 'socialist experiment'" (ibid., p. 198), and at one point the Chief Justice indicated that the judiciary might not recognize the law degree for purposes of admission.

At the same time, the faculty's proposal was supported by an amendment to the Post-Graduate Training Institute Act, sponsored by Buaki Singere as a private member's bill, which requires that a law graduate must have spent a year working with a community on customary law research or practice before he or she could undertake the study at the institute which is a prerequisite to admission to practise law. Some leading Papua New Guinean lawyers indicated support for such schemes at the 1976 Law and Self-Reliance Seminar (see Gawi, Ghai, and Paliwala 1976), but at the end of the first parliament in 1977 the faculty's proposals had not been accepted by the University Council and the government had not brought Singere's amendment to the act into effect. It seems that only a few Papua New Guinean students are enthusiastic about these proposals, and as more Papua New Guinean lawyers enter private practice and assume positions within the profession, it can be expected that commitment to the existing system will increase.

Underlying Law and the Law Reform Commission

The Constitution declares that it and the organic laws are "the Supreme Law of Papua New Guinea" (sec. 11). The Constitution enables parliament to legislate and allows that by legislation parliament may confer legislative powers and functions on other bodies (sec. 100). All these laws are of course in a written form. Schedule 2 of the Constitution then provides for an underlying law of Papua New Guinea which can be taken generally to mean the body of unwritten law which is recognized by the courts. The Constitution adopts custom as part of the underlying law and also adopts the common law of England "except and to the extent that [it is] inapplicable or inappropriate to the conditions of the country from time to time". In the task of evaluating the applicability or the appropriateness of the common law, and in formulating a new rule for the underlying law when no common law or customary law is applicable, the judges are instructed to have regard to the National Goals and Directive Principles of the Constitution. There is thus considerable scope under the Constitution for judicial creativity and a clear expectation that the common law will be adapted to the needs of Papua New Guinea. But the judiciary's post-independence record in this respect is not impressive (O'Neill 1976, p. 258).

However, the Law Reform Commission has tackled the problem of devising an indigenous body of underlying law which will have a national application, and in the post-independence period it has emerged as the most significant source of policy development in legal matters. The commission was established under the Law Reform Commission Act of 1975, and it began operations in May of that year. The act owes much to the initiative of John Kaputin. The concept of a law reform body had been supported by the Secretary for Law and others before Kaputin became Minister for Justice, but Kaputin's support as minister was of significance to the final form of the act, which gives the commission a considerable measure of initiative and independence. Bernard Narakobi, who had worked as a consultant with the Constitutional Planning Committee, was chairman of the commission from its inception until May 1978, and he quickly established himself and the commission as a significant influence on the development of legal policies. The act provides that the functions of the commission are to be exercised in accordance with references made to it by the Minister for Justice. The Constitution strengthens the role of the commission by providing a guarantee of its existence and giving it a "special responsibility ...to investigate and report to the Parliament and to the National Executive on the development, and on the adaption to the circumstances of the country, of the underlying law, and on the appropriateness of the rules and principles of the underlying law to the circumstances of the country form time to time" (schedule 2.14).

In its 1975 report, the commission signalled its intention to seek radical reform: "The Commission sees as its eventual goal the overhaul of the entire system and the building up of an entirely new legal order which takes full account of our traditions, our customs and our approach to life" (Law Reform Commission 1976a: 10). The Minister for Justice responded to this challenge by a series of references to the commission which provided it with an opportunity to review almost every major aspect of the legal system and the most significant aspects of the substantive law which affect Papua New Guineas. There has apparently been little opposition to the commission from the department. Narakobi had a close relationship with leading department officers such as Kearney's successors as secretary, Joseph Aoae and Buri Kidu, and department personnel in general have not shown enthusiasm for policy involvement.

The Constitution, while stating the primary sources of the unwritten law, provides little guidance on how the competing sources of law should rank in significance. In a working paper on the underlying law, the commission advocated a draft bill to replace the constitutional provisions. The bill provides that in relation to a particular issue, the principles of customary law should be adopted in preference to those of the common law. But both these sources of the law must be measured against the National Goals and Directive Principles, and if neither is appropriate the court should formulate its own rules in conformity with those goals and principles (Law Reform Commission 1976b).

Such provisions would require a revolution in the manner in which the courts of Papua New Guinea have gone about the task of ascertaining rules for decisions in particular cases, and it must be expected that some at least of the judiciary will not be sympathetic to such a revolution. At a seminar conducted by the commission at Goroka in March—April 1977, held to discuss the topic, Chief Justice Frost did not directly oppose the proposals but nevertheless was sceptical about the ability of the higher courts to develop customary law or to administer the law with the flexibility the draft bill seems to require (Law Reform Commission 1977, p. 4).

However, the problem that faces the commission is more deeply rooted. The commission has acknowledged that "it is the socio-economic characteristics, and in particular the level of technology the community employs, that have a decisive influence on the law" (Law Reform Commission 1976b, p. 15). In this acknowledgement lies the source of the major difficulty, for there are signs that policy-making in Papua New Guinea is becoming tied to the existing expatriate-created economy and to the laws that underpin that economy. Foreign business interests are also unlikely to oppose any alteration to the present legal system. The 1976 report of the Public Solicitor articulates the kind of general concern likely to be voiced by business interest, and the reaction of the local expatriate business community to the commission's working paper on fairness of transactions is illustrative. In this paper, the commission advocates that "the courts should have the power to re-write the conditions of contracts where one person enters the contract on unequal terms and accepts conditions which place the greater part of the burden of the contract on him. The contract should be re-written so that its terms and conditions are fair to both parties" (Law Reform Commission 1976c, p. 2).

These recommendations were based partly on the view that "the English common law of contract is often harsh and we are not convinced that it suits the needs of our country. It assumes that people enter contracts on equal terms" (ibid., p. 1). The paper advocates also that mediation should be a key element in the process of restructuring the transaction in question. Spokesmen for the expatriate business community have objected to the key recommendations of this paper and have claimed that the principles of English law are a protection to their business activities.

The commission advocates the use of the law to promote change, and agrees with the Constitutional Planning Committee that a "selective approach" should be taken to the adoption and promotion of customary values and the retention of "the debris and deposits of colonisation" (Law Reform Commission 1976*b*, p. 16). The evidence suggests, however, that there are wide differences of opinion within the Papua New Guinean community about what should be selected and adopted, and herein lies the difficulty for the commission and for any other person or body seeking to reform the legal system of Papua New Guinea.

THE SOURCES OF POLICY

This review demonstrates that the process of policy-making on legal issues varied considerably from one issue to another. For example, the persons involved in policy formulation with respect to the form of legal personality for Papua New Guinean customary groups differed entirely from those involved with the issue of legal representation by law students. Thus, it is not possible to analyse policy formulation on legal issues in the same manner as might apply in other areas where there were significant single issues that occupied attention over a long period of time. However, by considering the single issues collectively, and by taking account of some broader considerations, some generalizations about the process of legal policy formulation may be offered.

The influence of politicians on policy in relation to some legal issues was significant, but on the whole it was only sporadic. John Kaputin, the first Minister for Justice, was forced out of office somewhat embittered by the experience, and although his account indicates that disputes over specifically legal matters were important, it is not clear that they were paramount. However, Kaputin's term as minister was significant. One major reform, the creation of the Law Reform Commission, owes much to his initiative. Kaputin's policy speech at the Papua Hotel in November 1973 (Kaputin 1975) was also significant. In the speech he proceeded from a view that "the law does not stand as a set of mutual principles . . .

It has created, consolidated, and perpetuated class privileges", to propose radical reform to the legal system across a broad range of issues, and to call upon public servants to "become *development oriented*, to be *responsive* to the needs and wishes to the people, to become committed to the objectives of the *government*" (Kaputin 1975, pp. 4, 6). The speech raised political flak and it caused some lawyers to intensify their opposition to Kaputin's policies while leading others who were public servants to adopt a very narrow view of their role as legal advisers to the government as a preliminary, in some cases, to leaving Papua New Guinean altogether. On the other hand, the speech provided a charter for reform to those lawyers, both inside and outside the government, who were sympathetic to Kaputin's approach.

Ebia Olewale succeeded Kaputin and remained as Minister for Justice until the end of the first parliament. It has been seen that he sponsored the Business Groups Incorporation Act through the House of Assembly and he promoted village courts after the relevant regulations were promulgated in late 1974, but the initiative for these two important reforms came from elsewhere. He does not appear to have sought to use his portfolio as an instrument for legal reform. He was preoccupied with the Papua Besena challenge in 1974 and 1975, and in 1975 his time was taken up with negotiations concerning the Constitution and provincial government.

Apart from legislation that implemented reports of the Law Reform Commission and the Commission of Inquiry into Land Matters, the only legislation of significance to legal development to be presented to the first parliament after independence concerned what can be termed broadly the "law and order" issue. The government's attempt in August 1976 to enact a Public Order Bill was in effect defeated, but in March 1977 the Chief Minister introduced it in a modified form in the Peace and Good Order Bill. In November 1976 Olewale announced that the government would introduce an Inter-Group Fighting Bill and the parliament passed a Vagrancy Act in March 1977. All this legislation restricts the Basic Rights of the Constitution and can be attributed as much to the initiative of politicians as to any other group.

The review of particular issues in previous sections has revealed two occasions on which private members took up policy initiatives and secured the passage of legislation. There is a further example in the post-independence period — the Land Disputes Settlement (Amendment) Act 1976, promoted by Tom Koraea over opposition from the government — and private members' motions on legal issues have also been significant.

In a situation where the incumbent Minister for Justice was not, for various reasons, able or willing consistently to promote policy, it might be expected that the Department of Law would play a leading role in policy formulation. However, one conclusion that emerges from this review is that the department's role appears to have been one of reaction to pressures from other sources. The department did influence policy concerning the Law Reform Commission, but in respect of this issue John Kaputin's enthusiasm for the project was probably of significance to the final form of the legislation, if not to its acceptance by the government.

Another characteristic of the department's role that deserves comment, not least because it has given rise to criticism from other areas of the government, is the attitude taken by some senior officials towards the department's function of giving legal advice to the government. Officials in other areas (for example, mining, land, and finance) have expressed the view that some legal officers were on crucial occasions unwilling to present more than an opinion and have been reluctant to suggest means to avoid the legal difficulties inherent in some proposed course of action. Members of the team responsible for renegotiating the Bougainville Copper Agreement became frustrated with the attitude taken by Department of Law advisers, and this led ultimately to reliance on lawyers from the Commonwealth Secretariat.

It is possible only to speculate on the reasons for the low profile taken by the Department of Law in policy-making. The attitude may have been a product of Canberra control, in that the Port Moresby legal advisers were not accustomed to a policy advisory role. Watkins, Secretary for Law before 1969, acquiesced in Canberra's close control of policy, and most senior officers in the department were by temperament disinclined towards such a role. The department expanded considerably before 1972, but most of the additional personnel were relatively inexperienced as lawyers and had little knowledge of the country in general. In addition, the increasing emphasis on specialization which resulted from the growth of the public service meant that the contacts both older and newer staff had with non-legal administration personnel became more restricted. In 1972 the department was not in a position to play a strong policy-making role, and it has been argued here that the traumatic effects of the Boxtel cases served to put the Secretary for Law and some of the leading personnel in the department on the defensive.

The reasons for the very conservative attitude towards legal advice are more difficult to ascertain. The attitude is at variance with what is regarded as the normal function of lawyers. Generally, lawyers do not limit their function to that of giving advice only on the legal difficulties inherent in a proposed course of action, but see it their duty to advise on ways in which their client might avoid these difficulties to his best advantage. The department's unwillingness to take this latter role may have been a corollary of its reluctance to be involved in policy-making at any level. It may also have stemmed from a basic lack of sympathy on the part of some leading members to the direction of change that the National Coalition appeared to favour. Whatever the reasons, the result of the low profile of the department and its unpopularity with leading politicians and their advisers was that alternative sources of policy-making were more easily able to exert influence on the government.

The Coalition's willingness to accept advice from outside the boundaries of the traditional public service departments created opportunities both for non-public service advisers and for public servants whose influence on legal policy on some issues — Barnett in the Chief Minister's office, Ley in the Constitutional Planning Committee, and Fingleton in Lands. Some non-public service advisers to ministers also became significant at various points, for example, Fitzpatrick in the Office of the Chief Minister and elsewhere. These had links with the Faculty of Law and provided a means for the latter to influence policy. Some members of the faculty moved for periods into government positions (myself at the House of Assembly, and Jean Zorn and Abdul Paliwala at the Law Reform Commission), and others had advisory roles on more limited issues. There were also several non-lawyers who had an impact on legal policy: Nigel Oram in relation to village courts, Alan Ward in lands, and Stephen Zorn in mining. In the sense that members of this whole group were prepared at times to propose changes to the legal system, they might be described as "radical" in order to contrast them with other lawyers who were prepared to accept that the legal system should be retained in its fundamental elements. However, there was certainly no unanimity within this group, and in respect of some matters there was quite bitter conflict.

In contrast to the "radical" group, there was something of an "old boy network" which was on occasions active in support of the existing system. The key figures in this group were the judges, especially the two chief justices, and the persons who held the office of Public Solicitor. Some younger lawyers in the Public Solicitor's Office on occasions openly supported this group, and at other times the private profession was involved. Owing to the prestige of its members, this group did on occasions play an important role, but its potential was reduced as a result of the breach between some of its leading members and leading personnel of the Department of Law. (There had been a similar split in the 1960s involving different personalities, which may also have contributed to the long-standing low profile of the department.)

The Legislative Counsel, Joe Lynch, is not readily assignable to a group, although his position as draftsman meant that his influence on legal policy throughout this period was pervasive. His interest in proposing original and radical reforms to the legal system had placed him outside the mainstream of the Department of Law, and his role as legislative draftsman was in any event one performed in isolation. His long period of service in Papua New

Guinea meant that he had close contracts with the judges and other lawyers, but he also maintained links with several "radicals".

Papua New Guinean lawyers and law students did not play a significant role before 1975, but their influence in the post-independence period became crucial. Before independence there were only very few Papua New Guinean lawyers in a position to influence events, although Bernard Narakobi, and Ilinome Tarua in the Chief Minister's Office, played important roles in the development of the Constitution. Apart from the episode over legal representation in the lower courts, the students did not promote reform, although several were influenced by the more radical members of the Faculty of Law.

After independence there appeared to be a division in attitudes. On the one hand, the Law Reform Commission proposed quite radical changes which received public support from significant numbers of Papua New Guinean lawyers and students. On the other, the proposals that legal education should incorporate village work experience were frustrated partly because of opposition from students and from Papua New Guinean lawyers. A recent development has been the departure from the public service of several recent law graduates, some of whom are turning to private practice. The situation may be perhaps seen as a reflection of the tension that exists between the principles expressed in the Eight Aims and the National Goals and the pressures of the social and economic environment in which Papua New Guinean lawyers and students live and work. While this environment encourages maintenance of the Anglo-Australian elements of the legal system, and encourages lawyers to see their role as divorced from the villages, it is unlikely that many of them will actively propose radical change. The influence of this environment on legal policy is occasionally made explicit by those who argue that the legal system should accommodate the needs of foreign investors. At the end of the first parliament, the promise of substantial reform in the direction of a PNG legal system evident in the reports of the Law Reform Commission remained to be fulfilled, and there were signs that significant elements of opposition were forming.

Acknowledgements

I wish to thank those who contributed comments and information during the course of the preparation of this paper. John Ballard, Jim Fingleton, Peter Fitzpatrick, John Ley, Joe Lynch, Anthony Martin, Nigel Oram, Bruce Ottley, Christine Stewart, June Verrier, Tony Voutas, and Jean Zorn were of particular assistance. However, the opinions expressed remain mine alone. Statements of fact are based on information within my knowledge or on statements made to me by others which have, where possible, been verified by other sources.

The Framework of Economic Policy-Making

ROSS GARNAUT

Papua New Guinea had none of the characteristics of a national economy when the first Somare government was formed in April 1972. In attempting to establish a national economic policy, the new government could call on very few Papua New Guineans who were at all confident in the provision of economic policy advice. One of the striking developments in the first five, transitional, years of national government was the emergence of an effective PNG framework for economic policy-making. This framework, centred on the National Planning Committee of Cabinet and the Budget Priorities Committee, laid bare for political decision fundamental choices between dependence on aid, improvement in urban and public service incomes, improvement in various kinds of rural services, and reduction of inequalities in the amount of services provided within various provinces. By 1977 the principal operatives were all PNG nationals.

The Ministry of Finance played a central role in the evolution of the policy-making framework. It is important to understand the concept of the general economic framework that developed within the Finance Ministry over the five-year period. Economic stability and a policy-making framework that laid bare the fundamental choices for political decision were considered necessary preconditions for development. But the framework in itself could not generate development. Development grew out of the successful implementation of activities and programmes by individuals, groups of Papua New Guineans, local organizations, and national government agencies.

The first Minister for Finance, Julius Chan, described the role of general economic policies and the policy-making framework in his 1976/77 budget speech:

> I want to be a bit more precise about the role of the Budget and associated financial and economic policies in gearing up for true independence. As I see it, the task of the Budget in conjunction with other policies is to provide, as far as possible, an adequate and stable flow of revenue to finance Government services and development. The task of

ensuring that the money so provided is spent wisely and well does not belong directly to the Minister for Finance, but rather to other Ministers and to the Government as a whole.

The special job of the Minister for Finance is to look after the base: to safeguard the revenue, to safeguard the value of the currency, and to ensure as best he can that the economy proceeds on a steady course.

Without stable revenue, a stable currency and a sound economy the positive work of development would be undermined from the start – a fate, I must add, which has overtaken many developing countries that began with the highest hopes. [*NPD*, vol. 1, 3 August 1976, p. 1375]

The government as a whole came to place high value on "looking after the base" only after several years of decision-making within a relatively unintegrated framework. Questions of general economic management were given greater priority after 1974, when it had become clear to some Papua New Guineans in government that the absence of a stable macro-economic framework had contributed to the making of decisions which, in retrospect, seemed to have been inconsistent with national goals.

The institutional framework for economic policy-making established by the first Somare government made it very much easier for the government to evaluate the effects of various possible decisions on progress towards its ultimate objectives. Such a framework was essential to a government committed in principle to progress towards more equal domestic income distribution. Without such a framework the relatively wealthy in the Papua New Guinean community were in a strong position to take advantage of any weakness in policy co-ordination or vagueness in analysis of the effects of policy alternatives.

But the existence of an effective framework of policy-making in itself could not ensure that progress would be made towards any particular objective. Such progress depended on ministers' real commitment to the objective, and on the presence of all of the administrative, political, and other prerequisites of progress. The stable macro-economic framework reduced the risk that decisions at odds with the objectives of the government would be taken accidentally.

This paper describes the emergence of a framework for economic policy-making over the period 1972 to 1977. It does not cover the whole ambit of economic policy-making. It is concerned mainly with macro-economic policy, or matters that Chan described as "looking after the base". Much more of the time and effort of the government as a whole went into supervising or developing particular programmes than into "looking after the base", and a full assessment of economic policy would need to examine these programmes in some detail. Other papers in this volume discuss a few of the many programmes continued or initiated by the first Somare government.

THE COLONIAL LEGACY

The colonial authorities lacked the instruments and institutions within which policy is framed and implemented in a national economy. The budget aggregates were handed down from Canberra and there was no mechanism in Port Moresby for integrating decisions on these aggregates into wider aspects of decision-making by governments. There was no national currency and no means of effecting counter-cyclical fiscal and monetary policy or directing the use of credit.

In early 1972, Papua New Guinea's small and fragmented monetary economy was owned and managed almost entirely by foreigners. The only important exception was the rapidly expanding village production of export crops. But the greater part even of agricultural exports was produced within foreign-owned plantations. The economy was held together, and provided with its main impetus to growth, by extraordinarily large annual injections of Australian aid which contributed directly 53 per cent of public expenditure in 1971/72 (Garnaut 1978). Colonial power held in check resentment about huge differences between the incomes, wealth, and influence of indigenous Papua New Guineans and expatriates. It also held in check, with decreasing effectiveness over the course of time, regional resentments based on perceptions of unfair exclusion from enjoyment of the material benefits provided by the administration, and unwarranted exclusion from political power. People from the Highlands, Papua, the Gazelle, and Bougainville all felt deprived of what they considered to be their just share of public expenditure, of participation in national administration and, in the case of the Islands, of political power over matters of local interest.

The natural condition of Papua New Guinea was conducive to the emergence of great inequalities in the domestic distribution of power and income upon the withdrawal of the colonial constraints. There were rich natural resources in a few locations: the copper mine in Bougainville, coming into production in the month in which the first national government was formed, and the promise of riches in various other minerals deposits, potential hydro-electric sources and prospective petroleum geology. The fair distribution of this potential wealth, should it materialize, would require strong administrative systems and determined political commitment to equitable distribution, against the claims of the foreign corporations and personnel, national public servants and workers, local land-owners, and regional political organizations. Apart from these outstanding concentrations of potential minerals and energy wealth, there were marked variations in the potential for agricultural production and trade. The large islands and some coastal and Highlands areas had ready access to markets for agricultural products, while other areas were separated from opportunities for trade by difficult mountainous terrain, swamp, or long sea distances. The latter areas required large subsidies for their transport infrastructure to enable them to participate in national life and modern economic activities.

The historical distribution of educational opportunities was correlated strongly with access to other government services and opportunities for trade, so that the administrative system that was required to channel resources to poorer areas was likely to be operated mainly by people from better endowed areas. The desperate scarcity of trained people would make it difficult to contain the clear potential for the emergence of extreme inequalities in domestic income distribution. The shortage of qualified personnel was likely to place the first nationals who received relatively high levels of formal education in favourable positions to do well for themselves, through improvements in conditions of employment and in urban facilities. People from urban areas, and from rural areas already well endowed with education and other services, were likely to be the most skilled in national politics, and the best placed to apply pressure to policy-making processes.

Any national government seeking to contain the domestic inequalities that were liable to emerge with the withdrawal of the colonial constraints would have to manage pressures resulting from the predominance of foreign personnel, foreign investment and foreign aid, and their importance for effective administration and development. In 1972, the fifty thousand resident foreigners represented 2 per cent of the national population, a quarter of the urban population, and most of the skilled and managerial workforce. They were dangerous for the demonstration effect of their high incomes and consumption on the values and aspirations of urban Papua New Guineans, and the more so when easier race relations led to greater social intercourse in the late sixties and early seventies. They were likely to be most dangerous through the particular demonstration effects of white trade unions' pressures for improved conditions of employment (perhaps aided by links with aid donors), as they had been in Zambia and in other developing countries that were similarly dependent on expatriate skills and managements. The inherited dependence on Australian aid was a source of potential problems: a new government committed to the implementation of its own national development programme and requiring large amounts of foreign aid for many years was likely to be frustrated by the bilateral aid systems that were current around the world, with aid tied to projects that were selected outside the normal budgetary system through a variety of contacts between Papua New Guinean officials, foreign diplomats, and foreign consultants and businessmen. Heavy dependence on foreign private investment could lead to difficulties in the management of national economic policy, since independence would bring direct contact between Papua New Guineans and foreign corporations with considerable economic power and administrative strength.

Most foreign observers expected catastrophic consequences of rapid withdrawal of colonial administration in Papua New Guinea. Many resident expatriates had simple racist views about the incapacity of Papua New Guineans to perform well in positions of high administrative and political responsibility. But beyond such attitudes the experience of other countries suggested the possibility that a weak and ineffective central administration would try to accommodate strong domestic and neocolonial pressures by giving in to them all, bankrupting itself, and limping on in directions pointed out by project aid donors, officials provided under international aid programmes, and foreign investors who dictated the terms of their own agreements.

A national government could be expected to reduce many of the expatriate privileges that contributed to extreme inequalities in wealth and access to power between Papua New Guineans and foreigners in the colonial situation. But a weak and ineffective central administration, or a corrupt one, would open the way for the realization of Papua New Guinea's considerable potential for the emergence of domestic inequalities.

In the nautical metaphor later much favoured by Julius Chan in his budget speeches, the first national government was cutting adrift on a dangerous, shoal-ridden sea. But the new country carried with it assets, some of them clearly recognized at the time and some hidden in the hold, that were to be of considerable assistance on the post-colonial journey.

One advantage was the country's relatively rich endowment of agricultural and other natural resources, which made the pursuit of aggregate incomes growth rather less urgent and pressing than in many other developing countries. It was not that Papua New Guineans were rich, but that total incomes were above the bare requirements of survival by a sufficiently wide margin to allow a brief period of policy reconsideration, and possibly redistribution from foreign incomes, without a failure of growth directly causing great poverty. Closely related was the legacy of large-scale Australian aid which, if provided to the national government on suitable terms, could allow the continuation of programmes to raise incomes through the country and to improve services in poor areas and rural areas that could not possibly be financed for some time from domestic revenues.

One imporant asset that Papua New Guinea possessed at the transition from colonial government was the survival of the village as a viable and attractive, or potentially attractive, social and economic unit in many rural areas. Very few Papua New Guineans had grown up entirely outside villages. The idea of life in the village, improved by better services and opportunities to earn incomes, was to relatively few Papua New Guineans the unacceptably inferior alternative to urban life that it was in many other countries.

The retiring colonial administration had made most of the usual mistakes: an expansion of the secondary education system that was bound to overshoot requirements for highly educated manpower; a headlong rush into subsidized urban employment and urban growth through the agency of protection of urban manufacturing industries (fortunately too late to undermine the viability of village life); inadequate adaptation of metropolitan forms of administration to local conditions; too little involvement of Papua New Guineans in the administration of government and business. But there were positive aspects to the colonial legacy, some of them unusual in colonial experience: an administration that, in the Australian Commonwealth tradition, was on the whole non-corrupt; the dual salary system in the public service which, while extremely unpopular among Papua New Guineans, restrained the entrenchment of inequalities before national government; a simple, effective, and honestly administered taxation system (including taxes on personal and corporate incomes); and, despite the rhetoric about "concentration of effort" after the World Bank Mission in the early sixties, an impressive recent history of extension of the transport and administrative infrastructure into poorer areas, especially in the Highlands. The inherited parliamentary system of government may also have been suitable to PNG conditions and a constraint on possible neglect of poor regions and rural areas.

There was also some unusual quality in the Melanesian way of politics, some failure of dogmatic logic and propensity for humanity, that was capable of defusing political conflict short of irreconcileable rupture in communications. Closely related to this, there was little hysterical opposition to foreign influence which, as in the post-colonial situation in many countries, could easily have led to the "localization" of inherited structures without any consideration of complicated and important effects on other values.

The University of Papua New Guinea, established in 1966 and a very good university in the years immediately before 1972, also made an important contribution to the development of the system of ideas that was necessary to contain the emergence of extreme inequalities upon the retreat of colonialism. For example, in the Economics Department under Anthony Clunies Ross, an atmosphere of thoughtful search for solutions to emerging problems was important to the development of a number of students who were to play major roles in the post-colonial administration. This contribution encompassed distributional issues that went beyond the one-dimensional debate about the relative merits of growth and equality that was pursued energetically by overseas academics at that time. It was helpful in the orientation of new arrivals and visitors, including those on official missions, like Michael Faber and his team in 1972.

NATIONAL OBJECTIVES

The five-year life of the first Somare government saw the emergence of all the anticipated problems and pressures. The Eight Aims of the national government were announced in December 1972, with themes of localization, rural development, decentralization, self-reliance, and equal distribution of benefits. Through 1972 a number of initiatives were announced, almost all involving redistribution from foreigners to Papua New Guineans. These were the simplest politically, being conducive to solidarity among Papua New Guineans. Some had adverse effects on domestic income distribution incidental to their effects on distribution between expatriates and Papua New Guineans. A long period of relative inaction on important economic policy issues ensued, in which dispute over independence, national unity, and the Constitution reinforced a reluctance to come to grips with complex issues of domestic distribution. The instability associated with these great national disputes also made the government more cautious in handling its relations with foreign personnel and corporations. This was a costly period of *ad hoc* economic policy-making, extending well into 1974. After that, there seemed to be an increasing (although uneven) willingness to manage difficult questions of domestic distribution and foreign economic relations.

Independence, national unity, and politically cohesive national government were the over-riding concerns of the first Somare government. Many aspects of policy-making are misunderstood unless they are seen in the context of their contribution to national unity or cohesion and of the constraints imposed by these concerns. The critical judgements on many of the most important of these matters were made by Prime Minister Somare himself.

The first national government came to office without a clear economic programme. Neither did the individual parties within the Coalition have clear preferences on the objectives of economic policy. There was a widespread feeling within the government that incomes and services available to Papua New Guineans should be greatly increased relative to those available to foreigners in Papua New Guinea. This feeling was not shared in this general form by part of the United Party opposition at this time, although it was accepted by them after self-government as anxieties over expatriate departures declined. It tended to be felt most strongly within Pangu, several of whose leading figures had entered politics in the 1960s on the issue of opposition to salary discrimination. Michael Somare, as leader of Pangu Pati had made it clear in debate on the Development Programme in 1968 that "localisation of the Public Service and other categories is our prime aim in this country". As practical issues arose for decision over the next few years, there was relatively little general and consistent difference among the political parties in government on issues related to localization of business and the public service: as initiatives in this area were suggested from time to time by the Prime Minister, the Minister for Finance, National Party ministers, the Mataungan members, or the Constitutional Planning Committee (CPC), they almost invariably attracted support.

In contrast, there was relatively little agreement within the government and the parliament on desirable patterns of domestic income distribution. Individual ministers and members often had clear attitudes and preferences, but the differences did not consistently follow party lines. It was easy for politicians to agree on the importance of helping the poor and under-privileged, but there was no agreement on which groups were deserving of help. Members from urban electorates thought that the poor were urban workers and the long-neglected residents of urban villages; Tolais and Bougainvilleans thought that their own people required compensation for historical neglect and for the pain and suffering of colonial exploitation; Papuans pointed resentfully to the recent concentration of major public works and development projects in the Highlands and the New Guinea islands; Highlanders were concerned at how the late arrival of colonialism left them with less access than people in other provinces to education and other services; the embryonic class of Papua New Guinean businessmen saw themselves as being especially neglected in their struggle to survive in an alien business environment. Many MPs reminded the parliament that their own electorates lacked their fair share of roads, bridges, schools, aid posts, and fibro houses for public servants. The process through which these disparate attitudes, and similarly disparate attitudes on other matters, were developed into the Eight Aims is discussed by Tony Voutas in this volume.

The Eight Aims of the government as a whole were multi-dimensional, but they could be used by officials and members of the government, as well as by pressure groups and critics of the government, who were them-selves interested in promoting one particular objective by means that con-flicted with progress in other directions. A forestry bureaucrat could aim to have one large foreign-owned timber project in each province, and to some people that would look like equal distribution and maybe decentra-lization as well. A foreign businessman interested in investment in large-scale food production could show that he was contributing to import replacement. An agricultural extension officer (*didiman*) who opposed mechanized food production could criticize the businessman for the large scale of his project without acknowledging the difficulties of increasing food production by other means. A university lecturer could demonstrate that coffee exports were growing more rapidly than production of *kau kau* for the Port Moresby market and argue that this conflicted with the Eight Aims' emphasis on internal trade, without remarking upon the effects of growth in coffee incomes on equal distribution of benefits, rural development, or increase in Papua New Guinean incomes. Neither the bureaucrat nor the foreign businessman nor the *didiman* nor the university lecturer was necessarily wrong. The point was simply that, in seeking to make progress towards many objectives at once, it was necessary to judge any decision within an overall framework that took account of progress or retrogression in all relevant directions.

It was not possible for ministers to agree upon the weight they attached to various objectives, and the relative speed at which they should be approached, without an extended process of political debate, dispute, and compromise. But even when the government was clear on ultimate objectives, there was no machinery in December 1972 for laying bare to political leaders the multi-directional effects of various alternative programmes.

Some sense of priorities for objectives emerged from the political process at an early stage. Among the Eight Aims, the localization objective was listed first, and its statement was preceded by the requirement that progress be "rapid" (a requirement that was attached only to the advancement of women among the other aims): "A rapid increase in the proportion of the economy under the control of Papua New Guinea individuals and groups and in the proportion of personal and property income that goes to Papua New Guineans." This first aim was the most consistently and powerfully pursued. It was easier than other objectives to promote, often appearing to demand nothing in the way of choice about domestic income distribution unless rather complicated and indirect effects were examined. Pursuit of this aim seemed to be generally conducive to national solidarity and unity. It was the first aim of most elected politicians.

The emphasis on equal distribution in the second aim also seemed necessary for stability in an independent Papua New Guinea, but it did confront the interests of strong regions and groups and so was bound to be difficult to implement. To the extent that the leadership of the government in 1972 was aware of the potential for domestic political conflict inherent in this objective, the statement of the second aim was a challenge to privileged groups. Progress towards this aim could not proceed simply through the formulation of a precise objective, then the formulation of a policy, then the implementation of the policy. Michael Somare and others in the government who wanted more equal income distribution would have to wait, watch the politics, and see how far they could get.

Policy decisions in the early years tended to be dominated by single-minded pursuit of the first objective. In the period through to late 1974, the cumulative effect of policy was to favour redistribution from foreigners as a whole to nationals as a whole, at some cost to equitable rural-urban distribution and to equitable distribution between Papua New Guinean businessmen and others. Through the same period, a similarly single-minded approach to the decentralization objective, especially within the CPC, set in train a process that threatened adverse consequences for equitable distribution between provinces. Through the later years of the first Somare government's five-year term of office, incremental policy generally held the line on progress towards more equal distribution of benefits, although there were occasionally important conflicts within the government over the distribution effects of particular decisions. Even people very close to decisions in the two periods will never know how much the greater preparedness to hold the line in the latter period was the result of strengthening in the government's political position, a feeling that the localization that had already been set in train was moving fast enough, a more integrated system of national policy-making which revealed more clearly to ministers the consequences of decisions, or a change of heart among ministers on the relative importance of various objectives.

Unlike the guiding principles of economic policy in many other countries, the Eight Aims made no reference to economic growth. The omission of a growth objective did not accord with political demands, as almost everyone wanted more of almost everything. It was partly a reaction to the high foreign component of the extraordinarily rapid monetary sector growth of the immediately preceding years. It also reflected a confidence about growth: a feeling that growth would come, and that what mattered was the form it would take and the distribution of the resulting benefits. One clear difference from the attitude of the colonial administration was that it was only growth in the incomes of nationals that mattered to the new government and not growth in some aggregate like Gross Domestic Product which included incomes of foreigners.

The government certainly did not say that it was against growth. The Chief Minister early in 1973 and the Minister for Finance in a speech about foreign investment and the Eight Aims in June 1974 made it clear that political constraints meant that equalization must be up not down, so that progress towards more equal distribution and, simultaneously, greater capacity to raise revenue internally (the sixth aim) would require considerable growth.

Whatever the announced objectives of the government, it is a consistent theme of the whole period that threats to political stability and unity were handled as they arose as questions of ultimate priority, occasionally at considerable cost to the stated objectives of the government.

THE CO-ORDINATION OF ECONOMIC POLICY-MAKING *

In 1972 there were two established organizations that might have brought economic issues up to the new government in a coherent manner for political choice. In 1969 it had been decided that a General Financial and Economic Policy Division (GFEP) of Finance (then Treasury) would be established as part of the movement towards self-government. GFEP would be in a position to provide advice on the use of economic powers as they were released from Canberra. Graham Douglas arrived as First Assistant Secretary GFEP in early 1971 for a two-year term, and he was getting his staff together when the new government was formed.

The decision to establish GFEP developed from the view that the Office of the Economic Adviser had outlived its usefulness with the preparation of the first five-year development programme. But Les Johnson on his return to Papua New Guinea as Administrator thought that Bill McCasker and his office still had an important role to play. The office was renamed the Office of Programming and Co-ordination (OPAC), its establishment was expanded, and it took on some executive responsibilities for the first time.

When the Somare government arrived on the scene, OPAC's director was anxious to get on with the preparation of a second five-year programme. The first programme was to expire in June 1973, and the government's objectives and priorities had to be known by OPAC not long after mid-1972 if the second was to be ready in time to follow on. To advance the process of defining priorities, the director played the major role in preparing a White Paper on Development Priorities, which addressed a number of questions to members of the House of Assembly. The members never did come up with the clear statements of priorities that officials had hoped to prompt.

At about the same time a mission from the University of East Anglia Overseas Development Group led by Michael Faber, was engaged in consultations with ministers and officials over the general shape of the second programme. OPAC was asking Faber to come up with something "practical" upon which a programme could be built, not the "philosophical" views that were espoused in the draft report circulated in the middle of the year.

The head of GFEP thought that there was no useful role for OPAC. OPAC's director seems to have had in mind some division of responsibilities between Finance and OPAC along the lines of short- and long-run policy questions. The new Minister for Finance, Julius Chan, eventually formed the view that there should be a planning office within the Finance Ministry, which would be responsible for the generation and monitoring of

---

*   For a contemporary discussion of the early years, see Ballard and Garnaut 1973.

new projects and programmes in line with government priorities. Chan maintained this view of the proper role of the planning office throughout the period to 1977, although he later dropped his insistence that it be located within Finance.

The Office of the Chief Minister (OCM) felt that McCasker was out of sympathy with the aims of the new government and so did not want him to remain as director of OPAC. But neither was OCM prepared to allow the planning function to move to Finance, where it would be under the control of People's Progress Party leader Chan. The ensuing struggle over the location of planning generated the first political crisis under the national government. The issue was finally resolved in December, when the Chief Minister announced that OPAC would be abolished and a new Central Planning Office (CPO) established. The CPO would be located administratively within the Finance Department, but the director would report politically to a National Planning Committee of Cabinet, comprising the four Coalition leaders with the Chief Minister as chairman, and three senior Papua New Guinean public servants as advisers. The administrative location within Finance was never of much importance and ceased at independence.

Meanwhile the locus of economic policy-making initiative lay in OCM, although Finance through its minister was also very influential. OPAC was out of the mainstream of policy advice. OCM at this time had in mind a "presidential" concept of planning, with the Chief Minister himself actively and deeply involved at the centre of economic policy-making. This was supported by academic economists (including the present writer) with whom the matter was discussed. The weakness of this model was that the Chief Minister preferred to work things differently, relying heavily on trusted ministers and intervening frequently and in detail in economic policy-making only on highly political matters or where there were conflicts among ministers. The question of the location of planning having been resolved, OCM, Finance, and the large remnant of OPAC began to work together on the preparation of the 1973–74 Improvement Plan.

The position of CPO director was advertised, short-listed applicants for the position were interviewed in mid-1973, and a Canadian, David Beatty, arrived as director in late 1973. Beatty's interests and skills were in management rather than economic policy, and his appointment reflected concern that management problems were the greatest weakness at the centre of government. The CPO was nearly at full strength by the second half of 1974, after active local and overseas recruitment. The CPO's role at this time was influenced heavily by the political environment of 1974. This was a period in which the government was living from day to day, trying to hold the country's administration together through massive personnel turnover and through the political crises of the Constitution,

Bougainville, Papua Besena, Kaumi, and the ministry itself. These were also the days of high world-wide inflation, the oil crisis, and commodity scarcities. The government's time horizons were necessarily very short.

The CPO director was personally linked into high policy through his close relations with several senior ministers, through working closely with the Budgets Division of Finance on the estimates, and through management of the "crisis calendar" that was maintained to focus political attention on issues that required early resolution. The CPO had little in the way of hierarchical structure or formal internal channels of reporting. Individual members of the office worked closely with individual departments. On the major issues, the director would work closely with the relevant CPO operator. Much of the influence of CPO on departmental programmes was achieved from within and below, and the quality of its influence depended on the quality of the individual staff members. The main activity promoting internal integration was the preparation of *Strategies for Nationhood*, a survey of government policies, programmes, and capacity which accompanied the budget for 1974/75.

By contrast, the Finance Department maintained a fairly tight administrative structure throughout the period 1972 to 1977. This reflected both the department's major executive function and the preferences of its minister and leading officials. The formal reporting structures weakened somewhat through late 1972 and 1973, as the retiring expatriate secretary played a less and less important role. The minister frequently called directly upon relatively junior officers. The first Papua New Guinean secretary, Mekere Morauta, took office late in 1973, and he was concerned that some advice provided to the minister in this way might not have been adequately informed. Satisfactory working arrangements were soon established. In the case of GFEP, from mid-1975 the minister would make the first few hours of each working week available for briefings from each of the three branches — the latest assessments of relevant economic conditions, policy questions that had arisen, progress of work on long-term policy questions. Both the secretary and the First Assistant Secretary (FAS) GFEP would be present if they were not committed to other pressing business. The secretary and FAS were in daily, lengthy communication.

Through 1973 and 1974, the Finance Department was playing a considerable role in keeping the machinery of government turning but, like the CPO and the government as a whole, was living from day to day on policy questions. The main exceptions were its work on important new instruments of economic policy, including legislation to establish the central bank and the new currency, new domestic and overseas loans instruments, and new systems for price control and justification.

It was an important achievement of these middle years of crisis and rapid transition that Papua New Guinea avoided its own Khemlani loans affair, Lockheed affair, and Pertamina affair, any of which might have happened but for intervention by senior officials of Finance, CPO, and Prime Minister's, often enforced ultimately by the Prime Minister or Minister for Finance. (Some of the potential Lynch affairs were more difficult to handle.)[1]

The Finance Ministry's approach to policy-making, and its role, changed considerably between 1974 and 1976. The new Secretary for Finance, Morauta, with the support of his minister, initiated the changes, which were sustained by substantial restaffing of the GFEP. The Secretary for Finance arranged for the FAS position to be vacated and advertised in May 1974. The present writer was appointed FAS and took up the post in April 1975. The senior Papua New Guinean in the division, John Vulupindi, was appointed Assistant Secretary in charge of General Economic Policy, one of the three branches. Vulupindi worked closely with the FAS and secretary and became FAS himself late in 1976. Two of GFEP's three branches were strengthened considerably with the appointment of several new Papua New Guinean graduates and several well-qualified and talented expatriates. By early 1976, GFEP was fully staffed and in a strong position to perform the more central and active role that Morauta had in mind for it.

Through the first half of 1974 senior levels of the Finance Ministry gave considerable attention to the role and high priority activities of GFEP. GFEP was to concentrate on the aggregates, leaving policy questions relating to the allocation of public expenditure among various possible uses mainly to the Budget Priorities Committee (see below), which was serviced by the CPO and the Budgets Division. Thus GFEP's special role was to advise the secretary and the minister on matters related to "looking after the base". The Minister for Finance had taken a close interest in the reformulation of the role and the strengthening of GFEP. He and his office (especially the minister's research officer, Anthony Martin) were in close touch with the evolution of GFEP's work.

There were four closely linked areas of general economic policy that seemed to be of central importance to providing a framework within which the government could influence the direction of long-term development. First, it was necessary to provide for a stable flow of public expenditure, preferably with steady growth, known well in advance to allow senior officials and ministers to evaluate the relative merits of various activities of government in a long-term framework. This "stabilization strategy" required a long-term understanding on Australian aid and the setting of annual expenditures in line with the long-term capacity of the economy rather than the short-term availability of cash. Mechanisms were needed to allow and promote the accumulation of fiscal and foreign exchange reserves in buoyant years, so that it was possible to maintain steady or steadily growing levels of public expenditure in years of recession. The stabilization of the highly volatile flow of revenue from the Bougainville mine seemed to be the most important single aspect of the stabilization strategy. The use of highly progressive levies in times of high prices on exports of the main cash crops (copra, cocoa, and coffee), balanced by bounty payments to growers when prices were low, seemed to be useful in stabilizing domestic expenditure and economic activity (and hence internal revenue) through the trade cycle. Beyond these institutional mechanisms, steady trends in government expenditure would need to be supported by counter-cyclical variations in the level of government borrowing.

The second area of concern was the set of policies that later came to be known as the "hard currency strategy". These policies were designed to achieve a low rate of inflation and became important only upon the complete separation of the Australian and PNG monetary systems on 1 January 1976. The theory of the "hard currency strategy" had two main elements. First, foreign prices and the kina exchange rate were together the main determinants of the price level in Papua New Guinea. Second, Papua New Guinea could choose fairly freely the foreign exchange value it wished the kina to have so long as the average real level of public expenditure over a number of years was within the limits set by the average real level of internal revenue, plus grants from foreign governments, plus surplus savings of the PNG private sector, plus sustainable levels of foreign borrowings (the latter being kept low in line with the general objective of reducing reliance on foreign aid in the course of time). The art of the "hard currency strategy" was to establish mutually consistent and sustainable trends in *real* government expenditure, *real* wages, and *real* aid levels, and to co-ordinate changes in *money* levels of these variables with changes in the exchange rate and price level. It was essential that the exchange rate, and the kina-denominated levels of government expenditure, wages, and foreign aid, move in a consistent manner. Low inflation was considered to be important politically in itself (see below) and it would facilitate the careful allocation of resources in line with government priorities.

The third area of concern was government revenue growth. It was necessary to increase domestic revenue despite the reduced involvement of expatriate personnel and slower growth in urban incomes and employment, through means that were not excessively burdensome to low income groups and especially to villagers. The most important aspect of the revenue problem was fiscal policy on resources: renegotiation of the Bougainville Copper Agreement and then making the new agreement stick by ensuring that any subsequent resource agreements (especially for the Ok Tedi mineral prospects and petroleum exploration) were consistent with it. A number of other changes in the forms and rates of taxation were also required.

The fourth area of concern was the co-ordination of all decisions relating to the allocation of financial resources available to the government. Progress in this area was essential to progress towards national objectives, but it depended critically on the successful management of the first three concerns. Much closer co-ordination of government decision-making with implications for public expenditure was necessary for the identification and enforcement of priorities among the many claims on resources.

If progress in these four areas was to be made and maintained, it was necessary to ensure that the evolution of policy in other areas (including provincial government finances, non-Australian aid, and relations with such international agencies as the IMF, and the World Bank) was consistent with the overall strategy. If the system was to survive for any time, it was also necessary for it to be robust in the face of unexpectedly slow or rapid revenue growth and of important changes in the priority of various government objectives (for example, on more rapid reduction of foreign aid relative to improvement of services in poor areas).

The ideas that were important to the evolution of a satisfactory framework for economic policy-making had been around in Port Moresby for some time and had been discussed at length by Chan, Morauta, and their advisers. A clear programme of action began to emerge only in the second half of 1974. The timing of this change was related to the strengthened political position of the Minister for Finance (especially after the government's resolution of its attitude to citizenship), to the appointment of Morauta as Secretary for Finance, to the realization through 1974 that the absence of a satisfactory framework was leading to the closure of some desirable options, and to a strong feeling that if the system of policy-making (and especially of relations with foreign governments and lending agencies) was not established satisfactorily soon after independence and the monetary separation, it would be impossible to retrieve the situation.

The latter feeling engendered a considerable sense of urgency to work on the policy-making framework through 1975 and early 1976. And yet the timing of each of the half-dozen or so major initiatives that were most essential to the desired system of policy-making had to depend on the political situation from time to time. It seemed possible through late 1974, and 1975, and early 1976 that the circumstances might never arise for the implementation of some aspects of the programme. The Minister for Finance, working closely with the Prime Minister, often kept his own counsel on questions of the political acceptability of innovations relating to the evolution of the policy-making framework. The secretary and FAS GFEP checked off the major steps that had to be taken to establish an internally consistent macro-economic strategy. By the second half of 1976 the major elements had fallen into place.

The most important single element in the new policy-making framework was the Budget Priorities Committee (BPC), which played the central role in bringing issues with public expenditure implications forward for decision in a co-ordinated manner. The BPC was established in October 1974 and quickly became the central focus of overall policy co-ordination. It surfaced to public prominence in the situation of financial stringency in 1975–76 and is commonly thought to have been a response to that stringency. In fact, its establishment was in immediate response to a very different problem: the management of the use of the increased revenues that were expected to accrue from the renegotiation of the Bougainville Copper Agreement.

The receipt of large additional revenues from the Bougainville mine was expected to raise some special problems for public finance in general. The new revenues had been notionally spent at least three times by various government agencies and foreign governments before the terms of the re-negotiated agreement had been made public. The amount of revenue received from the mine seemed likely to shrink greatly (while still being spent at a rate three times its initial level) as copper prices retreated from the high levels of early 1974. The immediate problem was solved through the establishment of the Minerals Resources Stabilisation Fund, providing for a steady, and hopefully steadily rising, flow of revenue into the Consolidated Revenue Fund, beginning in the following financial year (1975/76). The establishment of this fund provided the government with some breathing space within which to consider carefully the use of the growth in revenues within a long-term framework and to develop wider support for the enforcement of government priorities in relation to public expenditure.

The BPC grew out of discussions between Chan, Morauta, and their advisers on systems for identifying and enforcing long-term priorities. Its membership was selected by senior Finance officers mainly from the central agencies of government, whose senior personnel had no special bureaucratic interest in the expansion of particular programmes. The Finance Secretary was to be chairman, and other members were drawn from CPO, the Public Services Commission, and the Prime Minister's Department and Office. Charles Lepani from the Bureau of Industrial Organisations was a founding member, as was the Secretary for Agriculture, despite his sectoral responsibilities, reflecting the political reality that the Minister for Agriculture would resist any entirely external co-ordination and reflecting also the high priority of agricultural development. All members were Papua New Guineans except the then director of the Planning Office (who attended as a member only for a brief period), and they formed a group that could be expected to work well together. The Minister for Finance took the submissions requesting approval for the establishment of the BPC and the Mineral Resources Stabilisation Fund to the first meeting of the National Planning Committee after the conclusion of the Bougainville Copper Agreement renegotiation. The BPC proposal was welcomed by the CPO as fitting in very well with its own evolving role; and the Budgets Division of Finance had undertaken a great deal of *de facto* assignment of priorities and was relieved to share some of that responsiblity.

The role of the BPC was described in the following terms in *Programmes and Performance 1975–76*:

> The Budget Priorities Committee is chaired by the Secretary for Finance and contains senior officers of departments concerned with co-ordination of policy. The main functions of the Committee are to:
>
> * Review past patterns of Government spending.
> * Make recommendations on the relative importance of the various activities of Government in achieving the national aims.
> * Review these recommendations with the National Planning Committee of Cabinet to develop priorities in the allocation of funds.
> * Make recommendations to the Minister for Finance on allocation of funds for the 1975–76 budget.
> * Develop priorities and guidelines for the allocation of Government funds over the next decade.
>
> The Budget Priorities Committee advises the Minister for Finance on the allocation of expenditures. It works within the macro-economic parameters (overall levels of revenue, aid, borrowing and total expenditure) given by the Minister and Secretary for Finance.

The role of the BPC was extended in August 1975, in immediate response to financial stringency, to ensure that no new expenditure commitments were made without their merits being assessed carefully in comparison with possible alternatives. The Prime Minister instructed the Cabinet secretariat that no submission with financial implications would be admitted for consideration unless Cabinet had first received the advice of the BPC and the National Planning Committee (NPC). The CPO (soon to be called the National Planning Office, NPO) was restructured to provide more effectively the services of a secretariat to the BPC.

The five years 1972 to 1977 saw the evolution of a simple but effective system for bringing economic policy choices forward for decision. The system worked politically because of the close relationship between the Prime Minister and the Minister for Finance. The mechanisms had evolved in ways that avoided the potential for destructive conflict between the CPO and GFEP. These two organizations had separate and complementary roles in the process of policy co-ordination. GFEP provided advice mainly on the macro-economic aggregates, while the CPO was concerned mainly with the content and priority of government programmes. There were good personal relations between the operatives of CPO and Finance. The mechanisms were thoroughly Papua New Guinean, operated by senior

Papua New Guinean officials on the BPC and ultimately by senior ministers in the NPC. The potential for conflict between the Prime Minister and Finance Minister, which had surfaced during 1972, was also avoided: in early 1976, when the Prime Minister asked whether the Minister for Finance still wanted the NPO in Finance, the latter replied that it was not necessary. The system was working well enough.

Not all resource allocation questions were handled through this mechanism. Ministers sometimes preferred to keep their own counsel, especially on matters not related directly to the budget. Some matters which senior officials and ministers judged to require co-ordination with the central stabilization and budget decisions were still being taken in isolation in early 1977, in particular in relation to the activities of statutory authorities and non-Australian aid, although there was considerable momentum towards integrating these decisions with wider policy-making. At the same time, ministers and departmental heads, sometimes found it useful to place questions only marginally related to public expenditure before the BPC and NPC, as a mechanism for generating clear and durable policy guidelines.

AGGREGATE GOVERNMENT EXPENDITURE AND ITS FINANCING

The Somare government inherited a level of public expenditure that was far beyond anything that could possibly be financed from domestic revenues for the foreseeable future. It inherited a political situation that seemed to demand increased expenditure to raise services and incomes at least in poor parts of the country. And it inherited a situation in which the relatively well off were able to resist strongly any reduction in their own incomes. In addition, the Somare government was at first prevented from making a forward-looking attempt to make way for important programmes through reduction in low priority programmes by balanced annual budgets (institutionally necessary until 1975/76) and annually determined Australian aid.

For its first three years, the government raised all the loans it could, encouraged by the Australian government which provided a guarantee until independence, raised taxes when it thought it was possible politically, held expenditure below levels it thought were necessary to implement some important programmes, and budgeted to spend all the cash it had year by year. The annual approach to the budget aggregates led to more obvious problems as time went by. But the government could not break out of this disastrous inheritance before it had (*a*) a long-term perspective on its own revenues and expenditures and (*b*) its prerequisite, a clear forward commitment on Australian aid.

The absence of a medium- or long-term perspective on Australian aid generated great uncertainty about planning for services. One senior OPAC official was studying Indonesian health services in the early weeks of the Somare government, because he thought that Papua New Guinea's would be something like them when aid was reduced after independence. By contrast, the Faber mission, which was recommending that major steps be taken towards reduction of inter-regional inequalities through improvement in services, thought that the real level of aid would need to rise by over two-thirds by 1978 (10 per cent per annum). When the government had articulated plans for raising standards of services in poor regions, the Health and Education departments, the big spenders, came up with careful programmes that required the real level of spending to rise by over 8 per cent per annum. These plans were never implemented, but it was not until about mid-1975 that it was generally recognized that the money simply was not available for their full implementation.

In the early period of national government there was pressure from urban workers for higher wages and from the Islands provinces for decentralization of taxing powers and receipts from royalties and export taxes. It was clearly going to be so difficult simply to hold the line on expenditure that no political leader contemplated reductions in the services available to any sizeable group of Papua New Guineans. To keep the budget balanced in cash required heroic efforts by Chan and his Budgets Division.

By about early 1974, some Papua New Guineans were becoming aware of the long-term problems that might be associated with high aid dependence. As it happened, they were often the same people who were front-line advocates of increased wages, new government programmes, or measures that would erode the internal revenue base. However, at least three Papua New Guineans had made the logical connection between becoming more self-reliant and spending less money. Of these, Julius Chan held the view (as in practice did every political leader) that it was impossible to take from those (nationals) who have. Equalization was required; equalization had to be up, not down; so a lot more revenue was required before much progress could be made in reduction of aid. Morauta, as Secretary for Finance, would probably have liked to try to achieve a radical reduction in expenditure, but recognized that these were matters with large implications for political stability, which could not be undertaken without strong commitment by senior ministers. John ToVue, newly appointed assistant director in the Central Planning Office, did advocate a radical reduction in wages, services, and standards of living in the interests of much greater self-reliance. ToVue expressed his view to aid donors as readily as to Papua New Guinean claimants for expenditure, and he returned home to the Gazelle Peninsula in late 1975 after a period of considerable tension in the Central Planning Office.

Through 1975, GFEP was suggesting that it was necessary to adjust downwards considerably expectations for medium-term internal revenue growth, and was also pointing out a very difficult short-term financial situation through to mid-1977. The annual perspective that had formerly characterized decisions on the budget aggregates became a two-year perspective in the preparation of the 1975/76 budget, facilitated by ministers' concern for the successful launching of the new currency (see below). A programme to reduce expenditure in the following financial year, 1976/77, had begun when Australian aid for 1975/76 was reduced to levels well below expectations, and below earlier official indications, in August 1975.

The aid cut produced an important decision point. Some Finance officials who had watched the Australian aid decision process for many years cautioned against any attempt to reduce public expenditure greatly in response to the reduction in aid except in the context of an effective long-term aid agreement. There was one view at senior levels in the government that no downward revision of expenditure should be attempted, because aid would come more readily if Papua New Guinea was near bankruptcy. GFEP, cautious about excessive borrowing in the first eighteen months of the independent currency, saw advantages in making necessity a virtue, slimming as far as possible in the following two years, and establishing a realistic base for a planned steady expansion in public expenditure and for an effective long-term aid agreement.

Ministers, backed by CPO and Finance, had been seeking an effective long-term aid agreement as a critical objective since mid-1974, when it was realized that the $500 million agreement of early 1974 had been aborted by the Australian government's insistence that the guaranteed level of aid included payments under the Employment Security Scheme to retired colonial civil servants. Chan had discussed long-term aid questions with the Australian Treasurer, Frank Crean, in 1974. Senior officials had met with a group of Australian academics (three of whom were in contact with Australian policy-making through this period) to discuss technical aspects of a possible agreement. There was also a growing realization in the new Australian Development Assistance Agency, now with former PNG Administrator Les Johnson as its director, of the importance of a long-term agreement for sound political relations between the two governments and for effective financial planning in Papua New Guinea.

Following the aid cut, PNG ministers pondered the politics of embarking on a major reduction in expenditure that would include some reduction in inherited services on the eve of independence and with an election year soon to follow. They decided to take the risks inherent in the reduction of expenditure and to work very hard for a forward agreement on Australian aid. From this point, Chan personally called the major shots on aid questions. The aid agreement was crucial to the whole macro-economic strategy towards which Finance and CPO had been working. Great care was taken in limiting aid-related information to senior ministers and a few senior officials to avoid premature disclosure of PNG positions to Australian diplomats. The effort and caution were rewarded in March 1976, when prime ministers Fraser and Somare agreed in Canberra to five-year arrangements that the PNG government judged to be consistent with the requirements of its general policies. Australian aid was to be provided as untied cash grants, minimum amounts of aid were specified forward for five years, and the terms of the agreement held out hope that clear princip-les could be agreed upon for upward adjustment of aid levels above speci-fied minima.

The Minister for Finance was also active in developing a political strategy to implement the new policy of financial stringency. The minis-ter began a series of major speeches which explained the importance of restraint in spending and wages to monetary stability and eventual national financial self-reliance at the launching of the new currency in April 1975. He established an Economic Affairs Council, which was designed as a forum for the exchange of views on the difficult economic policy choices between senior public servants, businessmen, and union leaders. A thrice-weekly series of broadcasts, at NBC prime time, in English, Hiri Motu, and pidgin were made through the second half of 1975 and the first half of 1976. They sometimes carried the Spartan message about "living within our means", and sometimes explained arcane points about economic policy or the workings of the Finance Ministry. Cabinet was briefed several times and key ministers more frequently about how the new independent currency worked and about the conditions that must be met if the mone-tary policy that the government had adopted was to be implemented successfully. A roster of senior Finance officials ensured that someone was always on hand at the parliament to aid the Prime Minister and Minister for Finance with information or advice when economic issues arose in or around the House. In July 1975 the Finance Department, with the minis-ter's encouragement, began to produce a new publication, *The Quarterly Summary of Economic Conditions,* which sought to describe graphically a government view on current economic conditions and issues. In their total effect these initiatives helped to bring about a very important change in political expectations on government expenditure.

The Secretary for Finance and members of the BPC had the main responsibility for explaining and enforcing the new stringency within the bureaucracy. The reaction at first was hostile, as it was in the community at large. But over the course of a year there was a major shift in commun-ity opinion. An atmosphere developed within which it was nationalist Papua New Guinean behaviour not to spend money. In most agencies of government — the Universities, the Minimum Wages Board, the Cabinet itself, even the Department of Foreign Affairs — there was acceptance among senior Papua New Guineans (after a period of crisis) of tight financial constraints. People who wanted to spend more money came to be watched carefully, especially if they were white. This reduction in expectations was necessary to economic stability and to political stability, and can be counted as one of the major successes of the early years of national government in Papua New Guinea.

Over the five-year period from 1972 to 1977, the real level of public expenditure rose by about one-third (with the real level of domestic revenue up almost by half, mainly through new taxation measures, aid down by about 10 per cent, and loans down as well). The increase in real expenditure was concentrated entirely in the first three years, and real expenditure fell considerably in 1976/77.

What made it possible for the first Somare government in its last two years to reverse the trend of rapid expenditure growth stretching back two decades? There were a number of linked but distinct causes. One cause was the gradual spread of the realization that nothing was free, resulting simply from the increasing experience of Papua New Guineans in government. The logic of necessity was also important in 1975/76, but too much should not be made of this since the tight kina limits on expenditure for 1976/77 that came out of the priorities work of 1975 were maintained despite the recovery of export prices in 1976, which would have supported temporarily an increase in domestic expenditure. The changes in the framework of decision-making — especially the longer-term view, and the focus on priorities within a given total expenditure — were very important. And the government's much more confident political position allowed it to take what appeared in advance to be a political risk.

Longer-term forward estimates of revenue generated within the General Financial Policy Branch of GFEP through mid-1976 suggested that a small steady annual increase in public expenditure programmes from the slim base established in 1976/77 would be consistent with a gradual modest decline in aid over the course of time, even if there were substantial delays in starting a new large resource project. Senior Papua New Guineans in the BPC and the NPC pondered the numbers, with attention focused concretely on the relative importance of expanding various services and reducing dependence on Australian aid. It was thought important to maintain a stream of new activities, growth "at a few per cent per annum", but a combination of necessity and virtue had caused the greater ambitions of earlier years to be put aside.

The Minister for Finance outlined the forward perspective on Australian aid and PNG public expenditure growth in major speeches in July and August 1976. The long-sought steady trend in real public expenditure was now a reality. The government moved ahead with the preparation of the National Public Expenditure Plan, which was to become a focus of policy-making after 1976.

THE ALLOCATION OF GOVERNMENT EXPENDITURE

When the Somare government wanted levers with which to redirect the efforts of government agencies, it came to rely most heavily on its financial powers. There were several reasons for this. Probably the most important was simply the constitutional requirement that the spending of money be supported by annual appropriation bills to be passed by the parliament. This most ancient of parliamentary controls meant that agencies had to keep going to the Minister for Finance and the Cabinet for their money, and the central co-ordinating agencies, under the most senior ministers, could then review their activities. Papua New Guinea from 1972 to 1977 may not have been the strongest bastion of Whig values, but the preparation of appropriation bills was always taken very seriously, and effective parliamentary supervision of expenditures was always supported by the Minister for Finance and Prime Minister through such means as increased staff for the Public Accounts Committee and the Auditor-General.

Other levers were sometimes used, but they were never as important as the budgetary controls. The central agencies frequently exhorted other departments to do their best to implement the Eight Aims, but this was not very effective unless followed up by the detailed attention of an alert minister. Only a handful of ministers were able to exercise such close supervision.

The preparation of the 1973/74 Improvement Plan brought people from OCM, Finance, and OPAC together to review programmes, but had relatively little influence on budget allocations. The CPO worked closely with the Budgets Division from late 1973, and this was more important in the shaping of programmes. However, the close working relationship between Budgets and CPO did not mean that funds were made available to support the expansion of services envisaged in various departmental plans (for example, Health and Education) which had sometimes been developed with CPO collaboration. The plans tended to be approved "in principle" by Cabinet, and remained as elaborate statements of what the various departments would like to do (and were valuable in this role). But funding was determined on the basis of annual availability of cash, and this was never sufficient to support the implementation of anything like the planned level of expansion.

The establishment of the Budget Priorities Committee brought a wider range of senior Papua New Guinean expertise and opinion to bear on the allocation process. The draft appropriations for 1975/76 were discussed at great length within the Budget Priorities Committee and the National Planning Committee, with both authorities making use of a numerical system developed in the CPO for assigning priorities across areas of expenditure.

Co-ordination of the activities of government through the budget process was corroded to a considerable degree by a tendency for the government to make decisions on extending funds to activities outside the periodic budget and budget review discussions. There was no problem when expenditure was pushing hard against available cash. But in the early years of transition it was sometimes the case that administrative failure led to under-expenditure in some activities, freeing cash for other uses. This effect was compounded through 1973 and early 1974 by buoyant revenues associated with high commodity prices. In these circumstances, the Budgets Division and the Minister for Finance could not tell Cabinet that no funds were available for some desirable increase in expenditure (and the dynamics of the aid relationship meant that they were often pleased to avoid a cash surplus). Commitments were often made to activities that would not have received funds in competition with other claims. The resulting distortion of priorities was greatest when commitments were made late in one financial year, not costing very much in that year, but carrying implications for continued spending.

This particular weakness was plugged in August 1975, when the BPC was required to review all mid-year requests for funds and to provide the NPC with advice on them within a comprehensive priorities framework. Despite this, the first priorities-setting exercise, for the 1975 Budget, was not an overwhelming success. By early 1976 it was apparent that low-priority activities, whose funding had been restricted severely, had continued in their old ways and overspent against their appropriations. High-priority activities which had been allocated increased funds were unable to mobilize for increased expenditure.

The priorities process had concentrated mainly on the allocation of funds amongst agencies up to this time, although direct contact of CPO and Budgets Division with departments did have some effect on the content of their programmes. There were problems, especially when it seemed that the headquarters of departments were passing an inordinate share of the burden of adjustment to financial stringency on to their provincial activities. The BPC became more actively involved in the allocation of expenditure within agencies through 1976/77. This involvement became very much deeper within the framework of the National Public Expenditure Plan.

The essence of the priorities process was that the BPC, NPC, and Cabinet kept under constant review the allocation of all public expenditure in line with long-term priorities. In the early stages, the system was far from all-embracing. Major decisions on the use of non-Australian aid, international agency loans, the works programme, wages, and activities of statutory authorities were taken independently of government priorities. The long, subtle process of bringing all public expenditure within the priorities process had begun on all of these fronts but still had a long way to go on most of them at the time of the 1977 elections.

Foreign aid was the most important and complicated challenge to the priorities system. Project aid dressed up as something for nothing, the use of funds that otherwise would not be available, had a certain appeal in a situation in which there was much development work to be done. The biggest danger was the possibility that Australian aid would be tied to projects. Several people in and close to the government in Port Moresby were alert to the danger in 1972, but Papua New Guinea's policy did not crystallize until the first half of 1973, in response to the insistence of the new Australian External Territories Minister, Bill Morrison, that Australian aid be committed to projects. Somare and Chan articulated a policy of firm opposition to Morrison's attempts to have aid encapsulated in project form.

The government stood by its policy despite great pressure from foreign diplomats, sometimes supported by people (often expatriate) in the employment of the PNG government who felt that their own priorities would be treated better if aid was allocated partly through a diplomatic process, rather than through the normal budgetary process. A few decisions were taken in conflict with announced policy. A few offers of special Australian aid "on top of normal aid" were accepted (and regretted). Nadzab Airport would never have been built and some activities under the cultural grant would never have been undertaken if PNG ministers had not thought they were using "free money". The same could be said of non-Australian aid, such as the Fisheries Training Centre built by the Japanese government and a number of New Zealand projects.

The boldest attempt by Australian officials to break the PNG priorities system arose when the Australian High Commissioner promoted the idea that Australian Prime Minister Malcolm Fraser should announce a gift of a "Unity Highway" between Port Moresby and Lae on his visit in early 1977. The High Commissioner encouraged the project amongst a few people centred on Transport Minister Bruce Jephcott who were thought to be unsympathetic to co-ordination by the central agencies. This and other misreadings of the PNG government's commitment to stated aid policies corroded confidence in the relationship between the Australian High Commission and the most senior and influential PNG officials. These Australian misreadings were never finally damaging to the aid relationship, because of the strength of political commitment in Port

Moresby and because some Australian ministers understood and were sympathetic to PNG policies.

In its early months, the second Somare government built on the momentum established in the period 1972 to 1977 and extended considerably the range of expenditures allocated through the priorities process. The most impressive extension was the effective co-ordination of major non-Australian aid (especially from Japan and the European Economic Community) into the budgetary and planning process, as a result of major diplomatic initiatives based on new aid policies developed through 1976 and early 1977. One important feature of the steady broadening of the scope of the priorities process was that it extended well beyond the membership of the BPC the range of senior Papua New Guineans who understood and supported the system.

MONEY AND PRICES

Papua New Guinea had no monetary independence whatsoever when the first Somare government came to office. In consequence it had very little control over prices. Variations in wages, price controls, taxes, domestic supplies of some commodities, and supply agreements for imports could each make some short-term impact on domestic inflation. But there was no means of insulating the PNG economy from overseas price developments.

The expatriate community had always been alarmed at any discussion of monetary independence for Papua New Guinea. Sudden rushes of speculative capital outflow had followed its discussion at an academic conference in Port Moresby in 1970 and at a Papua New Guinea Economics Society meeting in 1971. Academic commentators who addressed the question generally thought the sooner a new currency the better, so as to get business uncertainty associated with monetary transition out of the way before constitutional transition. But official nervousness on currency matters and then the acceleration of the transfer of powers caused Papua New Guinea to face a unique situation of introducing a completely new currency at the time of independence.

The idea of establishing a new currency was popular politically, and the Minister for Finance gave it careful attention and high priority from an early date. The government moved quickly to a decision in favour of full-blooded monetary independence, embracing all of the associated opportunities as well as the potential disasters, rather than some version of the currency board system employed by most ex-British colonies for some time after independence. (None of the interested academics had much enthusiasm for pushing things so far, although Ron May [1972] spelt out the full range of options.)

Legislation establishing the Bank of Papua New Guinea and the Papua New Guinea Banking Corporation was enacted in the months immediately preceding self-government, and legislation for the new currency over the following eighteen months. The technical aspects of the monetary transition were handled efficiently by officials in the Finance Ministry and in the Port Moresby branch of the Reserve Bank of Australia (many of whom joined the Bank of Papua New Guinea). The Reserve Bank benefited from an early concern for Papua New Guinean staff development and in particular from an able Papua New Guinean head in Henry ToRobert. The planning for the new currency was under Chan's careful supervision.

There were some advantages in membership of the Australian currency area through 1973: successive Australian dollar revaluations between December 1972 and September 1973 (about 10 per cent in all on a trade-weighted basis for Papua New Guinea and 20 per cent for Australia) helped to insulate PNG prices from much of the early effect of the world-wide inflation and commodity boom. But world prices were still rising rapidly after the completion of the Australian revaluations. The inflationary impact in Papua New Guinea was huge: the consumer price index rose by 10 per cent in the second quarter of 1974, 16 per cent in the six months to June, and 29 per cent for the whole of the 1973/74 financial year. This generated tensions throughout the country, even in rural areas which were benefiting from high export prices. Many people, especially in the Highlands, seem to have associated the loss in the purchasing power of their money with self-government, just as some of them blamed the increase in beer prices following tax increases in 1975 on independence.

Josephine Abaijah took up the inflation issue in Port Moresby in the second quarter of 1974. It was an easy winner, and large Papua Besena cum inflation rallies culminated in a spectacular invasion of the Chief Minister's office in Konedobu. Inflation went to the top of the "crisis calendar". On the initiative of OCM, the present writer was appointed co-ordinator of the anti-inflation campaign and given a week to stop inflation.

It was a good time to mount a political offensive against inflation, as there were signs that the boom in world food prices was abating. If the government used all of its instruments of policy to their useful limits, it could bring about an early and noticeable once-for-all reduction in the price level. It could demonstrate that it was using all of its resources to tackle a widely felt problem. Beyond the time when this immediate effect would continue to be felt, the easing of food price increases overseas would provide a period of respite. In the longer term, with the new currency, exchange rate policy could be used to insulate Papua New Guinea from overseas inflation as long as suitable restraint was exercised in domestic expenditure and wages.

The concentration of political influence in the group of people meeting each morning in the Chief Minister's office facilitated greatly an exercise like the anti-inflation campaign, which required the participation of many agencies. Within a day, working with Paliau Lukas of CPO, I had spoken at length to ministers and relevant officials in agencies that could be expected to play the major roles in the programme: Finance, Foreign Relations and Trade, Transport, Agriculture, and others. Two long days in Cabinet were then devoted to the inflation problem: what caused inflation; what Papua New Guinea could and could not do about it; proposals from a number of ministers. A series of initiatives were announced to produce an immediate effect: suspension of the 2½ per cent general import levy on the five basic imported foodstuffs; smaller wholesale and retail margins on basic commodities enforced by tighter supervision of price control; new price justification procedures for locally manufactured commodities (and support for a long-standing Finance request for a larger prices establishment); announcement of the rearrangement of coastal freight charges to lighten the burden on basic commodities and support for initiatives to lower international freight charges; the Foreign Minister to initiate discussions with suppliers of foodstuffs in Australia and in Asian countries with a view to longer-term supply arrangements at lower prices (and a few days later an offer by the Colonial Sugar Refining Company to reduce sugar prices well below world prices); the Department of Agriculture to accelerate its programme of fresh food supply and to submit to Finance a request for additional budgetary resources (and John Guise to make his own statement in parliament); and less dramatic moves in Forests and Business Development.

The anti-inflation campaign was directed mainly at a political problem. It was successful in that. It was not linked firmly to economic policy in general. It might have been quite useful for purposes of rural development if it had been used to resist pressures that were building up for huge urban wage increases. But by the time the new low inflation rates were coming out in the statistics, the due processes had ground out the 1974 Minimum Wage Board decision.

The desirability of using revaluation (and avoiding devaluation) as an anti-inflationary device, and of making this possible through the application of effective domestic stabilization policies, was discussed by some adademic economists in Port Moresby through 1974. This view was reinforced when a British economist, Fred Hirsch, visited Papua New Guinea under IMF auspices in late 1974, and later prepared a long and thorough report on all aspects of the workings of the new currency. The minister studied the report carefully and was confirmed in his commitment to policies that would maintain the kina's value in relation to major world currencies and to a low rate of inflation.

There was no difference in basic approach to monetary policy between the Bank of Papua New Guinea and Finance, although there were the usual differences about timing and amounts of changes in the main monetary policy variables. But outside these two organizations (and one or two people in the CPO) there was very little understanding of the links between inflation, the exchange rate, real and money wages, and real and money public expenditure. The Minister for Finance and the Prime Minister led the government in strong commitment to policies that would maintain a strong kina and low inflation, but the limited spread of understanding of monetary questions within the government meant that there was some danger that monetary strategy would fall prey to inconsistent decisions on indirectly related policy questions. Every possible forum was used by the Minister for Finance, his officials, and bank officials to explain the key relationships. By mid-1977 there was widespread support for the government's approach to monetary and related policies.

The government's monetary policies faced their greatest challenge immediately before and after the final currency separation on 1 January 1976. There was a massive flight of capital and potential reserves at a time when export income was very low, with anxiety about exchange control and possible devaluation compounded by uncertainty over Australian aid, the future of the Ok Tedi project, the secession attempt in Bougainville, and the World Bank's initial caution on Papua New Guinea's post-independence credit-worthiness. The new monetary instruments (interest rates, qualitative credit controls) were used to support the fiscal policies that had been prepared to weather this anticipated challenge to the new strategy. By about March 1976, some of the wider uncertainties (including Australian aid) had been resolved favourably, and the community was beginning to take the government at its word on monetary policy. The capital flight ceased, and within a few months, partly under the influence of rising prices for agricultural exports, foreign exchange reserves began to rise.

From early 1976, GFEP was incorporating a discussion of the exchange rate into its periodic review of economic conditions and budget strategy. By mid-year, developments in wages policy and economic conditions pointed the way to possible early revaluation. The minister began to weigh the possibility and discussed it with the Secretary for Finance, the Governor of the Bank, and the Prime Minister. The timing of the first revaluation, on 26 July 1976, was influenced by the need to consolidate the recently announced Minimum Wages Board decision and the forthcoming budget into a widely supported and long-surviving macro-economic strategy.

WAGES POLICY

The first Somare government did not formulate and seek to enforce a policy on wages until late 1975, by which time a large part of the increases in resources that became available to the government over the five-year period had been appropriated by urban workers and public servants. There were strong pressures from urban unions who had ready access to ministers from urban electorates, including the Minister for Labour.

During 1972 the earlier urban Pangu commitment to more equal pay between Papua New Guineans and expatriates was modified in favour of support for reduction in the real incomes of middle and upper level public servants, and increases for workers and public servants on lower incomes. The unions, including the Public Service Association (PSA), concurred in (and helped to shape) this approach, and there was a radical compression of pay differentials within the Papua New Guinean workforce between 1972 and 1976; at the same time, minimum (and, because of the preponderance of low-income workers, average) urban wages were increased very substantially.

There were early opportunities for an agreement with the PSA, the only powerful and effective union at that time, which offered to trade wage restraint for active redistribution from high foreign personal and corporate income, perhaps through taxation. The opportunities had been lost by early 1974, to a significant extent through the government's failure to act early in substantially raising taxation on personal and corporate incomes accruing to foreigners. These failures helped to create an atmosphere of cynicism about the government's approach to redistribution, particularly in the light of generous Employment Security Scheme (ESS) arrangements (underlined by the presence of more or less redundant expatriates in many parts of the administration, drawing high salaries and recalculating frequently their large termination benefits) and the generosity of the government's widely publicized pay arrangements for some of its new expatriate employees. All this was made worse by the absence of an effective stabilization policy in the boom year 1973/74.

All but the last of these failures were problems of the transitional situation. The Finance Department was worried about the effects of substantially increased taxation on the morale of expatriate personnel and business. The Office of the Chief Minister and the Public Service Board (PSB) were concerned about the morale of expatriate public servants and sought to maintain this with generous termination and salary arrangements. It is an open question whether this caution was necessary and inevitable, but it was certainly disastrous for wages policy.

When the Committee on Prices and Incomes, established by Cabinet in 1972, reported in early 1974, emphasizing the need for restraint in all urban (including expatriate) incomes, the force of its recommendations was destroyed by the cynicism about the government's commitment to equity in income distribution. The *coup de grâce* was applied by the high inflation of early 1974, which generated a political atmosphere in which it was possible for the Minister for Labour to sack an urban Minimum Wages Board whose interim decision failed to compensate fully for past price increases. A new board, which was more likely to grant a large wage increase, was appointed by the minister.

The union case to the new board was put forcefully by three Australians. They were able to raise without question some sound arguments and many fallacious ones because there was no government representation at the hearings. Papua New Guinea was "an Eldorado rich beyond the dreams of the conquistadores". Private employers who appeared before the board were mauled, and retired not too unhappily, since they represented mainly manufacturing and service industries which supplied urban markets and stood to gain as much as they would lose from a large wage increase. Two expatriate officials who had been associated with the preparation of the Prices and Incomes Report were abused. The CPO was kept out of wages policy by its director. A Department of Labour official raised arguments in support of the union's position. A timid Finance Department submission placed before the board information on the inflationary and immediate budgetary impact of the K40 minimum wage the unions were seeking. The only mention of the stabilization problem (i.e., that wages which appeared to be appropriate in the middle of a commodity boom would not be sustainable in normal times) was in a private submission introduced late in the board's deliberations at the request of the chairman.

On the evidence before it, and in the political circumstances, the board reached a moderate decision – to raise the urban minimum wage for Port Moresby from K13.80 per week to K25 in two stages, and to introduce indexation arrangements which would have the effect of further raising real minimum wages and lowering real wages of more senior personnel in the process of inflation. The PSB applied the increases to public service salaries with the concurrence of all departments. There was no immediate budgetary problem: revenue was still high on the tail-end of the commodities boom; borrowings were high on the pre-independence Australian guarantee; and in any case, the main impact of the increase would not be felt until the 1975/76 budget year.

In 1975/76, the government finally faced in the context of financial stringency the fundamental income distribution choices that are inevitable in wages policy. The BPC recommended and the NPC and Cabinet accepted that part of the stringency (which was in practice to be borne mainly by rural communities) should be carried by public servants through a variation from the indexation arrangements introduced by the 1974

Minimum Wages Board. The government was now in a stronger moral and political position to argue for wage restraint within the context of a range of policies to redistribute incomes more equitably across the whole community. There had been large increases in corporate income tax, import and excise duties on luxuries, the Bougainville Copper Agreement renegotiation and, in the 1975 budget, a progressive restructuring and simplification in the system of personal income tax. These strengths had been qualified somewhat by the introduction in 1974 of a five-year tax holiday for businesses owned by indigenous Papua New Guineans.

But the time for the deal offered by the PSA in 1972 and 1973 had passed: the government had nothing more to give away, and its overall policies required that it take something back. So for a year the government and the PSA slogged it out under the constant threat of a public service strike. The government was always solid in its resolve at senior minister (and hence Cabinet) level, but widely and at times bitterly divided at departmental level. The dispute was widened to affect private sector employees when the PSA raised relativity problems and the Prime Minister instructed the Minister for Labour to set up a new Minimum Wages Board. Before the new board, the government was represented throughout the hearings and provided a lengthy argument in support of its position. The publicity given to the hearings and the government's evidence, spread over many weeks in early 1976, helped to consolidate the widening community understanding for the government's policies of fiscal restraint, and heightened awareness of the problem of rural-urban imbalance in incomes and access to services. The Minimum Wages Board's decision did not follow the details of the government's proposal, but was judged by the government to be consistent with its general economic policies and distributional objectives.

As could be anticipated, the board's decision was received very unfavourably by the unions, and there were large demonstrations in Port Moresby and Lae. The government came under pressure again, with the PSA requesting an immediate public service pay increase, which would have cut across the board's decision. Meanwhile, the kina revaluation of July 26 promised (and in fact was to deliver) low inflation for the eight remaining months of the board's fourteen-month pause in wage increases. Some private sector unions said that they would live with the wage decision in the context of the revaluation. Soon after, the government and the PSA, again in the context of the prospects for lower inflation, reached agreement on terms that were consistent with the Minimum Wages Board decision. Subsequently, in the last months of the first Somare government, the PSC, Finance, and CPO, working within an explicit, official long-term expenditure strategy, came to a three-year agreement providing for full indexation up to inflation rates of 12½ per cent per annum (a proviso that had been included in the Minimum Wages Board's earlier decision). The government again argued a comprehensive case before a new Wages Board, and similar three-year arrangements were introduced to the private sector.

Over the five-year period as a whole, urban workers and lower-level public servants did rather better in improvement of their incomes than any other large group of Papua New Guineans. But by the end of the period there was widespread acceptance of arrangements on wages which would restrict the claims of urban wage and salary earners on future increases in financial resources that might become available for distribution among Papua New Guineans.

INVESTMENT CONDITIONS

There are two conceptually distinct but in practice closely intertwined policy areas under the general heading of investment conditions: the form and degree of assistance to one type of investment *vis-à-vis* other activities within the economy; and the terms and conditions upon which foreign-owned investments operate *vis-à-vis* domestic investments.

Colonial policy was little concerned with the distinction between Papua New Guinean and foreign investment. In consequence, an overwhelming proportion of modern business activity was undertaken by non-indigenous persons and corporations. The terms upon which this activity was conducted were highly favourable to investors: rates of personal and corporate income tax were set at very low levels and there was no withholding tax on dividends; tax holidays were granted for new activities under the Pioneer Industries Ordinance; there was no process of prices justification or control on locally produced manufactures which were often in a monopolistic position because of protection and the small market; the colonial state was prepared to hand over rights to non-renewable resources on terms which did not reflect their property value; the administration was prepared to provide a substantial part of infrastructure required for major private investments; tariff protection was handed out freely to manufacturers to the cost of the community as a whole; and there were no effective requirements for localization and training of the workforce.

These conditions were conducive to very rapid growth in monetary sector product. However, they were not conducive to the most rapid possible growth in Papua New Guinean incomes (counting government revenue as part of those incomes), since much of the growth took the form of rents to foreign capital and labour, and part, generated by protection and other subsidies, was illusory. Policies directed to maximizing crude aggregates like gross monetary sector product were especially inappropriate if high value was attributed to equal distribution among Papua New Guineans.

Three strands of criticism of the established (colonial) investment policy were of some importance in public discussion from 1972: an *economists'* critique, a *nationalist* critique, and a *neo-Marxist* critique. The three strands came together on some issues but not others and can best be examined separately.

A fairly consistent critique of the inherited investment policy regime emerged among the economists at UPNG and the New Guinea Research Unit and in the Faber mission. The essence of the critique was a technocratic judgement that more severe and carefully designed investment policies could lead to greatly increased national benefits from investment. This critique was based on the premises that no investment should be contemplated unless it raised total incomes of nationals, and that fiscal policies should be designed to yield the maximum possible national benefit from each investment. In practice, the first premise argued against the inducement of uneconomic manufacturing industry through public subsidy, especially by means of protection. The second argued for more concerted efforts to extract payments equal to the property value of natural resources made available to private investors.

The nationalist critique valued increased national ownership of business enterprises for its own sake. The major attempt to organize politically around this critique was led by John Kaputin and Father John Momis and the Constitutional Planning Committee, most notably through 1973 and 1974. The indigenous nationalist sentiment was supported in the early seventies by the populist economic nationalism that was influential in Australia and elsewhere at that time. The nationalist policy prescription was to bring enterprise under national ownership by any means whenever this was possible – although it was commonly allowed that new foreign investment was useful in areas in which effective national ownership was not yet possible.

Alongside the nationalist and economists' critiques, the neo-Marxist critique held that major problems in political economy were associated with high levels of dependence on foreign investment. These views were held mainly by non-economists at UPNG, and from 1974 by an increasing number of economists at that institution. At first the neo-Marxist prescription was similar to the nationalist – more national ownership by whatever means – although increasingly "state capitalism" was put forward as the most desirable form of business organization. The neo-Marxist position was not influential in policy-making between 1972 and 1977, although occasionally one or other minister (for example, the volatile sometime Minister for Agriculture and Transport, Iambakey Okuk, before his dismissal in January 1976) drew advice on particular policy issues from persons of this persuasion.

The main debate within the government was between supporters of the established investment policy and those of the economists' critique on the fiscal terms and conditions of investment. The main political debate was between supporters of the established investment policy and those of the nationalist critique on the ownership of the means of production. The nationalists commonly supported the economists on issues related to the fiscal terms and conditions of investment, but were much more concerned with increasing national ownership than with the fiscal terms upon which either nationally owned or foreign-owned firms were conducted.

To the extent that the established (colonial) position reflected more than a simple-minded attachment to high growth, it was based on a particular view or model of rural-urban migration and urban unemployment: there was an inexorable movement of people from villages to towns, and if jobs were not created in urban manufacturing industries, the migrants would simply join the ranks of the unemployed. In the alternative migration and employment model of the economists' critique, the rate of rural-urban migration depended mainly on the balance of benefits and opportunities between rural and urban life. Successful rural development in marginal areas of emigration would affect the rate of migration, as would the deterioration in urban conditions that would be caused by continued migration in excess of the rate at which urban jobs became available. There was no guarantee that a faster rate of growth in the industrial sector would reduce unemployment, and it might even raise unemployment if it were achieved through means that reduced rural incomes or services. Higher total revenues flowing from reduction of tax concessions to major investments would allow the government to provide more employment directly, although hopefully not mainly in urban areas.

The economists' critique was resisted fiercely by the established public service and business community. It was opposed strongly by OPAC (not so much by McCasker as by his lieutenants), by the Finance Department before the accession of Morauta to the secretary's position (but not under Morauta), and by the Investment Corporation (which opposed the Bougainville Copper renegotiation both before and after the event). The Tariff Advisory Committee was a battleground of the competing views through 1972 and 1973. Although part of the economists' critique was eventually absorbed into the government's approach to investment issues, it was never embraced by the whole of the government. The various arms of the Ministry of Labour, Commerce and Industry, which held major responsibility for investment policy, opposed the critique more or less consistently in the later years of the government.

The supporters of established investment policy rarely recognized differences between the different kinds of critique. To them, and especially to established foreign businessmen, there was little to distinguish opposition to subsidies for uneconomic investments from opposition to continued foreign ownership in a particular sector. Each was dangerous radicalism to be fought with whatever means were at hand.

The development of investment policy in relation to large minerals and petroleum projects proceeded along quite different paths from policy on other investments. The former were always managed directly by senior ministers and Cabinet, while the latter came to be handled within the framework of the National Investment and Development Authority (NIDA). The following discussion deals with each of these in turn, and then with policy-making on the ownership of the means of production.

MINERALS INVESTMENT POLICY

The development of minerals and petroleum policy can properly be told only as a long story in itself. There is space here only for the major mile-posts.

Although it contained such features as a three-year tax holiday, subsequent immediate expensing of all past capital expenditure, and the permanent exemption of 20 per cent of income from taxation, the original Bougainville Copper Agreement was widely acclaimed in Papua New Guinea (even by the Pangu opposition in the parliament) and in Australia, although there were a few academic critics (see, for example, my letter in the *Australian Financial Review,* 18 February 1969). The Faber mission suggested that the Australian government should renegotiate the agreement before self-government. The Australian government did not take up the suggestion, but the issue of renegotiation was kept alive, mainly by Bougainville political leaders and by Stephen Zorn in the Office of the Chief Minister. Somare and Bougainville politicians John Momis and Paul Lapun all made statements supporting renegotiation during the budget session of 1972 and in response the market valuation of the corporation was reduced by several hundred million dollars. The House of Assembly supported a statement by Momis on minerals policy, which became an important basis for the subsequent development of government positions. There was an inevitable progress towards renegotiation from that time, although events moved slowly.

A second element in the emergence of minerals policy began to be woven into the fabric in May 1973, when the writer was working for a short period in Finance Minister Chan's office. Chan said he wanted a system that would take as much money as possible from Bougainville Copper consistent with similar arrangements being applied to new mineral investments. Anthony Clunies Ross and the writer worked over the possibilities and took a resource rent tax proposal back to the minister. The company reacted quickly, strongly, and negatively to the proposal when given the opportunity to comment upon it in principle.

Meanwhile, the will to renegotiate had not permeated the whole of the government and, to demonstrate the respectability of changing the agreement (and the unrespectability of doing nothing about it), the Office of the Chief Minister arranged for a professor from the Harvard Business School, Louis T. Wells, Jr, to prepare a report on the existing agreement and to comment on desirable changes. Wells was of the view that the existing agreement was out of line with current practice in other countries and suggested a number of possible changes. The suggested changes would have realized a large amount of additional revenue, although Wells did not support the application of any profit-based tax in addition to the standard corporate income tax. Wells's role was to widen the range of people who thought that renegotiation was necessary.

From late 1973 the government had before it the Wells and Resource Rent Tax proposals, and did not really know what to do next. But political pressures for early renegotiation were accumulating rapidly, most importantly among government back-benchers and members of the Constitutional Planning Committee. Early in 1974 the Chief Minister picked his team to handle the renegotiation, headed by Beatty and Morauta as joint chairmen, with Leo Hannett, Bernard Narakobi, Moi Avei, Steve Zorn, and John Momis and John Kaputin from the Constitutional Planning Committee. The team appointed as consultants were the Commonwealth Secretariat's Technical Assistance Group, Marian Radetzki from the International Council of Copper-Exporting Countries (CIPEC), and myself from the New Guinea Research Unit. Staff of the Office of Minerals and Energy and the Law Department also participated in discussions. The Chief Minister and Cabinet developed the essential elements of Papua New Guinea's minerals and petroleum policies following consultations among this large group of national policy-makers and foreign consultants.

The first meeting between the government committee and company officials was held in May 1974, and the renegotiation process lasted until September. The government moved very little during the series of long meetings from the approach it had adopted at the outset, although adjustments were made to the detail of the additional profits tax in the course of the negotiations. Only a few of the original team of negotiators and advisers participated throughout the long process of negotiation. The experience of the Commonwealth Secretariat people (from time to time Gordon Goundrey, Michael Faber, Roland Brown, and Sumer Lallah) was crucial to the success of the renegotiation. The Chief Minister and Cabinet followed the proceedings very closely, and there were many lengthy Cabinet discussions on minerals policy and on the progress of the negotiations. Agreement came only after a credible threat that the government would legislate its own solution.

The last two negotiating sessions were handled by senior ministers themselves. The company's last big play, having failed to persuade the Australian government of its responsibility to intervene, was to offer taxation on the government's terms in return for nationalization of the mine on the company's terms. Sir Val Duncan, chairman of Rio Tinto Zinc (RTZ), the ultimate controller of Bougainville Copper Ltd (BCL), and Rod Carnegie, chairman of RTZ's subsidiary, Conzinc Riotinto of Australia, flew in on the company jet and asked to see the Chief Minister. The Minister for Foreign Relations, Maori Kiki told them that they could not see the Chief Minister whenever they wanted to. They could see Kiki instead. The Chief Minister sent two advisers to find out what the company wished to discuss with him.

The advisers reported to the full Cabinet early the next morning. Then the Chief Minister left the meeting, leaving Kiki in the chair, with Lapun, Chan, Gavera Rea, Ebia Olewale, Guise, and Okuk. Morauta, Rabbie Namaliu, and Hannett stayed on as advisers (and Cabinet secretary Mark Lynch as scribe), and the expatriate advisers left. This was Papua New Guineans' own business. The meeting lasted for several hours, during which time the ministers told Duncan that they did not wish to buy a further 50 per cent of shares in the mine. They wanted to proceed with negotiations on the basis of their own carefully considered proposal.

The final meeting came a week or so later, with Somare in the chair and the other ministers facing Duncan, Carnegie, Ray Ballmer, Don Vernon, and others from the company. This time both black and white advisers were present, but not participating at all. It was a long, tense, and tough meeting, during which the PNG ministers were consistently firm and often brilliant. All had a very strong awareness that they were standing at the beginning of the long history of Papua New Guinea. The new agreement, signed in September 1974, increased expected government revenues from corporate income tax, including a new additional profits tax, by several hundred million kina, including K65 million with respect to 1974 income, and secured for the government improved arrangements on environment, local business development, national control of future minerals development on Bougainville, and various other issues (Faber 1974). "Remember, they are stones, not trees," Kiki would say for a long time afterwards, emphasizing the importance of receiving a reasonable return to the PNG community for the sale of non-renewable resources.

Throughout the renegotiation of the agreement with BCL, the government was mindful of its possible implications for subsequent negotiations with the American mining company Kennecott, which held a prospecting authority over a promising copper prospect at Ok Tedi in the Star Mountains. But the government went back to other business and did not give the Ok Tedi negotiations very high priority during late 1974. Then those members of the BCL renegotiation team who were in Port Moresby regathered in the new year to face the reality that it would be difficult to reach satisfactory agreement with Kennecott, whose prospecting authority was to expire within a few months. The extensive information network established during the BCL negotiation was used to build up a view of decision-making processes within Kennecott and to develop possible government responses to the situation that would emerge should there be no agreement. Kennecott could be expected to try very hard to prevent other companies taking over the prospect. Josephine Abaijah and her supporters in Papua Besena could be expected to use the "neglect of Papua" theme upon the departure of Kennecott. But PNG advisers had talked to enough people overseas for the government to be mildly optimistic that it would not be stuck permanently without the means of continuing work on the project if Kennecott should pull out.

Kennecott did not undertake exploration work at Ok Tedi from 1972, while the corporation assessed the political situation under national government. In the meantime its capacity and willingness to undertake large new investments in developing countries had been reduced, since it had been expropriated in Chile and had run into severe and costly antitrust difficulties at home in the United States. The day that Kennecott rejected the government's last offer, the government considered its position at length and decided to refuse the company's request that the prospecting authority be extended. The same afternoon, the Chief Minister announced in parliament that a government company, the Ok Tedi Development Company, had been established to take over the prospect and that drilling would shortly be renewed under the supervision of a highly respected firm of geological consultants. Arrangements had been made to maintain education, health, and community services provided previously by Kennecott in the Ok Tedi area.

The proceedings of the Ok Tedi Development Company Board, the Ok Tedi Steering Committee, and subsequently the Minerals and Petroleum Policy Committee, reporting to Cabinet through the Chief Minister (as Minister for Natural Resources) and Minister for Finance, constituted the most effective, coherent, and harmonious work on policy I have observed in Papua New Guinea. Policy-making was facilitated by the clear principles articulated by the government and reinforced through the long BCL renegotiation process, by the active involvement of the most senior ministers, and by the excellent working relationships amongst officials that had been fostered by common participation in the BCL renegotiation.

The government came under considerable domestic criticism for refusing to extend Kennecott's prospecting authority: a barrage of more or less hostile questions in the House when Somare made his statement, and the expected criticisms from Papua Besena. Kennecott, as expected, was active in warning other companies away from dealing with the PNG government, and this complicated, without frustrating, the attempt to keep work moving at the prospect. However, Kennecott did co-operate by making all data from their earlier exploration available to the Ok Tedi Company. The new company proved to be successful in exploration and had extended substantially the ore reserves by mid-1976 (Davies 1978). The government then reached agreement with a consortium of Australian, American, and German firms (Howell et al. 1978) to take over the prospect on terms which, if applied to the Bougainville project, would have been more severe on BCL than the renegotiated Bougainville agreement.

The Prime Minister and Minister for Finance, acting with the advice of the Minerals and Petroleum Policy Committee, also developed petroleum policies parallel to and based on the same principles as the minerals policies. There was the same sorting out of corporations. One American corporation refused to accept the government's conditions. When the committee's negotiations were stalled, the Minister for Finance entered a meeting with executives of the company and told them that certain conditions were non-negotiable and that they might as well leave if they could not live with them. The company took him at his word and left. This company's prospecting commitments were taken over on the government's terms by a consortium led by Esso.

OTHER INVESTMENTS

Policy in relation to terms and conditions for smaller foreign investments was never given the high-level attention of minerals policy, and a number of basic questions remained unsettled throughout the life of the government.

In early 1972, GFEP had formal responsibility within the public service for "investment policy". It also had responsibility for advice on the use of the fiscal policy instruments which affected the profitability of investments. But in reality the Department of Trade and Industry had considerable autonomy in offering incentives to manufacturing industry (tariffs, and tax holidays for pioneer industries), and the Director of Agriculture had considerable autonomy in negotiating agreements on agricultural and fishing projects. New investment proposals from foreign corporations were received in GFEP unless, as was sometimes the case, they were quietly negotiated within the Department of Agriculture, Stock and Fisheries.

Other departments would be informed, and those with some interest in the matter would send representatives to negotiating sessions. The investors would be on one side of the table and a large number of representatives of PNG government agencies (who often had not reached agreed positions before the meeting) on the other. For a large and interesting project there might be a dozen or more representatives of Papua New Guinea, each of whom would have his say. General policies had not been established on many matters, so each department would put in a high bid on questions within its sphere of interest.

There were extremely complex policy and administrative questions to be resolved. A large number of politicians and officials held views on how some or other investment question should be handled, but the issues were never analyzed with sufficient clarity to allow basic differences in policy and approach to be debated and resolved. A small group of GFEP and OCM officers began work on investment guidelines and administrative arrangements for foreign investment. GFEP had public service, and the Minister for Finance political, responsibility. The GFEP/OCM group realized that they lacked the internal resources to settle the issues and in early 1973 hired W. D. Scott and Company as consultants on investment guidelines. The hiring of W. D. Scott meant that the major effort went into building an institution rather than into settling policy. The administrative issues were much less demanding politically and intellectually than the policy questions, and in any case foreign consultants were in a weak position to aid resolution of one of the country's most divisive political questions.

A committee of senior expatriate officials, led by Public Service Commissioner Norm Rolfe and including the head of GFEP and Tony Voutas from OCM, recommended in February 1973 the establishment of a National Investment and Development Authority, without specifying its role very clearly. It was to incorporate the Investment Corporation and the Development Bank, and presumably to co-ordinate the government's contact with foreign investors. The Rolfe Committee Report was rejected, but OCM continued to have in mind the need for some organization to act as a "watchdog" on foreign investment.

W. D. Scott suggested the arrangements in the Philippines and Indonesia as possible models for handling investment proposals, and provided the services of a consultant, Tom Allen, who had worked on investment questions in the Philippines. On the fundamental policy question of whether conditions should be set to facilitate a maximum rate of investment (the established position), or the amount of investment to be had without generous incentives (the critique), Allen declared himself to be neutral. What he had in mind, he would say, was a control mechanism, a mesh. The gauge of the mesh could be narrow or broad, depending on the preferences of NIDA's operators.

Beyond the gauge of the mesh, there was dispute about whether the proposed authority should itself make policy on the terms and conditions that would apply to investments, or whether it would work within policy that was established in detail by the government. There was one view that the effective co-ordination of foreign investment required the authority to work within quite general guidelines (like the Eight Aims), and have substantial discretion in relation to the application of incentives to investment. This was the W. D. Scott/GFEP view through 1973, and OCM mostly went along with it, although early OCM draft proposals had policy coming from the CPO and NIDA reporting to Cabinet through the CPO. There was an alternative view: that it was undesirable for an organization that had intense continuing face-to-face contact with foreign investors to have important discretionary powers over the terms and conditions within which projects were to be operated. At best, it invited the organization to be lenient on the people who would become its only clients. At worst, it invited corruption. This view was held by the chairman and majority of the Tariff Advisory Committee, and by those academic economists who held firm views about the question.

A similar dilemma arose in relation to enforcement of investors' contractual and legal obligations. The Scott/GFEP/OCM group thought that NIDA would enforce contracts and legal requirements. This cut across proposals that were being developed by Peter Fitzpatrick under John Kaputin (then Minister for Justice) to establish a specialized enforcement unit within the Department of Law where, they thought, it would be in less danger of deviation from firm and impartial administration of the law. The fundamental difference between the approach to investment policy developed around NIDA and the positions formed in the Kaputin-Fitzpatrick and economists' critique was that restriction in the former case was to be achieved through the exercise of administrative discretion and in the latter case through laws of general application.

GFEP began to put draft investment guidelines and proposals for a National Investment and Development Authority to the Minister for Finance in about April 1973. They never seemed quite right, and the minister sent them back for redrafting on several occasions. NIDA was still on the drawing board when the Chief Minister announced that ministerial responsibility would be shifted from Peoples' Progress Party minister Chan to Pangu's Minister for National Development, Gavera Rea, as part of the February 1974 ministerial reshuffle. Soon after, OCM staff arranged for Allen to be made interim director of NIDA, with the task of preparing legislation that could get through Cabinet and be made to work. The National Investment and Development Act was finally passed by parliament in late 1974.

The Pioneer Industries Ordinance was repealed at the time the NIDA

Act went to parliament (having been in suspension for some time). The other major policy development signalled by the act was the prohibition of new foreign investment from some areas of business as specified in the Priorities Schedule.

The powers established by the act were to be exercised by the Minister for National Development and the NIDA board. The board comprised representatives from all agencies that thought they should be represented (plus, after a while, a businessman from Lae). But the act was ambiguous on many aspects of the role of NIDA. Not long after its enactment, the heads of a number of departments asked the Secretary for Law whether or not, under the act, NIDA had a policy role. The opinion was that it did not, but that it was a co-ordinating and implementing agency.

But the adequacy of this opinion depends on how policy is defined. NIDA had wide discretion on the choice of investor, the extent of local processing, location, and much of the detailed shape of each project, although it had to share its discretion with the operative department (usually Agriculture, Forestry, or one of the other arms of the Ministry of Labour, Commerce and Industry). It also controlled the Priorities Schedule, through which foreign investors were excluded from some activities. In reality, the board and minister of NIDA were perhaps the major focus of policy-making on foreign investment except for large minerals and petroleum projects, and except for the offering of incentives to investors. There was an early decision to have investment policy questions managed by an investment committee of Cabinet, but this committee was never of any importance.

Some sections of the act seemed to convey policy powers in relation to matters of incentives, but others made it clear that NIDA had no power to control other agencies. Other ministers remained responsible for the legislation conferring powers over the use of many major instruments of policy. For example, the Minister for Foreign Relations and Trade remained responsible for tariffs. The Minister for Finance remained responsible for the taxation statutes, and for bills appropriating money for the purchase of equity of provision of infrastructure related to an investment. These ambiguities were of some importance to the evolution of policy, as the Ministry of Labour, Commerce and Industry came to be very much more anxious to encourage foreign investment through the offering of incentives than were the other major ministries.

NIDA had a clear power to promote foreign investment under its act and it was very active in the exercise of this power, with several large and widely publicized missions overseas. This emphasis on promotion probably helped to generate the impression that new foreign investment was rather more important to what was happening in the PNG economy in 1976 and 1977 than was actually the case.

By mid-1977 there was considerable national consensus on policy towards large-scale mineral and petroleum policy. The same could not be said for policy on small- and medium-sized investments, about which there was considerable public disquiet. There had been a noticeable shift in the direction of more restrictive and onerous conditions for manufacturing investments with the cessation of the easy granting of subsidies and protection to uneconomic new investments, but there were strong pressures from the business community and some parts of the public service for a return of hothouse industrial growth. The government had been ambivalent about large-scale investment in tourism. It was not obvious that the administration of investment proposals was more efficient than in 1972, and critics claimed that the formation of NIDA had simply added another stopping place to the investor's journey through the government. The need to settle policy on new small- and medium-scale investments had never been sufficiently pressing politically to be given priority on a crowded policy-making agenda, and a major task was handed on to the second Somare government.

THE OWNERSHIP OF THE MEANS OF PRODUCTION

The colonial administration had cared little about who owned productive assets, at least after the removal of restrictions on "Asian" investment in the late sixties. It seemed urgent politically in 1972 to do something about the overwhelming concentration of urban assets (and less extreme concentration of rural monetary sector assets) in the hands of foreigners.

The situation contained the usual "localization" dilemma. Colonial Papua New Guinea was a mixed capitalist economy. The role of the state was larger than in most mixed capitalist systems. Nevertheless, the indiscriminate transfer of privately owned productive assets from foreigners into private Papua New Guinean hands would massively change the distribution of incomes and wealth among Papua New Guineans. Probably very few Papua New Guineans wanted the type of income and wealth distribution that was likely to result from such transfer. But the reality of the situation was not recognized clearly, possibly because there were few wealthy Papua New Guinean capitalists at this time.

As time passed, a few Papua New Guineans decided that rapid localization of business ownership should be attempted, whatever the consequences for income and wealth distribution among Papua New Guineans. Expression of this view was often coupled with the statement that there would be time to worry about domestic distribution when most productive assets were owned by Papua New Guineans. Strangely, in Papua New Guinea the "localize now and redistribute later" view came to be thought of as a "radical" position.

There was never a coherent Pangu or PPP or government approach to the transfer of business ownership. The nearest to it was specific Pangu policy related to the establishment of large state enterprises in air transport and banking, and to the exclusion of foreign-owned firms from some activities that were suitable for small-scale investment by Papua New Guineans.

Through 1972, a "Chief Minister's Office approach" began to emerge, owing something to older Pangu positions and also to the Faber mission, and to the economists' critique. The only function of large-scale, modern enterprises (Faber's "bureaucratic sector") was to provide services and financial resources for more general development. These large enterprises would be either owned by the state or owned by foreigners and operated within carefully defined policies or controls which secured the national interest. Other economic activity would be conducted within medium-scale enterprises operated by provincial corporations or other broadly based businesses owned by Papua New Guineans. For the remainder, small-scale businesses would be owned by Papua New Guinean individuals and groups.

The greatest emphasis was to be placed on small-scale individual and group enterprises, the "informal sector", especially in rural areas. This was to be encouraged partly by freeing the business environment from legal and other restrictions that had the effect of deterring Papua New Guinean involvement in business, and partly by restricting the operations of competing foreign business. Policy was implemented more or less in line with this general scheme in relation to the largest modern sector activities – mining, air transport, banking. But ambiguities arose in other areas in the rush to promote Papua New Guinean ownership.

During 1972 the impetus to the development of policy to promote greater Papua New Guinean control and ownership of business came mainly from the Office of the Chief Minister. But it was not long before initiatives were coming from many directions. The wide-ranging origins of these initiatives, and the very great importance of personal initiatives by politicians, made this a rather special area of policy-making, commanding an unusual degree of political interest. OCM initiatives in the early period included those based on Fitzpatrick's work on unwinding restrictions on informal business and company law simplification, and on Jim Fingleton's work on plantation acquisition (the latter in response to pressing political problems). Ministerial initiatives became increasingly important through 1973 and 1974, and included the restriction on expatriate coffee buying, the restrictive tendering for some government purchases, the lifting of constraints on the Development Bank's financing takeovers of foreign business, the five-year tax holiday for businesses owned by indigenous Papua New Guineans, and the Village Economic

Development Fund. In late 1975 Julius Chan required the Development Bank to change radically its lending policies, which effectively ended substantial lending to foreign business.

The total effect of these various initiatives to increase Papua New Guinean ownership of the economy was large and likely to expand rapidly over the course of time. The distributional effects of rapid business localization, and especially localization that involved public subsidy, were brought to the surface as an important political issue first within the trade unions. There was considerable criticism of the tax holiday in the 1976 Minimum Wages Board case. Largely in response to this, the government decided to remove half the tax holiday privilege with respect to takeovers of established enterprises.

The politically important question of policies on the ownership of the means of production was never integrated into the general framework of economic policy-making in the period from 1972 to 1977, although late in the period some of the connections between these two areas of policy had become apparent to political leaders.

PROVINCIAL GOVERNMENT FINANCES

The system of macro-economic policy evolved against the backdrop of intense political debate about provincial government throughout the period from 1972 to 1977. John Ballard describes in this volume the complex events through which the arrangements for provincial government were established. Beneath the dense fog of tensions between the national government and provincial leaders and the Constitutional Planning Committee there was considerable continuity in the conception of provincial government financial arrangements through the original CPC proposals, the 1973 agreement between representatives of the Chief Minister and the Bougainville Interim District Government, the December 1974 agreement between a national government team led by Finance Minister Chan and Bougainville leaders, the proposals considered by the Follow-up Committee (FUC), appointed by the Chief Minister to recommend on the content of an organic law on provincial government in the second quarter of 1975, the agreement in October 1976 between the national government and Bougainville leaders to settle the secession crisis, and the Organic Law on Provincial Government that was passed by the national parliament in 1977.

The early pressures for provincial government came mainly from the politically well-mobilized provinces in the Islands, particularly Bougainville and East New Britain. They were motivated by a strong desire for local political autonomy that had its origins in confrontations with the colonial administration in the decade before the establishment of national government. The Islands provinces were the wealthiest in terms of monetary sector activity and established government services, and their leaders were generally relaxed about the potential inconsistency between their support for both political decentralization and interprovincial equity in the distribution of incomes and services. The strong Islands influence within the government, and Pangu's long-standing sympathy with decentralization, meant that there were proponents of Islands positions within the government.

The dynamics of national politics had by 1973 turned the Constitutional Planning Committee, forcefully led by John Momis from Bougainville and John Kaputin from East New Britain, into the main centre of opposition to Michael Somare's national government. The CPC's critique of the national government was, in the context of Papua New Guinea politics, from a radical nationalist position which attracted considerable support from elite groups outside the House of Assembly and from some opposition United Party members and government back-benchers within the House. The proposals of the Constitutional Planning Committee were thus able to draw support from outside the Islands, even on a matter like political decentralization, which had once been mainly of concern only in the Islands.

Support for decentralization also drew upon widespread suspicions of what was seen as an expensive and parasitical Port Moresby and an unproductive and unresponsive bureaucracy in Port Moresby. This suspicion was strong within the colonial administration, and among officials based outside Port Moresby these attitudes led to demands for administrative decentralization, including decentralization of financial authority, without the establishment of provincial political bodies.

The issues of decentralization of administrative and political power were, in principle, separable from the issue of distribution of revenues between the national government and the provinces, and among the provinces. Taxing powers and national government grants to provinces could in principle be designed to achieve any desired distribution of revenues between the national and provincial governments or among provinces. But the decentralization and distribution issues were indissolubly linked in the minds of the leading proponents of provincial government. To them it seemed that the maintenance of provincial autonomy required automatic control of sufficient money to finance provincial activities, whether by way of taxation powers or guaranteed grants.

One problem was that the overwhelming bulk of national revenue was collected in a few provinces and in the national capital, so that the granting of major taxing powers (such as personal and company income tax and import duties and excise duties) to provinces would force a major redistribution of public expenditure in favour of wealthier provinces. It was clear to national government officials that provincial activities would need to be financed mainly from national government grants, although this was not accepted until late in 1976 by some leading advocates of provincial government in Bougainville and East New Britain.

Vexed questions of distribution would arise in any system of grants to provinces. The CPC supported the use both of "equalization" and of "contribution to revenue" criteria for allocating grants among provinces. Among supporters of provincial government, the potential for dispute between wealthier and poorer provinces was obscured by the simple expedient of asserting that the total amount of expenditure on provincial activities could be increased above their current levels to allow for the devolution of major taxing powers to some provinces simultaneously with increased national government grants for equalization purposes to others. This view was put strongly, for example, by FUC members, who favoured a set of arrangements that would immediately and substantially increase the amount of money spent on activities taken over by provinces. If such guarantees caused difficulties for the national government in the financing of its own activities, it was argued, so much the better: the national government would be forced to reduce its apparently unproductive expenditure on the Port Moresby bureaucracy.

The CPC report and the 1973 agreement with Bougainville had provided for many elements of a system of national-provincial government financial arrangements that were eventually implemented, together with a few that were not. The following fiscal resources had been recommended: limited taxing powers (notably powers to levy and collect some sales taxes and a produce tax); the proceeds ("derived revenue") of some taxes levied and collected by the national government (notably royalties and export taxes); substantial untied grants related to historical levels of expenditure raised in line with growth in total government expenditure; other grants, some possibly tied, at the discretion of the national government, including an element of equalization of services across provinces; and a Fiscal Commission to establish or to advise upon national government grants to provinces. These arrangements were modified and set into national government policy in a series of discrete steps, each taken in an environment of political crisis, between 1974 and 1977.

The Finance Ministry's interest in the evolution of provincial government financial arrangements was focused on the need to ensure consistency with the framework of macro-economic policy which was taking shape from late 1974. Above all, it was necessary to prevent the provincial government arrangements giving form to the widespread belief or hope that all potential conflicts could be resolved by increasing the total expenditure by governments in Papua New Guinea, whether through the exercise of major provincial taxing powers, national government grants, or other means. To this end, Finance opposed provinces having major open-ended taxation powers, guarantees on grants that implied a significant increase in real outlays by the national government, and unrestricted access to long-term loans. Other centrally important concerns were that the national government should retain final powers with respect to the terms and conditions of large investments, and that the national government should be able to withhold final power for financial management from provinces that appeared to be incapable of exercising that power responsibly.

The debates and negotiations on provincial government were mainly conducted among politicians or among officials acting directly for politicians. The political heat associated with the decentralization issue created a difficult environment for technical work by officials, especially expatriate officials. Some officials felt obliged to withdraw from work on planning provincial government arrangements, when criticized by political leaders. Many national departments took the view that the whole issue was so highly politicized and so complex that the safest and most comfortable course was to hope that provincial government would go away, and to continue work on more manageable matters. Accordingly, they were continually being caught unprepared by the march of political events.

The Finance Ministry could not take this attitude, since the disputes with Bougainville between 1974 and 1976 were over issues with immediate budgetary implications. An amount of money equal to expected receipts from mineral royalties (1¼ per cent of the value of production), in addition to payments to maintain established services, was appropriated for payment to the Bougainville Interim Provincial Government (BIPG) in the 1974 Budget. Finance Minister Julius Chan led the national government team which agreed in December 1974 that BIPG should receive the mineral royalties on a continuing basis. The national government received Finance Ministry and other advice in resisting BIPG demands for the trebling of works programme expenditure in Bougainville for 1975/76, a response that led directly to the crisis in relations with BIPG in May 1975 and to a coherent attempt to organize for secession.

Beyond these immediate pressures, leading figures within the Finance Ministry were in any case inclined to keep closely in touch with discussion of an issue with important long-term implications within their area of responsibility. They were attempting to build a system of economic policy-making that would be useful for a long time to come, and so were concerned to ensure to the greatest extent possible that the provincial government arrangements would not undermine that system from the beginning.

The politics of the provincial government discussion clearly did not allow the Finance Ministry to play a central role. Finance tended to be distrusted by supporters of provincial government because its national perspective required it to oppose some proposals, and also because there was little understanding of or sympathy for the technical bases of assessment that sometimes had to be applied to proposals by Finance officials. Accordingly, rather than attempting to lead in the more general discussion, Finance officials developed clear positions on the financial implications of the provincial government proposals. They also remained sufficiently close to political discussion of the issues to ensure that Finance advice was available to senior ministers at all critical decision points, and ensured that they were available and helpful to all participants in the provincial government discussion.

The negotiations between the national government and Bougainville leaders which led to the decisive agreement of October 1976 were co-ordinated administratively by two NPO officers, who saw their role as that of facilitating agreement with Bougainville. This often placed them in the position of asking Finance for further concessions on financial matters. Some concessions seemed to be compatible with the maintenance of the macro-economic policy-making framework, but others were not. By October 1976, a year of negotiations had led to agreement on all issues except the financial arrangements, upon which the parties remained a long way apart. Prime Minister Somare, in a bold personal stand that was fully vindicated by subsequent events, had decided that he would accept some cost in reaching agreement with Bougainville, but that the risk of a major fracture in economic stability was too high a cost. It seemed possible that the negotiations would fail at the last moment until the Bougainville leaders agreed to withdraw demands with respect to produce and income taxation.

Although the Bougainville Agreement of October 1976 was not negotiated explicitly as the basis of arrangements for other provinces, ministers from virtually all other areas thought that similar rights and guarantees should be given to all provinces. The 1977 Organic Law on Provincial Government, which under the Bougainville Agreement had to be approved by Bougainville leaders, subsequently enacted and generalized many of the financial provisions of the Bougainville Agreement. The Organic Law provided more detail on the role of the Fiscal Commission and more precise arrangements for guaranteed minimum grants. It also left open the possibilities, at the national government's discretion subject only to political circumstances, that different provinces would establish provincial governments at different times and that some might never establish them, and that different provincial governments could exercise widely different powers.

The Organic Law was better suited than earlier proposals to safeguard the national government's discretion to alter the interprovincial distribution of expenditures in future, and to preserve the framework of macro-economic stabilization policy. The taxation powers were restricted to relatively minor sources of revenue, and these were subject to the Minister for Finance's power to place reasonable limits on them. Policy with respect to financial arrangements for large-scale investment, most importantly large natural-resource-based projects, remained the exclusive responsibility of the national government. Provinces required the approval of the Minister for Finance to undertake long-term borrowing. The CPC's derived revenue proposals, relating to royalties and export taxes, had been modified to reduce the advantage that they conferred on wealthier provinces (although not Bougainville, which had already been promised the benefits of royalties of the mine). The minimum grants formula provided that the minimum grants to provinces should be adjusted downward permanently in any year in which the real value of grant aid plus domestic revenue fell. This removed dangers that would have been associated with any commitment to maintain the real level of provincial grants through a severe recession, left open to future governments the option of reducing total expenditure in the interests of more rapid reduction in Australian aid, and increased the options of future governments to raise the level of expenditure in poorer areas. The formulation of the minimum grants provisions meant that provincial governments would bear the cost of increases in wages and salaries at the provincial level and so gave them a common interest with the national government in the containment of costs. An Organic Law provided that the Fiscal Commission would advise the national government each year on the distribution of untied grants to provinces in excess of the guaranteed minima on criteria that emphasized interprovincial equity, from a total sum specified by the national government.

The commitment to decentralization was bound to complicate the national government's project and programme planning and to reduce its influence on development at the local level. The successful implementation of provincial government was clearly going to require a huge concentration of political energies and administrative resources, which would impose costs on development in other ways. Critics of the government said that it was unnecessary to establish provincial governments at all, or that too much had been given away; that political stability and economic development would have been served best by the government simply rejecting demands for provincial government and sitting out the subsequent political crisis. Quite apart from its huge domestic benefit in reducing political tensions, the settlement of the Bougainville secession crisis removed an impediment to foreign perceptions of political stability in Papua New Guinea that had affected the country's creditworthiness and attractions to private investment. Within the Finance Ministry the prevailing mood late in 1976 was one of great relief that after years of policy-making in crisis conditions, it had been possible to reach a political settlement that would not in itself undermine the general framework of macro-economic policy-making. Neither would it prevent the allocation of much of the growth in national government expenditure to poorer provinces, in line with the government's equalization hopes, should this be allowed by the politics of future national-provincial relations.

SOME CONCLUSIONS

The period 1972 to 1977 saw the emergence of all the pressures on economic policy that had been expected. Urban workers, relatively wealthy provinces, urban-based public servants, and Papua New Guinean business-men all demanded higher incomes and better services. The expected external pressures also developed, especially over the allocation of aid funds and the terms and conditions of investment.

These pressures tended to be resisted more effectively in the latter part of the government's period in office. Economic policy-making was a junior relation to the transfer of power, the Constitution, and the great political disputes for most of the period 1972 to 1977. Long-term questions of economic policy were neglected during a period of political crisis. But after 1974, relatively little ground was given away through new policy initiatives to pressure for unequal distribution. However, some earlier policy decisions, notably the tax holiday for indigenous businesses, were having larger effects with the passage of time. The greater readiness to hold the line in later years was assisted by the policy-making framework. General principles such as those articulated in the Eight Aims were given more weight when the consequences of policy decisions were clearer and when decisions were made by groups of people who had committed themselves to support of the Eight Aims.

The four policy areas that had seemed to be central to the framework through late 1974 and 1975 were being managed effectively by mid-1977. Budget expenditures in each successive year were determined by adding a few per cent in real terms to existing real expenditures, and this trend in public expenditure was consistent with careful projections of revenue and with steadily declining aid in real terms. The aid agreement with Australia and the mineral resources and copra, cocoa, and coffee stabilization funds were assisting counter-cyclical borrowing policies in making the steady trend in government expenditure possible. Exchange rate policy was being co-ordinated effectively with public expenditure policy and wages policy, assisted by the agreements on wages, by acceptance of a modest and steady preannounced rate of increase in total real government expenditure, and by the form of the guarantees on grants to provinces. The indexation arrangements for wages and guaranteed grants to provinces carried caveats that would be triggered by economic difficulties, which allowed the essential features of the framework to be preserved through severe externally induced recessions or in the event of government decisions to seek greater national fiscal self-reliance through radical reduction in the level of aid and government expenditure. The government's fiscal policy on resource investments had been tested severely and had survived. A large proportion of decisions on the allocation of financial resources with the government's control were being taken within the Budget Priorities Committee system (although some important decisions continued to be taken outside it), in the framework of an emerging National Public Expenditure Plan.

Looking at the period as a whole, it is possible to identify several different phases in the approach to policy. After the major announcements of late 1972, originating mainly in the OCM, had laid out the desired basic direction of economic development, there was a period of gearing up for the implementation of new programmes. Then, when some institutional preparation, such as the setting up of the CPO, had been completed, major weaknesses appeared in the political centre and also in administration. There was an unfortunate coincidence of high-level political dispute, high turnover of key administrative staff, and difficult economic conditions. It is striking when looking across the various areas of policy that 1974 very often stands out as a year of great difficulty, and a year when commitments were made that would seem in retrospect to be of doubtful consistency with the Eight Aims. After 1974, the system of economic policy co-ordination facilitated the greater progress towards stated objectives that was permitted by the reduction in political tensions. But throughout the remainder of the first national government's period in office, there was no pressure among politically influential groups for rapid and radical movement towards the implementation of any particular objective, with the exception of decentralization. But the story of the dark year 1974 should not be taken too far. In economic policy-making this was the year of the renegotiation of the Bougainville Copper Agreement, the successful conclusion of which led on to the establishment of greatly strengthened policy-making processes.

One problem through the whole period was the extraordinary load that had to be carried by a few key figures — in particular Somare and Chan throughout the period, and Voutas (until his departure from government late in 1974) and others in the OCM in the early years. The problem of limited effective hands to do the work explains some of the unevenness of the government's efforts in economic policy-making. The government was effective when it turned its attention to a problem and was then as firm as any government in the face of domestic and external pressures. But it was never able to give detailed attention to all important problems. At any particular time, everyone in government was aware that some important issues were being let slide. There was no alternative to dealing with some and hoping that it would not be too late to catch the others. There was uneven government commitment to some stated objectives, although in the busy years of the first Somare government it was seldom clear that inaction resulted from an unwillingness to act rather than from the difficulty of taking new initiatives in an environment that was overcrowded with problems requiring decision.

The first Somare government succeeded in establishing a system of economic policy-making that laid bare fundamental choices for political decision. It also handed on the prospects of stable economic growth, steady expansion of public expenditure, and very low inflation by the standards of well-managed economies elsewhere in the world, which would allow the new government to develop programmes in the reasonable expectation that their implementation would not be frustrated by changes in financial conditions. It established something of a national consensus on a degree of expenditure restraint that was consistent both with progress towards reduced dependence on Australian financial aid and with domestic economic stability. In the politically contentious area of minerals development, it had developed a consensus on the financial arrangements within which foreign enterprises would operate that was acceptable as a basis of expansion of the industry both to PNG nationalists and to investors. Outside the minerals industry, however, a stable policy on foreign investment had not been established. Some of the high hopes and ambitions of 1972 were gone, and it is possible that there was less commitment to ultimate goals of equal distribution. But gone too were some of the worst fears that independence government in Papua New Guinea would be incapable of enforcing national policy in the face of strong external and domestic pressure groups.

1 The Khemlani loans affair involved several Australian ministers seeking to obtain large loans through a barely reputable intermediary during 1974 and 1975. The Lockheed affair involved ministers and senior officials in several countries receiving bribes and their political parties receiving cash contributions from the American aircraft manufacturer Lockheed, in return for agreeing to purchase aircraft for their countries' national airlines from Lockheed. The essence of the Indonesian Pertamina affair was that a semi-independent state-owned authority was taken to the edge of bankruptcy by financial mismanagement and corruption, and in the process created a major financial crisis for the Indonesian state. In the Lynch affair, Australian Treasurer Phillip Lynch in 1977 was revealed to have been involved in real estate transactions which, while not strictly illegal, would seem to have involved the use of political status to advance private business interest, as well as conflict of interest.

Policy-Making on Lands

J. S. FINGLETON

Land is a people's basic natural resource, and the policy a nation follows in the administration of its land is of central significance, as both an indicator and a determinant of its social and economic development strategy.

LAND ADMINISTRATION POLICY BEFORE 1972

The system of land administration inherited by Papua New Guinea at self-government reflected the aims and attitudes of the preceding colonial administration. Papua New Guinea's subjection to colonialism occurred relatively late, and by this stage "it had become a widely accepted principle that the native inhabitants of a colony should remain governed by their traditional laws until they had 'advanced' enough to live under the metropolitan laws of the colonising power" (Sack 1973, p. 5). Thus the colonial legislation preserved the operation of customary laws, and statutory recognition was given to customary title to land in both territories.

Since colonization, land in Papua New Guinea has been typically divided for administration purposes into customary land and alienated land. Customary land comprises that land still occupied and used in accordance with the body of local customs. Measures, more or less effective, existed since the beginning of colonial rule to protect the customary land rights of the indigenous people, the main safeguard being prohibition of dealings in customary land with any body other than the colonial administration or other indigenes in accordance with custom. At self-government 97 per cent of land remained customary land, almost completely excluded from governmental regulation but coming increasingly under the influence of official attitudes and introduced values.

Alienated land was that land removed by the colonial administration from the incidents of customary tenure, either permanently by acquisition (in most cases a purchase, for trade goods or, later, cash), or in a few cases temporarily by lease. The law applicable to this land was found in local enactments by the colonial administrations, and in the applied statutory and other law of the metropolitan powers. In accordance with concepts and processes then current in European land law, interests in this land were created, regulated, transferred, and otherwise managed.

During the colonial period the basic development strategy was to take land out of customary tenure and bring it under the regime of introduced concepts and institutions. Until the 1950s this was done almost exclusively through acquisition of the land and legal cancellation of all customary rights. Land development policies were primarily concerned with creating institutions for encouraging economic enterprise by expatriates on the land thus alienated from customary ownership. Statutory safeguards did exist for protection of the vendors but, given an almost unavoidable lack of consensus between the parties as to the nature of these early transactions, it is hardly surprising that they came to be the subject of increasing resentment and attempted repudiation as their full legal effects became clear.

From the 1950s the first serious attempts were made to extend the introduced legal system, with its clearer definition of rights and interests, to customary land. Expanding European contact brought exposure to a new cash economy, Western education, technology, and values, and greater personal mobility. People looked to their land as their sole resource for meeting new demands and expectations, and customary land tenure, which had developed to meet different needs, came under pressure (Crocombe 1971). In response to these developments, legislation providing for the conversion of customary land to individual freeholds was introduced in 1964. Customary tenure was officially regarded as unsuitable for cash-crop production and an impediment to economic development. The administration's ultimate objective was to introduce a single system of individual registered titles to land, following the Australian pattern (Bredmeyer 1975). Associated with these attempts to draw customary land into the Western formal institutions was the increasing promotion during the 1960s of settlement schemes, where administration-owned land was allocated by lease to individual Papua New Guinean small-holders. These schemes were intended to relieve population pressure and increase the production of cash crops.

While the very small extent of overall land alienation at the end of this period (3 per cent) could be argued as evidence of a liberal land policy, this percentage was not uniform throughout the country. For reasons partly historical and partly geographical, the greater proportion of alienated land at the end of the colonial era was located in areas of strategic value — in and near cities and towns — and in areas of high economic potential. On the remaining customary land the legal *status quo* was preserved, either by design or by neglect, but new demands on this land were exerting increasing pressure on customary institutions which, lacking the time necessary for gradual evolution, were becoming unclear in their effects. The Australian administration failed to provide any village-level system of land administration that could have responded to these pressures (Oram 1970).

As the momentum for early independence increased during the late 1960s, the land administration system and the policies on which it was based were straining under the emerging political, social, and economic demands associated with the transition to independence. However paternalistic the colonial philosophy might or might not have been, the apparent consequences were a serious inequality in social and economic opportunities, in particular in the almost total concentration of economic opportunuties in the hands of a small expatriate elite. Such a situation was unacceptable to the rising group of nationalist politicians. Just as colonial strategies for development had been based on their land administration policies and laws, inevitably the nationalist attack on the perceived social, political, and economic injustices centred on land policy issues.

Partly in response to these pressures, the administration in 1971 attempted to improve the machinery for settlement of land disputes and registration of customary land. In introducing four bills to the House of Assembly, it conceded that the existing legislation for tenure conversion had "not been very successful". In seven years of registration of title to customary land, only 270 titles had been issued as a result of tenure conversion, and there had been no single registration of communally owned land (cf. Bredmeyer 1975, n. 4). Despite an enormous amount of urgent work in Canberra and Port Moresby in preparation and presentation of the bills, they were strongly opposed by many elected members of the House of Assembly and sections of the public, and finally were withdrawn. While issues such as individualization of the ownership of customary land and the wide powers to be given to group representatives to deal in land on the group's behalf figured in the public debate, the general opposition arose from lack of consultation with Papua New Guineans in preparation of the new policies.

Although the administration's land law reform scheme failed, it was not without consequence. The exceptional controversy that attended consideration of the bills in the House of Assembly ensured that land would be a key policy issue after the 1972 elections.

THE COMMISSION OF INQUIRY INTO LAND MATTERS

When Michael Somare's Coalition government began its first term of office, it was apparent to most observers that a conflict between the inherited land administration institutions and the aspirations of the new nationalist government was inevitable. Evidence of the priority given to land law reform was the appointment of a Pangu leader, Albert Maori Kiki, as Minister for Lands.

The Coalition government's policy was a synthesis of the election platforms of its members, in particular those of Pangu Pati and the People's Progress Party. In the compromise, Pangu's call for restricting sectors of the economy to Papua New Guineans and promotion of customary-based groups rather than individuals in economic enterprise deferred to the PPP's commitment to protection of private ownership. But in response to the Governor-General's reference in his speech to Australia's intention to introduce land legislation, Somare assured the country that "there will be no new land laws without a very extensive committee of inquiry to look at the new proposals and to seek the views of Papua New Guineans in the first instance" (*HAD*, 24 April 1972, p. 22).

Tony Voutas elsewhere in this volume remarks that one "technique used by the Coalition Government to achieve policy control was the establishment of various Commissions and Committees". He mentions the Constitutional Planning Committee and the Commission of Inquiry into Land Matters as the most significant, and says that "they were important in softening up the bureaucrats and the public to accept major reforms." By setting up the Commission of Inquiry into Land Matters in February 1973, the Somare government implicitly rejected the policies then administered by the Lands Department.[1] The four bills promoted by the department in 1971 had been discredited and withdrawn, and the expatriate departmental head was one of the first to be localized in 1972. The wide terms of reference given to the commission of inquiry showed that the Somare government was looking for major reforms in land policies and administration, to come from recommendations by a body of senior and respected Papua New Guineans after conducting detailed village-level inquiry.[2]

The ten commissioners were all Papua New Guineans. The chairman, Sinaka Goava, was an experienced and highly regarded magistrate from Hanuabada in Port Moresby. The commissioners ranged widely in age, occupation, and experience. National politicians were not included, but two senior local government councillors were appointed. Only one commissioner, Posa Kilori, had had experience in official land administration, but this was in district administration and not in the Lands Department. Two were government employees, while the rest included farmers, a priest, and a recently graduated lawyer. There was a general spread of representation through the country's regions. The choice of commissioners was apparently made by Pangu ministers, with Kiki, as Minister for Lands, taking the lead.

The supporting staff, by contrast, was entirely expatriate. The commission's permanent consultant was Alan Ward, who had been a strong critic of the 1971 land bills while a history lecturer at the University of Papua New Guinea. Rudi James, at the time Professor of Law at Dar es Salaam, and Ron Crocombe, then Professor of Pacific Studies at Suva, acted as visiting consultants. The commission's secretary was Bill Welbourne, a projects officer with the Lands Department, Nick O'Neill from the Department of Law was counsel assisting the commission, and I was borrowed from the Public Solicitor's Office to be the research officer. Both O'Neill and I had acted on behalf of Papua New Guineans in land claims against the administration while in the Public Solicitor's Office, under the guidance of a champion of Papua New Guinean land rights, the Public Solicitor Peter Lalor. So, apart from the commission's secretary, whose main functions were administrative, no official from the Lands Department was included in the commission or its supporting staff. The commission did, however, consult with all senior lands officials and the majority were co-operative, if often guarded.

During its period of inquiry the commission conducted 141 public hearings throughout the country, met with fifty-five witnesses in private hearings, and received 258 written submissions. In June 1973 it presented an interim report on alienated lands, and its final report contained 132 recommendations, some in considerable detail. The commission of inquiry reported on 26 October 1973, barely eight months after its appointment, and its report was tabled in the House of Assembly, debated, and taken note of on 12 November. The report stressed the fundamental importance of land as the basis of social, political, and economic relations, and treated all aspects of land administration as an integral whole. Just as the colonial land administration system had underpinned the colonial development strategy, the commission of inquiry saw that the new system must provide the vehicle for social, political, and economic reform. The report was based squarely on the Eight Point Improvement Programme, and in order to implement these new development objectives the commission of inquiry felt that it would be necessary to repeal and replace all the existing land legislation.

PREPARATION FOR LAND POLICY REFORMS

The general thrust of the commission of inquiry's report challenged the established system of land administration and asserted priorities that threatened the privileges of dominant commercial entities in the country which that system had protected. It also represented a threat to the aspirations of the emerging Papua New Guinean class of entrepreneurs. Mindful of these factors, and the obvious limitations on its ability to affect policy by a report it had no authority to implement, the commission of inquiry had been concerned about the processes for consideration of its report. Final authority for land law reform rested with the House of Assembly, but the many procedural steps short of presentation of a bill provided fertile ground for the report to be subverted. The commission of inquiry tried to guard against bureaucratic inaction by promoting the establishment of a special section in the Department of Lands to prepare policy submissions, draft legislation, and work out detailed administrative proposals on its report, and was successful in gaining Cabinet approval for the establishment of a policy-planning and research body in the Lands Department.

Shortly before the commission reported, Albert Maori Kiki was replaced as Minister for Lands by the leader of the Highlands-based National Party, Thomas Kavali. This was intended to upgrade the ministerial status of the National Party in the Coalition, and to free Kiki for the new portfolio of Defence, Foreign Relations, and Trade. In the first instance this change-over meant a loss of impetus in following up the report of the commission of inquiry, and the Lands Department delayed setting up the implementation branch. With the single exception of the acting departmental head, Aisaea Taviai, all senior officers were still expatriates. Pressure was brought to bear by questions in the House of Assembly, however, and in March 1974 the Minister for Lands was able to advise the House that the new Policy and Research Branch had been approved and positions were being advertised. A former member of the commission of inquiry, Posa Kilori, was made acting head of the branch, and I was seconded on the request of Kavali to provide legal assistance. Two Papua New Guineans and two expatriates were appointed to subordinate positions.

This small new branch was viewed with considerable suspicion by the established order in the Lands Department. The main personalities in the branch, though public servants, were recruited from outside the department and had been part of the commission of inquiry team. But the government's localization policy had weakened the resolve of the old order in the department, and by the beginning of 1974 new staff committed to the government's aims had been appointed to key positions in the general bureaucracy and could encourage implementation of the commission of inquiry's report.

The House of Assembly had taken note of the commission's report, but no attempt was made to have the government adopt the report in full. Although the commission of inquiry looked at land policy "as a whole", and sought to make all its recommendations consistent in order to form "the basis of a new national land policy", it recognized that implementation of the report would need to be undertaken in parts. Only limited personnel were available to prepare reform legislation, and land reform was only one component of the government's work programme and had to take its place among other government priorities. Nonetheless, some attempt was made to maintain a rational programme for consideration and implementation of the report as a consistent entity.

Priorities for land law reforms were set by the Minister for Lands, after consultation with his three main advisors, Posa Kilori and myself from the department, and the former permanent consultant to the commission of inquiry, Alan Ward, who was engaged as a part-time honorary consultant by the minister. These priorities reflected the apparent political urgency of the major land problems facing the government, and presumably the minister received counsel on this from the Chief Minister and Cabinet.

THE PLANTATION REDISTRIBUTION SCHEME

The former Australian administration had attempted unsuccessfully to recover undeveloped freehold land, and had also negotiated fitfully for the purchase of a few expatriate plantations which were under considerable local pressure, but the asking prices in these latter cases had exceeded the Valuer-General's valuations by up to three times. So seriously did the commission of inquiry view the problems concerning plantations that it produced an interim report only four months after its appointment, recommending urgent measures to defuse an explosive situation. These included the acquisition by the government without compensation of all undeveloped rural freehold and leasehold land and its redistribution with first preference to land-short people in the locality and, as a last resort, the power to acquire compulsorily for redistribution developed rural land in areas of land shortage.

In trying to moderate the popular outcry for return of land, the commission of inquiry itself appears to have been too conservative to satisfy the requirements of the Coalition government. The nationalist drive was gaining momentum in early 1974, and Papua New Guinea leaders, informed by the new staff of the Central Planning Office, were increasingly aware of the enclave that expatriate planters occupied.

Until the returns from Bougainville copper started to influence export revenue, cash-crop production clearly dominated the sources of national income. With the exception of coffee, most cash crop production came from plantation estates, almost entirely owned by expatriates. The total contribution to direct and indirect tax revenue was very small, and the greatest part of profits was being expatriated. Plantations were to be found in all areas of the country where land was cultivable, and there was a strong link between plantation ownership and foreign firms with control over marketing and transport. The new national leadership felt that to embark on independence with a dominant and pervasive sector of its economy under the ownership and control of foreign interests was not tolerable.

While controls might have been exercised by fiscal or monetary measures, the political climate necessitated a policy of transferring ownership to Papua New Guineans. This was most obviously essential in areas where remaining agricultural land was insufficient to meet the present-day subsistence and economic needs of a rapidly growing population. But lack of action had allowed resentment of expatriate ownership to increase and generalize, and there was a growing incidence of squatting and harassment of plantation management. The only final solution seemed to lie in the localization of all expatriate plantations. Such a policy was in line with the government's social and economic objectives, and reflected its faith in the ability of its people to develop the capacity to manage cash crops without reliance on foreign capital and skills. The Land Act 1962 provided that land could only be validly transferred with the minister's approval, the purpose being to prevent speculation in land. The minister's discretion was unqualified, and now assumed new significance, becoming the vehicle through which the new policy could be implemented.

The first step was the announcement by the Minister for Lands in January 1974 of Cabinet's decision that approval of plantation sales to foreign interests would be refused. To this general prohibition there were two exceptions: where there were special circumstances making joint ventures desirable under an approved programme for full Papua New Guinean ownership; and where there were overriding national considerations, for example the introduction of new technology, which would justify the sale. There followed a long series of meetings convened by the Lands Department, aimed at establishing the guidelines for localization of plantation ownership. Participation at senior level from the Office of the Chief Minister, the new Central Planning Office, the Departments of the Chief Minister and Development Administration, Agriculture, Finance, and Business Development, and the Development Bank reflected the wide range of issues involved in such a policy. The debate was clouded by the then unresolved question of what should happen to the property rights of expatriate plantation owners, for the citizenship issue and the property rights of non-citizens were still under consideration.

The departmental arguments seemed endlessly circular. There was general agreement on the need to start a programme for recovery and redistribution of properties in areas of genuine land shortage, but the more conservative departments (in particular Agriculture) saw overwhelming difficulties with a policy of eventual complete localization of plantation ownership. They judged that any redistribution of plantations, even in areas of land shortage, would be the thin end of the wedge, and so were loath to interfere with the *status quo*. They produced figures on expected production drop, management shortfall, and enormous training requirements, all of which seemed designed to scare Lands away from plantation localization. The Minister for Agriculture at the time, John Guise, did not endorse this scepticism.

We made great efforts in the Lands Department to accommodate views of other departments and arrive at consensus, but finally Kavali felt that he had sufficient support in Cabinet, and the department's recommendations were submitted. In June 1974 the new policies were approved, and in August of that year the House of Assembly passed the supporting legislation.

The major policy components of the Plantation Redistribution Scheme were for all plantations (with the exception of the new and heavily capitalized tea plantations and nucleus oil palm estates) to be brought under a programme for transfer of ownership to nationals. In so "nationalizing" plantations, preference was to be given to the former customary owners of the land where each plantation was situated. The manner of redistribution was to be determined by a body representative of the groups claiming to have been the former customary owners of the land, an approach reflecting the government's realization that for a permanent settlement of grievances the new indigenous ownership must be representative of the interested local groups.

Localization of plantation ownership was to proceed by outright transfer in areas of acute land shortage, but otherwise would be by gradually increasing equity acquisition. Valuation of plantations was to be calculated solely by reference to remaining income-earning capacity and not on the basis of market value. The new legislation gave the government a power of compulsory acquisition and set out a formula for assessment of compensation. The new group owners were to be required to pay for plantations the commercial value of the asset *to them,* taking into consideration the realities of the new use to which they could reasonably be expected in their circumstances to put the plantations. Acquisition of ownership and equity was to be substantially assisted by soft-terms government loan finance. So far as possible, consistent with all the requirements mentioned, productivity from plantations was to be maintained and improved.

Finance for mounting the Plantation Redistribution Scheme was to come partly from internal revenue and partly from Australian aid, both grant and medium-term loan, which was the subject of a special request to the Australian government. It was a strongly and widely held view, from the top national leadership down, that Australia had a clear moral responsibility to assist in the resolution of the serious alienated land problems it had left as a legacy to the new national government. But quite apart from this moral obligation, Papua New Guinea put to Australia a range of factors which in its view demonstrated the critical role of special Australian aid.

In the first place, an immediate injection of substantial capital was necessary to allow for the purchase of a number of properties coming under extreme pressure in land-short areas. Secondly, there was a heavy element of subsidy implicit in the government scheme. The aims of the scheme were as much social and political as economic, and the government was mindful of the results of the sale of "White Highlands" properties in Kenya where much of the land ended up in the hands of a small number of wealthy Kenyans. Heavy and unrealistic debt obligations would soon subvert the social objectives of the scheme. Further, the government recognized that it would have to allow for a drop in production, at least in the short term, as a result of the transfer of ownership. The government had its own strong reasons why payments to expatriate planters should be in keeping with their reasonable expectations. Obviously this would have the greatest single effect in gaining their co-operation, an essential requirement for a gradual and orderly transfer of interests and minimum dislocation of cash-crop production. It was accepted that a fairly long period of transition to national ownership of all plantations was necessitated by the heavy manpower demands in settling claims in the redistribution process and the general need to build up a management capacity to replace the outgoing owners. Acquisitions of an expropriatory nature would also undoubtedly damage the new nation's international image, to the detriment of investment and aid initiatives then current. In broad terms, Papua New Guinea asked Australia to cover by a special grant the difference between what planters (the great majority of whom were Australians) could reasonably expect to receive and what the new national groups could reasonably be expected to pay.

As far as payments by the local groups were concerned, it was apparent that many groups would depend heavily on government loan finance. This presented the PNG government with a further problem in that most plantations were concentrated in the best-developed areas of the country. Despite the seriousness of the alienated land problems, the inevitable consequence of their solution under the scheme would be to increase the benefits of areas already in a more advantageous position than the rest of the country. It was quite unacceptable to the government's development priorities, which favoured the less-developed areas, for substantial government funds to be directed to these comparatively prosperous areas. It was for this reason that Papua New Guinea looked to a special allocation of loan funds by Australia as a major component of the loan finance required.

The domestic political situation and the government's commitment to concentrate expenditure on the less developed areas thus made it essential that any allocation of Australian funds to the Plantation Redistribution Scheme should be clearly earmarked for that purpose, so that it would be isolated from the fierce competition for shares in general revenue allocation according to national priorities. In that the final recipients of the funds would be almost exclusively Australian, such a special fund would have seemed politically acceptable to both countries. To fail to identify and isolate any Australian finance would have the result of forcing the PNG government to isolate the funds, now knowing how much they represented of the global aid grant. Politically at the national level it would be quite unacceptable for Papua New Guinea to give funding of the scheme a high priority, no matter how much it wanted to do so.

In the event, the Australian government pressured Papua New Guinea into including the request for funds for the scheme in the general aid bid, availing itself of Papua New Guinea's new policy to avoid tied aid. Funding of the Plantation Redistribution Scheme was accepted by Australia as a suitable project and, one assumes, appeared anonymously somewhere in the aid grant. As was expected, in the distribution of funds under the Papua New Guinea budget, the scheme received only a modest allocation quite insufficient to launch it at the level that had been proposed.

After three years' operation of a scaled-down version of the original scheme, about forty-five plantations had been acquired under the scheme. These were carefully selected so as to give a national spread, but a case study by Tei Mark (1975) illustrates the vulnerability of the selection process to political pressures. Other properties had been bought by national groups under the guidelines of the scheme, but without recourse to government funds. Only one plantation, a soldier-settler block heavily in debt, was acquired by compulsory process. The ability to resort to compulsory acquisition, however, obviously put the government in a strong bargaining position.

The scheme was not without its problems, and certainly its critics. It was blamed for drops in crop production, but, significantly, these were confined to copra and cocoa, where the expatriate plantings were old and had been deteriorating for some years before the scheme's introduction. The scarcity of experienced staff available for supervision of the sensitive redistribution process among claimant groups caused delays, and lack of managerial skills in the new operators led to repayment difficulties. Despite these problems, the basic objectives of the government's policy were never seriously challenged. The scheme received the general support of those groups most aggrieved by expatriate plantation ownership, and there is no doubt that it enabled the government to recover the initiative out of the dangerous emergency facing the country only three years previously.[3] In its initial stages it was clear that a rapid transfer of some plantations was essential as an act of good faith by the government to people who had long since given up hope for resolution of their problems through the normal channels. Perforce, economic considerations took a back seat to political and social exigencies as the government strove to gain credibility. Once the government had retrieved the initiative, it was possible to give economic objectives their rightful position in the scheme.

At the close of the Somare government's first term a greater willingness to commit resources, in particular skilled manpower, to the scheme became apparent. The government set up the National Plantation Management Agency to act as a bridge in the management of plantations acquired under the scheme during their transition to full local ownership and control, and a plantation management training course was started to which persons were nominated by the new owning groups.

A final point should be made about the first three years of the scheme's operation: all the plantations transferred to local groups under the scheme were transferred *as plantations*. As its name suggests, it was originally envisaged by the Plantation Redistribution Scheme that many properties, particularly in areas of land shortage, would be split up into individual holdings for members of the acquiring group, with the occupation and use being individual, although the title would be held by the group as a whole. This was consistent with the recommendations of the Commission of Inquiry into Land Matters on the types of interest in land which should be registrable. On the advice of the government's agriculture experts at the time, an initial loss of production from conversion of unitary plantations to small holdings was allowed for in assessment of the finance requirements and economic impact of the scheme. The scheme's policy did not, however, involve a commitment as to the most suitable cash-crop production unit.

The evidence of the scheme's operations suggests that by the end of 1977 the government had formed a commitment to the retention of plantation estates as such, albeit under national ownership. The institutional constraints of government and industry certainly favoured retention of the familiar form, but the opportunity was not taken during this time of reform to have a critical look at plantations as units of production. At the time a senior officer in the Department of Agriculture, Stock and Fisheries, Bob McKillop, criticized plantations as an inefficient form of agricultural production whose essential weakness was the low productivity of labour. He urged that the opportunity be taken under the Plantation Redistribution Scheme to convert these holdings to forms of organization that would allow producers greater identity with and control over the final product. McKillop's views were well broadcast in his department but apparently fell on barren ground. By 1977 the possibility of any radical restructuring of plantation operations seemed remote. A review of the scheme was under way, after which it was possible that the rate of acquisitions might accelerate to something like the level intended in the scheme's original conception.

SETTLEMENT OF DISPUTES OVER CUSTOMARY LAND

The colonial legacy of processes for land dispute settlement was no more satisfactory than that for dealing with claims on plantations. As with international conflicts, the main traditional method by which tribal land boundaries were adjusted was conquest.[4] At the risk of oversimplifying the complex of reasons for tribal fighting which led to the alteration of territories, acquisition by conquest can be said to have produced a rough measure of social justice in that the larger groups with greater members supplied their requirements for expansion by annexing the lands of their less populous and less powerful neighbours. Alliances were made and broken, and boundaries shifted with fluctuations in the balance of power.

This aspect of customary practice was not afforded legal recognition in colonial law, being regarded as contrary to the "generally acknowledged principles of justice and equity". The official approach to land acquired by conquest was revealed by Max Orken, a former district officer who was at the time he wrote a senior commissioner of the Land Titles Commission, the body charged with the settlement of customary land disputes:

> I almost invariably found in favour of the group which could prove their occupancy and control over the subject area since the time of effective Administration influence. This was not an arbitrary step on my part. It was settled (if unwritten) Administration policy to act in this way, and from the point of view of the practicabilities of the situation, it is difficult to criticise. Surely, in the name of common sense, a start must be made at some specific time and what better time to select than the time of effective Administration control, i.e. when tribal fighting has been put down, census taken, missions and private enterprise permitted to come into the area and, in general, when *pax Australiana* was established and recognised? [Orken 1974, p. 147]

Despite Orken's appeal to (Western) layman's logic, such an approach *was* an "arbitrary" element of "pacification" and imposition of the white man's institutions, rather than a process for determination of claims according to their merits. The same author admitted that it sometimes led to hardship for groups, but he seemed to regard this as the price of progress.

The problem with this approach was that it did not lead to the effective settlement of land disputes. The fundamental reason for its failure is expressed in Peter Sack's summation of "primitive law" which, he says "is not a battle between right and wrong where one side has to win and the other to lose; primitive law is not an attempt to establish the higher order of justice, its aim is to maintain and to restore social balance. This is why there is and can be no finality in primitive law. There are no binding decisions: primitive law is an endless series of compromises, each side trying to get the best possible deal, a dialogue which can be reopened at any time" (Sack 1973, p. 18). But this still does not solve Orken's problem about the "practicabilities" in finding a solution, and Sack concluded that "primitive law and the primitive group as a political unit have to be destroyed and a colony has to become a state before a Western type of law can begin to rule" (ibid).

Entry into the new way of life and access to its institutions were exerting pressure on customary law and practice, which had evolved to provide for different needs. In communities with a fairly long history of contact with the colonial administration and introduced values, a period for development of customary law in response to the new needs and demands had been available. In the areas more recently subjected to the incursions of foreign values, mainly the Highlands districts, such a period for evolutionary adjustment was not available. In these areas the tensions consequent on rapid change manifested themselves in increased levels of tribal fighting, a recourse to the only "valid" mechanism for handling conflict — valid to the protegonists, but illegal under the new rule of law.

On 20 December 1972 the Chief Minister appointed a Committee to Investigate Tribal Fighting in the Highlands Districts. In the light of increased fighting in the Highlands over the preceding three years, the government stated its "genuine concern . . . that the situation might deteriorate to the stage where the Government could no longer effectively administer parts of the Highlands, without the use of excessive force" (PNG 1973a, p. 1). In its report of May 1973, the committee noted that "most of the fights are connected with disputes over land". Pressures on land, created by population increase and the redefinition of land rights for cash cropping, had produced high levels of anxiety and uncertainty and the undermining of traditional authority (pp. 4—5). In relation to the settlement of land disputes, the committee concluded that the introduced system had never worked (p. 6), and recommended in place of the Land Titles Commission machinery a decentralized system of village-based courts with wide powers to "dispense justice based on local customs and sanctions and which will have the full legal backing of the Government" (p. 7).

With the Land Titles Commission lacking credibility and virtually inoperative by the end of 1974 as a result of retirement of commissioners, and with the number and gravity of land disputes increasing, reform in this area was an obvious government priority. In 1975 Kavali, the Minister for Lands, adroitly steered through the House of Assembly the Land Disputes Settlement Act. Despite the crucial nature of the bill, it was not accompanied by the intense media-supported discussion and controversy which had attended the passage of the scheme of legislation relating to plantation redistribution — a pithy comment on the preoccupations of certain interest groups.

The new act followed the recommendations of the commission of inquiry in close detail. In an attempt to balance the flexibility of the traditional open-ended and temporal settlements with new demands for a clearer definition of land rights and a degree of finality of settlement results, the act established a three-tiered process of mediation, arbitration, and appeal. Mediation is conducted by a land mediator, whose primary obligation is to promote the settlement of disputes by agreement between the parties. At this level, the new machinery reflects the traditional open-ended nature of dispute settlements, with the added important novelties that the process is conducted within the framework of the official system, and the result is recorded for future reference.

Where mediation had not been successful in reaching a settlement, a dispute can be brought before a local land court. This court is chaired by a land magistrate, and has membership from land mediators for the area involved in the particular dispute. At this level, also, the dispute-settlement machinery is flexible, and the local land court may make a wide range of orders which allow it to relate the decision specifically to the root cause of the dispute. Its jurisdcition and powers are designed to promote compromises which restore the social balance. Having vested such a representative body with wide functions, powers, and duties, the act gives only restricted rights of appeal from the local land court, to the provincial land court.

The Land Disputes Settlement Act is an attempt to balance traditional flexibility with the increasing need in some areas for greater certainty in land rights, by providing for dispute settlement at different levels which reflect the gravity of the dispute, and for determinations of ascending conclusiveness depending on the degree of finality required of the settlement. In a final rejection of the legalistic approach to the settlement of disputes over customary land, legal representation is excluded from all stages, except in limited cases on appeals to the provincial land court.

The administration of the act is decentralized, with district land disputes committees being responsible for declaring Land Mediation Areas and appointing land mediators. Provincial and local land courts have been established in every province, but otherwise there has been no attempt to cover the country. In many areas traditional dispute settlement authorities are still able to handle disputes satisfactorily, and official mediation is only introduced where there is a clear need and popular demand for it.

After its first two years of operation, as was to be expected, the new machinery was having most impact in the five Highlands districts. It was not expected that the act would be able to do much about disputes that had escalated over the previous years into almost institutionalized hostility. Indeed, in order to prevent the act being brought into disrepute through the inability to apply to long-established conflicts measures designed to take up disputes at an early stage and channel them into formal processes, the act made special provision for such disputes to be withdrawn from the ambit of the act and dealt with by executive regulation or order. At the end of the first term of the Somare government, harsher measures were being proposed to suppress such conflicts. Of their nature they invite dramatic treatment from the media, but little publicity was being given to the success the new measures were having in stopping land disputes from becoming headlines material.

The new act was being well received by the public and administrators, and its contribution to land peace in some Highlands areas was impressive. The act was described by the Chief Justice, Sir Sydney Frost, in 1976 as one of the three most important laws passed by the government during its first term.[5]

THE CONSTITUTION AND LAND RIGHTS

During the period leading up to independence a difference of opinion emerged between the Chief Minister and some members of his Cabinet on the one hand, and the Constitutional Planning Committee (CPC) on a number of key issues. One of these issues was citizenship — the qualifications for automatic citizenship and naturalization. Intrinsically tied up with citizenship was the question of property rights.

By far the most contentious aspect of the debate over property rights which raged during this period was the effect that the constitutional provisions would have on the property rights of expatriates, in particular plantation owners, who were at the time considering the advantages and disadvantages of applying for Papua New Guinean citizenship. The Australian Minister for External Territories, Bill Morrison, had pre-empted any real test of commitment to Papua New Guinea through renunciation of Australian citizenship by announcing that recovery of Australian citizenship would be readily available to any Australians who took out Papua New Guinean citizenship. Clearly the effective tests now had to be applied by Papua New Guinea.

The CPC's approach was to confine important constitutional safeguards and privileges, particularly in relation to property rights, to citizens, and to deny the benefits of those protections to expatriates by requiring eight years' residence *after* Independence Day as a qualification for naturalization. The Chief Minister and other ministers and members reflected a vocal body of public opinion in seeing these proposals as unduly harsh, and branding them as racist.

It looked for a time during the debate on the Constitution as if the government did not intend any restrictions to be imposed on the rights of naturalized citizens *vis-a-vis* automatic citizens. At the last minute Thomas Kavali proposed an amendment to the draft Constitution which would have the effect of suspending the enjoyment of the property right protection by naturalized citizens for a period of five years after Independence Day. Having lost the battle on delaying naturalization, the CPC members adopted this amendment, and after a long and bitter debate (Wolfers 1977, pp. 371—76), it was accepted by the Constituent Assembly. Despite endorsement of the amendment by a joint government parties meeting, People's Progress Party ministers and members absented themselves from the chamber during the vote, and defections by opposition members to support the amendment were crucial in the result. The effect was that while expatriates could gain citizenship by naturalization immediately after Independence Day, they did not gain the benefits of the constitutional protection of property rights for a further five years. They did, however, have the same constitutional protection as non-citizens to the extent that compulsory acquisition of their property could only be effected in accordance with an act of parliament.

Regardless of the merits or demerits of this approach (some naturalized citizens calling themselves "second class citizens"), its effect as far as property rights were concerned was substantially the same as would have been the case under the CPC approach. Such a qualification was essential to the success of any measures for redressing the great imbalance in economic benefits between expatriates and nationals which existed at the time of independence. The most important consideration exercising the minds of most expatriates who were considering applying for citizenship was whether their existing material position — their property rights — would be safeguarded. Had that safeguard been afforded, then any test of commitment to the national goal in the Constitution of equality and participation would have been illusory, and government measures for social and economic reform would have suffered the constant upset of constitutional challenge.

Two years after independence, the predictions of "gross injustice" and "destruction of investment confidence", had proved to be totally unfounded. The constitutional provisions on property rights facilitate the creation of a climate in which greater social and economic equity are attainable, and upon such a base the welfare of any individual ultimately relies. The legal fetters on economic redistribution and social reform had been struck away, but the realization of these objectives depends upon the constancy of the government's purpose in wearing down other links with the colonial past.

The CPC sat during and beyond the period of the Commission of Inquiry into Land Matters, and made specific provision to implement certain recommendations by the commission of inquiry which finally appeared in the Constitution. Its recommendations on citizenship and property rights were designed to protect the operation of the Plantation Redistribution Scheme, and the Constitution excludes from the property rights protection parliament's power to enact a law for the recognition of state title to government land required for a public purpose. Again following the commission of inquiry, the Constitution provides that only citizens may acquire freehold land.

PROTECTION OF STATE TITLE TO GOVERNMENT LAND

The passing by parliament of legislation to protect the state's title to government-owned land was allowed for in the Constitution as an exception to the property rights protection, provided the state had a genuine basis for its claim that the land in question was owned by the government, and provided the land was needed for a particular public purpose.

At independence the government inherited all the problems associated with the manner in which customary land had been acquired in order to provide a development base. The government's strategy for the resolution of these problems had a number of aspects. Where alienated land was under commercial development, the general aim was to create a climate that promoted the transfer of equity and control in existing businesses to national interests. This was to be done by foreign investment controls, provision of finance facilities, and the giving of preferences and tax concessions, in addition to more direct measures of government intervention such as the Plantation Redistribution Scheme. So far as practicable, such assistance was to be concentrated on representative Papua New Guinean groups from the locality where each business enterprise was conducted. In this way national ownership and control of the economy would be expanded and decentralized and at the same time much of the heat could be removed from local land grievances.

The second aspect of the government's strategy was to return vacant government land to the original customary owners in areas of land shortage, and 220,000 hectares were returned in this manner. Much of this land had been acquired by "waste and vacant" declarations during the colonial period and was a source of bitter resentment which posed a threat to the credibility of the new nationalist government. But there still remained many areas of government land that were being used for public purposes but were tainted by early colonial acquisition. As hostility mounted over claims to such land, particularly land in cities and towns where educated people had ready access to the media, the government increasingly tried to buy its way out of trouble. A number of *ex gratia* payments around the K100,000 mark were made to the most insistent claimant groups, but predictably this served to increase the rate of claims and the amounts of compensation demanded.

These selective payments did nothing to produce a lasting settlement of the grievances. Instead of being used as a base for entry and continuous involvement in the new monetary economy (exclusion from which was in most cases the real reason for revival of old claims), the gratuity was either appropriated by the more grasping self-seekers in the claimant group for their own purposes, or scattered so thinly among the group members that it represented only a temporary and useless palliative.

In moving to arrest this irresponsibility, the Minister for Lands, Thomas Kavali, who had opposed *ex gratia* payments from the outset, succeeded in gaining Cabinet's approval for preparation of a bill which would enable the state to register its indefeasible title to disputed government land where that land was required for public purposes, and providing for the payment of limited compensation for proved rights extinguished as a consequence of that registration. In the press of new organic and other laws following on the Constitution, the preparation of this bill was delayed. Given its sensitive political nature and the potential for tendentious interpretation of its effects in an election campaign, it seemed a risky bill to attempt to bring in during the build-up to the 1977 national elections. The resentment over unsettled land claims was exploited by some anti-government candidates, but under considerable pressure the government maintained its resolution to refuse any further *ex gratia* payments and promised to bring in the new law as soon as possible after the elections.

Customary land owners are likely to approve and support the release of their land for development only if they are guaranteed continued involvement in the new opportunities and lifestyle which the development of their land affords. The Lands Department took steps together with other governmental bodies to see that instead of the once-for-all purchase of land rights that colonial administrations had employed, new development proposals contained preferences for the former customary land owners in the new business and employment opportunities and services associated with the proposed project. The government was also looking at ways of facilitating joint ventures with customary owners for the development of customary land in urban areas.

As a further step to recovering the national interest in alienated lands, Cabinet approved the drafting of legislation for converting all freeholds owned by non-citizens to government leases to be held under development conditions. As part of the law elaborating the constitutional prohibition on acquisition of freeholds by non-citizens, machinery had been provided for the voluntary conversion of freeholds to government leases. Full systematic conversion of all non-citizens' freeholds to government leases was a legislative priority at the finish of the Somare government's first term.

LAND ADMINISTRATION TRAINING

Under the colonial administration no comprehensive course existed for the training of officials in general land administration. Specialists were trained in surveying, valuation, and other technical areas, but these disparate disciplines were held together by a network of bureaucratic procedures and not by any overall philosophy other than that land was essentially an economic article of production to be exploited by virtue of, and in accordance with, the dispensations of a paternalistic central administration. The fact that land administration was separated into compartments of technical expertise largely explains the difficulties that the Lands Department experienced in attempting to adjust to the dramatic change in development strategies brought in by the Somare government. As a primary vehicle for conveying new social, economic, and political priorities into action, the department was sorely lacking in resources and for the first few years lurched about aimlessly trying to find direction.

The Commission of Inquiry into Land Matters declared its belief that "for too long land administration has held too low a place in the Public Service" (para. 11.8), and recommended the establishment of courses in land administration, giving the opportunity for theoretical study but emphasizing practical training. In 1975 the Lands Department set up with the Administrative College a ten-week certificate course in land administration, and in 1976 a two-year course for a Diploma in Land Administration was introduced at the University of Papua New Guinea.

A REVIEW OF LAND POLICY REFORMS AND THEIR IMPLEMENTATION

Those associated with the commission of inquiry were fairly optimistic about the prospects for implementation of its report in the climate of change promoted by the Somare government and reflected in the Eight Point Improvement Programme. Indeed, initial results were fairly prompt and encouraging. In mid-1974 the Lands Acquisition Act, Land Redistribution Act, Land Groups Act and Land Trespass Act were all passed by the House of Assembly, furnishing the government with the legislative basis for its plantation redistribution policy. The government moved immediately to acquire a small number of desperately pressed plantations, but general introduction of the Plantation Redistribution Scheme was delayed until the middle of 1975, when the extent of the Australia grant-in-aid was known, and when, as has been noted, a much scaled-down version of the scheme originally planned was begun. In June 1975 the Land Disputes Settlement Act was brought into operation to make available the machinery for settlement of disputes over customary land. It was at about this stage that impetus in implementing the report began to diminish.

From the latter part of 1975 until the national elections in 1977, only three minor land acts were passed, and they can hardly be regarded as important land policy reforms. The first was the Land (Wuvulu) Acquisition Act, which expropriated an expatriate-owned tourist development on remote Wuvulu Island, north-west of Wewak, which in the government's view had assumed heavy elements of land speculation, and fixed a compensation figure for claims and interests thereby abolished. Then in 1976 came the Land (Ownership of Freeholds) Act, which defined the forms of ownership to be regarded as freeholds, for the purpose of the constitutional prohibition on the acquisition of freehold land by non-citizens. The final act in this period was the Land Settlement Schemes (Prevention of Disruption) Act of 1976, which was prepared by the Lands Department after a request by a member of parliament and was introduced to parliament as a private member's bill. It allowed for the compulsory acquisition with compensation of the leasehold of a person in a declared land settlement scheme who was found by a court to have committed misconduct that had led or was likely to lead to disruption of the scheme. The act followed on a series of payback killings between ethnic groups on oil palm settlement schemes in West New Britain.

The preoccupation of politicians and legislative institutions with the Constitution and subsequent organic laws partly explains the loss of momentum in bringing forward land policy reforms and new land laws. But there was another, at least additional, reason for delay. The manpower available to promote the land policy reform programme consisted of Posa Kilori (until late 1975), myself, and our staff of three in the Policy and Research Branch. We also had assistance from Alan Ward, who made fairly regular visits as an honorary consultant, Nick O'Neill, then secretary of the newly formed Law Reform Commission, and Rudi James and Abdul Paliwala from the Law Faculty of the University of Papua New Guinea, but all these outsiders were available only when their normal duties allowed. The bulk of the work in preparing submissions to the National Executive Council (NEC), and following the lengthy processes through NEC consideration of submissions, instructions to the Legislative Counsel during the drafting of bills, presentation of bills and their debate in parliament, and final implementation of new legislation, had to be carried by the Policy and Research Branch, and its limited resources imposed a critical constraint on policy reform. In addition, under a cabinet system of government the participation and co-operation of all affected ministries is essential to the gaining and survival of any policy reform, and in the case of land administration this spread the net of involvement very wide. The Land Development Board, which had operated from the 1960s as a top-level planning and co-ordinating body, was defunct by mid-1973, and the new Central Planning Office had not immediately taken over a co-ordinating role.

Apart from reforms initiated in Lands, the Somare government was developing new policies on equalizing the distribution of government services and economic opportunities, preference to local business institutions, decentralization of planning and administrative functions, environment protection, and setting guidelines for foreign investment and major resource industries. To a large extent land administration policy underpins these activities, and depending on its manipulation can either promote or frustrate the desired progress.

It is a grand thing to make new policies, with all the attendant drama and rhetoric. But a conservative administration has one final defence — its own inertia. Despite the climate of change brought in by the Somare government, institutionalized obstructions seemed to be an inherent part of the whole machinery of government. In the first place there was the sheer size of the public service, which was bound to make any government, particularly a government of change, unwieldy. Secondly, notwithstanding moves to politicize and localize the public service, most expatriate officers, working in a system that reflected their own imported values and processes and in which they were experienced, were resistant to change. Replacement of senior personnel by Papua New Guinean and some hand-picked expatriate officers certainly improved the situation in many key areas, but as far as implementation of new policies was concerned, the resilience of middle-level operators was a constant threat to sustained reform.

In addition to these general constraints, there were the traditionally conservative arms of government to reckon with, and in this respect the Department of Law (later Department of Justice) must be singled out for special mention. Land administration is an area of government in Papua New Guinea where policies depend largely on legislation for their effect. In this respect, land policy may be distinguished from economic or agricultural policy, for example. Land policy reform, therefore, necessitated legislative reform, a fact that was apparent to the Commission of Inquiry into Land Matters, which saw adoption of its report as requiring the replacement of all current land laws. The Crown (later State) Solicitor's Office of the Department of Law employed lawyers in its Property Advisings, Conveyancing, and Property Litigation branches. During the later part of the period under consideration, reforms that clearly fell within the responsibility of the Lands Ministry were subject to almost constant obstruction, during introduction and later implementation, from certain government law officers in these branches. Government lawyers will argue, of course, that it is their duty to protect the state against the possibility of litigation, and they certainly brought to bear a lively imagination regarding the risks involved in any proposed course of action. In keeping with the Australian practice, they also maintained the provision of legal advice to the government as their exclusive entitlement. A major problem was, however, that when Lands Department officers sought advice or assistance from the Law Department in accordance with this requirement, the replies were frequently negative, non-responsive, or dismissive. A lawyer giving that sort of service would not last long in private practice!

Having witnessed the emergence of this trend from my position in the Lands Department, I cannot help concluding that some of the legal officers concerned were simply hostile to the policy changes emanating from the department. They certainly demonstrated an appalling lack of touch with the current political, social, and administrative realities of Papua New Guinea, which is hardly surprising when it is considered that some of the people concerned seldom left the theoretical cosiness of a Port Moresby office. Nor, as might have been expected, did this indifference diminish as senior positions in the Law Department were localized — rather, the contrary seemed to be the case. Some Papua New Guinean lawyers showed signs of succumbing to a Western notion that law is a technology separate from its social and political context. Experience in Western and developing nations alike shows that such an artificial separation can only lead to law being increasingly dissonant, or at best irrelevant, to people's needs.

I should hasten to add that the statutory bodies within the administrative embrace of the Law Department were striking exceptions to my general remarks, and considerable assistance was given in the formulation of policy by the Registrar-General, staff of the land courts secretariat, and the Law Reform Commission. Nor were lawyers in general so inflexible. The two legislative counsel brought to bear considerable versatility and experience in the drafting of the new land legislation. The Law Faculty at UPNG and other lawyers were used by the Somare government in the promotion of its new goals in land and other areas.

To the extent that new policies were successfully translated into action, direction was maintained only as a result of a constant campaign of attrition against the bureaucratic monoliths. This required personal attention almost to the last detail of implementation, and even then continuous review of performance was often necessary to prevent a slide back to the previous position. As more reform legislation was introduced, the available energy was increasingly tied up in overseeing its operation. This was, I feel, the main reason why the drive that characterized the first eighteen months of work on implementing the commission of inquiry's report started to dissipate in late 1975.

In so far as the impetus was maintained through this period, a large share of the credit is due to Alan Ward, based at La Trobe University in Melbourne. He made an important contribution in making himself available to visit Papua New Guinea at the minister's request to conduct research together with Lands Department officers, hold meetings, and prepare papers and outlines of NEC submissions. The follow-up work was carried out by the Policy and Research Branch, but Ward had the happy talent of being able to get things moving.

It is only fitting to conclude these personal comments by paying tribute to Thomas Kavali, the Minister for Lands during the most energetic period of land policy reform. Albert Maori Kiki, the Lands Minister until late 1973, played an important role in the establishment of the Commission of Inquiry into Land Matters, and in events during the inquiry, in particular the consideration of its Interim Report on Alienated Lands. But it was Kavali who handled the contentious plantation redistribution policy and laws, facing attacks from its expatriate critics which sometimes bordered on hysteria. He faced further onslaught over his amendment to the constitutional provisions on property rights protection, which was critical to the government's promises of wealth redistribution. He also steered the sensitive bill for settlement of disputes over customary land through the House of Assembly. In all these matters he acted with resolution and showed shrewd political acumen. His creation of the National Party shortly before the 1971 elections was one of the crucial factors in the formation of the Coalition government, not only in helping Somare get the numbers, but most significantly in giving the new government a credible base in the conservative Highlands. As leader of one of the three Coalition parties, he developed considerable influence.

After Kavali's dismissal in February 1976,[6] the Prime Minister assumed the Natural Resources portfolio, which had recently been established to combine Lands with the Office of Minerals and Energy, and he continued to hold it until the 1977 elections. Not only did Lands have to take its place among all the other commitments of the Prime Minister, but it also had to compete for attention with the more glamorous mineral and oil exploration activities. This was another reason why land law reform drifted into the wings.

Perhaps, after the first fever of activity, it was as well to have a period of consolidation. After a time of rapid localization in the Lands Department, many fairly young Papua New Guinean officers were still finding their feet and gaining confidence in senior and demanding positions. The remaining major areas of reform — registration of title to customary land, and the complete overhaul of the laws concerning the administration of government land — were certainly daunting. The slackening-off period did allow for research to be done in the former delicate area, while the introduction of provincial governments in 1977 was going to have important implications for land administration. An encouraging sign for the future was that by 1977 the National Planning Office, under the leadership of Charles Lepani, had elevated the role of land administration to a central position in the planning process. There was little doubt at the end of the Somare government's first term of office that the report of the Commission of Inquiry into Land Matters had maintained its integrity as the basis for land law reform, and that the return of a Somare-led government would see its continued implementation.

In countries with a long history of evolving political institutions, the activities of governments, no matter what their complexion, tend to form a continuity and to be reasonably predictable. For a nation newly independent from the dictates of colonialism, the easy course is to maintain continuity with the inherited policies and institutions. In the short term this may maintain stability, but where serious inequalities are entrenched in the existing order then more and more does it become necessary to sustain that order by force. The more ambitious course is to try to reset priorities and reform institutions, in order to redress inequalities. Such a course destablizes the existing order, and does so intentionally, as a necessary factor in the rearrangement of priorities. The Somare government set out in 1972 to redirect Papua New Guinea's course, and land policy gave its weight to the tiller. Towards the end of its first period in office, critics were accusing the government of having lost this direction, but so long as the government of whatever political make-up remains committed to the land policy reforms under way by 1977, and sees those reforms through to completion, no fundamental loss of direction will be possible.

ACKNOWLEDGEMENTS

I am grateful to John Ballard, Nigel Oram, David Hegarty, Bill Standish, Theo Bredmeyer, Bob McKillop, and Alan Ward for comments made on earlier drafts of this paper, and to Nick O'Neill, who provided information on the establishment of the Commission of Inquiry into Land Matters.

NOTES

1. For the sake of convenience, the term "Lands Department" is used throughout this paper to denote the department responsible for land administration, which was called during the period under consideration Department of Lands, Surveys and Mines, and later the Department of Natural Resources. Similarly, the terms "Lands Minister" and "Minister for Lands" are used to denote the minister responsible for land administration, who was called during this period Minister for Lands and Environment, then Minister for Lands, and finally Minister for Natural Resources.

2. John Ley, then House of Assembly Counsel, made an important contribution to the establishment of the Commission of Inquiry into Land Matters. He drafted the motion to set up the commission of inquiry, which was passed by the House of Assembly on 27 June 1972. He also drafted, together with Nick O'Neill, the commission of inquiry's terms of reference.

3. Field staff of the Division of District Administration had prepared a list in 1974 which showed that around the country some sixty properties were illegally occupied, either totally or partly, and another forty properties were threatened with occupation. On 19 August 1971, East New Britain District Commissioner Jack Emmanuel was murdered while in the company of a police party summoned to remove a large group of Tolais occupying Kabaira Plantation under a claim of right.

4. Crocombe points out that "warfare was seldom undertaken with the overt purpose of acquiring land, but adjustments in population or land boundaries often occurred as a result of warfare" (Crocombe 1971, p. 22, n. 18). Other, peaceful, methods of territory alteration included incorporation of smaller neighbouring groups and land grants negotiated between groups. These depended on the degree of cordiality of relations between the groups.

5. The Chief Justice made his remarks in welcoming newly admitted barristers and solicitors to the National Court. The other legislation he mentioned was the Village Courts Act 1973 and the Business Groups (Incorporated) Act 1974, which latter act copied the Minister for Lands' Land Groups Bill 1974 in close detail.

6. In the Cabinet reshuffle in December 1975, Kavali kept his Lands portfolio, which was extended to take in Minerals and Energy in a new Ministry of Natural Resources, but Iambakey Okuk, the deputy leader of the National Party, was transferred from his Transport portfolio to Education. Under pressure from Okuk, Kavali spoke out strongly against the Prime Minister and the reshuffle and, after they refused to resign, both were dismissed from the ministry.

Agricultural Policy-Making

R. F. McKILLOP

Agricultural policy during the first Coalition government often appeared to be an obsession among Papua New Guinean politicians. For example, the ministerial post assumed a status that made it keenly sought after by the most senior politicians, the government's publicity suggested that it was giving increased priority to agricultural projects, and the Department of Agriculture, Stock and Fisheries was in fact given first priority in the allocation of new resources by the Budget Priorities Committee.

In order to examine policy-making in agriculture we must first consider the meaning of *policy*. Traditionally policy has been thought to represent the matters of principle or objectives which politicians and organization executives decided were desirable by a process of rational decision-making. If we accept this view, then we need only look at the decision of formal policy-making bodies such as Cabinet or the Agricultural Standing Committee in order to understand the policy-making process; but an examination of policy-making in real organizations proves this an inadequate explanation. A wide range of actors appears to influence the outcomes of decisions or commitments which might be thought of as policy. As Hal Colebatch points out in his paper in this volume, actors at the local level may make a series of "micro-decisions", which are reinforced by "non-decisions" further up the line, to bring about a major change in the commitment of important resources. Thus we may view policy in a broader context where policy-making is the outcome of actions which serve to promote a movement away from existing patterns of commitment, while policy-reinforcing decisions are those that serve to reinforce existing patterns of commitment. It is this perspective that will be applied to an examination of policy-making in agriculture during the period 1972–77.

The discussion here is confined to agricultural policy as seen from within the structural framework of the Department of Agriculture, and concerns the extent to which new policy initiatives were achieved during the period 1972–77.

AGRICULTURAL POLICY-MAKING IN DEVELOPING COUNTRIES

The available literature points to a widespread concern about the effectiveness of agricultural policy decision-making and programme implementation in developing countries. Part of the problem lies in the nature of agriculture itself, which is intolerant of administrative inefficiency and is very complex (Joy 1967). The range of policy instruments relative to agriculture is large, and there are differences in agricultural techniques which are appropriate to different areas and even to individual farms. These demands of agriculture call for great flexibility in the implementation of programmes and make co-ordination especially difficult. It is therefore not unexpected that the agricultural sector usually has significant shortfalls in policy implementation (ibid, p. 5). Extension services, which are given the responsibility for implementation of agricultural policies, are frequently criticized for lack of effectiveness and efficiency. In Africa extension services have been said to suffer many deficiencies, summarized as lack of high-level manpower, poor attitudes among public servants, lack of integration and co-ordination, and inappropriate structures (Schulz 1977). In part these problems lie in the origin of the services which were introduced by the colonial powers and have grown out of colonial development strategies.

As new governments have come to power and new policy initiatives have been announced, there have been frequent attempts to change the structure of agricultural departments or to introduce new organizations. Extension services, for example, are frequently restructured. Examining the rural development agencies of Kenya, J. R. Moris (1972) notes that there is a wide and complex range of agencies involved in programmes. In Nairobi the overall complex of institutions, specialists, and services for rural development "has reached the threshold of self-sustaining interaction", but "the attention of the Nairobi-based administrators is becoming involuted because of the sheer complexity of the many different agencies and interests caught up in this interaction. It is not stretching the point to say that most rural development initiatives in Kenya are launched from Nairobi; many never leave Nairobi" (ibid, p. 113).

An important point made by Moris is that although there is an increasing trend towards centralized authority in East African administration, very little rural development activity, as opposed to policy, is initiated, shaped, or controlled by the formal plannning structure. Thus, although national officials at the centre spend considerable energy on policy formulation, their decisions do not necessarily influence the activities of local officials.

Looking at the changes in post-war agricultural policies in Jamaica, Carl Stone (1974) notes that the policies have evolved from incrementalist strategies of change. However, more radical changes have taken place in the wider society — there has been a decline in the influence of the planter class, corporate estate agriculture has become non-viable, new parties have come to power under populist banners, and there has been a national economic crisis. The minor changes that have occurred in agricultural policy under an incrementalist approach have not matched these changes. Stone suggests that a situation has now been reached where a more "radical" and "structural change" approach to policy will be required before results are achieved.

Some other important themes emerge from the literature on agricultural policy. An "urban bias" thesis that the governments of most developing countries have endeavoured to maximize national savings at the cost primarily of rural consumption, through mechanisms such as low prices for agricultural products, has been promoted by Michael Lipton (1976). Dupe Olatunbosun (1975) argues a similar case for Nigeria, where, he says, agricultural development remains virtually unaffected by independence and it is the regressive pattern of distribution of public expenditure in favour of urban communities that has created inequality and social injustice where none existed before. Agricultural policies, especially pricing policy, have been concerned to keep down the price of food and raw materials for the growing industrial sector, and to increase the investment profits from trade in agricultural commodities to the benefit of the cities.

Another aspect of policy implementation that has received widespread attention, especially in East Africa, is that extension services themselves have a bias toward wealthy farmers and therefore operate to accelerate rural inequality (Leonard 1972). This bias has also been shown to exist in Papua New Guinea (McKillop 1975). Where national policies seek an equal distribution of economic benefits, this bias means that agricultural programmes are implemented contrary to national policies.

THE FRAMEWORK OF AGRICULTURAL POLICY IN PAPUA NEW GUINEA

The Department of Agriculture, Stock and Fisheries (DASF) was formed in 1946 by the Australian colonial administration (McKillop 1976). It followed Australian models with five divisions, each with its share of responsibilities, except that one division had responsibility for all agricultural extension. The post-war administration followed "dual policies" in agriculture, actively encouraging the plantation sector and strengthening DASF "to give settlers the full benefits of modern agricultural, scientific knowledge" on the one hand, and promoting a smallholder peasant proprietorship on the other (ibid., p. 23). The specialist technical and research sections of the department were primarily concerned with plantation agriculture, and plantation managers formed direct links with research staff. The local smallholders were the responsibility of the large extension service.

By 1972 DASF and its Australian structure were coming under increasing criticism. The Faber mission which reported to the government on development strategies in mid-1972 felt that the organization, methods, and objectives of DASF would need to be reviewed in order to implement their recommended strategies. They commented adversely on the preoccupation with establishing a broad-based extension service on the patterns of the rich countries of the world and with individual farm business profit irrespective of its relationship to national goals. They recommended a development strategy for the domestic food sector to concentrate on replacing imports and spreading on a wider basis for the growing of rice, maize, and legumes. However, they felt that the existing organization of DASF would give little hope for a noticeable impact on the domestic food sector for many years to come (Overseas Development Group 1973).

The difficulties of generating new policy initiatives from within the structural constraints of a colonial institution such as DASF go beyond those envisaged by the Faber team. Following the Australian pattern, DASF was a specialist and technically oriented department. There was no place for the generalist administrator; each section was led by professionals trained in a narrow technical field. Policy initiatives originated within the specialist sections and they therefore expressed the specialist or commodity structure of the department. In this there was a preoccupation with export crops such as cocoa and coffee. The structure effectively precludes an approach to agricultural policy that focuses on all aspects of the land-use system. For a start, land uses such as forestry and mining were the responsibility of other departments. Concern with land tenure and social aspects of rural development was also foreign to the department. It is significant that the very important debate over the future of plantations that emerged during the period was initiated elsewhere and barely penetrated DASF. The extent to which DASF was committed to the existing structure was evident as late as 1976 when the Assistant Secretary for Economics in the department appeared before the Minimum Wages Board to argue for rural wage cuts in open support of plantation interests (*Post Courier*, 11 March 1976).

The period 1972–77 was one of political and administrative instability, and officials at the centre were preoccupied with interactions and attempted administrative reform to cope with these demands. In 1972 DASF was still in the process of implementing a reorganization designed to further strengthen a regional structure first introduced in 1967. The reorganization was very much the creation of the director, W. L. Conroy, and based on anticipation that the future political organization of Papua New Guinea would follow a regional basis (Conroy, pers. comm.). It involved a rapid build-up of specialist staff at national headquarters, especially in economic research, training, extension research, and planning, and the creation of a team of technical experts in each of the four regional centres. A regional economist, who was expected to have a planning function, was a member of this team. For policy formulation the four regional controllers joined the headquarters assistant directors on the Agricultural Standing Committee, which met every six weeks and advised the director on policy matters. This committee was dominated by expatriate officials throughout the period.

The new Coalition government brought new actors into power who wished to change existing patterns of policy commitment. Among these people, implementation of more effective agricultural and rural development programmes had a high priority. The first Coalition Minister for Agriculture was Iambakey Okuk, from Chimbu District. Okuk demonstrated an enthusiasm to involve himself in policy initiatives, but was generally kept isolated by DASF officials. He frequently sought advice from academics and others outside the department. In the area of fisheries development he managed to establish a working relationship with a key research officer, which meant that he was well informed in this area, but this was an exception. On 23 February 1973 a frustrated Okuk took the initiative of calling a meeting of agricultural officials at Goroka and addressing them on his views on a number of topics including the slack attitude towards work by many of the staff and continued expenditure on research projects which he considered to be irrelevant to the country's needs.

During 1973 the expatriate director, Conroy, was transferred to another department and John Natera took up the position, becoming one of the first nationals to head a major department. He was, however, separated from other Papua New Guinean officers in DASF by a solid wall of expatriate technical experts, many of whom had held their positions for considerable periods. This tended to increase the power of the technical sections and orient the department further towards a commodity approach to policy.

On 27 February 1974 a Cabinet reshuffle resulted in Dr John Guise becoming Minister for Agriculture. The new minister soon made it clear that he intended to play an active role in policy formulation, and his status in the government as Deputy Chief Minister commanded some respect from officials. The minister was closely associated with Papuan interests which were politically vocal at this time, and the Papuan-dominated and Port Moresby-based public service was sensitive to their voice.

By 1974 it was becoming apparent that the department's regional structure was out of step with emerging trends for the future political structure of the country. The Agricultural Standing Committee appointed a working committee to report on the "abolition or modification of the Regional Organisation". In an interim report on 13 August 1974 the working committee reported that a regional structure was anachronistic, but that alternatives needed to be examined further. The committee also commented at length on the dangers of political interference in departmental activities at district level and emphasized the need for "loyal" public servants insulated from politicians. Such concern with organizational structure and policy-making machinery dominated DASF headquarters, and indeed all public service departments, throughout 1974—75. Officials at the centre undertook a continuous round of meetings to discuss future headquarters organization, leaving district officials largely to their own devices.

Some progress was made. By April 1975 the director announced a further reorganization of the department at headquarters level. The purposes of the review were said to be to:

(a) Rationalise allocation of Departmental functions at the national level to meet political changes and the development of a new constitutional framework for PNG.
(b) Cater for the needs of increasing responsibilities.
(c) Open up promotional opportunities to staff engaged in rural development work in field situations. [DASF circular 9/75]

Concern for a structure that would facilitate an integrated approach to rural policies based on indigenous land-use systems and social factors was notably lacking in this explanation.

In the reorganization, regional lines of communication were abolished and a process of delegating substantial powers to provincial officials was begun. Regional staff were to continue to act as technical advisers or trouble-shooters, but they would gradually be absorbed into national headquarters positions. A feature of the changes was that the four regional controllers were localized and designated area co-ordinators within a new headquarters Policy Review and Co-ordination Branch. This group held responsibility for contact with field staff, policy advice to the director, and direct liaison between the director and the minister. The branch had emerged as a result of moves by Guise to establish a policy secretariat within the department which would be responsible to him, but the Public Service Board would not accept this proposal and the branch was set up under the department head.

On 11 December 1975 the National Executive Council decided on a major restructuring of the public service. In this reorganization DASF was amalgamated with Forestry to form the Department of Primary Industry (DPI). However, the internal structure of the old department remained. Natera, in accord with some other department heads, successfully resisted a planned transfer of heads among departments.

Since its inception, the Policy Review and Co-ordination Branch has attempted to initiate a more systematic approach to policy formulation. Richard Doery, a former DASF officer, was recruited from the Central Planning Office to head the branch over the four Papua New Guinean area co-ordinators. A circular was issued in August 1977 to advise field staff of the policy-making machinery that had been established. According to this circular, policy recommendations were made by the Agricultural Standing Committee at its meeting every six weeks. Commodity papers were prepared for the different crop and livestock industries, and twelve of these had appeared. They reflect the orientation of the department toward export crops. A commodity approach to agricultural policy is still dominant in the department, but papers have also been prepared on topics that vitally affect primary industry, such as rural credit, land tenure, land settlement, land use, and agricultural training. However, basic policy issues such as that of the type of agricultural holding that would be applicable to Papua New Guinea have not been tackled to date. Other areas, such as policy for agricultural research, continue to reflect previous patterns of commitment.

Essentially this policy machinery still serves primarily as a rubber stamp for policy decisions originating within the technical branches, although some issues, such as agricultural education, have provoked intense and lively debate. It is possible, indeed common, for agricultural policies on different commodities to be based on assumptions and strategies that are in conflict with one another, and there is a considerable risk in generalizing from a few policy initiatives. Throughout the period of the first Coalition government, however, there was one constant theme which preoccupied the government in its agricultural initiatives — a drive for self-sufficiency in food. This was the only rural policy issue that clearly established itself as a front-running political item over an extended period, leading the government to make new commitments. A lot of publicity was given to government programmes to increase fresh food production, to grow more rice, and to establish a sugar industry. All three were promoted under the emotional banner of self-sufficiency.

Efforts to promote rice production have been a feature of PNG agricultural policies since the 1920s. Programmes under the Coalition government in fact involved less commitment than some of those attempted in earlier eras. The emergence of clear policy initiatives to promote the marketing of fresh foods in urban areas and to establish a sugar industry were, however, new policy initiatives characteristic of the Coalition government. It is therefore to these two areas of agricultural policy that the present study is addressed.

FRESH FOOD POLICY

The establishment of a wholesale fruit and vegetable market in Port Moresby was first recommended by the administration's Project Planning Team in 1965 (Yeats 1975). It is a project that had long been put forward by the urban elite of Port Moresby in response to high vegetable prices. It had also been enthusiastically supported by plantation interests in the expectation that new marketing opportunities would emerge. In 1968 the Controller of Supply proposed a fresh food handling centre to cost $750,000. This resulted in the establishment of an inter-departmental committee, the Fresh Foods Committee, the following year. This committee obtained eight hectares of land in the Gordon industrial area and proceeded with a modified plan for a wholesale market which was estimated to cost $250,000. The committee then attempted to pass over the carriage of the project to a department, but none would accept the responsibility. At this time senior officials within DASF viewed Port Moresby as a natural market outlet for North Queensland produce and assumed supplies would be developed from this source by private enterprise.

Later, following an Asian Development Bank loan for the Hiritano Highway which put pressure on the government to improve fresh food marketing, DASF decided to establish a wholesale fruit and vegetable market in Port Moresby. This was put to the Administrator's Executive Council on 29 August 1972, where it was decided that DASF and the Department of Business Development should jointly investigate the practicability and need for establishing a wholesale facility in Port Moresby. In June 1973, following pressure from the Public Service Association for an increase in urban wages, Cabinet directed the establishment of a committee to look at the most appropriate means of reducing the import of fresh vegetables in order to restrict increases in the cost of living. A draft report was prepared by the committee, but it never reached Cabinet. Policy-making in this area was largely confined within DASF, mostly in the form of *fait accompli*, as the result of activities already initiated by enthusiastic officers (Yeats 1975, p. 4). In November 1973 a Cabinet Information Paper was prepared to tell Cabinet what action had been taken to promote self-reliance in local foodstuffs. This action was the appointment of Mick Mead as national co-ordinator and of Clive Troy as manager, Port Moresby market, and the rental of Troy's private freezer complex. The appointment of a national co-ordinator was the first indication that a national marketing system, rather than a local Port Moresby operation, was being considered. Again this paper was apparently never presented to Cabinet, but a group of senior ministers met on 14 November 1973 to discuss the need for increased reliance on locally produced foods.

From this point most of the fresh foods "policy" originated in the form of papers presented by Mead to the Minister for Agriculture, the Director of DASF, and his immediate supervisor, the Assistant Director, Planning and Development. The first of these papers appeared in November 1973 and broadly outlined a development programme to be considered in the establishment of a national wholesale marketing organization. The Port Moresby market was established, and in April 1974 Mead minuted the minister on "approvals required for further development of Wholesale Fresh Food Marketing, P.N.G.". The minute requested the development of a wholesale market establishment in Lae, cool shipping space from Lae to Port Moresby, and a permanent Port Moresby market.

This was the general procedure for "policy" formulation during 1974. From the papers and minutes prepared by Mead it emerged that the following aims were being pursued for the industry:

(a) To improve marketing and facilities for smallholder and large scale grower.
(b) To cater also for fish, meat and preserved foodstuffs.
(c) To lower marketing costs, to increase returns to growers.
(d) To provide a more effective arm for use by the Government.
(e) To assist the Government's aim of greater self-sufficiency in food-stuffs and consequently to lessen the rate of growth of imported food.
(f) To assist the Department's aim of improving the nutritional status of the population.

These policy papers were primarily concerned with problems of marketing vegetables as seen by administrators. Many of the actions initiated were in conflict with the claimed objectives of the project.

During 1974 a rapid increase in food costs provoked unrest among urban people, especially in Port Moresby. Josephine Abaijah, the parliamentary leader of the newly formed Papua Besena movement, was able to mobilize this unrest for her cause. In June 1974 she led a number of marches by women in support of demands for more money for their husbands, a price freeze, and cuts in politicians' salaries. On successive days angry women, led by Miss Abaijah and inflamed by her numerous speeches, laid siege to the Chief Minister's office, rampaged through a conference room, attacked the Chief Minister, the Minister for Foreign Relations, and their advisers, threw stones, caused damage to both the main stadium and the airport terminal, and tried to prevent Somare from boarding an aircraft.

The Somare government quickly responded to the demonstrations. Within a week import levies and profit margins on imported foods were cut and an increase in the urban wage was announced. Cabinet approved an acceleration of the Fresh Food Project (FFP) and implementation of the programme. The following week John Guise made a detailed speech to the House of Assembly setting out his department's programme to "relieve high food prices and promoting the Government's aim of reducing food imports and encouraging the production and marketing of fresh foods by our people" (*Post Courier*, 28 June 1974). The statement set out a number of activities which DASF was initiating to promote vegetable production and better marketing and commented that the people in *urban* areas were most affected by inflated prices and the government's priority would be to serve their interests.

The announced expansion of the FFP fortuitously corresponded with an unexpected increase in government funds due to the renegotiation of the Bougainville Copper Agreement and favourable prices for exports. The FFP rapidly expanded its facilities and staff. Depots were established in most main centres, coolroom facilities were obtained at Lae and Port Moresby, and staff were transferred from other branches of DASF. The FFP established a policy of purchasing all fresh food offered by farmers, and vehicles combed the countryside buying lavishly. Wastage of purchased food was high.

The activities by the fresh food market did not take long to provoke a hostile reaction from rural interests. In Goroka the Lowa Marketing Co-operative (LMC) had been established for some years, and one of its main purposes was to provide a vegetable marketing service for its members. In 1974 Mead visited Goroka and told the directors that the co-operative would be phased out and replaced by the government wholesale market (Gerritsen 1975). The directors of LMC mounted a campaign against the fresh food market and obtained space in the national press (*Post Courier*, 5 November 1974). A period of intense political lobbying directed at the Minister for Agriculture followed, in which Fred Leahy, a plantation owner representing the rival Asaro-Watabung Rural Development Corporation, competed with the LMC directors for the right to control sweet potato marketing in the Goroka area. Leahy made a number of direct telephone calls to Guise. However, the LMC appeared to win out when Guise made a personal visit to Goroka on 5 November 1974 and agreed that LMC should be the monopoly buyer within a clearly delineated area and that the government market would buy LMC surpluses and sell to them if they were short of foodstuffs for the local market (Gerritsen 1975, p. 24). Thus a "big peasant" interest group had emerged to influence agricultural policy directly.

However, the government wholesale market paid little attention to the agreement between the minister and LMC directors. It continued to operate the Goroka depot and offered a higher price to growers than did the LMC, which had to deduct its expenses. The action of FFP officials provoked bitter reaction from DASF field staff who were advising the

LMC. This reaction was a specific instance of a deteriorating relationship between the FFP and the DASF extension service. The rapid expansion of the FFP had taken many experienced staff from extension, throwing a greater burden on the few remaining experienced officers.

On 5 May 1975 the LMC achieved headlines in the national press with a report that the co-operative was being bankrupted by the government's fresh food scheme. In January 1976 the LMC was closed by order of an adviser from the Department of Business Development after continued losses of K300 per month. The managing director of Waso Ltd, a large vegetable marketing company based in Enga Province, also expressed fears that the FFP would stifle the development of New Guinean businesses and co-operatives in the marketing of fresh produce (Weier 1976).

Meanwhile, farmers in the Central Province began to voice a frequent complaint that the prices paid by the fruit and vegetable market were too low. The minister responded to these criticisms by claiming that the reason for farmers receiving low profits was the small scale of their operations. He advocated the use of machinery in vegetable production to reduce costs. This response reflected the orientation of DASF officials who were preoccupied with individual farm profit irrespective of its effect on national policies and who saw the problem in terms of marketing efficiency for the FFP. In a lecture to agricultural students at the University of Papua New Guinea on 15 October 1975, Mead stated that his policy was to centralize buying of produce at large warehouses in the main centres and that he hoped to see the development of about fifty large-scale farms which would be sufficient to supply the nation's needs for fresh vegetables. He also stated that over 60 per cent of the sweet potato purchased by the FFP was being produced by expatriate plantations.

By this time the 1974 situation of excess government funds had been reversed and a serious budgetary crisis had developed. The FFP reversed its decision to buy all fresh food offered for sale and only took what it required to meet demand. This caused still further outcry among rural interest groups, and the combination of this criticism with concern over the escalating cost of the project prompted the DASF Standing Committee on 11 June 1975 to undertake a thorough review of fresh food policy. The standing committee meeting considered background papers from George Yeats, Robert Densley, and myself which gave a summary of policies and events to date and posed some of the policy issues that had been overlooked. The meeting noted that "not all sections of the Department were aware of the various policies and objectives of the programme — generally as a result of the various and informal lines of communication used to transmit Ministerial policy directives". The meeting sought a response from the minister to clarify conflicting aspects of the current policy, noting that the objective of supplying cheap food to the towns was in conflict with that of increasing income to rural producers, and that many of the actions undertaken by the programme would have the result of making urban living more attractive. It pointed out that the present programme favoured large-scale commercial farmers who were located close to the urban areas and who could use mechanical means of vegetable production. Such a policy, the meeting said, would increase imports of machinery, fuel, fertilizer, and technical experts and would be very costly in terms of extension services. The conflicts between proposed government production of food and the objective of providing more income for rural areas, between purchasing food in the Highlands and the objective of cheaper food for towns, between paying a single national price and the objective of a fair return to farmers, and between monopoly control of marketing by a government authority and the objective of encouraging local marketing organizations were brought to the minister's attention. However, no further action was taken and the programme's existing momentum was maintained.

The officials of the FFP continued toward their next goal, which was the creation of an autonomous food marketing authority. A further proposal from the project was for the establishment of a state farm on the outskirts of Port Moresby to produce vegetables. This had the direct backing of Guise, but it was in conflict with government policies to support smallholders and was backed by very dubious budgeting. The proposal was blocked by the standing committee on 31 October 1975 — an action that was perhaps more boldly taken on account of Guise's recent promotion to the position of Governor-General.

Throughout the remainder of the first Coalition government the marketing project continued to gain regular publicity from dissatisfied clients, customers, and competing interests. In July 1976 the new Food Marketing Corporation achieved headlines when it was revealed before the Public Accounts Committee that the fresh food market lost K1.3 million in 1974–75. The chairman of the committee reacted to the huge loss by calling on the "people who are responsible for the decisions" to appear before the committee in order to obviate financial mismanagement. The new Minister for Primary Industry, Boyamo Sali, reacted by blaming the inefficiency of other departments for his department's problems. Subsequently the Minister for Labour, Commerce and Industry, Gavera Rea, called for a full investigation into the loss by the Fresh Food Market and pointed out that the K1.3 million loss was more than two-thirds of the amount received by the Department of Business Development to carry out all its programmes.

As no one was concerned with resolving the basic issues of the fresh food policy, particularly the question of whether priority should be given to urban development or to rural development, the second Coalition government began its term with much the same rhetoric on self-reliance in food and the same demands from interest groups for government assistance as had marked the previous four years. The new Minister for Primary Industry, Julius Chan, forecast the introduction of new policies to increase food production rapidly; the Premier of the Central Province complained that the prices paid by the Food Marketing Corporation were too low; and a corporation spokesman said that producers lacked continuity of production.

SUGAR POLICY

Sugar provides another area of agricultural policy which indicates the sorts of changes that emerged during the period. Dreams of a PNG sugar industry are not new. Captain John Moresby wrote of the tens of thousands of acres of land that could profitably be developed for sugar cane in 1875. He set a theme that was constantly repeated by explorers, adventurers, administrators, planters, and Papuan nationalists over the next hundred years. Considerable effort and expenditure was put into a sugar project at Sangara in the Northern Province in the 1930s, but its failure was soon forgotten (McKillop 1977) and a belief that Australian interests had forced the abandonment of the project persisted. In 1942 Lewis Lett wrote: "It is Papua's misfortune that Australia's policy does not permit competition with Australian growers of the products . . . for which Papua is best equipped" (Lett 1942, p. 119).

As the prospects of PNG independence emerged, those who saw the possibility of agricultural development free from Australian influence again became vocal. Expatriate planters were prominent in raising the prospects of new industries, and a favourite subject was a local sugar industry. In May 1973 the managing director of Tanubada Dairy Products, W. Groeneveld, claimed that Papua New Guinea had been held to ransom by Australian sugar interests and called for the rapid development of a local sugar-cane industry. A year later the Chief Minister told a meeting at Kaiapit that the Australian administration had lied to Papua New Guinea about her potential for agricultural development and had put its own interests first in preventing the establishment of a sugar industry in the Markham Valley.

The agricultural policy-making machinery readily responded to these inputs. In 1964 a Department of Territories investigating team had suggested that the establishment of a sugar industry might be feasible by 1975 provided a sugar research programme gave satisfactory results. DASF conducted research in the Markham Valley which demonstrated that sugar could be grown successfully there. There was some debate within

DASF on the type of development strategy that might be pursued for a local sugar industry. Earlier planning had naturally looked to the Australian industry as a model. This assumed an industrial agricultural system based on high energy technology and high capital investment. The 1964 investigating team had recommended an industry based on a 30,000-ton vacuum-pan factory which would have cost $50 million. For comparison, an investigation into the establishment of a sugar industry in the Ord River area of Western Australia in 1974 had estimated that a 120,000-ton industry would have a capital cost of $111 million. Thus the cost of a sugar industry on the Australian model appeared to be beyond the capacity of the PNG economy, and DASF officials looked for alternative models which would suit small-scale farmers and low-technology capacities. The department sent two officers to India to study processing equipment. They recommended the open-pan processing method, which produced a rough raw sugar but could be established at a fraction of the cost of vacuum-pan factories.

During 1974 Australian assistance was sought for a sugar project, and the firm Sugar Consultants Australia Pty Ltd was hired to draw up the details for a mill. They recommended a mini-vacuum factory, a recently developed technology which would enable the establishment of a smaller scale industry than previously envisaged. In June 1974 the Minister for Agriculture announced that K500,000 would be made available for the initial work on two sugar plantations. One of these was to be in the Markham Valley and the other in the Kemp Welch Valley in the Central Province. DASF officials were concerned at the inclusion of the latter area as they did not have research data to determine if commercial sugar could be grown there. They saw the announcement as a political one in response to the Papua Besena movement and associated with Guise's contacts with the area. Guise's announcement also mentioned that his department would look into small-scale sugar production at village level.

Strains between departmental officials and the minister over sugar policy were becoming apparent by October 1974. Guise stated that he would take a village man from the Rigo area with him on a trip to Fiji to study sugar, adding that this was "better than sending officers who come back and put their experiences on paper for impractical committee discussion" (*Post Courier*, 31 October 1974). In a fast-moving tour of Fiji's cane-growing areas and sugar mills, Guise rejected advice from Fiji officials on the economics of the sugar industry on the grounds that costs were irrelevant. On 22 April 1975 Guise personally made a decision to reject the open-pan factory for Papua New Guinea, saying that he would have only the best equipment for his factory. Two days later the press carried a statement from the minister that the government planned to build a sugar mill capable of producing a thousand tons of raw sugar at Niuruku village on the Kemp Welch River. The mill alone was estimated to cost K440,000. Two months later he issued another press release on the proposed Kemp Welch mill which by then was said to have a future capacity of three thousand tons of raw sugar.

These actions by the minister caused concern among DASF officials who saw them as irrational and politically motivated. A news item appeared in the national press which suggested that farmers in the Markham Valley were upset at being overlooked for a sugar industry and claimed that money for sugar should be invested there first because feasibility studies had proved that commercial sugar could be grown in the Markham (*Post Courier*, 26 June 1975). This provoked an angry response from Guise, who said that "plans to set up a sugar mill in the Kemp Welch River area would go ahead regardless of the demands of farmers in the Markham Valley" (ibid., 27 June 1975). He also promised an investigation to locate the officer responsible for the statement and to take appropriate action. However, the damage had been done: the member for Usino/Bundi, Marcus Kawo, followed up with a strongly worded letter accusing Guise of deceiving the Markham people and demanding that a sugar mill should also be established in the Markham Valley.

Budget restraints and the appointment of Guise to the position of Governor-General provided the opportunity for the sugar controversy to be quietly dropped by the department. When the Department of Finance demanded that departments reduce their budgets in 1975, the allocation for the sugar project was first to be cut. Guise maintained his interest in the project, and in June 1976 he used the opportunity of the Port Moresby Show opening to attack the government for using delaying tactics in starting the sugar project. In August 1976 the new Minister for Primary Industry, Boyamo Sali, MP for the Markham Valley's Morobe Province, reported to parliament that a World Bank report had said that the Kemp Welch area was too small to be profitable for a sugar industry. He said that potential investors in sugar had failed to make firm offers of aid or investment. Sali added that in order to offset the disappointment of villagers who had been waiting to take part in sugar projects, a major effort would be made to encourage village production of maize in the Markham Valley and small-scale production of stock feed in Kemp Welch.

The project has not yet been laid to rest. In January 1978 the Minister for Primary Industry in the second Coalition government, Julius Chan, announced that a British firm was to study the feasibility of a sugar industry which could produce 30,000 tonnes of sugar per year. He added, however, that a local sugar industry would have to produce at the cost of imported sugar or less.

CONCLUSION

The two cases presented show very clearly that the realities of policy-making and implementation are very different from the rational decision-making model that is often presumed to exist. Occasionally an economic argument has been introduced to rationalize a decision after it has been made, such as the abandonment of the sugar project or the decision to reverse the fresh-food buying policy, but it is difficult to support a view that such rational factors have really determined the decision-making process. Rather, the new commitments that were made and succeeded in establishing themselves came about as a result of a combination of outside political pressures and the availability of additional resources.

Although this examination has been confined to the two areas where there were new policy initiatives, we are left with an overriding impression of an organization that was impervious to change. A central thesis that emerges is that the policy assumptions built into the structure of DASF — a commodity approach to agriculture, a technical production orientation with an emphasis on export crops, support for an estate plantation system, concern for individual farm profit, and an Australian technology base — tied the department to a reinforcement of previous policies. Policy initiatives only emerged when there was strong pressure from external groups, and even then remained peripheral to the central activities of the department.

In the case of the fresh-food policy, external groups applied political pressures that the government readily responded to. Sometimes the sources of pressure might not have been anticipated. For example, it is not clear that in accepting a loan from the Asian Development Bank for the Hiritano Highway the government appreciated that it would be subjected to pressure from an outside agency to commit itself to the FFP. Other key groups who influenced the government to make new commitments with the FFP were the Public Service Association and the women who marched in Port Moresby. Both were clearly voicing urban interests. These groups were able to push the government into a panic reaction. In contrast, rural groups, although gaining some publicity and an unfulfilled promise of support from the minister, were not able to influence policy in their favour. The FFP developed as a programme that aimed to keep down the price of basic foods to the urban people, and it maintained this position despite the complaints of farmers.

Of the two projects examined, the FFP was implemented with a large commitment of resources while the sugar project was shelved. Why was one implemented but not the other? Part of the explanation lies in the nature of the projects. Urban interests in Port Moresby were demanding an immediate response to the inflation crisis of 1974, and officials were obviously shaken by the anger of the women's marches. The FFP offered an opportunity to give an impression of activity in the short term, but sugar was a long-term project and would probably result in a higher-priced and lower-quality product than imported sugar. However, there were other important differences.

The FFP was fortunate in gaining Mead as national co-ordinator. He had little time for formal procedures and regulations and got things done, but he did so within the value framework of the department. There was little support for the promotion of fresh food marketing through small entrepreneurs within the informal sector, the emergence of local producer organizations such as the LMC, or the use of price mechanisms to stimulate production. It was assumed as a matter of course and tradition (McKillop 1976a) that the market would be controlled by a government monopoly; that collection, distribution, and sale of produce would be carried out by government officials; and that there would be one national price. When the farmers complained, they were told they were inefficient and that they must reduce their costs by mechanization. These assumptions fitted into DASF values without too much friction, so that Mead, using the support of the minister to advantage, was able to get the FFP established and operating before other branches moved to block the initiatives. Hindsight reveals that this was possible only because of the special conditions of 1974 when the government found itself with additional funds. This enabled the FFP to be established from additional resources rather than by cutting into those of other branches of the department. At this time the important limiting resource was experienced staff, and a resistance to the FFP gradually built up as it took staff from other branches. Open rivalry with the extension service emerged once the operations of the FFP began to hurt some of the extension clients, but the feelings of field staff were poorly represented at the headquarters level. By mid-1975, however, finance was also a limiting resource and other branches of DASF were being asked to make budget cuts. It was then that the Agricultural Standing Committee called the FFP to account and attempted to find out what commitments had been made and what the fresh-food policies were supposed to be. By this stage the FFP had been clearly established as a policy commitment even though formal policy approvals had not been obtained, and they had already achieved a K1.3 million loss on their operations.

The sugar project, on the other hand, did not have the support of a key official prepared to circumvent bureaucratic procedure in order to get the project under way. More importantly, there was not a clear strategy for implementation which fitted the value framework of the department. The cost of a capital-intensive high-technology industry appeared prohibitive, so there was some search for alternatives. However, the small-scale, low-level technology approach recommended by the officers who visited India did not mesh comfortably with the overall preoccupations of the department, resulting in a lack of clear support for the project. The initiatives for sugar were largely left to the minister, and the departmental response was mainly a negative reaction. Little had been achieved by mid-1975 when the financial crisis hit, and no branch of the department had a strong commitment to its preservation. Thus, when the necessity for budget cuts emerged, the branches were unanimous that the sugar project should be the first to go.

The agricultural policy commitments that did emerge during the period, then, were the result of an interplay of political and resource factors which combined in such a way that enabled them to overcome bureaucratic inertia. The outside political forces that were able to influence the government tended to have an urban bias.

Another important point arises from the analysis. The basic value orientation that emerges from the DASF structure is one that favours an industrial agricultural model based on high energy technology and high capital investment. This results in a clear policy bias towards those few farmers able to afford the capital and management for large-scale operations. Expatriate plantations were favoured by the FFP executive, and there were hopes that all the nation's food needs would be produced by only fifty large farms.

In these two areas at least the government has followed policies that lead to more technologically advanced farming. However, this trend is creating precisely the kind of demand for services that the government administration is becoming less able to cope with. As Moris so clearly points out (1972, p. 127), such farming demands higher standards of husbandry which must be backed by increased sophistication of management. This in turn will not be effective unless supported by well-administered producer services. Thus the strategy of leaving producers to be passive recipients of centralized services and of selecting sophisticated technology carries with it an immense organizational load for the agencies responsible. However, the changes that have taken place within DASF have made the organization less able to cope with this load. Not only has the organization maintained the bureaucratic structure and behavioural patterns inherited from Canberra, but the "remedies" tried have reduced the planning capacity of the organization by withdrawing resources from the field and concentrating them in the centre. Instead of developing field staff that seek lateral communication, take initiatives to re-evaluate commitments, and formulate contingency plans, the field operations have been left to inexperienced staff with a strong bureaucratic orientation. When a crisis strikes, the field organization goes into immediate paralysis until higher orders are received from above. In place of "engaged planning" to meet the crisis, one finds what Robert Chambers terms "planning without implementation" at the centre and "implementation without planning" in the field (Moris 1972, p. 128). Both the fresh food and sugar projects provide excellent examples of this trend.

ACKNOWLEDGEMENTS

I would like to express my thanks to W. L. Conroy and J. A. Ballard for their assistance in the preparation and revision of this paper.

Policy-Making for Rural Development

H. K. COLEBATCH

This paper stems from what might be called an exercise in the archaeology of public policy. My initial concern was with a current field of governmental activity — the Rural Improvement Programme (RIP) — whose proclaimed aim was to link central financial resources with local initiative in order to improve the way of life of rural people (see Colebatch 1977 for a preliminary account of this study). The National Coalition government placed great stress on this programme, particularly in its early years in office, as a means of translating into action its concern for improving the lives of rural people (as opposed to what it saw as a narrow concern for economic growth). In presenting the 1973/74 budget, which more than doubled the allocation for RIP, the Minister for Finance described the increase as reflecting "major changes in policy". He went on:

> The change in name not only emphasises the much greater importance your Government attaches to rural improvement; it also symbolises a new approach. The emphasis is now not so narrowly on economic development, but more broadly on social improvement and an enrichment in the quality of the lives of the village people . . . The increase in funds shows that we are prepared to do much more to help the underprivileged areas of Papua New Guinea. [*HAD*, vol. 3, p. 2312, 28 August 1973]

In other words, the RIP was seen by the government as a major policy initiative, reflecting its determination to use the resources of government to achieve a particular sort of social change. It therefore offers an opportunity for a study of what happens when a government attempts this sort of change — i.e., what "policy-making" means in the context of the working of the machinery of government. This paper is an attempt at such a study. It begins with a consideration of some analytical questions about policy, looks at the situation of the incoming government in 1972 and the way it made its commitment to the RIP, examines the development of policy in relation to the three main characteristics of the programme, and in its conclusions tries to assess what can be learned from the RIP that is relevant to the more general study of policy.

WHAT IS "POLICY"?

It is useful to start with the question of what *policy* means in relation to the activity of government. Classical liberal political science distinguished between policy and administration. This distinction was seen as being (at least ideally) parallel to a role-division between politicians and public servants: politicians made policy, and public servants carried it out. Policy was concerned with matters of principle, administration with matters of detail.

This model had its attractions, but it became increasingly difficult to relate it to the actual process of liberal cabinet government. It was clear, for instance, that formally identified "policy decisions" did not spring fully formed from the heads of the ministers with whom they were identified, and that public servants were significantly involved in their formulation. It was suggested then that ministers made policy by selecting from policy options presented to them by public servants, but this did not seem very satisfactory. It was not clear, for instance, that ministers always had options to choose from, or even that they wanted them. And in any case, the power to decide what the options were, and in what terms they were to be presented to the minister, was clearly of great importance. A further difficulty was that ministers did not always seem to want to concern themselves only with matters of principle and leave the detailed administration to their public servants: often, it was the details (rather than the principles) that ministers wanted to affect.

Another obstacle in the way of a clear-cut definition of policy was the way in which the term was used in government; it had great potential as a defensive weapon in the arsenal of the bureaucrat. G. E. Caiden, reporting to the Royal Commission on Australian Government Administration, made the point pungently:

> The word "policy" is used loosely to refer to what the Minister says, or what Cabinet decides, or what one has always been doing, or what one did yesterday, or what comes within guidelines, or whatever anyone wants it to mean. Both officials and politicians are prone to resort to oracular mystification by announcing that such and such a practice is "policy." . . . Respect for policy is too often co-extensive with reverence for precedent and past practice. This awe for received guidance is related to the authority of Cabinet and the difficulty of securing change. [Caiden 1975, p. 85]

The slipperiness of the concept has led one academic writer on policy to adopt what might be called a definition of despair: "Public policy is all the courses of action carried out by the authorities" (Forward 1974, p. 1). This is a definition that has its appeal: it is certainly comprehensive, and it avoids some of the definitional red herrings that abound in discussions of policy — e.g., the classical distinction between policy and administration, and the attempts to discuss something called "the problem of implementation", which is seen as being in some way distinct from the making of policy (on which see Schaffer 1976, n. 5). But it does seem to throw the baby out with the bathwater: in escaping from formalist distinctions between policy and administration, it makes policy synonymous with governmental activity as such, which seems to deprive the term of most of its analytical value. To paraphrase Wildavsky, if policy is everything, maybe it's nothing.

John Dearlove (1973, pp. 2–6) is particularly helpful here. He recognizes that the term *public policy* relates to "the substance of what government does", but does not equate it with governmental activity as such. Rather, he sees it as the way in which governments commit resources in response to perceived problems; in that case, it is "the product or output of governmental activity". Defining policy by reference to commitments focuses our attention on its function in stabilizing the operation of the government machine. The outcomes of governmental activity are not entirely unpredictable: some matters are more or less settled, with participants' scope for action being limited by previous commitments; some matters, on which no such commitments have been made, are more open. To the extent that the course of government action is settled, we may speak of "policy", which can be seen as "a committed structure of important resources" (Schaffer 1977, p. 148). For this reason, "policy" can be (as Caiden complains) a shelter for the conservative and unadventurous bureaucrat. Equally, as is implied in the ministerial statement quoted on p. 257, it can be a force for change in the nature and direction of governmental activity. The minister clearly expected that a change in the resources allocated to the programme would lead to a significant change in the impact it had on rural development.

This means, as Dearlove points out, that is is important to distinguish between "policy", in this sense, and "policy-making", particularly when this is taken to mean decision-making in relation to policy. Dearlove argues that in the London council which he studied, there certainly were policy decisions, in the sense of particular points at which significant commitments of resources were made. But equally important was the process of policy maintenance: the pattern of small, routine actions which stemmed from an initial policy commitment and reinforced it. The initial major commitment (e.g., to give a loan to a housing trust) can be followed by a succession of increasingly routine decisions (e.g., to give subsequent loans to that trust). Dearlove argues that policy maintenance is a very important and much-neglected aspect of the policy process.

A considerable amount of activity within organisations is, in fact, devoted to avoiding and resisting the necessity for taking trauma-producing decisions of this kind in favour of confining activity to the taking of decisions that are only routine and work within the framework of established policies maintaining the pattern of commitments and implementing the implications of earlier policy decisions. [Dearlove 1973, p. 5]

Now while this is a very valuable insight, caution must be exercised in applying it to empirical situations. It is often the case that a substantial policy commitment leads to a series of relatively routine decisions. But it is also often the case that a string of apparently routine decisions can lead an organization into a quite different pattern of commitments — Lindblom's "disjointed incrementalism."

It is also possible that the initial commitment may not be followed and reinforced by a stream of routine decisions. For instance, in 1974 the Chief Minister issued a circular about the RIP in which he said, among other things, that the programme "should ideally result from a long term view or plan rather than be developed on an *ad hoc* basis". This implied a series of subsidiary decisions reinforcing this desire for planning (e.g., by giving some sort of preference to proposals that formed part of a plan). In fact, there were no such decisions, and it soon became clear that whether or not a project resulted from a plan made absolutely no difference to its chance of being funded, and no clients made any serious attempt to draft (still less to adhere to) a long-term plan. Not all those involved in the policy process agreed with the attempt to link RIP grants to the building-up of a planning process in the districts. Others argued that the RIP was meant to be a compensatory programme, filling the gaps in the overall pattern of government activity, and that it was therefore not possible to plan for RIP projects. I am not concerned here with the contradiction between these policy themes. I am simply pointing out that a directive issued to the public service at one point embraced the "pro-planning" view, but that in the absence of supportive decisions lower down the line, it had no impact.

Here, it would seem that the impact of the "policy" decision was dependent on the existence of "routine" acts stemming from it. This suggests, perhaps, that the extent to which a decision should be regarded as substantive "policy-making" rather than routine "policy maintenance" is not so much something inherent in the decision itself as something derived from the extent to which the decision actually alters the flow of resources within the governmental machine. In other words, it may be more useful to think of policy-making decisions and policy-reinforcing ones as ideal types rather than as empirical categories, so that actual commitments within the policy process are examined in terms of the extent to which they reinforce existing patterns of commitment or contribute to a movement away from them. And it is obviously important to look for non-decisions (as in the planning example quoted above) as well as decisions – the dogs that did not bark in the night, as it were.

POLICY AND THE INCOMING GOVERNMENT

When considering the specific case of policy-making in Papua New Guinea under the National Coalition government, the question is not simply: What did the incoming government want to do, and how did it do it?, but the rather broader question: What was the pattern of commitment that shaped the direction of governmental activity, and to what extent, and in what ways, did the actions of the new government change these commitments or reinforce them? It should not be assumed, for instance, that the government was primarily concerned with changing the pattern of policy commitments: quite apart from the normal weight of inertia in the governmental process, the incoming actors had (or acquired) interests in the maintenance of existing commitments as well as a concern for the adoption of new ones. They did have to make commitments of resources: the question is how *purposive* these were (in terms of either policy innovation or policy maintenance), and how *effective* they were in terms of the purposes being pursued.

Before moving to the particular case of policy for rural development, it is worth noting three points about the policy situation applying to the incoming government in its early years. The first is that the incoming figures (both ministers and new [Papua New Guinean] departmental heads) were concerned with a great deal else apart from policy. They were, for instance, concerned to work out their respective roles: the ministers were the first to be appointed in Papua New Guinea, and there was considerable uncertainty about their roles – among bureaucrats as well as among politicians, among the well-established actors in the policy process as well as among the newcomers. The ministerial member role of 1968–72 offered some cues about the role of a minister, but there had been much dissatisfaction with this role (particularly among Pangu MHAs, then in opposition), and it was not one the incoming government wanted to use as a model. As localization proceeded, there was a high turnover in the upper ranks of the bureaucracy, and consequently a need to learn the roles as they then existed (and by implication, to service the existing pattern of commitments rather than to introduce radical changes).

The second point is that the incoming government was a "Coalition of the Outs" – i.e., a loose alliance of all those who for some reason wanted to form a government without the United Party (which had up to that time had a numerical preponderance in parliament). This meant that it incorporated a range of political actors, with quite different styles and aspirations. It also meant that the policy objectives expressed in the early days tended to be couched in terms of broad polarities — Then and Now — rather than in terms of specific proposals for action. The old order (i.e., the colonial administration and its United Party supporters) stressed economic goals; the new government would stress social goals. Similarly, large-scale development was to be replaced by small-scale development, centralization by decentralization, and "betting on the strong" by the equal distribution of benefits. These policy themes may have provided an ideological rallying point for a disparate coalition, but they did not indicate specific courses of action for the government to follow.

Thirdly, the inexperience of the incoming actors meant that to a large extent they were unsure of just *how* they could affect the policy process. They were ambivalent in their attitudes towards the bureaucracy, which they saw as mainly responsible for the policy stance from which they had to some extent dissociated themselves. In many cases they sought alternative advice from academics, outside consultants, and personal staff. But this did not always help them find their way around the government machine, for these outsiders were not necessarily more experienced in government than they were themselves. This could be of particular importance, as some sorts of question present themselves for policy attention (e.g., budgetary allocations) while others do not (e.g., the actual outcome of these allocations). Those who want to change the outcomes of government action have to find out the points at which existing commitments are subject to review before they can fight any battles over the worth of those commitments.

EXISTING "RURAL DEVELOPMENT" COMMITMENTS

Turning now to rural development as a field of policy commitments, one sees that the commitments are very extensive, and also highly bureaucratized. A number of government agencies were involved in seeking to influence the pattern of rural change — departments such as District Administration and Agriculture, statutory authorities such as the Development Bank, and bodies outside the formal structure of government, such as co-operatives and local government councils — and they had increased considerably in both size and complexity in the 1950s and 1960s. Bob McKillop (1977, pp. 12–13) points out that in the Eastern Highlands the number of staff involved in agricultural extension grew from 1 in 1953 to 16 in 1963 and to 164 in 1973 (plus thirty administrative staff). These structures of bureaucratic intervention had available to them a range of benefits, inducements, and controls, and built up their client contact networks through which to distribute them (see, e.g., McKillop 1975).

In addition to the maintenance of its own bureaucracy, the government also provided funds under the Capital Works Programme for "rural development". These funds were first made available in 1967 and enabled district-level officials to secure funds for small, local projects. The initial allocation was $200,000, of which half was earmarked for "rural development roads", $25,000 for village water supplies, and the remainder for "aid to council projects". By 1971/72 the allocation had grown to $1.4 million, but this was still a relatively small proportion of the whole Capital Works Programme ($38.5 million). (Ordinary departmental expenditure was $96.2 million out of a budget total of $208.1 million). Roads and bridges accounted for 90 per cent of the funds spent, water supply projects 9 per cent and all other projects only 1 per cent. Recommendations for grants were made by the District Co-ordinating Committee (DCC), and each proposal was to provide for a local contribution, generally supposed to be 50 per cent of the total cost.

The policy situation in 1972 was therefore marked by the presence of a new set of actors who wished to demonstrate the impact of the new government in general, and to manifest in particular its concern with rural development, but were uncertain about how this could be achieved through the existing machinery. The government had extensive commitments which at least purported to be concerned with rural development, but these largely sustained an existing bureaucracy, and it was a political commonplace that this bureaucracy was immersed in its own concerns and was not sensitive to the needs of villagers or particularly effective at consciously changing their behaviour. (For empirical investigation of this, see McKillop 1975.) It is in any case difficult for outsiders even to take in the nature and operations of large bureaucratic organizations, let alone work out how to control them and use them for their own innovative purposes. Grants programmes, by contrast, are attractive because they can be focused clearly on a particular target, brought into action quickly, and become a clear symbol of the policy intentions of the government. This, at any rate, is how the situation often appears to policy-makers. Of course, the organizational problems involved in, for example, promoting very small public works projects, do not go away when a government chooses to pursue this aim by making grants to outside bodies to do the work: the problems are simply transferred to the outside body. It may or may not be able to cope with them better than a government department could do, but the advantage from the point of view of the government is that it cannot be held responsible for the problems and may only have the sketchiest knowledge of them.

It is not surprising, then, that the concern of the new government for promoting rural improvement came to focus on what was then called the Rural Development Fund. It was a clearly labelled manifestation of governmental concern for the rural areas. Moreover, it was quantifiable: changes in the commitment it represented could be clearly identified and publicized. Increasing the allocation under this heading would not conflict directly with the interests involved in the other established commitments of the government. And the stress on local project initiatives appeared to circumvent the problem of getting innovative behaviour out of an established bureaucracy and could at the same time be represented as a move towards the decentralization of decision-making, which was another declared policy aim of government.

THE RIP AS A POLICY COMMITMENT

The outcome of the expressed concern of the incoming government was, therefore, an increased stress on an existing programme of grants – the Rural Development Fund (RDF) – including its renaming as the Rural Improvement Programme, and a substantial increase in the funds allocated to it (see table 1).

Table 1.

Expenditure on the Rural Development Fund (1967/68 to 1972/73) and the Rural Improvement Programme (1973/74 to 1977)

	Budget Appropriation	Actual Expenditure
	$	$
1967/68	200,000	141,118
1968/69	502,000	587,910
1969/70	1,000,000	1,007,400
1970/71	1,440,000	1,289,048
1971/72	1,450,000	1,446,558
1972/73	1,507,000	1,431,581
1973/74	3,300,000	3,636,928
1974/75	5,250,000	5,971,027
	K	K
1975/76	6,000,000	6,185,700
1976/77	6,200,000	
1977 (½ year)	3,298,000	

Source: Rural Improvement Programmes; Budget papers; Conyers 1976, p. 18. In some cases there is disagreement between the sources on the correct figure.

The defining principles of the programme, as expressed in official statements, were (*a*) that proposals originated as *local initiatives,* filtered through local decision-making bodies, (*b*) that government grants were a matching contribution to local self-help efforts, and (c) that projects were to promote *improvements in the quality of life* of rural people.

On the face of it, these were not new principles, but restatements of the formal rules of the RDF. Even the "social improvement" theme (as opposed to economic development) emerged from a review of the RDF made by officials in 1971, which had resulted in the preparation in March 1972 of a set of detailed proposals to give greater emphasis to "social" projects in the RDF. But what was really important was what these rules meant: what was the *operational* definition given to them in the course of the ordinary working of the programme?

The process whereby a pattern of specific commitments of resources is built on the foundation of these vague policy aspirations is clearly a fundamental part of policy formulation. But it does not nearly fit into Dearlove's distinction between policy decisions and routine decisions. For instance, the question of whether or not a project can be counted as improving the quality of rural life is clearly not a routine or trivial one, either to the client or to the programme itself (although it may seem so to an administrator confronted with a great many such "micro-decisions"). Nor is it adequately described as the "implementation" of already-formed "policy": clearly, it would be fatuous to say that the policy was to promote improvements in the quality of rural life, and that the question of what this meant was simply a matter of implementation. What the policy is can only be expressed in terms of the sort of commitments that can be successfully attached to this particular ideological flag. This paper is therefore concerned in some detail with the way in which these policy themes were defined and refined in the course of the programme's operation.

This process of definition consisted not so much of formal decisions about the nature of the programme, it was more a series of small decisions (sometimes implicit rather than explicit) and non-decisions about what projects would be funded under the programme. There were, at least in theory, a number of filters through which proposals had to pass. They were proposed by councils or local groups, scrutinized by the District Co-ordinating Committee, assembled into district lists by (from 1974) area authorities or conferences of councils, forwarded to the Co-ordinator of Works in Waigani, and, eventually, included in a list presented to Cabinet by the Minister for Finance for its approval. At any stage in this process, proposals were open to challenge; in practice, however, especially in the earlier years of the programme, there was usually little objection to the inclusion of projects on council lists, or even to the inclusion of all council projects on district lists.

The critical point in the filtering process was the consideration of district lists by the Co-ordinator of Works and the minister. The programme had only one minister for the whole of this period, and he maintained a close interest in it, giving the Co-ordinator general directives on the sort of projects he would like to see included in the programme and those that should be excluded. The Co-ordinator's office would then draw up lists within these guidelines, and the minister would make the final ruling on any marginal cases. The programme then had to be submitted to the National Executive Council, but it appears that it was unusual for the programme to be subjected to further detailed consideration at this level.

To some extent this process can be described in Dearlove's terms — the Minister laying down the guidelines ("policy decision") and the officials making a number of smaller decisions within these guidelines ("routine, reinforcing decision"). But there were important differences. One was that the guidelines were not consistently applied. The guidelines were said to exclude the purchase of vehicles from RIP funds, and in 1976/77 the Gumine Council was refused funds to buy a four-wheel drive vehicle for the maternal and child health clinic; the Central New Ireland Council, however, received a grant to buy a truck for the Lemeris school. Similarly, the guidelines were said to preclude the use of RIP funds for departmental purposes, and in the same year the New Ireland Area Authority was refused funds for a rat control programme on the grounds that this was already a Department of Primary Industry project. But in East New Britain, the Department of Business Development received an RIP grant for "Village Industries Training and Development" which would appear to be a departmental function.

The binding effect of the policy guidelines was also eroded by the use of fairly open subterfuges. For instance, the maximum grant per project in 1974/75 was $10,000. In that year, the first five projects on the West Sepik programme were:

10-1	Lumi-Aitape road (Gravelling Stage 2)	(Grant $10,000)
10-2	Lumi-Aitape road (Mokai Construction)	(Grant $10,000)
10-3	Lumi-Aitape road (Gravelling Stage 3)	(Grant $10,000)
10-4	Lumi-Aitape road (Gravelling Stage 4)	(Grant $10,000)
10-5	Lumi-Aitape road (Sibi River bridge)	(Grant $ 5,000)

All of these projects were funded. Another such subterfuge was the funding of a church on the grounds that in remote and sparsely settled areas, the church functioned as a community centre. (The church in question was in fact at the provincial headquarters.)

What this all means is that the laying down of "policy" guidelines did not in fact diminish the importance of individual admission decisions. It is important to note here that the bodies doing the bidding (area authorities and council conferences) were not being given clear cues about the sorts of projects that would or would not be admitted: no formal criteria were promulgated, and the *de facto* rules appeared to vary from year to year and even within a single year. As only a very small proportion of proposals were rejected (in 1975/76, only 20 proposals were rejected of the 1,140 submitted), local bodies had every reason to try their luck with any given proposal and see if it would be accepted.

In this context, it is significant that responsibility for the programme lay with the Department of Finance, rather than with any of the agencies more directly concerned with rural development. Finance had no field staff of its own (or none who were used in connection with the RIP) and therefore had to deal directly with district- and local-level bodies who were clients rather than agents, without the benefit of any independent source of information or administrative support in the field. There were several attempts by the Office of Local Government (OLG), to take over responsibility for the programme, on the grounds that it was essentially a grants programme for local councils and that the OLG was much more closely attuned to what was actually going on in the operation of the programme, but these were vigorously and successfully resisted by Finance. The programme was administered by a section of the department which was primarily concerned with the channelling of money to the district engineers of the Public Works Department (PWD) under the Capital Works Programme; in terms of administrative procedure, then, the RIP was seen as a works programme executed by bodies other than PWD.

"LOCAL INITIATIVES"

To speak of "local initiatives" immediately raised the question: What is local?. Does it mean simply those people living in some geographically defined area, or does it imply those people who could be regarded as forming a local "community"? "Local" groups who might conceivably put forward project proposals under the RIP could include:

1. Customary groups based on kinship (purportedly?)
2. Locally based officials of the agencies of government (who are quite likely to be foreign to the area, or even to the country)
3. "Contact structures" under official sponsorship, such as local government councils
4. "Non-sponsored" groups, such as anti-council movements, student-initiated development associations, etc.

The RDF had operated through an institutional framework consisting of locally based officials working through official contact structures. Proposals went to the national level from the (official) District Co-ordinating Committee, and the effective channel to the DCC was through kiaps in the field (although councils might be listed as the formal sponsor).

The RIP continued to operate as the RDF had, through councils and kiaps, though increasing weight was given to elected representation at the district level, where the (indirectly elected) Area Authority (or, in its absence, the Combined Councils Conference) took over from the DCC responsibility for formulating district priorities and submitting requests to Port Moresby. The increasing identification of the RIP with councils reduced the possibility of smaller community groups (type 1 or 4 in the formulation used above) successfully tapping the RIP. Few such groups are listed in the annual programmes as project sponsors (see Colebatch 1977, p. 9), and while some may be subsumed under the general umbrella of the relevant council, there is no evidence to suggest that this is at all common. Indeed, the fact that many groups of this nature are either explicitly or implicitly anti-council makes it unlikely that the councils are putting their projects forward for RIP grants. In November 1977, one regional MP told some dissident constituents from an anti-council part of his electorate that RIP grants could only be given to legally constituted councils, and that this explained why that particular area had done relatively poorly in the annual allocation (*Post Courier*, 24 November 1977).

Several points should be noted here. The first is that the procedures of the programme reinforced the tendency for allocations to be limited to councils. Projects had to be proposed on a form, with costings and justifications, and had to be formally submitted by a particular date each year, for funding approximately nine to twelve months later. These procedures had been devised and administered by kiaps, and the organizations best able to comply with them were the councils, who in most cases had kiap advisers (who were, in an indeterminate but large proportion of the cases, the people responsible for the actual drafting of the council RIP proposals). Without going into the question of the extent to which non-council groups would be capable of executing projects of the sort actually funded by the RIP, it is evident that even in only procedural terms they would be starting from well behind scratch.

A second point to be noted is that as the relationship between councils and kiaps changed, adherence to the norms of "efficiency" held by kiaps and the Finance Department became more difficult to enforce. ("Efficiency" in this context can be taken to mean spending money only on the projects as quickly and economically as possible; it does not take in considerations of the purpose of the project or of the programme as a whole.) Councillors increased their political confidence, and at the same time there was a decline in both the confidence and the competence of the kiaps. Consequently, there was more pressure (or more effective pressure) for councils to assume real control over the funds allocated to them. This usually meant less "efficient" use of funds in the sense outlined above: a higher proportion of grants spent on labour (an important point, to which we will return later), more uncompleted projects. and more waste of materials and effort.

One official response to this trend was to try to improve the efficiency of the administrative machinery of the RIP. Kiaps were seconded to area authorities full-time to work as "RIP Managers"; technical staff were made available to area authorities by Public Works to supervise projects; outstanding uncompleted projects were consolidated; there was a manifest desire for fewer and bigger projects so that they could be effectively supervised; and so on. This approach culminated in a proposal (which was current in the early stages of thinking about provincial government) that something like the top two-thirds of the RIP should be absorbed into a "provincial works programme" to be run by PWD for the provincial government, while the small local projects would remain with something like the present RIP (which would presumably operate in much the same way as it does at present). The proposal has not been carried very far in policy circles, largely because it became clear that provincial governments would swallow the RIP whole, and that for this reason there was little point in debating what form it might take after the event. It is significant, though, as evidence of a common sentiment among officials concerned with the RIP − that is, that the trouble with the programme lay in its being handled by local bodies of low competence, and that one solution would be to put it into the more "professional" hands of the PWD.

In a situation where money was being made available through local channels for ill-defined purposes, one might expect that field officials of the various departments (other than DDA) might try to place departmental projects on the RIP. Certainly, this has happened to some extent, but perhaps to a lesser extent than comparable experience in other countries might suggest (see, e.g., Collins 1976). The Department of Education realized the potential of the RIP at a relatively early stage and managed to get large numbers of primary school classrooms and teachers' houses (formerly a responsibility shared in an uncertain fashion between councils, the Education Department, and the local community) placed on the RIP. The department subsequently managed to transfer much of the financial burden of the construction of new high schools onto the RIP as well. Other departments, however, seem to have been less active in tapping the RIP as a source of funds.

One consequence of the effective redefinition of "local initiatives" to mean "council initiatives" has been that RIP projects are increasingly identified as council projects (rather than "community" projects). Villagers who perceive RIP projects in this way are unlikely to feel any personal commitment to them and will be reluctant to contribute to them (other than through their council tax); consequently, local labour will be paid labour, and local materials will have to be paid for. There is considerable evidence that this is already the case over a large area of the country.

As well as asking What is local?, we must also ask What is an initiative?. The formal model of the programme implies that the action of the central government is in response to activities that have already begun on the ground. But the fact that a total budgetary allocation is made for the programme is in itself an inducement to spend, since both ministers and public servants need to justify the allocation for which they have struggled by showing that it can all be spent. In the early years of the RIP (1973–75), when allocations were rising rapidly and were outstripping demands, district officials were specifically instructed to ignore the normal rules limiting spending and to spend at the maximum possible rate. (This was not simply a case of following the ground rules of the budgetary process: the amount of unspent RIP funds remaining with councils had been raised by the Australian side at aid negotiations in Canberra.) Breaking down the national allocation into provincial figures gives the provinces a specific inducement to spend up to that figure. The fact that there is a specific figure to be spent, and that it comes up for grabs at a particular time, has meant that, to a large extent, local "initiatives" have arisen in response to the existence of the programme rather than vice versa, and the "initiatives" are limited to the formal requirements of the programme – that is, a declaration of intent coupled with a request for financial support. In many cases, council lists of RIP projects have been compiled by the kiap adviser in order to meet the deadline, with the council giving its formal assent.

We can see, therefore, two trends at work: one is the routinization of RIP projects, the close involvement of government officials in them, and their consequent identification as governmental projects. The other is a tendency to increase in scale. Both of these trends make it increasingly difficult to discuss the RIP in terms of the language of "local initiative" which is found in some of the official pronouncements about it.

"LOCAL SELF-HELP EFFORTS"

The idea of local self-help activity is an important component of central rhetoric about the RIP. In introducing the 1976/77 programme, the Minister for Finance stated: "The programme should not be thought of as a list of hand-outs. Rather, it should be seen as embodying the determination of the Government to back-up the efforts of the people themselves."[1]

"Self-help" has been discussed in relation to the RIP largely in terms of the amount or proportion of "local contribution" to the project. In other words, although the rhetoric speaks of a central government contribution to local activity, the discussion of detail assumes that it is the local community that is making the contribution and the government that is actually executing the project. The RDF had had a requirement for 50 per cent of the cost of a project to be met by the local contribution, but even by 1969 this was described as "not automatic".[2]

For the RIP, there was the question of what constituted a local contribution. Cash contributions were relatively straightforward: in most cases they became routinized as votes from the council budget. Since the councils were the construction authorities for most RIP projects, the only real evidence of the "local contribution" was the fact that the council had spent more on the project than the grant it had received. (Conversely, if this were not the case, then clearly there had been no local contribution.) But in addition to cash, local groups could make their contribution in kind — materials or labour. This was recognized as being particularly important, since a reliance on cash contributions as criteria for a grant has a regressive impact ("To him that hath, more shall be given . . . "). The supply of materials for projects was also straightforward, and in any case declined in importance as projects became more "formal" in nature and there was less call for bush materials.

The idea of local contributions in the form of labour raised more problems. Papua New Guineans had long been required to contribute free labour (usually one day a week) for road maintenance and other public purposes, and the assumption with the RIP was that people would be willing to contribute their labour for local projects, and that this could then be costed and counted as part of the local contribution. This assumption rested on two other assumptions: first, that villagers would identify with the goals of the project and get intrinsic satisfaction from their participation; secondly, that there would be no alternative uses for projects to be seen as government ones (not an unreasonable perception given the clear interest of government officials in getting such projects completed) and from the start, a very clear reluctance to provide free labour. There were, in fact, alternative uses for the apparently untapped labour time of villagers (not necessarily wage labour). And one consequence of the pattern of political change was an increasingly strong demand from villagers that the governmental machine provide them with some positive benefit in exchange for their loyalty and their taxes. In this atmosphere it became difficult enough for councils even to maintain their tax collections, let alone ask for new contributions of free labour.

The solution devised by the officials who handled the RIP was that it would be possible to pay people for work on RIP projects, but less than the rural minimum wage, the difference being counted as their contribution to the project. For instance, if a project required 1,000 man-days of labour, the calculation would go like this:

1,000 man-days at K2.00 per day (the rural minimum wage)	K2,000
1,000 man-days at K0.50 per day (amount actually paid)	K 500
Amount saved	K1,500

This amount of K1,500 is then counted as the local contribution to the project.

Leaving aside the question of whether or not is is realistic to consider this notional K1.50 per day as income foregone and therefore as a contribution to the project (on which see Colebatch 1977, p. 21), it is clear that the decision to pay a wage of some kind represents a dramatic transformation of the significance of the RIP for the villager. Where labour is contributed freely, the potential value of the RIP to the villager is the completed project: the road, the classroom, the aid post. Where a wage is offered, a very important benefit is the employment which the project offers. In most rural areas, there is little wage employment available, the employment benefit offered by the RIP may outweigh the benefits offered by the completed project. In these terms, a road project, which offers jobs for large numbers of labourers, may be valued more than an aid post constructed by council carpenters with little additional labour. Furthermore, it is not necessary for the road to be completed to yield its value: in fact, an uncompleted road project represents not a failure (as outside observers might see it), but a successful source of employment this year, and a possible source of further employment next year. Those who consider this a cynical formulation should ask why so high a proportion of roads built under RIP are not trafficable. One kiap in the Gulf stated that on one occasion, a group of villagers working on an RIP road presented a wage demand of such proportions that it would not have been possible to complete the road. He pointed this out to the group (who did not dispute it) and asked, "What do you want: the money or the road?" The unequivocal answer was "The money."

The next question, after determining what could be regarded as the local contribution, was to determine what level of contribution should be required. From the administrative point of view, the simplest answer would be to require all councils to contribute a fixed proportion of the total project cost. But because council areas vary widely in their wealth, the concentration of their population, and the cost of providing services, it could be argued that it would be inequitable to require all councils to meet the same proportion of project costs, and that councils in richer, more central areas should pay proportionately more than councils in remoter, poorer areas. A variable rate of contribution would enable more equitable dealings as regards the councils' capacity to pay, but it would equally enable variations on many other grounds and would also raise the question of who was to decide what rate of contribution was appropriate in any particular case. The outcome was that no firm rule was prescribed, and it was left to project sponsors to propose the level of local contribution they felt appropriate, and to area authorities and the Co-ordinator of Works to challenge the proposal if they felt so inclined. I have no detailed information about the way in which the control system worked in the earlier years, but the level of local contribution appears to have declined. By 1976/77, the claimed level of local contribution ranged from 49.1 per cent (Western Highlands) to 12.8 per cent (Gulf). In this year it was announced that some provinces had had their allocations reduced because of low rates of local contribution; the following year it was stated that some projects had been deleted for the same reason. It was not made clear, though, what rate of local contribution was regarded as unacceptable, or what screening procedures would apply in the future.

Finally, there was the question of how anyone in the central government would ever know what the rate of local contribution really was. Certainly, there were figures stated on the application form, but there was no procedure for determining if these targets were in fact met. The cash contribution was, in effect, paid by the council to the council, and only an investigation of the audit reports would show if there had been any real transfer. The contribution in kind was described by one kiap as "almost without exception the figment of someone's imagination[which] bears absolutely no relation to the amount of subsidised labour that can be expected to be applied to a project". There were wide variations in the level of contributions in kind claimed which are not necessarily explicable by objective differences between the provinces in question, and are just as likely to reflect instead variations in the practices of kiaps. It was technically possible for the Department of Finance to determine (after the event) what the actual level of local contribution had been by consulting the council audit reports held by the Commissioner for Local Government, and this seems to have been done in particular cases (though not necessarily by Finance). But the small staff in the Co-ordinator's office would not have been able to do this for all RIP projects. While a pooling of staff by the Co-ordinator and the Commissioner for Local Government might have circumvented this problem, it appears that the two offices were not accustomed to working together as closely as this.

It can be seen, then, that although self-help contributions occupied an important place in the rhetoric of the RIP, there was not a great deal of detailed concern at the central government level about this aspect of the programme, so that decisions about definition were left to officials further down the line. They had to decide what level of local contribution they could hope to achieve and how this could best be presented in the application forms (which was the only information about local contribution available at the time to those making the allocations). In the course of this micro-decision-making by officials, the significance of the RIP from the villager's viewpoint was completely transformed by the general acceptance of the practice of paying wages for RIP work. That so fundamental a change could happen in this way illustrates the importance of middle-level actors in the process of policy formulation.

TO ACHIEVE IMPROVEMENTS IN THE QUALITY OF RURAL LIFE

As has already been noted, policy statements in the early years of the new government stressed that the RIP should not concentrate on roads and bridges, as it had done in the past, but should focus more on "the quality of the lives of village people". As the same pronouncements also stressed that the RIP was an example of decentralized decision-making, the possibility immediately arises of a conflict between these two values (decentralization and the stress on "social" projects). What would happen if the preferences of decision-makers in Port Moresby and the provinces did not coincide? As it happened, in most cases the officials and clients at the provincial level and below did not share the concern of people in Port Moresby to shift the emphasis away from roads and bridges. They saw road projects as being tangible, known, within the technical capacity of sponsors, and representing a source of employment for large numbers of people with little other income.

This implicit conflict was a continuing one: the Department of Finance continued to stress the importance of "social" projects, but did not actually veto the project proposals it did receive. (Projects were deleted from provincial submissions for a variety of reasons, but it does not appear that this was done systematically in order to increase the proportion of social projects.) At the same time, officials in the field made efforts to drum up projects of the sort desired by Finance, and to present projects as having a "social" dimension wherever possible. Fairly soon, the Education Department became aware of the situation and realized that it offered the possibility of securing funds for the replacement of bush material classrooms and teachers' houses which would free headmasters of the need to badger the local community incessantly to renew and replace these buildings. Some misgivings were expressed in Finance about the incorporation of classrooms and teachers' houses into a programme for rural improvement, but provinces included them in their submissions in considerable numbers, and then were funded.

To some, this inclusion of primary school construction projects represented an increase in the "social benefits" side of the RIP ledger. But it can just as well be viewed as representing a consolidation of the tendency for the RIP to become an alternative works programme, whose function was to accommodate projects which for one reason or another could not be included in either of the government's other programmes (Capital Works and Minor New Works). And it is open to question how much projects of this sort can be regarded as contributing to the "enrichment in the quality of the lives of village people" to which the minister referred.

The point, however, is not whether or not an outside observer, looking back at the programme, would regard any given project as having improved the quality of rural life, but to what extent the programme was geared up to ask this question. For instance, to take one example, I do not know whether the purchase of a bus for the Namatanai Day High School[3] enriched the quality of the lives of the village people; what seems to me more important is that this question would have been dealt with only in an incidental way during the processing of the application. The applicant did not have to show that the project would have any village impact; the official receiving the application would have had very little information on the subject, fairly vague guidelines to work on, and a general disposition to make a grant unless there was some good reason not to do so.

There would have been, moreover, no evaluation after the event of the impact of this project on the quality of life in the area served. The Department of Finance did try, from time to time, to obtain from local councils or kiaps certificates of completion in respect of RIP projects (as were required under the Capital Works Programme), but with little success. Its exhortations were generally ignored by field officials, and it refrained from applying any sanctions (e.g., delaying or suspending funds) to bring about compliance. Given that it was unable to ascertain even if the projects it financed had been constructed, it is hardly surprising that it would have been unable to assess the impact they had on the quality of life.

In short, the proclaimed aim of the programme proved to be a difficult thing to give a clear operational meaning to within the particular organizational structure through which the RIP was run. The rather worn categories in which projects were placed in official discussions of the RIP did little to illuminate the actual impact of the programme and the real benefits it represented to village people. Roads were classed as "economic" projects — a hangover from the days of the World Bank Report and OPAC and internal rates of return — even though it was clear that many of the roads were untrafficable either on completion or shortly thereafter, and that the real benefit was the employment offered by their construction. Conversely, schools were seen as "social" projects, in the face of all the evidence that parents regard education as an investment aimed at securing salaried jobs for their children. Neither the top officials allocating the funds nor the middle-level officials distributing them made any systematic evaluations of the impact of the programme. Indeed, it can be argued that it was not in their interest to develop a concern with the impact of projects, since they all had a personal interest in maintaining the flow of money through the programme, and any study that questioned the ultimate utility of the whole exercise posed a potential hazard.

CONCLUSIONS

It remains to ask what light this account throws on the policy process under the National Coalition government. It may help to begin by outlining a formal model of policy-making, and then considering the extent to which the process we have been discussing can be described in these terms. In the formal model, the election of a new government is of great significance in policy terms because it brings in new policy-makers at the top of the government machine. Attention is focused on the policy concerns of the incoming actors in the political process, the decisions they make about the future course of government action, and the way in which, and the extent to which, these decisions are implemented.

In practice, as we have seen, the arrival of the new government does not necessarily have the dramatic impact on the policy pattern that the model implies. New governments do bring new (or at least different) sets of policy concerns with them, but they also inherit an existing pattern of policy commitments and strong structural inducements to maintain these commitments rather than to abandon them in favour of new proposals. In this particular case there was an extensive set of existing commitments supporting various forms of government intervention in rural areas (i.e., policy for rural development), and while the incoming government felt some dissatisfaction with the way the governmental machinery operated in rural areas, it did not pursue this to the point of seeking radical changes to the way the existing machinery worked. Rather it sought to compensate for this by building up an alternative form of governmental activity at the side, as it were — the RIP. And in doing this it was not adding something completely new to the machinery of government but building up a programme that was already there.

Moreover (and more importantly), it appeared that the role of government in the policy process could not really be described as taking big, important decisions, with minor questions of administrative detail being left to officials. The "decision" (ministerial) that projects should have a self-help component was less significant than the "decision" (official) that people could be paid a wage and still be counted as having made a self-help contribution.

Furthermore, it did not necessarily make sense to talk about "decisions" in this context. As the use of quotation marks in the previous paragraph implies, it is not clear that there were in fact specific, identifiable decisions in either of these matters. The ministers inherited a Rural Development Fund that provided for a self-help contribution, and the assumption that this would continue to be required was implicit rather than explicit. Similarly, the practice of paying villagers for work on RIP projects would have stemmed from a series of "micro-decisions" in particular cases by individual field officials, reinforced by "non-decisions" by officials and others further up the line (i.e., implied decisions not to intervene). The concept of a policy decision implies a major, binding commitment in principle, which brings in its train a number of consequential, administratively determined decisions which implement the major decision: in practice, key choices about the RIP were made in a very specific and local context by actors at the local level. The concept of a decision has more to do with the analytical constructs of the observer, such as the presumption of rationality and purpose, than with the actual processes of the RIP. As Bernard Schaffer put it: "Drama is continuous. Decisions are convenient labels given post hoc to the mythical precedents of the apparent outcomes of uncertain conflicts" (Schaffer 1975, p. 6). As was noted in the "planning" example cited earlier, a policy pronouncement from the Chief Minister could be quite ineffective in the absence of specific changes in the day-to-day handling of project applications. What counts is not so much who made the decision but whether or not it "sticks". If it does, one could talk about a decision, but it would be more precise to speak of a commitment.

The role of officials, then, is not one of implementing formed policy, but of making, maintaining, and changing commitments of important resources within ideological guidelines and some specific reference points determined (implicitly or explicitly) by ministers. In the RIP, the ministers' role was, broadly, to manifest their concern for rural people by allocating a new name, higher prestige, and much more money to an existing programme of grants which declared itself to be promoting rural development. These were the tools that came most readily to hand: other ways of achieving a more direct impact of government on rural change were possible, but would have required other resources — better channels of information, for instance — which were perhaps not as readily available. In any case, this financial commitment was made, and to it were attached ideological statements of the government's intent.

Within this broad framework, officials directed resources to particular projects. The most significant group at the centre was the Office of the Co-ordinator of Works, which controlled the actual allocation of funds. It was essentially a central office, with no field staff of its own, and was therefore dependent on proposals and reports sent in by clients for its information on the progress of the programme. (It tried to ensure that these reports were submitted by delaying the payment of fund allocations.) It resisted any suggestions that control of the programme should be transferred to the Office of Local Government, which would have been better placed to advise councils and exercise restraints on the use of funds. This is perhaps partly explained by, or partly rationalized by, the technocratic argument encountered in Finance that the department has no concern with the way in which, or the effectiveness with which, funds are spent, but only with seeing that funds are spent on the purpose for which they are voted.

This meant that field officials dealing with the programme, who were largely DDA staff of one sort or another, were to some extent cut off from headquarters officials dealing with the programme, since they were from another department and were not formally regarded as agents of the Co-ordinator of Works. They were also, in many cases, in an ambivalent positions *vis-à-vis* the RIP, since they were, in effect, clients of the programme themselves, or at least brokers. It was at this level that most of the critical interpretative choices had to be made: Did this sort of activity qualify for the programme? Did the limited amount of local contribution proposed satisfy the programme requirements? On occasions, the Co-ordinator of Works' office would intervene in these matters, but in general they were left to field staff.

What this meant was that the RIP could mean quite different things in different parts of the country: it was very much dependent on the relationship between the kiap and his constituents, and this was of course very variable. In some areas, such as parts of the Southern Highlands, a kiap (particularly an expatriate kiap) who enjoyed the confidence of his council could effectively control the RIP in his area. In other areas, such as the Gulf, kiaps had to stand helplessly by as councils voted away their RIP grants in the form of roadwork contracts, at rates which seemed to the kiaps ludicrously excessive (I asked one council kiap in the Southern Highlands what he would do if his council attempted this. He replied "I just wouldn't let them do it.").

What was common to the programme in all areas was money: essentially, the RIP was a spending programme. Public discussion of the programme was nearly always about the allocation of grants among different areas, or (more rarely) about inefficiency and waste in the spending patterns of particular councils. The volume of spending becomes an end in itself in official pronouncements: "Since the National Coalition Government came to power a total of K21.5 million has been allocated compared with K4.506 million in the previous five years. This shows quite clearly the Government's intentions in the field of Rural Development."[4] Whatever the purpose of the programme may be held to be, one of its most important functions has become that of the pork barrel — the fund of government largesse available for distribution to demonstrate the good will of the regime.

We can see, then, that the policy question in relation to the RIP is not simply: What were the government's intentions, and were they fulfilled? The government's intentions were not necessarily clear, or constant, or mutually consistent. And they were certainly not the only significant factors in the policy process; such things as the diffusion of bureaucratic responsibility for the programme, the emphasis on formal budgetary procedures, and the pressure to maintain spending rates for demonstration purposes were all as significant as any formal statement of government intentions in shaping policy (i.e., establishing commitments) relating to the RIP. Obviously, one could take formal statements of the aims of the programme — raising the rural standard of living, promoting self-reliance, etc. — and try to assess to what extent these things had or had not happened, leaving one with a balance sheet — almost certainly in the red — and a conclusion about the effectiveness of the RIP. But to do this would be to take a simplistic view of the powers of government and the nature of governmental commitments. In effect, in setting up the RIP the government was creating an opportunity, giving scope for rather freer access to public funds (for some sorts of claimant) than was normally allowed. Once this opportunity, this arena for action, had been created, the hopes and preferences of the government became one of the several alternative perspectives on appropriate modes of government action. Several observers have spoken of the alleged inefficiency, confusion, and waste associated with the RIP but have not taken the point that the possibility of this outcome is inherent in anything like the RIP. The real policy question is What happens to the pattern of governmental commitments in rural areas when the normal restraints are relaxed? It is to this question that this paper has been addressed.

NOTES

1. *Rural Improvement Programme* for 1976/77 (Port Moresby: Government Printer, 1976), p. 3.
2. Administrator's Circular Memorandum of 28 May 1969, "Rural Development".
3. Project 15–64 of the 1975/76 RIP. It attracted a grant of K9,000 with a local contribution of K9,000 in kind. It was unfortunately not spelt out what sort of contribution in kind can be used to buy a bus.
4. *Rural Improvement Programme* for 1976/77 (Port Moresby: Government Printer, 1976), p. 3.

"Maunten na Barat": Policy-Making in Chimbu Province

BILL STANDISH

It is tempting to say that there has been no policy made by Chimbu leaders in recent years. Very few, if any, major changes in governmental activity resulted from the work of either the Simbu Interim Provincial Government (SIPG) in 1977 or its predecessor, the Chimbu District Area Authority (subsequently referred to as the AA) in the years 1972–76.[1] This assessment echoes the complaints of several Simbu Assembly members in late 1977, and is made despite the passing of many hundreds of resolutions and the dispatch of dozens of letters to the national government. One reason might be the dramatic inconsistencies and reverses of opinion, common in Chimbu politics, which have often reminded me of the spectacular mountains and ravines of the Chimbu landscape —hence the title of this paper. I was still in the Highlands[2] when asked to discuss policy-making in Chimbu for this symposium, without the attractions and distractions of a library. I was thus forced to consider *a priori* what the word *policy* meant to me, a middle-class white Australian, who was watching the activities of a group of Papua New Guinean Highlands big-men on their home ground.

Firstly, I assumed that policy was made with a conscious awareness of the implications of the decision and course of action being taken: that it was a deliberate process. Secondly, I assumed that policy formulation involved an examination of problems, goals, available resources, alternative approaches, and explicit implementation and monitoring once a decision had been taken. This idea really involves planning, rather than mere decision-making, and conforms with the rational approach advocated by Robert S. McNamara (Schaffer 1977, p. 147). Thirdly, I assumed that policy decisions established general principles which could then be applied to a variety of specific cases, providing guidelines for future action and enabling both the avoidance of repetitious discussion and the maintenance of consistency. Policy in this sense is strategy rather than tactics. Fourthly, as a variation on this theme, some decisions commit political and social resources of such magnitude that they determine future courses of action, and even though the precise subject never arises again they thus involve policy.

Against such criteria, the Chimbu provincial politicians had indeed not been making policy. They did not explicitly isolate the policy aspects of the decisions they made during their formal meetings, nor (so far as I could determine) in their informal sessions at the rowdy men's house known as the Kundiawa Hotel. In fact, I noted only one occasion on which relatively abstract criteria were laid down so as to establish policy priorities. This was to do with the recommendations for Rural Improvement Programme (RIP) allocations for 1976/77. In January 1976, with the recommendations three weeks overdue in Port Moresby, with less than two sitting days remaining before the end of the AA's meeting, and with 142 applications for grants quite unsorted by the staff, the AA set up a subcommittee to rank the submissions from the nine councils and various non-governmental bodies. Presumably because I was thought to have some clerical skills, I was named to this subcommittee along with some educated young Chimbu men and one of the AA's three functionally literate politicians. In order to cover myself against later charges of meddling, and to give some coherence to our task, in one of my few activist moments I summarized what appeared to me to be the AA's consensus on desired types of project. This was firstly to open up a road to the Bomai area of southern Chimbu (of which more later), secondly to promote business, and thirdly to assist high schools. This statement of priorities was then implicitly accepted by the AA. We worked until 3 a.m., and when the AA's Chimbu clerk submitted our recommendations they were accepted by the AA — if only because it was Friday afternoon and the meeting was scheduled to end. This was an a-typically "rational" process. The Chimbu politician is a strong-willed person, and, as this paper shows, if a desired course of action goes against an agreed set of abstract principles then he or she has no qualms about dropping the general and implementing the particular.

Yet Chimbu politics is not without conflict over issues, and if my initial assumption had indeed been correct, then five years of my own work could be seen as rather sterile. Although little had resulted from the furious activity of AA and Simbu Assembly meetings, they *had* involved conflict over issues, however ill-formulated. Furthermore, there was a difference in emphasis between the concerns of the provincial leaders (who are mostly small businessmen) and whose deliberations often centred on their own perquisites and the large prestige projects which they have hope of controlling, and the concerns of rural village people with their emphasis on finding markets for smallholder produce and on social problems (Howlett et al. 1976, p. 340). Indeed, it was only at the instigation of a foreign-led team of consultants that the AA members in 1975 held meetings in rural settings, remote from the forbidding formalities of the provincial capital Kundiawa. Furthermore, as an observer I had found myself reacting silently in agreement, disagreement, or confusion to the resolutions of the provincial politicians. Being better informed than most of them about measurable social indicators for most parts of the province, I was well aware that adequate information for rational decisions did not exist, but that did not inhibit them. In other words, issues *were* at stake, which involved conflict over development strategies for the province, and policy decisions *were* being made — even if only implicitly.

After sketching the Chimbu geographic and social context, this paper summarizes the Chimbu politicians' vacillations over four key broad issues during the last five years: (*a*) land, population, and migration; (*b*) education; (*c*) clan warfare; and (*d*) coffee and provincial revenues. I have out-lined institutional arrangements in some detail in another study (Standish 1979), and the political struggles are to be analysed in much greater depth elsewhere (Standish forthcoming). My emphasis here follows Schaffer's formulation of "the public policy process", which he describes as "a multi-person drama going on in several arenas, some of them likely to be complex large-scale organisational situations. Decisions are the out-come of the drama, not a voluntary, willed, interstitial action. 'Drama is continuous. Decisions are convenient labels given *post hoc* to the mythical precedents of the apparent outcomes of uncertain conflicts' " (Schaffer 1977, p. 148, quoting Schaffer 1975, p. 6). Indeed, as this paper shows, policy-making is not always a consistent or rational process.

CHIMBU SOCIETY AND LEADERSHIP

Despite a history of endemic warfare, Chimbu — with good soils and a healthy climate in its northern sector — is the most densely populated province in Papua New Guinea. Preliminary estimates from the 1978—79 provincial census, the first for six years, indicate that there are 213,446 Chimbu people, 35,006 of them absent from the province. The annual growth rate since 1971 was thus 2.5 per cent, which is below the national average of about 3 per cent, but still enough to place strain on arable land in Chimbu. The area of the province is 5,879 square kilometres, of which some 13 per cent is above the upper limit of cultivation (2,400 metres above sea level). Population densities below 2,400 metres in the Gembogl District are over 200 persons per square kilometre, and in the Kundiawa District over 120 (Howlett et al. 1976, pp. 93, 95). In contrast, the Karimui Administrative Area, which forms the southern half of the province, is in the altitudinal range of 600—900 metres, and supports only 9,536 people. Unless otherwise mentioned, when referring to "the Chimbu people" this paper is discussing the 95 per cent of the Chimbu population who live in the northern sector of the province, mostly between 1,300 and 2,400 metres above sea level.

The Chimbu people are vigorous, and competition between clans and tribal groups is intense. Given the pressures on land, which have intensified since the introduction of the permanent tree crop coffee, those Chimbu who are keen to advance in the modern economy have frequently migrated out to less densely settled coastal areas or to urban areas throughout Papua New Guinea. Along with other Highlanders, they have contributed to rising levels of tension and strains on national unity when conflicts of interest, or physical violence, occur with host groups. Highlanders have become known collectively as Chimbu, and the degree of uniformity of environment and culture means the Highlands have the largest potential political bloc in Papua New Guinea, but between and within the Highlands provinces there are important political and cultural divisions. Within Chimbu Province thirteen languages are spoken, the largest — Kuman — by about eighty thousand people. Most adult men speak Melanesian pidgin (*tok pisin*), the national lingua franca. The Chimbu people live in named exogamous clan groups numbering up to a thousand people, with some phratries (allied clans) and tribes as large as five thousand.

The Chimbu people are now organized administratively into six districts of about thirty-five thousand each, and politically into nine local government councils. In the northern Chimbu, councillors represent one or two clans, an average of around one thousand people. The province has six members in the national parliament representing open electorates, and one from a provincial electorate covering the whole of Chimbu; the latter, Iambakey Okuk, in 1978 became opposition leader in parliament. The administrative and political arenas for decision in Chimbu have been fairly constant during the last decade, but the politicians now have weight they previously lacked. Much more dramatic than institutional change in the last ten years has been the socio-economic revolution begun during the colonial period, involving the spread of modern education, including five high schools, and the entry into cash cropping of most families with suitable land in northern Chimbu. A fleet of some one hundred trucks owned by private buyers uses an effective road network to carry coffee to Kundiawa and to other provinces for processing before export.

These social and economic changes did not alter the style of political leadership in Chimbu fundamentally in the colonial period, and despite the cessation of warfare for two decades and the banning of sorcery there is a great deal of continuity in the political culture. Paula Brown (1963) has argued that pre-colonial clan leadership was the relatively open big-man system which is often attributed to Melanesian societies (Sahlins 1963). In contrast, I have persuasive evidence that there was a strong hereditary element in leadership. Given the wealth available before the first European contact in 1933, there was considerable economic differentiation and stratification in Chimbu society, along with occasional "despotism" in a

CHIMBU PROVINCE

leader's relations with his group (Standish 1978*b*). In the arena beyond the clan — i.e., in the tribe — the situation was more competitive, and leadership might depend on the numerical and fighting strength of the constituent clans. The domineering style of Chimbu leaders remains, along with their conspicuous displays of wealth and their occasional demonstration — especially in the 1970s — of prowess in warfare.

Access to leadership positions has opened up with the creation of modern institutions, in that electoral arenas are larger than any single clan or tribe. Now many educated young men have aspirations in politics as well as ambition for business and public service careers. Because of the fragmentation of the electorate along kinship lines, and because most clans have their own contenders for political office, it is frequently possible for a man to be elected, even in council wards, with a minority of votes as small as 15 per cent. Provided this small constituency, comprising often just his own kin, is kept happy, the rest can be ignored. Similarly, if a candidate manages to neutralize potential rivals within his own group, perhaps incorporating them with generous inducements, and then encourages a few stooges to stand so as to split his rivals' clan vote catchments, he then has a good chance of election (Standish 1978*a*). The vertical kinship divisions within the social structure are suited to the development of small patronage networks within clans, which are the real basis of most elected office.

Yet the members of the dominant elected political elite, who usually become businessmen soon after election if they are not so already, have a great deal in common which often leads to co-operation. The first of these interests, of course, is to stay in office, and the second is to make that stay repay the investment made to get there. The competing claims of electorates for increased allocations of government resources often seem relatively insignificant in Chimbu politics. The reasons may well be that throughout the colonial period, and to a lesser extent since, local politicians in Papua New Guinea have not, themselves, had to raise the bulk of the revenues they expended, and something of a supplicatory "handout" mentality developed. Since money came readily, it could be spent easily. Partly, too, because of the power of the bureaucracy, there was little sense of competition between electorates for scarce budgetary resources.

THE FRAMEWORK FOR POLICY-MAKING IN CHIMBU

The Interim Assembly is an appointed body, having no electoral base. It grew out of the Chimbu AA, which was set up in December 1972 comprising two representatives chosen by each of the nine Chimbu councils. From 1974 onwards this body was keen to emulate Bougainville and win provincial government powers, and in 1976 it resolved that its membership should become the Interim (appointed) Provincial Assembly, with the addition of a representative of the Chimbu women's movement and one clergyman from each of the major churches in the province, Catholic and Lutheran. These twenty-one people were specified as members of the Simbu Assembly in November 1976 by the National Executive Council (NEC), under a charter drawn up under the Provincial Government (Preparatory Arrangements) Act 1974. The same membership was reappointed in 1977 by the NEC under transitional provisions in the new Constitution of the Simbu Province drawn up under the Organic Law on Provincial Government 1976. The Assembly elects one of its number to be Premier, and he in turn chooses an executive of five from the Assembly. The Interim Premier since 1976 has been Siwi Kurondo, MBE, a former policeman and member of the House of Assembly for Kerowagi from 1964 to 1972.

An election for the Simbu Assembly is not required until August 1979. At least one local government council has failed in an attempt to change its "representative" in the Assembly. Whereas previously AA members had to keep their council happy and retain their council membership, the bolder Assembly members now feel they can afford to ignore their original bases of support, the councils. Although this would appear to be a short-sighted approach, some have indeed turned their backs on their home councils. In future, they will face electorates of around ten thousand people. Given the kinship and occasional linguistic divisions within Assembly electorates, and the lack of political party machines, they might after their election well find themselves almost as isolated from most of their voters as are members of the national parliament, whose electorates hold three times the population.

The former AA members of the Simbu Assembly are in many ways "middle men", neither traditional nor modern. Their average age is in the mid-forties, and while nine claim literacy in *tok pisin* I would class only three as functionally literate. Yet they value modern education, as is shown by the fact that 59 per cent of those with children old enough have sent them to high school. Sixty per cent are polygynous. All but one claimed to have six or more pigs, with an average claimed ownership of twenty-eight pigs and a median of sixteen, figures which I suspect to be too high (Standish, forthcoming). In the northern Chimbu area twenty years ago only 10 per cent of men were polygynous (and the figure is about half that today), and average ownership of pigs today is around four per adult male in a sample of the same age as the AA members. So by the simplest criteria these are "big-men", an impression reinforced by their modern sector business activities. Almost 60 per cent own or have owned pig projects with imported stock; 52 per cent have or have had cattle projects; 94 per cent grow coffee, and 76 per cent own coffee hulling machines; almost 60 per cent have owned or still own trade stores; 47 per cent have owned or still own motor vehicles; 53 per cent are engaged in coffee buying. In addition to these business activities, allowances and salaries accruing to them from their official political activities in 1977 totalled some K3,600 each, and 71 per cent employed paid workmen. The three additional appointees were all much better educated, and apart from the priest had business connections, but they were not prominent in Assembly debates. Given that the per capita income in Chimbu in 1977 during a coffee boom was K100, and in a year of average coffee prices is around K50, the Assembly members are clearly part of a very small economic, as well as political, elite.

The SIPG was served in 1977 by a secretariat of six young men, who are well educated but mostly not highly educated. They had received substantial promotions from their previous positions with the AA when they won out during the intense political lobbying and faction fighting that surrounded the appointment of the secretariat. There is a shortage of qualified people willing to compete for these positions. None of the secretariat staff in 1977 had extensive public service experience, and all owed their position to the interplay of political forces. Policy matters in 1977 were handled by the Provincial Secretary and the Planner, with the Legal Officer holding a narrow but unspecified brief and the Administrative Officer operating as a minutes and correspondence clerk. The Research Officer, a former magistrate, complained that he was given no research to perform and he mainly worked as manager of the RIP grants. A system of weekly staff meetings broke down soon after it was initiated, a reflection of the factionalism riddling the secretariat. This phenomenon was promoted by the Premier himself, who along with other executive members played "favourites" in a divide-and-rule ploy apparently designed to neutralize potential future rivals. The executive members, and to a lesser extent some of the secretariat, became embroiled in the volatile four-month campaign leading up to the national parliament elections held in June—July 1977. It is fair to say that this environment was not conducive to forward planning and teamwork. Staff members were constantly engaged in political manoeuvres merely to ensure the preservation of their own positions, which rarely allowed time or energy for considered policy initiatives.

Co-ordination of the public service in Chimbu has usually been poor. Chimbu was separated from the Eastern Highlands District in 1966, and although by 1977 it had elements of some seventeen national agencies, many of these were smaller than the normal provincial establishments and remained subordinate to departmental branch offices in neighbouring provinces. With its reputation for turbulence — in the form of tribal fighting, occasional highway stonings and frequent urban burglaries — Chimbu was usually not able to fill all of its rather small quota of established posts, and often did not attract the highest quality staff. Given that the departmental officers-in-charge (OICs) in Kundiawa lacked the delegations held by most district administrative authorities, it is not surprising that the informal teamwork which developed in the Southern and Eastern Highlands never reached a high level in Chimbu's Provincial Co-ordinating Committee, consisting of departmental OICs, which met in Kundiawa until the inauguration of the SIPG. Chimbu thus suffered from the worst defects of the overcentralized bureaucracy inherited by the Somare government and identified by the Constitutional Planning Committee (CPC) in 1973, for which the CPC prescribed the essentially political step of devolution to provincial governments (PNG 1973*b*, chap. 4; PNG 1974*c*, vol. 1, chap. 10).

Tensions and morale problems arising during decolonization and localization were exacerbated because of the lack of hard information on just what provincial government would entail. The worst-affected part of the bureaucracy has been the previously dominant field service of generalist administrators, the kiaps. These are the government's basic data collectors and they carry much of the burden of implementing development activities, often performing "agency" functions for other government departments, including the police. The senior kiap, the District Commissioner (after independence, Provincial Commissioner) was most vulnerable to provincial government pressure, as his position symbolized national government power. The Provincial Commissioner never had real power of administrative co-ordination, but without his co-operation government programmes had little chance of success. In March 1977 the Romney Committee, set up by the Public Services Commission, recommended that the PC's position be abolished with the inauguration of provincial government, but the PCs were left in doubt about their future throughout most of 1977. In October the new Minister for Decentralization (Father John Momis) told the PCs that they were likely to become the new administrative secretaries, the senior national government public servants in every province who now hold full co-ordinating powers. This rash statement was soon withdrawn, although in December 1977 most of the men recommended by the provinces for temporary appointment as administrative secretaries had previously been senior kiaps. In the case of Chimbu, the doubt and uncertainty had considerably worsened the relations between the SIPG and the acting PC (a young man from the Premier's home area, who was automatically therefore seen as a political rival).

The commencement of the SIPG in early 1977 appeared to be a suitable occasion to initiate a new order of coherent administrative action to develop and carry out provincial policies. Although there was some improvement in Chimbu in 1977, the structures are still evolving. The final gathering of the departmental OICs meeting as the Provincial Co-ordinating Committee was held in February 1977, but the first meeting of a new body, the Provincial Development Team (PDT) was not held until May. This body comprised the provincial OICs of the key developmental agencies — Education, Health, National Works Authority, Provincial Administration, and Bureau of Management Services — who met monthly with the Planner under the active chairmanship of the Provincial Secretary (succeeded in 1978 by the Administrative Secretary). The Premier attended meetings frequently in 1977, but his occasional comments were not noteworthy for their pertinence. This body had been designed to act as a channel of expert opinion on matters arising within Chimbu, either on referral from the provincial executive or arising from departmental operations. It proved educational for secretariat members, and helped establish friendly contact between the senior government officers in Kundiawa, but it was not a suitable forum for interchange between specialist bureaucrats and non-literate politicians. The PDT worked quite well in 1977 to co-ordinate routine matters (such as staff housing), and it also initiated for provincial executive approval some worthwhile health and minor works proposals. It is too early to assess the results from this innovation, and so I return to my principal focus, the involvement of Chimbu politicians in policy matters in the years 1972–77.

THE "GREEN BOOK"

It was largely to overcome the paucity of data required for coherent planning that the Central Planning Office in 1975 commissioned an Australian National University team led by Dr Diana Howlett to prepare a base-line study for Chimbu. The team's report (Howlett et al. 1976) became generally known as the "Green Book" and sometimes as the "Chimbu Bible" to the more optimistic. The latter appellation is misleading in that the report explicitly seeks to present the issues in Chimbu development and makes no attempt to provide a plan or to prescribe detailed policies. However, the book opens with a quotation from E. F. Schumacher's *Small Is Beautiful* that "economic development is something much wider and deeper than economics", and is in line with Papua New Guinea's Eight Aims (Lepani 1976), the Constitution's National Goals and Directive Principles and the *National Development Strategy* (PNG 1976). The Green Book highlights social and geographic inequalities and is opposed to large-scale agricultural projects and to capital-intensive secondary industry. Rather, it advocates the development of small businesses using "appropriate technology" wherever possible. The main problems identified are land shortage, population pressures, employment, and the quality of rural life. In short, it is an egalitarian document. Its English version was presented to the Chimbu AA in November 1976 and a *tok pisin* version became available in November 1977.

Upon receipt of the Green Book, the SIPG with the lead of its secretariat seemed to be taking a sophisticated approach to the policy-making process. Several seminars were planned. In mid-January 1977 the Assembly was briefed at a special meeting on the issues raised in the study. But this meeting ended two days early, because the members were more keen to elect their executive and to set their levels of remuneration. Most of the SIPG's energies for the next two months were directed towards organizing its spectacular inaugural ceremonies. This legitimating ritual over, a "Green Book Seminar" was held in March 1977 for Simbu executive members, departmental staff, and some community leaders. The points raised in the Green Book were commented upon by the departmental representatives, who gave their own policies. These contributions were in turn discussed by the gathering at large. In early May 1977 a three-day seminar was held on provincial powers in the decentralized system, and in June another was held on provincial government and education. Some months later, in October, a further half-day session was held to discuss agriculture, but by this stage the seminar approach had lost momentum. From these meetings the Simbu Planner drew up a draft "First Priority Schedule (June 1977–June 1980)", which was accepted by the Development Team and passed by the Simbu executive. After an hour's explanation, it was endorsed by the Provincial Assembly in July 1977 (SIPG 1977). This document follows the tradition of the Green Book, stressing rural development in the sense of improved living standards and small industry development, improved public health and community-oriented education with an emphasis on the dissemination of skills useful in village life, and the improvement of social services and infrastructure for rural people. The Priority Schedule was announced with well-orchestrated media fanfare and was praised by the National Planning Office.

There were signs, however, that this textbook approach to provincial priority-making was too good to be true. During the January seminar some of the Assembly members rejected outright the Green Book's advocacy of an increase in the number of vocational schools and technically oriented high schools. They wanted more academic high schools and, indeed, a university as well. While in favour of improved rural credit, they were opposed to any restrictions upon private enterprise and in particular were against any slowdown in the development of cattle projects, whose stratifying impact has been noted (McKillop 1976*b*). They resented being lectured (as they appeared to be) by idealistic young university students, who not only tried to explain the Green Book (sometimes in very academically jargonized *tok pisin*), but who also promoted their own vision of communal rather than individual enterprise. As noted above, the seminar broke up early.

During the March seminar, the same policy conflicts again emerged, but the exercise did not involve substantial participation by the provincial executive members, none of whom have sufficient literacy in *tok pisin* to handle the issues being raised in the documents circulated. They did not contribute to the consensus that emerged, which largely echoed the Green Book and which was expressed subsequently in the Priority Schedule. Yet the March seminar was useful in bringing various sectors of the community together and enabled the Provincial Secretary to display some of his talents for diplomacy at a time when there was considerable apprehension within the bureaucracy in Chimbu. But this policy discussion stopped at the level of talk, instead of leading to action. It was not until October 1977 that a secretariat member was detailed to examine implementation of the Priority Schedule. The SIPG members ostentatiously carried around their English language versions of the Green Book, but when the *tok pisin* version arrived in Kundiawa late in 1977 no special effort was taken to disseminate its points. In summary, then, there are signs that the SIPG was using the study by Howlett et al. merely as a symbolic legitimating device, as has happened to similar studies and to development plans in many countries, and that the SIPG had no depth of commitment to it as a policy guide.

LAND, POPULATION, AND MIGRATION

The problems of responding to pressures on land have been examined spasmodically by Chimbu authorities over the last ten years, with the general reaction being that more land must be opened up for resettlement. But where? Highlanders are unpopular settlers in coastal areas, and Chimbu settlers have had difficulties in the Western Highlands. Even though their labour is crucial to the success of much plantation agriculture — including that which is owned by nationals — Highlanders are often simultaneously hated, feared, and looked down upon in coastal areas. Chimbu politicians have for over a decade cast covetous eyes on the thinly populated Ramu Valley to their north in the Madang Province, and also to their own southern portion, the Karimui and Bomai census divisions in the Karimui Administrative Area. These areas are lightly populated and have similar environments. When the tropical forest in the Karimui is removed, the soils leach quickly because of the warm climate and heavy rainfall. The people suffer from high rates of malnutrition, malaria, and leprosy, and so not surprisingly there are few of them

(Simpson 1975). In late 1976 the Simbu executive chartered an aircraft to examine a route for a road across the Bundi gap into the Ramu, connecting with the Madang Highway, which consultants had costed at K19 million four years previously. In September 1977, in five minutes flat, the Simbu Assembly resolved to spend K500,000 on a minor road to Bundi, over the border in Madang Province. There was no consultation with the Madang authorities or the national government, no feasibility study, no costing. The best that can be said of this exercise is that it was not a formal appropriation, although the members thought it was. The Bundi people have traditional marriage and trade links with some Chimbu groups, but the Madang leaders are very much concerned about urban immigrant problems and indeed have resolved that they do *not* want a direct road to the Highlands.

The Karimui/Bomai sectors of the Great Papuan Plateau have long been seen by Chimbu leaders as a land of milk and honey, and bearing in mind the activities of politicians this is certainly a much-promised land. In late 1973 a Chimbu AA delegation flew to Karimui and reported that 800 hectares and possibly 2,400 hectares would be available for resettlement at Karimui. In recent years the spice cardamom has proved to be a valuable crop there. It has a high value for its weight, making it suitable for air transport, and furthermore does not require destruction of the forest cover. Production of cardamom on a major scale would require large areas of food gardens for plantation workers, however. Over the years, various patrol officers have dreamt of large-scale resettlement in the area, despite negative assessments arising from the only serious studies by agriculture and soils experts. A scheme that was being planned in Kundiawa in 1969 received adverse publicity (Wagner 1971) and was scotched by the Administrator, L. W. Johnson. Then in 1973, at a time when his electoral standing was low, the Minister for Agriculture and Member for Chimbu Regional, Iambakey Okuk, revived the Karimui dream once more. His National Party colleague, Minister for Lands Thomas Kavali, boldly announced at the end of 1974 that the government would buy 20,000 hectares for resettlement and issued an instruction to that effect. A departmental officer had ascertained that only 440 hectares was available in Karimui, and it appeared that a major conflict over the issue was arising in national government circles. At the end of 1974 the Office of Environment and Conservation commissioned a feasibility study which collated all available data (Simpson 1975). This report stressed the need for caution; it was calculated that there was no spare land at Karimui after future needs of the local residents were taken into account, and that at the most the Bomai area could only support eight hundred families, or a few thousand people. This would be the equivalent of Chimbu's annual population growth, and so resettlement would have negligible long-term benefits at considerable development expense. The report recommended that research be carried out into more intensive agriculture for Chimbu, and furthermore that a national family planning programme be adopted for Papua New Guinea as a whole.

The Chimbu response to this report was dramatic. In June 1975 the AA chairman (now Simbu Premier) and several prominent public servants from Chimbu reacted angrily at an illustrated briefing on the report given in Port Moresby. They denied that Chimbu had a population problem, although somewhat paradoxically they stressed the need for more land, especially to "make business". The Simpson report increased Chimbu determination on the issue. In January 1976, following the initiative of a road-building kiap in the neighbouring Gumine District, the Chimbu AA voted to recommend the expenditure of some K50,000 of RIP money on an access road to Bomai for resettlement purposes. But following the sacking of Kavali and Okuk from the national ministry for insubordination later that month, this proposal was quietly blocked again by the central government. Gardens were prepared to feed road workers along the proposed route, but from mid-1976 access to the roadhead was prevented by sustained clan warfare in the Marigl Valley. All work ceased. Nonetheless, the SIPG acquired 160 hectares of land at Bomai for a cardamom plantation during 1977, as a forerunner to major resettlement. Should the small self-help road ever be completed, it will have to be duplicated on a new alignment if a major "Bomai Highway" is built to southern Chimbu and Gulf Province, a long-term possibility projected in the draft National Transport Plan drawn up while Okuk was Minister of Transport.

Such proposals inevitably open up political conflict. For instance, the Gumine and Chuave members of the Simbu Assembly are divided on whether an all-weather access road to Karimui should pass through Chuave and Nomane, or through Gumine and Bomai. The Karimui people themselves want a road to join the existing road south of Lufa in the Eastern Highlands, which would be a smaller construction job but which would take the area out of the Chimbu sphere of interest. Another road being built through the Kambia in the Western Highlands is approaching the Chimbu border near Bomai, and might have a similar impact on that area. Meanwhile small-scale spontaneous resettlement continues at Karimui and Bomai, with tensions between settlers and the land-owners. The problem may escalate if construction of a major hydro-electric dam ever proceeds at Wabo as part of the Purari scheme, for Wabo is only a short distance south of the Chimbu border in the Gulf Province. The impact of a direct road link from the Highlands down to the Papuan Gulf could well rescuscitate fears of a Highlands takeover which led to moves for Papuan secession in the years 1973–75.

The public health activity "family planning education" in the draft

Priority Schedule was the only item changed when this document was put to the Assembly at its July 1977 meeting. It was dropped at the insistence of the Premier, who argued that there was no land shortage problem in Chimbu. He said (in all seriousness?) that Chimbu needed warriors, and should aim at a population as large as that of China. No members expressed dissent, not even those who themselves had arranged tubal ligations after their wives had borne numerous children. The PDT was not so quiescent, and in September 1977 wrote to the Premier that it felt "obliged to advise the provincial government [that] population control is still a national priority and the national government recognises the dangers of severe social problems associated with an unrestricted rate of population growth especially in an area of such intense population pressure as exists within Simbu Province". As so often occurs with the SIPG, there has been − to my knowledge − no reply to this letter. Meanwhile, public demand for family planning services is continuing, encouraged in some instances by Catholic missionary priests. The existing programme is likely to continue quietly, fulfilling as it does a demand from village couples for information. But if ever this matter becomes one of public controversy, the professional health workers could find themselves in a difficult conflict situation. Similarly, the Simbu Provincial Government could well find itself in disagreement with the national government and other provinces if present stances on this sensitive issue are maintained.

Several coastal and island provinces have frequently expressed concern about Highlands migration to coastal areas, with those on the mainland taking a more moderate stance than the Islanders (*vide* the recent threats of pay-back and expulsion emanating from North Solomons and East New Britain [Talyaga and Olela 1978]). In 1974 the Morobe AA raised the question of prostitution among Highland settlers in Lae, and the Chimbu AA's response was the rather unworkable proposal to set up checkpoints on the Highlands Highway at the Daulo and Kassam passes, with identity cards being required for travel to the coast. These cards would be issued by local leaders. At the internal migration conference of interested AAs held in Goroka in January 1976 the Chimbu delegates were notable for their silence, but then their trip had been regarded as a junket and the policy issues involved had not been discussed by the Chimbu AA in advance.

The interests of ordinary Chimbu villagers and those of their political bosses on the migration question do not necessarily coincide. With limited opportunity at home, migration is the only option for many villagers. The leaders want to keep up the numbers at home, ostensibly to promote local development but also to raise tax collections and per capita revenue grants from the national government, to maintain or increase the number of electorates, and quite probably also to boost their strength in local disputes, which often degenerate into armed conflict. These reasons may explain the approach of the Simbu Premier during the November 1977 Premiers' Conference, when he agreed to North Solomons' highly divisive suggestions for limitations upon (constitutionally guaranteed) freedom of movement.

In summary, the SIPG's approach to these crucial land, population, and migration policy issues has been erratic and unpractical, and at best simplistic. It may be that the Assembly members appreciate the magnitude of the issues but find them too big to handle, and therefore easier to put aside. In so far as Chimbu migration continues to create problems for them, other provinces will not want this approach to continue.

EDUCATION

The SIPG's Priority Schedule for education gives first listing to the improvement and expansion of existing vocational schools, which provide primary school leavers with some farming, trade, and business skills, and suggests upgrading the curriculum and directing the centres more towards village life. The schedule follows this suggestion with a proposal for the incorporation of appropriate skills for village living in community (primary) schools. It seeks the promotion of adult and technical education. Apart from mentioning the consolidation of existing high schools, the schedule argues that what is needed is "consideration of change in curriculum to spend more time on village improvement skills. To include nutrition, food production, village hygiene, appropriate technology skills and technical education" (SIPG 1977). These curriculum changes might be made outside the core curriculum, which is of course a national government responsibility and not subject to provincial authority. But these policy priorities were twice put to the test in 1977, and twice the SIPG's commitment to them was found wanting.

The unusually flat tract of land known as Gui on the Highlands Highway in the Kerowagi District has for five years been occupied by a vocational school and thus as an educational institution would normally become a provincial asset. The Corrective Institutions Service (CIS) has long sought this land, which apart from being fertile is virtually the only non-urban government land in the entire province. The site of the prison at Birane near Kundiawa is both too small and geologically unstable: it has the alarming tendency to slip off into the Wahgi River. In March 1976 the Provincial Co-ordinating Committee endorsed the CIS request, without first making a full examination of the files on the matter. Nothing happened for nine months. With hundreds of men being jailed after clan warfare, Chimbu leaders have for several years wanted a larger prison within their province. They also allege that sorcery has led to the deaths of Chimbu men who have been transferred to other provinces to serve their time. The Simbu executive resolved on 15 December 1976 that Gui should be handed over to the CIS and that the vocational school should "move out somewhere else". As so often occurs — because of other demands on his time or political tensions with his ministers — the Provincial Secretary was not present to advise during this meeting, and the Planner was overseas on leave. The executive was not aware that a side effect of their decision was that the provincial government would thereby surrender to the national government control of Chimbu's prime piece of real estate, perhaps the only area suitable for light industry in the province.

Opposition to the Simbu executive decision soon grew both within the bureaucracy and among the public. Following statements from irate local villagers, the kiaps examined their files and discovered that before acquisition in 1971 the original land-owners had been promised that the Gui land would only be used for educational purposes. On these grounds the Co-ordinating Committee reversed its earlier recommendation in favour of the CIS. It considered that government credibility on land matters was at stake, and that if pledges made over Gui were broken then all future land purchases would be jeopardized. Politically ambitious young men organized two protest marches in Kundiawa, the participants being vocational centre students and other community school leavers, as well as local land-owners who were reluctant to have a jail next door. The SIPG members faced the first of these demonstrations, but reacted angrily to this defiance of their ruling when they returned to an Assembly meeting then in progress. The executive members avoided a second confrontation on the issue by going at short notice to Goroka in a spontaneous attempt to open negotiations with the owners of the Collins and Leahy trading empire to purchase the Kundiawa Hotel. The executive dug in on this issue when the Provincial Secretary tried to persuade them to change their minds. They also rejected their Planner when he nobly took the blame upon himself for failing to advise them adequately on this issue.

As Robert Price (1974) shows for Ghana, "big-men" are determined to put down others and show them up as "small-boys". Despite a final plea to the Assembly from the Education Superintendent, in April 1977 the vocational school was given two weeks to vacate the site. It was the middle of a school term. In a move reminiscent of the tactics of Highlands warfare, the CIS then destroyed a valuable crop without consulting the vocational centre staff. Education Department staff have refused to move to the Birane site, not unreasonably saying that if it is unsafe for prisoners it is unsafe for children. Very few alternative pieces of land are available in the area. Two portions were subsequently offered to the SIPG, one in the Western Highlands, the other too small, and both in areas of probable future land shortage. The net result of this saga is that one of the province's two vocational centres has literally folded up. (The Catholic Church had withdrawn its girls centre from the Education system in 1977 so as to maintain autonomous control over its curriculum.) The remaining centre is inside the urban area of Kundiawa, and so cannot conform to the SIPG's rural priorities. This case shows that the first point in the SIPG priority schedule proved of no practical effect.

Following the successful June 1977 seminar on education, the Simbu Planner heard about the national government's proposed trial Secondary School Community Extension Programme (SSCEP). This aims to relate high school work to problems of rural life, to involve students in village life and agriculture, and to carry new ideas out into the villages. The proponents of the scheme argued that despite time spent with villagers, students would not suffer academically, but in fact would be more self-reliant individuals, better informed about their own societies, better equipped to relate to them upon graduation, and quite probably more self-reliant academically. The Planner immediately saw that this scheme appeared tailor-made to fit the Priority Schedule requirements, and he quickly persuaded the Simbu executive to put in a bid for a SSCEP project under the National Public Expenditure Plan. He suggested that Kerowagi High School was suitable, because it has sufficient land, but he considered that the incumbent headmaster was a traditionalist who would have to be transferred elsewhere to get the scheme going. The executive agreed in principle, and the Assembly appropriated K3,000 as a voluntary provincial contribution, a tangible sign of serious intent to help swing the national government behind the Chimbu bid.

The provincial leaders lacked knowledge about the scheme, and the Kerowagi High School's board of governors, comprising local dignitaries, raised doubts about the impact of SSCEP on the academic careers of students. The SSCEP approach does not match Chimbu conceptions of a "proper" education, which were expressed as early as 1959 by the man now Premier. He told the then Director of Education at a primary school opening ceremony: "We want our children to be exactly like you" (Smith 1975, p. 46). When in October 1977 Education Department officials from Port Moresby came to Chimbu to test the depth of public commitment to the SSCEP idea, the Premier joined the Kerowagi board of governors in rejecting the scheme. In this he was being utterly consistent with his earlier attitudes, although this meant abandoning the designs of both the Planner and the Provincial Secretary, and ignoring the executive and Assembly decisions. Some secretariat members blamed their colleagues for the switch, and the headmaster was accused of sabotaging the scheme, responses which I believe were unwarranted. The executive briefing had been rushed and was obviously inadequate, given entrenched attitudes towards education. In addition, the proposal goes against the perceived self-interest of the Chimbu elite who want white-collar jobs for their children. These men are socially conservative, and once again the Simbu Priority Schedule was ignored.

CLAN WARFARE

Chimbu and other Highlands politicians have generally taken an authoritarian line on clan warfare, arguing for draconian police tactics, including shooting to kill. While fights in Chimbu can last for months and involve thousands of people, leading to dozens of deaths and injuries each year, as well as to the destruction of many houses, economic trees, and food gardens and the complete disruption of government extension services, there has been an unwritten moratorium on the use of modern weapons. The armoury is confined to traditional bows and arrows, shields, spears, and axes. Warfare, which erupts from traditional causes such as disputes over land, women, and pigs, is now also often a response to accidental road deaths caused by liquor. This manifestation of clan solidarity is, I would argue, an expression of political insecurity in the period of decolonization. It is thus a complex social question (Standish 1973; PNG 1973a; Kerpi 1976), and the national government which has constitutional responsibility for keeping public order has resisted pressures from Highlands leaders to use punitive tactics with modern weapons.

In late 1976, angered and shamed by the three years of intermittent fighting between the Endugwa and Kumai clans of Kup in the Kerowagi District, the Simbu executive threatened to withdraw all government services such as schools and aid posts, to cease agricultural extension work, and to close roads until fighting ceased. The threat had no obvious immediate effect, but in January 1977 peace descended upon the Kup area – probably because the body count (or "kill ratio") had evened up. A separate fight started in Kup in October 1977 involving the Kumai clan who had been party to the 1973–76 conflicts, and continued for six weeks until stopped by a concerted kiap-led police operation. Clearly, the SIPG's threat had not been an effective deterrent. Similar threats to withdraw services in the upper Marigl and Mon areas of Gumine (in the Yuri/Yani fights of December 1976–January 1977) were ineffective, in that the participants lobbied the SIPG to withdraw the sanctions (before themselves burning down a school and an aid post). Where memories are long, government bluff has only to be called once to fail for ever. Later in 1977 the Yuri were again involved in a major series of battles. Given the deep social roots of the fighting, governmental sanctions – including the wholesale imprisonment of participants – are rather like cutting off sword grass above ground level and then expecting it to wither away. Yet peace is a prerequisite for any social and economic development to get under way. A conundrum.

The Chimbu leaders have tried to help the national government to stop fighting, on several occasions visiting battlegrounds and speaking with the participants, hastily organizing peace ceremonies and the like, and officers have been grateful for such political support as has been forthcoming. Unfortunately, the provincial politicians lack the necessary degree of credibility on this issue. Indeed, one has built his reputation as a fight leader in recent years and another tried to start a clan fight after the 1977 national elections. I have myself witnessed a Simbu executive member congratulating his fellow tribesmen on the particularly grisly mutilation of a victim in a clan fight. The Simbu Premier wants the same powers as an Australian state premier, and has often claimed to "boss" the police, which he knows to be beyond his authority. He is reported to have attempted to stop the police moving to block a Kumai (Chimbu) advance into Goligup (Western Highlands) territory on the provincial border near Kup in early November 1977 (*Post Courier*, 8 November 1977). One Chimbu AA member was killed in fighting at Gumine in 1976, and six Gumine councillors were jailed for fighting at this time. So local politicians are not seen as impartial in fight situations. Nor can they be, as this would weaken their leadership position, given Chimbu political culture. Since the local political interests of individual leaders are in conflict with those of the national government — and indeed with those of the provincial government as a whole — consistency between policy and behaviour are unlikely.

The Inter-Group Fighting Act, passed in November 1977, legislated proposals emanating from Highlands politicians for group punishment of persons belonging to those clans which are party to conflicts within declared fight zones. Yet the draft bill had a turbulent history even before it reached parliament. The Simbu Premier used the National Broadcasting Commission to criticize publicly patrol officers, lawyers, and others working up these proposals for being power-hungry in failing to consult the provinces, when they were in fact — at the request of the national government — following provincial suggestions. He also walked out of a meeting of local leaders held by the Kerowagi MP at Minggende in Kerowagi District — within the Premier's own area — which was designed to gain public acceptance for the legislation. These incidents may reflect poor briefing of the Premier, but they certainly show the domineering style of a Chimbu leader wanting to be on top. The Premier is now a member of the province's Inter-Group Peace Committee, which was set up under the new law, with national government officials forming the majority. Because they serve the provincial government, kiaps are excluded from membership of this committee, although they are the only staff with the necessary local intelligence and the negotiating expertise required to assist in bringing peaceful settlements to such conflicts. Kiaps can sometimes bring about a reconciliation before a squabble becomes a fight and finally a war. The police, on the contrary, are national government officers, and have proved themselves loath to work under provincial governments, as indeed a Police Commissioner has stated. Police-kiap co-operation has been poor in the past, and the present procedures do not augur well for consistency between policy and practice with regard to clan warfare. On a wider front, the premiers collectively showed at their 1977 conference that they wanted provincial governments to take over control of the police force, which constitutionally is a national institution.

COFFEE, THE ECONOMY, AND PROVINCIAL REVENUES

As in other Melanesian societies, there is in Chimbu a close nexus between politics and business. Businessmen frequently go into politics and politicians usually try to become businessmen. Few Chimbu assemblymen are commercially successful in their own business ventures. But they desire to build up the resources at the provincial government's disposal by expanding its business arm, whereas the biggest businessmen in Chimbu resent governmental intrusion into what they see as their province. Chimbu Holding Enterprises Pty Ltd, 94 per cent owned by the SIPG, is active in passenger carriage and transport, petrol sales, and leasing urban real estate, and is trying to enter liquor retailing as well. It has started a cardamom plantation at Bomai in southern Chimbu, and one for coffee and chillies in Kerowagi. While still in its early days, and quite dependent upon its Canadian volunteer management, Chimbu Holding Enterprises has so far been a modestly profitable company despite the lack of relevance of most of its activities to the SIPG's proclaimed development policies.

Smallholder-grown coffee is a far larger source of income than government expenditure. Smallholders in years of normal prices receive only about K50 each, and in the boom years 1976 and 1977 were lucky to receive about K200 each. The big money is to be made in the marketing and processing of the crop, where energetic and tough-minded operators can, especially on a rising market, make huge profits. In 1976 the two main processors in Chimbu made profits of between K500,000 and K750,000, and the most successful buyers, who purchase the crop at the roadside from smallholders using cash advances provided by the processors, made profits of up to K20,000 in that year. While there are forty thousand smallholders in Chimbu, there are only a hundred buyers and three processing factories. Of these, Chimbu Coffee Ltd (formerly the Chimbu Coffee Co-operative) has the largest plant, but has a patchy financial history. A smaller, but generally highly profitable, factory is run by Chimbu Developments Pty Ltd, which is 30 per cent owned by an Australian with almost all the balance owned by the giant commodity exporter Angco Pty Ltd (which in turn is controlled by the PNG Investment Corporation, a national government body). Okuk on several occasions has failed in attempts to gain control of Chimbu Coffee, and so in late 1976 started building his own coffee factory. He assiduously cultivated the Chimbu AA members before this exercise, as their endorsement of his plans was required before the national government's Coffee Industry (formerly Coffee Marketing) Board would issue him with the required processing permit.

State regulation of trade has always been a rich harvest for politicians, whether directly or by backdoor means. We have noted the involvement of Simbu Assembly members in coffee growing and buying. Many are also prominent shareholders in Chimbu Coffee, and in 1977 the Provincial Secretary was a director of Chimbu Coffee. Throughout 1977, SIPG was negotiating to buy shares in Chimbu Developments, negotiations which ultimately broke down but which had real potential at the time. Policy questions concerning the licensing and taxing of buyers, the protection of the Chimbu market from outside buyers, and hence also the major issue of the size of "derivation grants" (refunds of export taxes based upon the amount of commodities produced and processed in the various provinces) are all matters in which the Chimbu politicians have a direct stake, individually and collectively, and yet the SIPG was the main source of Chimbu opinion consulted by the Coffee Industry Board in its regulation of coffee buying, and particularly of the trade in unprocessed coffee between provinces.

For all but ten weeks between January 1972 and 31 July 1977 a "coffee border" imposed by the Coffee Marketing/Industry Board operated with the aim of preventing the export of unprocessed coffee from Chimbu to the neighbouring provinces. The border was designed to reduce competition and thereby enable Chimbu Coffee to recover from bad management and low prices in the late sixties and early seventies. The board is required to consider growers' interests first and foremost, but the Chimbu representatives on the board since 1970 have been coffee buyers and usually held office as the chairman of Chimbu Coffee. The board argued that a side-effect of the imposition of the border was to lower prices paid to growers, and it several times consulted the Chimbu AA and SIPG on this matter with the aim of lifting the restrictions upon outside buyers. Although often divided on the question, the Chimbu politicians generally desired to keep the border. The protectionists' long struggle was almost lost in early 1976, but then several influential politicians again changed their minds, and the border stayed. The issue is a delicate one but worth probing.

The public activities of the Chimbu politicians on the coffee border question directly reflected their private interests. In several cases it is possible to link their policy waverings with their business dealings with Chimbu Coffee, Chimbu Developments, and processors in the Wahgi Valley of the Western Highlands Province. The dealings in question usually involved credit arrangements for vehicle purchase, and cash advances for roadside buying, both of which can involve thousands of kina. Some coffee factory managers have written off many thousands of kina lent to politicians as a necessary operating expense, a form of "protection money". The pressure to remove the coffee border often increased just at the time when managers sought to recover unacquitted advances at the end of each coffee season. One politician changed his vote when a factory bought his old vehicle at a handsome price; others attacked the Chimbu factories when denied credit and started dealing with Wahgi processors, which required the illegal transport of unprocessed coffee. It is not clear that the border did serve to suppress roadside prices for coffee in Chimbu, but certainly it served the interests of the owners and management of the Chimbu factories, the buyers, and the politicians.

With full provincial government powers imminent, and feeling the need to secure derivation grant revenues (which are based on national exports from each province and are higher if the commodity is processed within the province of origin), the SIPG early in 1977 once again appeared to be united behind the coffee borders. This was despite the fact that several powerful politicians, as well as directors of Chimbu Coffee, were themselves selling coffee across the border to Wahgi Valley factories. The Provincial Secretary received little support from the Coffee Industry Board when he wanted to tighten border supervision, so he negotiated with Chimbu Coffee and Chimbu Developments to fund two vehicles for this purpose. (The processors had previously funded the operations of the board's officially licensed inspectors.) A small detachment of extra-legal "inspectors", appointed by SIPG and not the board, and chosen for their loyalty to the Provincial Secretary, their brawn, and their courage, policed the border in June and July. They managed to hamper some of the more important Chimbu buyers who had been exporting unprocessed coffee, and netted some interesting catches, including seventeen bags of coffee owned by a prominent Simbu Assembly member. The Provincial Legal Officer was not keen on the border patrols, and his prosecution of a test case failed. In late July the Coffee Industry Board resolved that since Chimbu Coffee had made a large profit in 1976/77, the buying restriction should be revoked from 1 August 1977. This step was taken and, despite heated public exchanges with the board and the Minister for Agriculture, the SIPG was not able to persuade the board to change its mind or the national government to give the SIPG legislative powers over coffee marketing. The patrols ceased, and the SIPG kept the vehicles.

Once again, this issue could become the subject of inter-provincial dispute. The derivation grants are calculated by the national government according to Coffee Industries Board estimates of production in each province, allowing for transfers of unprocessed coffee — which even with the border restrictions in operation were probably about 50 per cent of Chimbu production. In 1977 the Simbu Planner questioned the board's estimates. It is also noteworthy that in 1976 the Highlands provinces were unable to agree on a proposal for a uniform tax upon coffee, an idea that originated in Chimbu. Similar disputes could arise over cocoa and copra exports from Island provinces.

In the SIPG's search for revenues, it is at present negotiating for joint enterprises with foreign breweries, and soft drink, ceramic, and cement producers. Aside from the fact that some of these industries duplicate activities already covered in national plans for foreign investment, the nature of these activities is likely to vitiate the proclaimed policy intentions of the Simbu Provincial Government and damage the welfare of many of the Chimbu people.

IMPLICATIONS AND CONCLUSIONS

The conclusions to be reached by deduction and induction from these few brief case studies have important policy implications, not just for Chimbu but for Papua New Guinea as a whole. As Hugh Heclo nicely puts it, "an assembly of cases can be used to unfold the pathology of a particular disease" (Heclo 1972, p. 88).

First, let me extract some general points from the material here presented.

1. The interests of provincial government personnel as members of a tiny elite are not the same as those of the mass. Yet given Melanesian political cultures and the fragmented social structure, there is no effective electoral accountability, because politicians need only cultivate a tiny sector of their electorate and can afford to ignore the majority and still survive.
2. Provincial leaders are likely to seek simplistic solutions to complex problems, without being fully aware of the consequences of their actions or of alternative approaches. Inconsistency and irrationality in provincial policy-making are more likely than not.
3. There is in most — if not all — provinces a shortage of the trained, experienced, competent, and confident staff required for coherent policy formulation, advice, and implementation. This shortage is likely to continue.

4. Although valuable initiatives have emerged in the recently improved co-ordination structures within provinces, mutual suspicions between officials and politicians are likely to inhibit the open exchange of ideas in policy formulation.
5. Interests of the different provinces vary, and hence their policies will often conflict.
6. Provincial policies may undermine national planning processes, and/or the conservatism of provincial elites may stultify creative approaches to growing social issues. The national government does not have clear power to impose its will in such cases. Although it can offer financial inducements to sway provincial governments, this undermines the fundamental rationale of the decentralized political system, raising doubts not only about its viability but also its desirability.

Second, we might consider whether the characteristics of the present appointed interim provincial assemblies will change for the better after provincial elections. Recent national and local government elections in Chimbu (and elsewhere) have demonstrated increasing fragmentation of the electorate. Given the lack of mobilization of the public along class lines, the wealthy have decided advantages. Although young and better-educated candidates have sometimes emerged victorious, they have continued to play patronage politics within their narrow parochial bases. Nor have they always proved more perspicacious, although they have been better equipped than their elders to manipulate the political-administrative system, and particularly the agencies of financial credit, to their advantage.

Third, we must ask whether Chimbu is *sui generis*, and whether generalization is possible. My material on other provinces is necessarily in the form of second-hand, word-of-mouth reports from participant observers and media reports. Perhaps three provinces seem to be running well according to administrative criteria, and several appear to be quiet politically. But there is little administrative or policy innovation and most have suffered serious upheavals over both staff and policy matters as well. Having myself observed the hasty shoot-from-the-hip approach to decision-making collectively demonstrated by the provincial premiers at their 1977 conference, and noted their cavalier attitude towards national policies and indeed towards the national Constitution, as well as their petulance when national ministers were unavoidably absent from their meeting, it is my belief that the operational style of other provincial governments is probably not very different from that of Chimbu. And certainly the preoccupation with the symbols and perquisites of office — cars, houses, overseas trips, and allowances — has been general.

With a few exceptions, such as the North Solomons, the incoming provincial governments do not have strong policy orientations of their own. They have taken power because it has been offered to them on a plate, but it is rather like a smorgasbord, where it is easy to take so much that indigestion is inevitable. The national government's rush to decentralize has now gone well beyond administrative deconcentration (taken too far too fast, in my view, but along the right lines), and it has opened up political prizes beyond the dreams of most Papua New Guineans and perhaps beyond the capacity of the country to provide. Provincial government has become a fad, much as local government was in earlier days. Now, the creation of community governments under provincial control is being discussed, without a hard look at the roots of the malaise that led to the failure of local government councils. The basic political elements have been left out of consideration in all this institution-building, but this time the stakes are higher; once entrenched, provincial elites will not readily forgo their gratuitous gains.

The saga of provincial government has been a go-stop-go process since 1973. It has long been my belief (Standish 1974–76, 1979) that there are serious pitfalls in this process, some of which I have here tried to demonstrate. National government policy-makers appear to have been oblivious of how politics works at the local level. The prospect in the Chimbu mountains is rather chilling, and the depths have been plumbed more often than the heights achieved. While this case study of policy-making in one province is only part of the story, it reinforces the argument that the hurried steps being taken by the national government at this time will be regretted in future years, not only by the national government but also by those whom provincial governments are intended to serve — the mass of the people of Papua New Guinea.

NOTES

1. The colonial districts were renamed provinces at independence, and the old sub-districts thereafter became districts. The leaders of Chimbu have chosen "Simbu" as the name for their provincial government rather than "Chimbu", because it better transcribes the triumphal shout used at ceremonies to greet visitors. Until the national parliament legislates to change the name, the province is still technically "Chimbu", which usage I will retain here.
2. Thirty months of fieldwork in the years 1972–77 have been funded by the University of Papua New Guinea, the Australian National University, and the Papua New Guinea Institute of Applied Social and Economic Research. I am grateful for this support, and thank the SIPG and its staff for co-operating with my study.

References

Ballard, J. A. 1971. "Administrative Origins of Nigerian Federalism." *African Affairs* 70: 333–48.

———. 1972. "The Politics of Localisation in Papua New Guinea." Paper delivered to Seminar on the Politics of Bureaucracy, Department of Political Science, Research School of Social Sciences, Australian National University.

———. 1976a. "Public Administration in Papua New Guinea, 1972–1976." *Australian Journal of Public Administration* 35: 229–43.

———. 1976b. "Wantoks and Administration." Mimeo. Waigani: University of Papua New Guinea.

———. 1977. "Students and Politics in Papua New Guinea." *Journal of Commonwealth and Comparative Politics* 15: 112–26.

———. Forthcoming. "Ethnicity and Access: Political Incorporation in Papua New Guinea." In *Problems of Access to Government Services in Papua New Guinea*, ed. J. A. Ballard.

Ballard, J. A., and Colebatch, H. K. 1976. "Provincial Administrative Structures: An Interim Report." Paper presented to the annual conference of Provincial Commissioners, Port Moresby.

Ballard, J., and Garnaut, R. 1973. "Economic Policy-Making During the Transfer of Power in Papua New Guinea." Seminar Paper, Department of Political Science, Research School of Social Sciences, Australian National University.

Bayne, P. J. 1975a. "Legal Development in Papua New Guinea: The Place of the Common Law." *Melanesian Law Journal* 3, no. 1: 9–39.

———. 1975b. "The Village Courts Debate." In *Lo Bilong ol Manmeri*, ed. J. Zorn and P. Bayne, pp. 40–41. Waigani: University of Papua New Guinea.

Bayne, P. J., and Colebatch, H. K. 1973. "Constitutional Development in Papua New Guinea, 1968–1973: The Transfer of Executive Power." New Guinea Research Bulletin, no. 51. Port Moresby: New Guinea Research Unit.

Bredmeyer, T. 1975. "The Registration of Customary Land in Papua New Guinea." *Melanesian Law Journal* 3, no. 2: 267–87.

Brown, P. 1963. "From Anarchy to Satrapy." *American Anthropologist* 65, no. 1: 1–15.

Burns, T., and Stalker, G. M. 1961. *The Management of Innovation*. London: Tavistock.

Caiden, G. E. 1975. *Towards a More Efficient Australian Government Administration*. First report presented to the Task Force on Efficiency, Royal Commission on Australian Government Administration. Canberra: Australian Government Publishing Service.

Colebatch, H. K. 1974. "Local Services and the Governmental Process in Kenya." PhD thesis, University of Sussex.

———. 1977. "The Rural Improvement Programme: Does It Improve Access?"

Institute of Applied Social and Economic Research, Discussion Paper no. 14.

Collins, P. D. 1976. "Decentralisation and Local Administration for Development in Tanzania." Institute of Development Studies, University of Sussex, Discussion Paper no. 94, May 1976.

Conyers, D. 1975. "The Introduction of Provincial Government in Papua New Guinea: Lessons from Bougainville." New Guinea Research Unit, Discussion Paper no. 1.

———. 1976. *The Provincial Government Debate: Central Control versus Local Participation in Papua New Guinea.* Monograph 2. Boroko: Institute of Applied Social and Economic Research.

———. 1979. "The Office of Implementation: A Case Study of Administration for Development." *Administration for Development* 13: 44–56.

Crocombe, R. 1971. "Overview: The Pattern of Change in Pacific Land Tenures." In *Land Tenure in the Pacific,* ed. R. Crocombe, pp. 1–24. Melbourne: Oxford University Press.

Davies, H. L. 1978. "History of the Ok Tedi Porphyry Copper Prospect, Papua New Guinea: The Years 1966 to 1976." *Economic Geology* 73: 796–802.

Dearlove, J. 1973. *The Politics of Policy.* Cambridge: Cambridge University Press.

Derham, D. P. 1960. "Report on the System for the Administration of Justice in the Territory of Papua New Guinea." Mimeo. Canberra: Department of Territories.

Faber, M. L. O. 1974. "Bougainville Re-negotiated: An Analysis of the New Fiscal Terms." *Mining Magazine* 131: 446–49.

Fenbury, D. M. 1979. *Practice without Policy: Genesis of Local Government in Papua New Guinea.* Development Studies Centre Monograph no. 13. Canberra: Australian National University.

Fitzpatrick, P., and Blaxter, L. 1974. "Legal Blocks to Popular Development." *Yagl-Ambu* 1: 303–10.

Forward, R. 1974. "Introduction." In *Public Policy in Australia,* ed. R. Forward. Melbourne: Cheshire.

Garnaut, R. 1978. "Australian Aid and the Papua New Guinea Economy." Seminar Paper, Department of Economics, Research School of Pacific Studies, Australian National University, October.

Gawi, J. K. ; Ghai, Y. P.; and Paliwala, A. 1976. "National Goals and Law Reform: A Report on the Goroka Seminar." *Melanesian Law Journal* 4, no. 2: 259–69.

Gerritsen, R. 1975. "Aspects of the Political Evolution of Rural PNG: Towards a Political Economy of the Terminal Peasantry." Paper to Canberra Marxist Group, 26 October.

———. Forthcoming. "The Politics of Ambition: Damuni, From Micronationalism to Provincial Government." In *Micronationalist Movements in Papua New Guinea,* ed. R. J. May. Canberra: Research School of Pacific Studies, Australian National University.

Griffin, J. 1972. "Bougainville – Secession or Just Sentiment?" *Current Affairs Bulletin* 48, no. 9: 258–80.

———. 1973a. "Kivung Bougainville – *Em nao em Kantri bilong yumi.*" *New Guinea* 8, no. 2: 41–50.

———. 1973b. "Movements for Separation and Secession." In *Alternative Strategies for Papua New Guinea,* ed. A. Clunies Ross and J. Langmore, pp. 99–130. Melbourne: Oxford University Press.

———. 1976. "Bougainville – *Occultus Sed Non Ignotus.*" *New Guinea* 10, no. 4: 44–50.

——— . 1977. "Local Government Councils as an Instrument of Political Mobilization in Bougainville." In *Local Government Councils in Bougainville*, ed. J. Connell, pp. 29–57. Christchurch: University of Canterbury, Department of Geography.

Gunther, J. T. 1970. "Trouble in Tolailand." *New Guinea* 5, no. 3: 25–37.

Gyles, R. V. 1975. "Law and Lawyers 1972." *New Guinea* 9, no. 4: 33–41.

Hasluck, P. 1976. *A Time for Building.* Melbourne: Melbourne University Press.

Hastings, P. 1976. "Bougainville and the Solomons." *New Guinea* 10, no. 3: 33–41.

Hawker, G.; Smith, R. F. I.; and Weller, P. 1979. *Politics and Policy in Australia.* St Lucia: University of Queensland Press.

Healy, C. 1969. "Companies in Papua New Guinea: The Legal Framework." Mimeo. University of Papua New Guinea.

Heclo, H. H. 1972. "Review Article; Policy Analysis." *British Journal of Political Science* 2, no. 1: 83–108.

Helleiner, G. K. 1972. "Beyond Growth Rates and Plan Volumes: Planning for Africa in the 1970s." *Journal of Modern African Studies* 10: 333–35.

Hirschman, A. O. 1975. "Policymaking and Policy Analysis in Latin America – A Return Journey." *Policy Sciences* 6: 285–402.

Hood Phillips, O. 1973. *Constitutional and Administrative Law.* 5th edition. London: Sweet and Maxwell.

Howell, W. J. S.; Fardon, R. S. H.; Carter, R. J.; and Bumstead, E. G. 1978. "History of the Ok Tedi Porphyry Copper Prospect, Papua New Guinea: The Years 1975 to 1978." *Economic Geology* 73: 802–9.

Howlett, D.; Hide, R.; and Young, E.; with Arba J.; Bi H.; and Kaman, B. 1976. *Chimbu: Issues in Development.* Monograph no. 4, Development Studies Centre, Australian National University.

Hyden, G.; Jackson, R.; and Ikumu, J., eds. 1971. *Development Administration: The Kenyan Experience.* Nairobi: Oxford University Press.

International Commission of Jurists. 1970. *The Rule of Law in an Emerging Society.* Sydney: International Commission of Jurists.

Joy, L. 1967. "Problems of Agricultural Administration and Extension Services." Paper to 13th International Conference of Agricultural Economists, Sydney. Mimeo. Institute of Development Studies, University of Sussex.

Kassam, F. M. 1974. "Ex Officio Indictments: An Aspect of Criminal Justice in Papua New Guinea." *Melanesian Law Journal* 2, no. 2: 248–62.

Kaputin, J. 1975. "The Law – A Colonial Fraud?" *New Guinea* 10, no. 1: 4–15.

Kerpi, K. 1976. "Strains, Tensions and Tribesmen: Clan Warfare in Kup." *New Guinea* 10, no. 3: 2–18.

Kerr, J. R. 1968. *Law in Papua New Guinea.* Melbourne: Australian Institute of International Affairs.

Law Reform Commission. 1976a. *Annual Report 1975.* Port Moresby: Law Reform Commission of Papua New Guinea.

——— . 1976b. "Declaration and Development of an Underlying Law." Working Paper no. 4. Port Moresby: Law Reform Commission of Papua New Guinea.

——— . 1976c. "Fairness of Transactions." Working Paper no. 5. Port Moresby: Law Reform Commission of Papua New Guinea.

——— . 1977. "Summary Report on Underlying Law and Customary Law Seminar." Port Moresby: Law Reform Commission of Papua New Guinea.

Law Society. [1973]. *Report on Village Court Proposals.* Port Moresby: Council of the Law Society of Papua New Guinea.

Leonard, D. K. 1972. "The Social Structure of the Agricultural Extension Services in the Western Province of Kenya." *African Review* 2: 323–43.

Lepani, C. 1976. "Planning in Small Dependent Economies – A Case Study of Papua New Guinea." Seminar Paper, Institute of Development Studies, University of Sussex.

Lett, L. 1942. *The Papuan Achievement*. Melbourne: Melbourne University Press.

Ley, J. F. Forthcoming. "Nation Building in Papua New Guinea 1972–1975: The Role and Contribution of The Constitutional Planning Committee." La Trobe University Centre for Pacific Studies, Occasional Paper.

Lindblom, C. E. 1959. "The Science of 'Muddling Through'." *Public Administration Review* 19, no. 2: 79–88.

Lipton, M. 1976. *Why Poor People Stay Poor: Urban Bias in World Development*. London: Temple Smith.

Lukes, S. 1974. *Power: A Radical View*. London: Macmillan.

Lynch, C. J. 1965. "Aspects of Popular Participation in 'Grass-Roots' Courts in Papua New Guinea." Mimeo. Port Moresby.

———. 1969. "Legal Aspects of Economic Organization in the Customary Context in Papua New Guinea." Mimeo. Port Moresby.

———. 1970. "Group Ownership of Business." Mimeo. Port Moresby.

———. 1972. "A Note on Conciliation and Arbitration as a Form of Settlement of Disputes." Mimeo. Port Moresby.

McKillop, R. F. 1975. "Catching the Didiman." *Administration for Development* (Port Moresby), no. 3: 14–21.

———. 1976a. *A History of Agricultural Extension in Papua New Guinea*. Extension Bulletin no. 10, Department of Primary Industry, Port Moresby.

———. 1976b. "Helping the People in Papua New Guinea? A Case Study of a Cattle Introduction Programme." Conference Paper, Sociological Association of Austrlia and New Zealand, La Trobe University.

———. 1977. "Sugar." In History of Agriculture Discussion Paper no. 2, ed. G. T. Harris and F. Wieland. Mimeo. UPNG/Department of Primary Industry, September.

———. Forthcoming. "Problems of Access: A Case Study of a Cattle Development Programme in Papua New Guinea." In *Problems of Access to Government Services in Papua New Guinea*, ed. J. A. Ballard.

Mamak, A., and Bedford, R. 1974. *Bougainvillean Nationalism: Aspects of Unity and Discord*. Christchurch: University of Canterbury, Department of Geography.

Mark, T. 1975. "Acquisition and Redistribution of Alienated Land: A Study in Access." *Yagl-Ambu* 2, no. 1: 65–70.

May, R. 1972. "Pennies from Heaven: Problems of a Separate Currency." *New Guinea* 7, no. 3: 43–51.

———. 1975. "The Micronationalists." *New Guinea* 10, no. 1: 38–53.

Moore, M. P. 1976. "The Bureaucratic Perception of Policy Options." *Institute of Development Studies Bulletin* 8, no. 2: 27–30.

Moris, J. R. 1972. "Administrative Authority and the Problem of Effective Agricultural Administration in East Africa." *African Review* 2: 105–46.

Murray, D. J., ed. 1970. *Studies in Nigerian Administration*. London: Hutchinson.

O'Connell, J. 1967. "The Inevitability of Instability." *Journal of Modern African Studies* 5: 181–91.

Olatunbosun, D. 1975. *Nigeria's Neglected Rural Majority*. London: Oxford University Press.

O'Neill, N. 1976. "The Judges and the Constitution – The First Year." *Melanesian Law Journal* 4, no. 2: 242–58.

Oram, N. D. 1970. "Land and Race in Port Moresby." *Journal of the Papua and New Guinea Society* 4, no. 1: 5–28.

————. 1978. "Grass Roots Justice: Village Courts in Papua New Guinea." Mimeo. Department of Pre-History, La Trobe University.

Orken, M. B. 1974. "'They Fight for Fun'." In *Problem of Choice: Land in Papua New Guinea's Future,* ed. P. G. Sack, pp. 164–69. Canberra: Australian National University Press.

Overseas Development Group. 1973. *A Report on Development Strategies for Papua New Guinea.* Port Moresby: Office of Programming and Co-ordination, February.

Paliwala, A.; Zorn, J.; and Bayne, P. J. 1978. "Economic Development and the Changing Legal System of Papua New Guinea." *African Law Studies,* no. 16: 3–79.

Papua New Guinea (PNG). 1973a. *Report of the Committee Investigating Tribal Fighting in the Highlands.* Port Moresby: Government Printer.

————. 1973b. "Second Interim Report of the Constitutional Planning Committee." Mimeo.

————. 1973c. *Report of the Commission of Inquiry into Land Matters.* Port Moresby: Government Printer.

————. 1974a. *Constitutional Planning Committee Report 1974: Draft Recommendations.* Port Moresby: Government Printer.

————. 1974b. *Constitutional Planning Committee Report 1974: Draft Narrative.* Port Moresby: Government Printer.

————. 1974c. *Final Report of the Constitutional Planning Committee.* 2 volumes. Port Moresby: Government Printer.

————. 1974d. *Government Paper: Proposals on Constitutional Principles and Explanatory Notes.* Port Moresby: Government Printer.

————. 1974e. *United Party Proposals for the Constitution.* Port Moresby: Government Printer.

————. 1976. *National Development Strategy: Papua New Guinea Government White Paper.* Port Moresby: Government Printer.

Parker, R. S. 1966. "The Growth of Territory Administration." In *New Guinea on the Threshold,* ed. E. K. Fisk, pp. 187–221. Canberra: Australian National University Press.

————. 1972. "Public Administration." In *Encyclopedia of Papua and New Guinea,* ed. Peter Ryan, pp. 982–93. Melbourne: Melbourne University Press.

Pratt, C. 1976. *The Critical Phase in Tanzania 1945–1968: Nyerere and the Emergence of a Socialist Strategy.* Cambridge: Cambridge University Press.

Price, R. 1974. "Politics and Culture in Ghana: The Big-Man Small-Boy Syndrome." *Journal of African Studies* 1, no. 2: 173–204.

Public Solicitor. 1976. *First Annual Report, 1975–1976.* Port Moresby: Public Solicitor of Papua New Guinea.

Ross, S. D. 1977. "A Review of the Judiciary in Papua New Guinea." *Melanesian Law Journal* 5, no. 1: 5–25.

Sack, P. G. 1973. *Land Between Two Laws.* Canberra: Australian National University Press.

Sahlins, M. D. 1963. "Poor Man, Rich Man, Big-man, Chief: Leadership Types in Melanesia and Polynesia." *Comparative Studies in Society and History* 5, no. 3: 285–303.

Sam, P.; Passingan, B.; and Kanawi, W. 1975. "Bringing Law to the People." In *Lo Bilong ol Manmeri,* ed. J. Zorn and P. Bayne, pp. 161–67. Port Moresby: University of Papua New Guinea.

Sawer, G. 1967. *Australian Federalism in the Courts.* Melbourne: Melbourne University Press.

Schaffer, B. B. 1965. "Advising about Development: The Example of the World Bank Report on Papua and New Guinea." *Journal of Commonwealth Political Studies* 4, no. 1: 30–46. Reprinted in Schaffer 1973.

———. 1970. "Public Employment, Political Rights and Political Development." In *The Politics of Melanesia*, ed. M. W. Ward, pp. 402–417. Canberra: Australian National Press. Reprinted in Schaffer 1973.

———. 1973. *The Administrative Factor: Papers in Organization, Politics and Development.* London: Frank Cass.

———. 1975. "Editorial:: The Problem of Access to Government Services." *Development and Change* 6: 3–11.

———. 1977. "Review Article: On the Politics of Policy." *Australian Journal of Politics and History* 23, no. 1: 146–55.

———. 1978a. "Administration Legacies and Links in the Post-Colonial State: Preparation, Training and Administrative Reform." *Development and Change* 9: 175–200.

———. 1978b. "Comparing Administrators: Researching and Reforming." In *Dynamics of Development: An International Perspective*, ed. S. K. Sharma. Vol 2: 131–54. Delhi: Concept.

Schaffer, B. B., and Lamb, G. B. 1974. "Exit, Voice and Access." *Social Science Information* 13, no. 6: 73–90.

Schulz, K. 1977. "Organising Extension Services for Integrated Rural Development in West and East African Countries – the Commodity Approach." *Sociologia Ruralis* 17, no. 1/2: 87–106.

Schumacher, E. F. 1974. *Small is Beautiful: A Study of Economics As If People Mattered.* London: Sphere.

Simbu Interim Provincial Government (SIPG). [1977]. First Priority Schedule June 1977–June 1978. Mimeo.

Simpson, G. J. 1975. "A Report on the Karimui Resettlement Scheme: Problems and Prospects." Mimeo. Office of Environment and Conservation, Port Moresby.

Smith, G. 1975. *Education in Papua New Guinea.* Melbourne: Melbourne University Press.

Somare, M. T. 1975a. "Law and the Needs of Papua New Guinea's People." In *Lo Bilong ol Manmeri*, ed. J. Zorn and P. Bayne, pp. 14–18. Port Moresby: University of Papua New Guinea.

———. 1975b. *Sana: An Autobiography.* Port Moresby: Niugini Press.

Standish, B. 1973. "The Highlands – *ol i no save harim mipela.*" *New Guinea* 8, no. 3: 1–30.

———. 1974–76. "Papua New Guinea Review." *The Australian Quarterly* 46, no. 1: 88–103; no. 3: 113–28; 47, no. 1: 104–27; no. 3: 112–23; 48, no. 2: 106–19.

———. 1978a. "Pork, Talk and Beer: Colonial and Post-Colonial Electioneering in Chimbu, Papua New Guinea." Conference Paper, Australasian Political Studies Association, Adelaide.

———. 1978b. "The Big-Man Model Reconsidered: Power and Stratification in Chimbu." Discussion Paper no. 22, Papua New Guinea Institute of Applied Social and Economic Research, Port Moresby.

———. 1979. *Provincial Government in Papua New Guinea: Early Lessons from Chimbu.* Monograph 7, Papua New Guinea Institute of Applied Social and Economic Research, Port Moresby.

———. Forthcoming. "Roads to Power: the Politics of Decolonisation in Chimbu Province, Papua New Guinea." PhD thesis, Australian National University.

Staniland, M. 1969. "Frantz Fanon and the African Political Class." *African Affairs* 68: 4–25.

Stone, C. 1974. "Political Aspects of Postwar Agricultural Policies in Jamaica, 1945–1970." *Social and Economic Studies* 23, no. 2: 145–75.

Talyaga, K. K., and Olela, C. 1978. "The Debate on Repatriation of Squatters and Vagrants from the North Solomons Province (1977–78)." Mimeo. Port Moresby: Papua New Guinea Institute of Applied Social and Economic Research.

UPNG. 1973. *Calendar of the University of Papua New Guinea.*

Voutas, T. 1977. "Managing Political Stability in P.N.G." *Pacific Defence Reporter* (May): 22–23.

Wagner, R. 1971. "When a Chimbu Meets a Karimui." *New Guinea* 6, no. 2: 27–31.

Ward, R. G., and Ballard, J. A. 1976. "In Their Own Image: Australia's Impact on Papua New Guinea and Lessons for Future Aid." *Australian Outlook* 30: 439–58.

Weier, R. O. 1976. "Problems in Marketing." In *1975 Papua New Guinea Foods Crops Conference Proceedings,* ed. K. Wilson and R. M. Bourke. Port Moresby: Department of Primary Industry.

Weisbrot, D., and Paliwala, A. 1976. "Lawyers for the People: Reviewing Legal Services in an Independent Papua New Guinea." *Melanesian Law Journal* 4, no. 2: 184–210.

Welch, R. V. 1976. "Manpower Planning Problems and the Public Service of Papua New Guinea." *Australian Journal of Public Administration* 35: 264–72.

Wettenhall, R. 1976. "Modes of Ministerialization II: From Colony to State in the Twentieth Century." *Public Administration* 54: 425–51.

Wolfers, E. P., 1977. "Defining a Nation: The Citizenship Debates in the Papua New Guinea Parliament." In *Racism: the Australian Experience,* ed. F. S. Stevens and E. P. Wolfers. Vol. 3 (2nd ed.), *Colonialism and After.* Sydney: ANZ Book Co.

Yeats, G. 1975. "Submission to Standing Committee: DASF Fresh Foods Policy." Typescript, 22 April. Held in UPNG Library under "Documents on PNG Fresh Food Policy."

Young, L. K. ed. 1971. *Constitutional Development in Papua and New Guinea.* Sydney: International Commission of Jurists.

Zolberg, A. R. 1966. *Creating Political Order: The Party-States of West Africa.* Chicago: Rand McNally.

Index

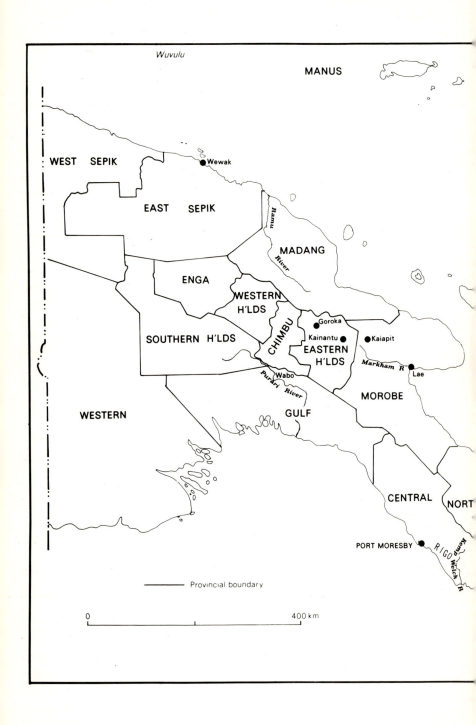